# of North America

SOCIETY, WASHINGTON, D.C.

*Pronghorn in Wind Cave National Park, South Dakota,*
*by Bates Littlehales, National Geographic photographer*

*Another volume in the*
NATURAL SCIENCE LIBRARY

*Foreword by* MELVILLE BELL GROSVENOR
*President and Editor, National Geographic Society*

*Consultant:* A. REMINGTON KELLOGG, *noted mammalogist
and Director, U. S. National Museum, 1948-62*

*Edited and prepared by the*
NATIONAL GEOGRAPHIC BOOK SERVICE,
MERLE SEVERY, *Chief*

*Chapters by*

| | |
|---|---|
| AGNES AKIN ATKINSON | A. REMINGTON KELLOGG |
| WAYNE BARRETT | ROBERT M. McCLUNG |
| VICTOR H. CAHALANE | EDWARDS PARK |
| GOODE P. DAVIS, JR. | WILLIS PETERSON |
| MELVIN R. ELLIS | DONALD A. SPENCER |
| DONALD R. GRIFFIN | ERNEST P. WALKER |
| JAY JOHNSTON | STANLEY P. YOUNG |

*407 illustrations, 266 in full color*
*by* WALTER A. WEBER, LOUIS AGASSIZ FUERTES,
*and other artists and photographers*

*Staff for this book*
*Editor-in-chief:* MELVILLE BELL GROSVENOR
*Editor:* MERLE SEVERY
*Associate editor and staff mammalogist:* ROBERT M. McCLUNG
*Writers:* WAYNE BARRETT, EDWARDS PARK
*Editorial assistant:* MARY SWAIN HOOVER
*Design:* HOWARD E. PAINE, PAUL JENSEN, ROBERT M. McCLUNG
*Engravings:* WILLIAM W. SMITH

*Composed on Linofilm by National Geographic's
Phototypographic Division,* HERMAN J. A. C. ARENS, *Director*
ROBERT C. ELLIS, JR., *Manager*
*Printed and bound by*
*R. R. Donnelley and Sons Co., Chicago*
*First through fourth printings: 390,000 copies*
*Fifth printing, with revisions, 1971: 75,000 copies*

# Foreword

*Mountain Lion in Big Creek, Idaho, by Wilbur Wiles*

As a youngster, I was fascinated — like youngsters before and since — by the wild animals that live around us. I would bombard my father, Gilbert Grosvenor, with questions and at bedtime wheedle "just one more" story about the bears, rabbits, and whales that roused my youthful curiosity. As Editor of *National Geographic*, he realized that he could answer a great popular demand for this exciting scientific knowledge (and at the same time "rescue" harassed parents!) by publishing colorful accounts of wild animals and their ways.

So he commissioned artist Louis Agassiz Fuertes, the Audubon of his day, to illustrate two articles by the adventurous naturalist Edward W. Nelson, which

5

appeared in the magazine in 1916 and 1918. We children were so enthralled with those stories and pictures that my father published them as one of The Society's first books. Two editions of that 1918 wild animal book sold out. Long out of print, it now commands a premium in rare-book stores.

Remembering my fondness for the book, I read it to my children, and they were as fascinated as I had been. Later, my grandsons called for "just one more" from the dog-eared volume. It was high time Society members had the opportunity to explore the realm of bison and beaver, mountain lion and mole with such a guide.

With this book they do.

Over the years, the study of nature has taken great strides. Armed with high-speed color camera, the naturalist can now capture the most elusive game, and modern printing displays his trophies with startling realism. But the lens can only supplement, not replace, the patient observation and skilled brush of the artist.

When I sat down with Merle Severy, talented chief of the National Geographic's Book Service, and Dr. A. Remington Kellogg, then the distinguished director of the U. S. National Museum, to plan *Wild Animals of North America,* we agreed that some of the original Fuertes paintings could not be improved on, and you will see them here. Old-timers will recall such favorites as the dramatic scene of wolves attacking the Peary caribou, on page 88. But that was only a beginning.

The Society's own staff artist, Walter A. Weber, further enriched the book with his striking portrayals of animals in the wild. Ranging the continent from Alaska's glaciers to the jungles of Veracruz, he tracked down his subjects in their native habitats. On field trips that took him 137,000 miles, he filled notebook after note-book with on-the-spot sketches, shot 60,000 feet of color film and 10,000 slides. From these he created an incomparable gallery of wild animal studies. While many will be familiar to Geographic members, 51 paintings and drawings appear here for the first time.

Dr. Kellogg himself headed a unique team of scholar-adventurers who wrote — and lived — the 90,000 words of vivid text. Victor H. Cahalane, Assistant Director of the New York State Museum and well-known author of *Mammals of North America,* takes us into forest and desert to meet the deer and the big cats. Biolo-gists Stanley P. Young, noted author of *The Wolves of North America,* and Donald A. Spencer draw on their many years of field experience with the U. S. Fish and Wildlife Service to introduce us to wild dogs and porcupines. With Harvard pro-fessor Donald R. Griffin, who wrote *Echoes of Bats and Men* and *Listening in the Dark,* we explore caves where bats sleep the winter through.

These enthusiastic experts — and others — reveal to us the entire panorama of our wild neighbors. With them we follow the daily life of each species, see what it looks like, where and how it lives.

Animals have fed, clothed, and intrigued mankind for thousands of years. Now a new generation of Geographic members can come to know them, growing up as mine did with a book they will read and reread — their constant companion and an open-sesame to a wondrous world.

*Melville Bell Grosvenor*

# CONTENTS

*Top: Varying Hare by Warren F. Steenbergh*
*Center: Bighorn Sheep, © Wendell Chapman*
*Bottom: Alaska Brown Bear by Cecil E. Rhode*

# Gnawing Mammals

# Survivors of Ancient Orders

# Ocean Dwellers

*Top: Prairie Dog by Warren E. Garst, Walt Disney Productions*
*Center: Armadillo by Leonard Lee Rue III, National Audubon Society*
*Bottom: Walrus by Mac's Foto, Anchorage*

*This and all other Part Dividers drawn by*
*Walter A. Weber, National Geographic staff artist*

# Animals in Fur

BENEATH WINTER'S BLANKET of white, a fur-clad marmot
snuggles in his burrow. Under a snow-packed roof,
a paunchy bear in black parka sprawls dead to the world.
But not all furred creatures are asleep. Racing
through earthen corridors, a tiny shrew pursues a mouse
and catches it. Exploding from cover,
a cottontail stays one jump ahead of a gray fox
and death. And life goes on.
A whitetail buck, antlers held high, steps out of blue shadows.
A family of otters, wrapped in satiny fur, careens down a snowbank, while
a red squirrel on his woodland balcony churrs indignantly.
These denizens of wintry woods belong to the world of mammals.
In the following two chapters Dr. Kellogg tells of
their heritage, their ways of life, their importance to man.

CHAPTER 1

# Mammals and How They Live

By A. REMINGTON KELLOGG

THE DAY WAS SULTRY for late summer. I had finished lunch and was stretched on a grassy bank beside a stream north of Yellowstone National Park. Eyes closed, I drowsed, the sun warm on my face. In the distance a jay called. All was peace. Then *whoof!* A loud snort brought me to with a start. There, barely a dozen feet away, towered a gigantic bull moose, velvet antlers black against the sky. We stared at each other, and I held my breath as he pawed the ground. Would he charge? Luckily, he tossed his head, wheeled, and bolted into a growth of scrubby pines. Three-inch trunks bent like grass as he crashed through.

That, my first face-to-face encounter with America's biggest deer, happened in my college days. But my interest in mammals goes back to childhood.

Toads, snail shells, turtles, caterpillars, and bits of fossils filled my pockets, impressed my playmates, and fortunately were tolerated by my parents. I still recall vividly my excitement at meeting a fearless little weasel, her five bright-eyed young strung out behind her, or finding a hoary bat hanging to the limb of a pawpaw tree. I skinned and mounted the bat and it held the place of honor in my bedroom. For now I was hooked. I was going to be a zoologist.

The years have passed all too quickly—years of study, field work, research, years full of interest as I have pried into the ways of animals. I began my career with the Bureau of Biological Survey, under Dr. Edward W. Nelson, author of the first wild animal book published by the National Geographic Society in 1918. Finally I went to work for the Smithsonian Institution; I have been there ever since.

13

**Bull moose,** mightiest of deer, crunches a salad of water plants in Yellowstone National Park, Wyoming. Antlers, still growing, are sheathed in summer's velvet.

FRANK AND JOHN CRAIGHEAD

I get thousands of questions about mammals from school teachers, children, housewives, businessmen, farmers, crossword puzzle addicts, college students, and scientific colleagues. Oddly, I have seldom been asked what is the fiercest, largest, or tallest flesh eater. When told that the largest known mammal is the 100-foot blue whale, weighing some 150 tons, and the smallest a tiny shrew that weighs less than a dime, some people are dubious. They've never seen either. One year everyone wanted to know the number of quills on a porcupine (around 30,000). This must have been a question in a contest, judging by its popularity. Here are a few others:

*What's the fastest mammal in America?* The pronghorn, with bursts of speed up to 40 or 50 miles per hour.

*What is our commonest mammal?* The mouse. Some species have populations estimated in the billions. No one has taken an actual count in more than a small area.

*The rarest?* Perhaps the black-footed ferret. Other species such as the musk ox and Guadalupe fur seal have barely escaped extinction.

*What mammal lives longest?* Man. Then the elephant, 50 to 75 years. Whales can live 40 to 60 years, bison 20 to 30 years. Bears may live 30 or more years in captivity. Very few wild animals die of old age.

*How far can a porcupine shoot its quills?* It can't.

*How do whales breathe?* Through blowholes. They have lungs just as we do.

*What's the smartest mammal?* Man. The chimpanzee and porpoise are leading contenders for second place — but so far, devising an IQ test that could rate them fairly has defied man's intelligence.

But in telling the story of mammals, the first important questions are: Just what *is* a mammal? How does it differ from other animals?

A mammal has a bony skeleton. But so do birds, reptiles, amphibians, and fish. Except for the egg-laying platypus and echidna of the Australia region, all mammals bear live young. But so do some fish, reptiles, and insects. Mammals are warm-blooded with body heat controlled internally, regardless of outside temperature. But birds have the same advantage.

MAMMALS *differ* from other animals in two ways: They produce milk with which they nurse their young; and they grow a covering of true hair or fur. The sheep's kinky wool, the mole's velvet fur, the peccary's bristles, and the porcupine's quills are all modified hair. So are the cat's whiskers. Fur bearers have a soft, thick undercoat, overlaid with coarser guard hairs. The walrus and manatee grow sparse hair, and whales a few bristles near the lips. Even the armadillo sprouts wisps of hair between its bony plates.

Hair protects the mammal's skin from strong sunlight, rain, snow, thorns, and sharp rocks. It holds body heat. Just as we put on a warm winter coat, many mammals grow heavy fur every fall, then shed it for lightweight summer wear. Shaggy patches make a molting animal look unkempt until sleek new hair grows in.

Compared to brightly plumed birds, most mammals dress somberly. But one dandy, the jaguar, sports gay yellow and black spots. And the skunk lets would-be attackers know who he is in striking black and white. A few mammals boast distinct color phases. Black bears may be black, brown, cinnamon, bluish, or whitish.

**Author teams with a budding naturalist to give a gray squirrel a midday snack**

Young, and fascinated by animals? No one understands better than Dr. A. Remington Kellogg, former Director of the U. S. National Museum and now a Research Associate of the Smithsonian Institution.

Helping Judith Marshall of Washington, D. C., feed her baby a formula of milk and water (whole milk can kill baby squirrels), he recalls his own first friendships with wild animals. His youthful hobby grew into a life's work in field and laboratory.

A professional mammalogist for more than 40 years, and long a member of the National Geographic Society's Research Committee, Dr. Kellogg is a world authority in his field.

He dips unstintingly into his vast reservoir of firsthand knowledge to enrich the pages of this book.

BATES LITTLEHALES, NATIONAL GEOGRAPHIC PHOTOGRAPHER

Red, silver, and cross foxes are all one species. Albino or pure black individuals pop up in everything from shrews to whales. The legendary Moby Dick was albino. To add even more variety, young mammals often wear clothes quite different from their parents'. Fawns and baby pumas are spotted, their elders plain; a bison calf is red or yellowish, its mother dark brown; young harp and gray seals are born with snowy white coats, then shed them to adopt the dark pelt of adults.

We try to dress our children appropriately. Nature does the same with many mammals, for their very lives may depend on camouflage. Thus desert animals are generally pale and drab compared to forest dwellers of the same species. With northern weasels, varying hares, and collared lemmings, nature performs a minor miracle. By the time the first snow falls, they have replaced brown summer coats with winter fur of pure white to blend with their surroundings.

As though jealously proud of their fur, wild animals instinctively care for it with

15

the zeal of beauty-conscious debutantes. They take dust baths, apply mud packs, and nibble and scratch, grooming one another as well as their young. A mother otter and her infants take turns combing each other with their claws. And no one who has seen it can forget the desert kangaroo rat busily rubbing a paw over a gland on his back that secretes oil, then sleeking down his hair with all the absorption of a teen-ager getting ready for a date.

Hoofed animals, cats, and dogs are born covered with fur. But marsupials, bats, and most rodents arrive practically naked. The opossum gives birth to hairless young, embryos really, only 11 or 12 days after mating. But the elephant carries its young 20 to 22 months; at birth they are well developed, with more hair than the parent.

A newborn opossum weighs only about one fourteen-thousandth as much as its mother. Cubs of a 400-pound black bear may weigh only six to eight ounces apiece. On the other hand, a newborn whale may be half its mother's length. It's born tail first; otherwise it would drown during labor. The mother snaps the umbilical cord with a quick twist or jerk, and the massive youngster starts right in swimming.

**Light-colored calves** scamper to keep up with their milk supply as bison cows lope across the Black Hills of South Dakota. Like the domestic calf, which he resembles, the baby bison sucks at his mother's nipples. Only mammals nurse their young and have coats of hair or fur. The word mammal comes from the Latin *mamma,* meaning breast.

This herd of about 1,000 roams Custer State Park, sanctuary also for deer, elk, pronghorns, and bighorn sheep.

TED SPIEGEL, RAPHO GUILLUMETTE

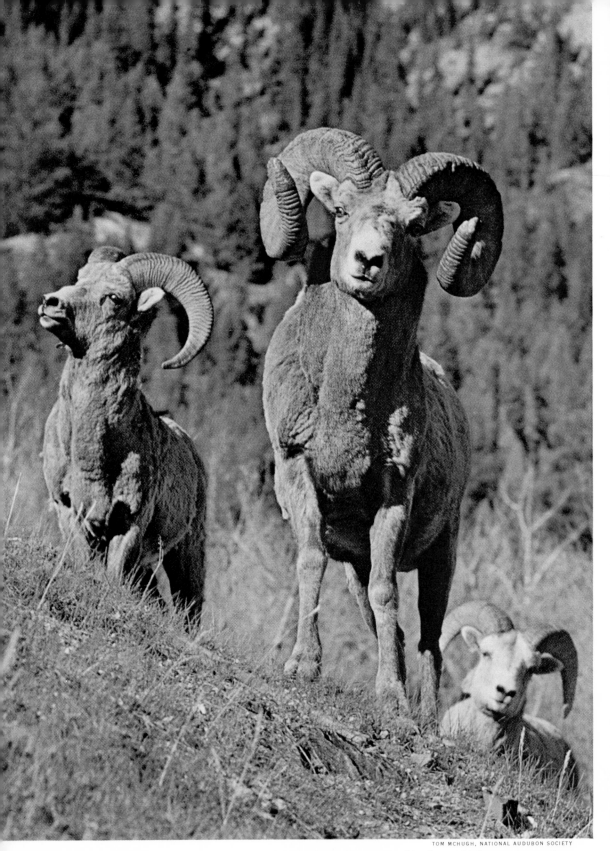

**Bighorn sheep display** proud headgear the year round, unlike deer, which grow new antlers each summer. These sure-footed, stouthearted alpinists haunt Rocky Mountain heights.

RECENTLY I WATCHED a baby bottle-nosed porpoise snuggling close to its mother, cavorting around the tank at Miami's Seaquarium. Every now and then it would nose in to her flank, stay for a moment, then swim on with a contented look. It was getting a quick snack—on the fly, so to speak.

Young whales and porpoises nurse quickly while partially or completely submerged. The mother rolls on her side, contracts muscles, and pumps milk into the baby's mouth. Other mammals suck in the standard way. Soon after a mother has licked away birth tissues and cleaned her newborn baby, he instinctively nuzzles around for a nipple and takes his first meal. Cow's milk is four or five per cent fat, but a reindeer's has up to 22 per cent, and some seals top 50. Colostrum, the mother's first milk, is even richer in solids to fill the newborn's needs.

Buffalo, deer, and mountain sheep usually stand to nurse their young. Bats may nurse on the wing, and sea otter mothers float on their backs, cuddling infants against their breasts. Nursing generally goes on every few hours, provided mother is available. An infant fur seal gulps as much as a gallon at a sitting, then fasts for several days while his milk bar goes to sea to hunt food for herself. Each gray and hooded seal nurses her offspring daily for two or three weeks, and the baby soaks up weight. Then the female abruptly abandons him. Weaned without warning, the youngster fasts until hunger drives him into the sea to fish for his supper.

Mice have several litters a year and nurse each for only two or three weeks. But an indulgent she-bear may nurse her cubs a year and a half, even though they are eating solids long before their first summer is over. And a walrus baby nurses nearly two years—until it sprouts tusks for digging mollusks.

Most meat eaters are helpless at birth and need a long period of mothering. On the other hand, their future victims, the hoofed animals, can generally follow their mother within hours or days. A two-day-old pronghorn can run like the wind for a short distance, yet its mother keeps it hidden except to nurse it.

Whatever the mammal, mother love is a powerful instinct—strong enough to drive a man up a tree in the case of a bear with cubs or a moose with calf. Even the timid mouse may fight to the death for her young. And when danger threatens, wild mothers carry their infants to safety in a number of ways. A black bear gently grasps her cub's entire head in her mouth to carry him. A swimming polar bear may nestle a small cub against her chest. When he's older, he may hang onto his mother's tail with his teeth and hitch a ride through the water.

A crowd of New Yorkers gathered at the Bronx Zoo to watch a mother gray squirrel transfer her young to a new nest by scrambling about 75 feet up a slanting cable. She tried to persuade one baby to follow, but with no luck. Then she tried pushing it out onto the cable, but the little one would have none of that. So she ended up pushing the youngster over until it hung upside down from the wire like a sloth. Then she gripped the skin of its chest with her front teeth, and the baby clung to her neck with its little paws and tail. Carefully, the mother made the perilous trip, sometimes slipping and catching herself at the last moment while the onlookers gasped. When she delivered the infant to the nest, a cheer went up.

On a sadder note, porpoises have been seen trying to support their dead young with their pectoral fins—thus the ancient belief that porpoises would carry ashore mariners washed overboard in a storm.

H OWEVER LONG they're cared for, the young eventually must face life on their own. To escape daily dangers they learn to rely on keen senses, cunning, concealment, flight, and fight.

Hoofed animals ordinarily flee a predator. But if cornered they use sharp hoofs or horns. Naturalists Frank and John Craighead saw a strange winter drama enacted in the snow-clad Tetons of Wyoming. A band of mule deer, exhausted by plunging belly-deep through drifts, paused on the edge of a cliff to rest. A golden eagle, sensing their vulnerability, attacked with raking talons, trying to panic them over the cliff to the rocks below. But the deer held together, reared and flailed at the eagle with sharp forefeet, finally driving it off.

A bobcat would have slashed with claws and teeth.

Even small mammals use their teeth most effectively, as I know from sad experience. Once I was setting a trap in a burrow when its occupant came out in a hurry — a dark blur of fur. Without thinking I grabbed at it; all that my enthusiasm got me was a nasty bite from an angry mink.

Skunks have a chemical defense which few opponents care to test. One winter night in Kansas, my hunting companion and I were asleep in our tent when I was awakened by a nudge and a whispered comment that something had been licking my friend's face. He grabbed his shotgun, intending to shoot the intruder. Fortunately for all three of us, the animal reared to get a drink from a bucket and we recognized it. A big skunk! We both lay still, hardly daring to breathe. Finally the skunk sauntered unconcernedly out into the night.

Another time I wasn't so lucky. On a narrow ledge I ran smack into a little spotted skunk who promptly let me have it with both barrels full in the face. My eyes

**Crashing head on** from 20 feet, young whitetails cut capers when battle is done. But in their antlered prime at five years, bucks may fight to the death at mating season.

**Frisky whitetail fawn** clears a low hurdle. Born in June, he'll lose his spots in September.

burned with liquid fire until I staggered to a stream where I could wash them.

The porcupine is too slow to flee from enemies, but he doesn't need to. His sharp quills are a persuasive defense. The armadillo carries armor-plating, but prefers to run to a hole if an enemy appears.

As well as being effective weapons, the teeth of every mammal are adapted for the food it eats. Rodents and rabbits have chisel-shaped incisors for gnawing and cutting vegetation. These teeth grow continuously, uppers wearing against lowers to keep the length constant. If the teeth don't make contact, they keep growing in a great arc until, unable to eat, the animal dies.

The sharp canine teeth of carnivores pierce and tear, and specialized cheek teeth cut meat. Sharp-cusped molars of shrews and bats crack the hard bodies of insects, while the armadillo's peglike teeth grind the same fare. The aquatic, plant-eating manatee grows molars in succession, new teeth coming in from the rear and moving forward as front molars wear down.

M AMMAL FOOD HABITS vary from season to season, depending on what is available. Hoofed animals — browsers and grazers — live off lush vegetation in the growing season, but in winter nibble on twigs or paw through snow for withered tufts. Insect eaters may find easy pickings in summer, but in cold weather must scrounge in litter, under bark, or in the soil for grubs and larvae. Some bats migrate south. Others hibernate, as do some rodents.

A few mammals are picky about food. Porcupines eat the bark of coniferous trees that no other mammal likes. Red tree mice of the Pacific Coast die if deprived of fir needles and twigs. Baleen whales gulp tiny crustaceans by the ton, while the regular diet of the mighty sperm whale consists of giant squid and octopus. Vampire bats of the tropics flourish on blood.

Gathering, curing, and storing food is a seasonal job for many rodents. Making hay while the sun shines, the little pika of our western mountains cuts plants and spreads them to dry. When it rains, he pulls his harvest under a sheltering rock. Such rodents as ground squirrels and chipmunks have hair-lined cheek pouches for carrying seeds and other food. At night the giant desert kangaroo rat fills his built-in satchels with green seed pods of peppergrass and evening primrose. He scoops out inch-wide hollows in the soil and stores his loot, covering each cache with sand. In one 55-square-foot area around a single burrow, a naturalist counted 875 caches. The seeds soon cure in the sun-heated sand. Then the busy little hoarder transfers them to underground chambers that hold perhaps eight quarts.

Pumas and jaguars gorge themselves on a fresh kill, then sometimes cover the carcass with brush and leaves to hide it while they sleep. One bloodthirsty mink dragged the bodies of 13 muskrats, two mallard ducks, and one coot into his den in

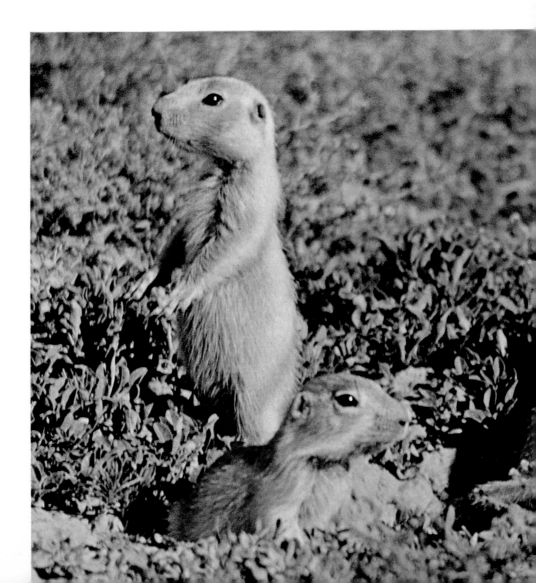

**Surprised in the open,** a prairie dog races for its life as a falcon swoops down with needlelike talons. The rodent barely escaped to its tunnel on the Great Plains.

**Heads-up sentinels** stand guard at the door of their burrow, ready to bark a warning to the rest of their prairie dog town before disappearing below. But safety may not await there. Rattlesnakes and ferrets can follow them underground; the raking claws of the badger can dig them up.

January as winter supplies. The wild canines are generally excellent providers. The wolf often hauls a large share of his kill home to feed the entire family.

Some wolves and foxes mate for life, the faithful husband helping his mate to care for the young. But such marital fidelity is rare. Many a male stays with his mate one season, then gets a new one. Most rodents are promiscuous—the male mates with the first accommodating female that comes along, then sets off happily for the next conquest. In his carefree wake, deserted spouses bear

23

and bring up their litters alone. Some of the deer and seals build up harems, proud males herding their many mates together, ruling them, and fighting off rivals.

In a mild climate, rodents produce litters all year long. Many mammals mate only during a limited season. At this time, males battle and court feminine favors. A male humpback whale often leaps spectacularly around his ladylove. The pronghorn buck prances in front of an interested doe, head erect, slim legs stepping high, white pompon flashing in the sun.

M ANY LAND MAMMALS construct elaborate nests or burrows where they rear their young. Highly social rodents like prairie dogs often co-operate in digging their homes. They live peacefully together, sometimes several in the same burrow. If a stranger from another neighborhood intrudes, they chase him away.

I was watching a dog town in Kansas when a black-footed ferret—the prairie dog's mortal enemy—entered an unoccupied burrow. I set two traps at the entrance and sat back. The ferret soon reappeared and stepped into a trap. He thrashed about, spitting and biting. Two old prairie dogs rushed at him and bit him through the small of the back. The ferret died in minutes. When the odds are right, the inoffensive prairie dog will retaliate against any enemy.

The muskrat makes a dome-shaped house of cattails and rushes that sometimes measures six or eight feet across. The beaver builds an even larger lodge of branches and muck, locating it in the still water behind his own dam. Tree squirrels and wood rats often make bulky leaf nests high in trees. Others live in hollow logs or tree holes.

Sometimes one mammal usurps another's home. The hollow tree where a raccoon usually lives may hold a surprise—as I once found out.

While doing field work in southeastern Alabama, I went on a coon hunt with local

24

**Home:** mother's back affords opossum offspring a mobile haven after they leave the pouch. A youngster ventures on daily forays for food until he decides to strike out on his own.

LOIS M. COX, PHOTO RESEARCHERS, (CENTER) ROBERT C. HERMES, NATIONAL AUDUBON SOCIETY, AND (RIGHT) © WENDELL CHAPMAN farmers. Shortly after midnight the dogs found a trail and took off in hot pursuit. Soon their frantic barking told us that the quarry had been treed. We hurried up to find the dogs baying under a huge tree with a big smoke-blackened hole at its base. We built a fire and tried to smoke out the animal. No luck. Smoke was coming out another hole halfway up the trunk. One man climbed up and stuffed the upper hole. Another held a sack over the lower hole.

In a few minutes things began to happen thick and fast; there were snarls and shouts and confusion. The man with the sack lay rolling on the ground, yelling for help and clutching at the bag, which was alive and jumping. The captive—a spitting, clawing bobcat—escaped.

WHEN snow and ice make living hard, some mammals go into hibernation. Their heartbeat and breathing slow down markedly, and their body temperature falls to only slightly above that of the surrounding air. Many bats and rodents pass the

**Home:** a flying squirrel's hollow tree; a black bear's den at the end of a one-way street.

winter this way. Such meat eaters as the black bear, grizzly, and skunk also retire in cold weather, but do not truly hibernate. They may wake up during thaws.

Estivation is a period of similar summer sleep, evidently brought on by hot, dry weather, in an arid area lacking succulent green food. Ground squirrels often estivate, plugging their burrow entrances.

Bears, mountain lions, and wolves may patrol hunting territories 50 miles wide. On the other hand, a field mouse may never venture more than 50 feet from its door. Deer and mountain sheep may band together and wander far afield searching for food. Barren Ground caribou travel several hundred miles north in spring, south in fall, or shift erratically from place to place seeking lichen forage.

Fur seals may swim 3,000 miles to and from north Pacific feeding grounds. The hoary bat has been found summering at Southampton Island in Hudson Bay; but in winter it may fly to Michoacán, Mexico.

MAMMALS FLOURISH practically everywhere. Some live underground, others in treetops. Whales never leave the sea; bats take to the air. The cactus deer mouse thrives in the southwestern desert, while its first cousin, the northern deer mouse, takes arctic temperatures of 60° below zero in its tiny stride.

Some mammals are extremely prolific, others bear only one baby every two years. Why don't the species with large families take over? One statistic-minded scientist figured that *one pair* of fast-breeding Norway rats theoretically could balloon to 350,000,000 in three years. Why aren't we knee-deep in rats? Simply because predators, disease, and famine cut the population. Prolific species face greater hazards in life than those with smaller or infrequent litters.

Some mammals rise and fall in cycles. Numbers of varying hares are apt to increase at 10-year intervals, eastern red squirrels boom every five or six years, lemmings burgeon every four or five. Abrupt die-offs, "crashes," always follow. Then the animals slowly begin to multiply again.

Man has been the prime factor in upsetting nature's balance. Before the white man came to North America, primitive tribesmen barely dented the hoofed herds that grazed on prairies, the abundant deer of eastern forests, the predators that stalked everywhere. Then came the settlers—and firearms. Men cleared the forests, built towns and cities, pushed across the continent. They killed game not only for food and clothing, but to market the hides and furs. For several centuries the slaughter continued unrestricted.

From 1764 to 1773, more than two million pounds of deerskins, representing the hides of nearly half a million animals, passed through a single port, Savannah. Just think how many hides must have been exported from all the colonies! No wonder deer eventually became scarce in many parts of the country.

The fur trade spurred America's exploration and settlement and garnered astronomical numbers of pelts. In 1788 the State of Franklin—now eastern Tennessee—authorized salaries to civil officers in pelts: the governor got 1,000 beaver skins a year, the state treasurer was worth 450 otter skins, the governor's secretary 500 raccoon skins, and each county clerk earned 300 beaver skins.

**Deposed monarch,** the grizzly ruled the West until the repeating rifle overcame his size and strength. When enraged, he is still the most feared and respected of North American carnivores. At birth this serene Yellowstone giant, like other grizzlies, was no larger than a squirrel.

FRANK AND JOHN CRAIGHEAD

Colonists, hungry for land, sometimes wiped out every animal within miles as though they feared any lingering trace of wilderness on their chosen acres.

Col. H. W. Shoemaker describes an animal drive in central Pennsylvania organized by Black Jack Schwartz, "the Wild Hunter," in 1760. Under Black Jack's direction, settlers massacred "41 panthers, 109 wolves, 112 foxes, 114 mountain cats, 17 black bears, 1 white bear, 2 elk, 98 deer, 111 buffaloes, 3 fishers, 1 otter, 12 gluttons [wolverines], 3 beavers, and upwards of 500 smaller animals.

"The choicest hides were taken," Shoemaker continues, "together with buffalo tongues, and then the heap of carcasses 'as tall as the tallest trees,' was heaped with rich pine and fired. This created such a stench that the settlers were compelled to vacate their cabins in the vicinity of the fort, three miles away. There is a small mound, which on being dug into is filled with bones. . . ."

Shoemaker notes as epilogue that "Black Jack's unpopularity with the Indians was added to when they learned of this animal drive. The red men, who only killed such animals as they actually needed for furs and food, resented such a wholesale butchery. The story has it that the Wild Hunter was ambushed by Indians while on a hunting trip and killed."

As the frontier moved westward so did the guns of hunters. Hide hunters ruthlessly slaughtered whole herds of bison on the plains. Stockmen and farmers declared war on predators. Sportsmen took to the wilds with high-powered rifles and telescopic sights to hunt the elusive bighorn and mountain goat in their craggy citadels. Airplanes now fly hunters over the Arctic to gun down polar bears.

But throw nature too far off balance and disaster may follow. In 1905 the Kaibab Plateau in Arizona supported a herd of about 4,000 mule deer. In an enthusiastic campaign to protect the deer, hundreds of mountain lions, wolves, and coyotes were killed. The herd increased alarmingly, numbering about 100,000 by 1924.

Catastrophic overbrowsing followed. Malnutrition and disease decimated the deer. By 1939 the herd had plummeted to some 10,000 and the plateau was practically a desert. The slaughter of predators had ruined nature's method of holding deer in check.

**Hot-blooded bull elk,** swinging like boxers, erupt amid docile does at the herd's wintering grounds in Jackson Hole, Wyoming.

**A thrifty Westerner, Douglas squirrel** may keep ten bushels of cones in a single savings account in Washington's Olympic National Park. Smaller deposits go into shallow holes.

Conservation, as Theodore Roosevelt said, means the wise use of natural resources. Wildlife is a valuable natural resource which man has plundered recklessly for centuries. Now at last men are working to save what is left, to restore nature's own way of ruling its wild domain.

Fortunately, many of the pockets of wilderness that shelter today's remnants of once-great herds of wild game are preserved as national or state parks, forests, or game reserves. The U. S. Fish and Wildlife Service has set up a number of wildlife refuges, game management areas, and winter ranges. State governments have done the same. Food and cover for game are being restored and improved. Game wardens live-trap deer, elk, antelope, mountain goats, raccoons, beavers, and muskrats and transplant them from unfavorable or overpopulated districts to new areas that need restocking and offer room to forage and raise families in peace.

Wildlife censuses determine game abundance, so that hunting and trapping seasons can be set. Deer have burgeoned into nuisances in many areas. But regulated hunting holds them in check. Hunters kill millions of cottontails, jack rabbits, and varying hares, yet the animals remain plentiful. The man with a gun is playing the necessary role of predator.

Yet as human population increases, civilization squeezes certain wildlife species into corners. Farmers and bison both want the same land—they simply don't mix. So the buffalo can only browse in a few protected ranges instead

**Eastern chipmunk** in a Maryland yard neatly unties peanut after hauling it up. Dubbed Clifford, "he" promptly had four babies.

of covering the prairie as its herds once did. Man hunted the bison, fur seal, and sea otter almost into oblivion. Yet the fact that they exist today is to man's credit. An alert public backed sound conservation programs, and most Americans now look upon wild animals as something to be proud of—not to kill indiscriminately.

Zoologists divide mammals into 19 orders on the basis of anatomical differences and relationships. Eleven orders appear in North America above the Rio Grande (page 51). Each order contains smaller groups—families—and each family is subdivided into genera. A genus includes one or more species. And that's not the end of it. Species are split into races or subspecies varying in size and color.

Thus the white arctic wolf and the eastern timber wolf are just two of the 24 races of the gray wolf, *Canis lupus.* This species, together with the red wolf and coyote, are the American members of the genus *Canis,* one of the divisions of the

**The coyote may look like Rover,** but his eyes speak death. He'll stalk a jack rabbit, get the jump, and snap! Wild dogs live in other lands, but this one's as American as the Wild West.

wild dog family, *Canidae.* They belong to the order of meat eaters, *Carnivora,* of the class *Mammalia,* the scientific name for mammals.

In 1758, when Linnaeus, the pioneer classifier of living things, listed the animals known to science, he put down only 86 different kinds of mammals. Zoologists have since named between 15,000 and 20,000 different species and subspecies. Close to 800 species with 3,800 forms (more than half of these are rodents!) are found on the North American continent alone.

A race in one area may differ from its neighboring race in color, size, or other characteristic. But along border areas where the races interbreed, a blending of traits occurs. A new species may be in the making.

Outside forces sometimes play a dramatic role in evolution. Take the Kaibab and the Abert squirrels, on opposite rims of the Grand Canyon. They were one form, hundreds of thousands of years ago. But the Colorado River, deepening and widening its canyon, separated them and they developed along divergent paths. The result? These brothers under the skin wear different coats.

The structure of a mammal's limbs usually shows how the group is adapted for some particular type of locomotion. Bats, the only true fliers among mammals, have greatly elongated forelimbs. The fingers stretch into a ribbing for the membranes that form wings. Some bats beat their wings rapidly, flying like swifts or swallows. They glide for short distances, but none can soar like a hawk or gull. A few bats have the knack of hovering hummingbird fashion.

The feet and toes of hoofed mammals are adapted for running, while the clawed feet of predatory animals help them climb as well as to seize their prey. The mole, armadillo, pocket gopher, and badger all have short, broad forelimbs with large, strong claws for digging.

Adaptations for aquatic life are even more marked. The beaver, muskrat, and otter — all equally at home on land or in the water — have broad webbed hind feet. The sea cow or manatee, which spends its life in the water, has lost its hind limbs, but flippered forelimbs and platterlike tail serve it well. All four feet of the aquatic carnivores, seals and walruses, are adapted as flippers. Graceful and speedy in the water, seals are awkward when they waddle ashore.

Whales, however, are the most perfectly adapted of all mammals for life in the water. Their forefeet have evolved into flippers, and all external evidence of hind limbs is gone, giving them torpedolike forms. The whale's flippers bear little resemblance to the forelimbs of most land mammals. Shaped like paddles, thickly coated with blubber, they still cover the same bone structure the bat has.

**Armadillo,** plated above but soft underneath, digs for his life when a coyote lopes by.

**Bats are mammals too.** This little brown bat banks steeply, wings puckering like sails in a sudden gust. Forearms and extra-long fingers form a framework for the membrane. Clawed thumbs protrude from the wings. He hangs by his feet, whether sleeping during the day or hibernating for the winter.

HAROLD E. EDGERTON

Whales use their flippers mainly for steering and balancing, while they propel themselves with their horizontal tails, powerful enough to shatter stout boats, as old-time whalers learned. I once watched an eight-foot bottle-nosed porpoise being netted off Cape Hatteras and was astonished by the strength in his tail. A foolhardy onlooker tried to stand on the flukes. With an effortless flip, the porpoise tossed him several feet. Like the whale, the porpoise swims with up and down strokes of his flukes, reaching impressive speeds and easily leaping twice his body length.

Mammal tails serve many uses. The beaver swings his broad tail like a sculling oar. Approach him and he'll slap the water with it to alert his neighbors. The muskrat's tail functions as a rudder, and the flying squirrel steers with his flat, furry tail when he's gliding.

Tree squirrels spread their bushy tails as parachutes when they tumble from limbs, and wrap themselves in these fur comforters to sleep. Kangaroo rats and mice use their long, slender tails as props when resting on their haunches, and as counterbalances when they jump. Without them, they'd somersault helplessly in air.

The opossum sometimes uses his naked prehensile tail for hanging from a limb, or for carrying leaves to make a nest.

Marvelously endowed with special equipment for land, sea, and air, adapted for extremes of climate, mammals fill every ecological niche. Blessed with greater brain development than any other group of living things, they rule the world. Man himself is a mammal, with the finest brain of all. And on man must rest the responsibility for conserving all the others. The wild animals of North America are a priceless, living heritage for this and future generations to understand and enjoy.

**Baby porpoise** (above) at Florida's Marineland enters the world tail first, else it would drown. Most mammals bite the umbilical cord; this mother snaps it with a whirl. She will nurse baby for nearly a year. The porpoise can remain underwater only a few minutes and usually surfaces every 30 to 45 seconds to breathe. Like the bat, he emits beeps which, bouncing back, tell of obstructions or food ahead.

    **Finback whale,** a mere handful when a six-week-old embryo (right), measures 20 feet at birth, 80 feet full-grown.

*André Durençeau*

**Trapped mastodon roars** as primitive Americans stone it to death. Bones of this flat-headed cousin of the elephant have been found with human relics from Florida to California. Colonials, discovering its manlike molars, thought them giant's teeth! The coarse-haired beast stood 10 feet at the shoulder; its dome-skulled relative, the imperial mammoth, as high as 13 feet, with tusks curling 16 feet. Muck pits in Alaska still yield frozen mammoth remains.

CHAPTER 2

# The Rise of Modern Mammals

By A. REMINGTON KELLOGG

SCREAMING IN HELPLESS RAGE, the mastodon rolled a bloodshot eye at its puny, two-legged tormentors. It had blundered into a deep pit gouged by great glaciers. Wedged tight, it probed its prison walls with furry trunk, trumpeting and lunging uselessly as primitive hunters gathered, drawn by the uproar. Here was a vast prize — a mountain of meat for the whole tribe.

Encircling this huge, witless beast, the hunters stabbed it with stone-tipped spears and battered it with rocks. They brought it to its knees and finally slew it. Mothers and daughters helped skin it and hack it apart.

This scene took place in the California of 15,000 years ago, when Ice Age glaciers were withdrawing and lush grasslands and forests again carpeted much of North America. Man was no newcomer. Nomadic hunters had groped across the misty Bering land bridge some 15,000 years before — "discovering" America perhaps 300 centuries or more ahead of Columbus, according to recent estimates by anthropologists. The mastodon's ancestors had arrived from Asia 15 to 20 million years before man. In fact, mammals have lived in North America 130 million years or more. Their saga is one of the most fascinating chapters in what Chinese villagers call "The Book of Ten Thousand Volumes" — earth's bedded strata that reveal, in fossils, the story of life.

For billions of years after its creation, a lifeless earth spun through space. And then, scientists theorize, somewhere in warm primeval waters, more than two billion years ago, the overwhelming miracle occurred, the union of organic compounds to form a single cell that could split and duplicate itself. Life began.

Those very first microscopic blobs of protoplasm left no marks on the rocks of past ages, but they spelled a teeming future for this planet. From them, scientists believe, multicelled plants and animals evolved: simple fungus to sturdy oak, primitive protozoan to modern mammal. Most dramatic of early fossils come from trilobites — flattened, hard-shelled animals that ranged from the size of an oyster to a serving tray. Waving long antennae, they scavenged along muddy seabottoms, dominating Cambrian life of half a billion years ago.

Like a television camera under the sea, the fossil sequence chronicles the first vertebrates: jawless fish, fantastic armored fish, finally tiny sharklike fish. Some 300 million years ago, plants invaded the land. And a footprint in Devonian sands records the portentous moment when a lunged amphibian crawled ashore to spend part of his life out of the mothering sea.

REPTILES DEVELOPED from amphibians. They spread quickly over the now green earth and ruled it throughout the Mesozoic era. These were the days of dinosaurs, of Tyrannosaurus rex, "King of the Dragon Lizards," who towered 20 feet, stretched 50 feet from scaly snout to tail tip, and with rows of six-inch teeth slashed his way to fame as the fiercest predator the world has ever known. Brontosaurus, a mild-mannered vegetarian, grew even longer— 70 feet. He would wallow in a bog, grazing on tropical plants.

But earth's mild climate was gradually changing, the land itself was changing, and the great lizards were doomed. Warm seas receded. Friendly marshes dried up. Forests of giant ferns and cycads, conifers and ginkgoes were pushed aside by magnolias, dogwoods, laurels, oaks, and willows. Mountains thrust up raw crests. The dinosaurs couldn't adapt. At some moment about 70 million years ago, the last Tyrannosaurus died. The king is dead! Long live the king!

And who would earth's new rulers be? During the Age of Reptiles two offshoots emerged from reptilian ancestors — birds and mammals. The latter consisted of insignificant little insect eaters, many living in trees. But they had an improved system for raising their young. Before birth, baby mammals developed inside their mother's body instead of in eggs. Born alive, they were nursed and protected instead of having to fend for themselves. These warm-blooded animals had internal "thermostats" regulating their body heat. Climatic changes killed off the dinosaurs, but the adaptable mammals were able to endure.

Timid, but marvelously equipped, down came the mammals from their trees. At first they were all about the size

**Resurrected from a muddy grave,** the skeleton of a Columbian mammoth is prepared for exhibition at the University of Wyoming in Laramie by Dr. Paul O. McGrew (left) and Dr. George Agogino. National Geographic Society support helped recover the bones from a bog in southern Wyoming where human hunters slaughtered the mired beast 11,000 years ago. Kin to the present-day Indian elephant, this specimen weighed 5 tons and towered 11 feet at the shoulder, not quite as tall as the imperial mammoth (page 36) with whom it roamed North America during the Ice Age.

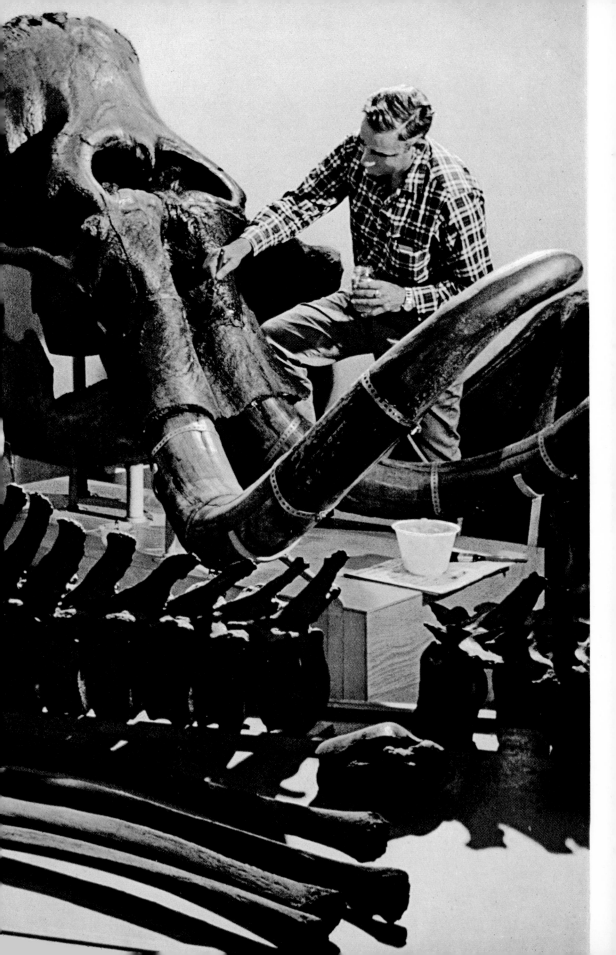

PRE-CAMBRIAN
ERA

PALEOZOIC ERA

Cambrian

Ordovician

Silurian

Devonian

Diagram scales geology's four grand eras and their subdivisions to show relative duration. Exceptions are the Pre-Cambrian, which would occupy five extra pages in this book, and the Quaternary, which is rightfully entitled to only 1/50 inch. Dating of animal and vegetable life reflects current scientific thought.

| | | | |
|---|---|---|---|
| 1. Microscopic Algae | 16. Meganeuron | 31. Mosasaur | 46. Tulip Tree |
| 2. Segmented Worm | 17. Eogyrinus | 32. Elasmosaurus | 47. Maple |
| 3. Archaeocyathus | 18. Shark | 33. Hesperornis | 48. Pine |
| 4. Snail | 19. Seymouria | 34. Water Lily | 49. Whale |
| 5. Trilobite | 20. Edaphosaurus | 35. Palm | 50. Bluefin Tuna |
| 6. Starfish | 21. Plesiosaur | 36. Ginkgo | 51. Crocodile |
| 7. Giant Nautiloid | 22. Cynognathus | 37. Triceratops | 52. Saber-toothed Cat |
| 8. Corals | 23. Cycads | 38. Tyrannosaurus | 53. Equus |
| 9. Heterostracan | 24. Plateosaurus | 39. Pteranodon | 54. Bison |
| 10. Acanthodian | 25. Araucarites | 40. Diceratherium | 55. Woolly Mammoth |
| 11. Osteolepis | 26. Ichthyosaur | 41. Uintatherium | 56. Teratornis |
| 12. Ferns | 27. Brontosaurus | 42. Diatryma | 57. Sequoia |
| 13. Ichthyostega | 28. Stegosaurus | 43. Alticamelus | 58. Black Oak |
| 14. Lepidodendron | 29. Archaeopteryx | 44. Mesohippus | 59. Monkey |
| 15. Calamites | 30. Archelon | 45. Amebelodon | 60. Man |

AGE OF

AGE OF MARINE INVERTEBRATES

MILLIONS OF YEARS AGO

520    440    360    320    265

## Life's endless miracle parades out of the mists of time

No fossils record when creation first stirred in the warm Pre-Cambrian seas. Earliest traces of life were left by one-celled algae and fungi, dead two billion years. Until half a billion years ago the threads of evolution remained almost invisible. By then sea creatures without backbones (figures 2 through 8) had developed; they live on today as sponges, corals, worms, mollusks, and crustaceans.

Fishes swam into prominence as the first ani-

of rats and mice, but they quickly began to specialize and so to vary in size and form. Spreading over the face of the land, the meek inherited the earth.

A few of the most ancient mammal lines still flourish today—the opossum, for example, and some of the shrews. But many experimental models proved impracticable and died, like the six-horned Uintathere. Massive in size but tiny in brain, it finally gave up the struggle for survival to smarter creatures.

Other ancient mammals were the forerunners of more progressive types. Among these were the raccoonlike creodonts, ancestors of modern carnivores, and the condylarths, from which all modern hoofed mammals descend.

About 50 million years ago new mammals migrated from Asia to America— among them the first little camels and Eohippus, the dawn horse. No higher than

Mississippian

Pennsylvanian

Permian

Triassic

Jurassic

Cretaceous

Tertiary

Quaternary

Paleocene
Eocene
Oligocene
Miocene
Pliocene

Recent
Pleistocene

Carboniferous

AGE OF REPTILES

AGE OF MAMMALS

FISHES, AMPHIBIA

MILLIONS OF YEARS AGO

| 265 | 235 | 210 | 185 | 155 | 130 | 70 | 2-3 |

JOHN W. LOTHERS, NATIONAL GEOGRAPHIC STAFF

mals with backbones (9-11); they were progenitors of the amphibians (13), whose legs and lungs enabled them to waddle out on land. From them evolved the mighty dinosaurs (27, 28, 38), destined to rule the earth for 100 million years. But as the day of these giants waned, a vital new age was dawning.

Cold-blooded reptiles gave way to warm-blooded birds (29) and mammals. The Cenozoic, which embraces our time, produced the world's largest animal, the whale (49), and the smartest, man (60).

Meanwhile, the vegetable kingdom evolved from primitive seaweeds (1) through flowering plants (35).

a fox terrier, Eohippus browsed North America's subtropical lowlands, unaware that his remote kin, lithe and long-limbed, would someday set hearts beating at the Kentucky Derby. Eohippus had four toes on his forefeet, three on his hind feet. As millenniums rolled by, the primitive horse would grow larger and the number of toes diminish until a single functional toe — or hoof — remained.

In the Oligocene, beginning about 40 million years ago, volcanoes spewed ash over much of western North America, the climate cooled, and grasses, conifers, and hardwood trees edged out the lush subtropical flora of earlier epochs. By now rodents have expanded mightily and meat eaters have branched into catlike, doglike, and weasel-like forms. Great herds of massive Titanotheres, stupid and ungainly, wander the plains like bison of a later day. Wolflike animals raid the fringes of the

41

herd, picking off stragglers. Foraging beside a swamp is Archaeotherium, a giant
six-foot-high pig with bony knobs on its jaws and below its eyes. And bounding
underfoot is a gnawing mammal much like the rabbit of today.

Great grasslands flourished in the cooler, drier climate of the next epoch, the
Miocene, from 28 to 12 million years ago. Here was the golden age of mammals,
when grazing animals spread and developed—as did the meat eaters that preyed
on them. Horses abounded, big and handsome now, well equipped to gallop across
the plains escaping catlike carnivores. Many forerunners of deer and antelope

## From Eohippus to modern mount, the horse trots through 50 million years

Parading skeletons trace the rise of the horse (above). Dobbin's story begins with foot-high Eohippus, dawn horse of the Eocene (above right). A Lilliputian who could look a prairie flower in the eye, he cut tiny trails through brush country of the ancient West. His four-toed front feet and three-toed hind ones gave no hint of the horseshoe; his arched back gave little promise for the saddle.

But time wrought its changes. Four toes gave way to three, legs grew long and strong, maned neck stretched above the shrubs. Such was Hypohippus (right), who browsed deer-like in Miocene forests. He lost the race for survival during the Pliocene, but other forms,

blood of champions-to-be coursing in their veins, lived on. A million years ago donkey-size *Equus scotti* (lower right) kicked up Texas dust with his single flat-tened toes—now hoofs. With the coming of the Ice Age, horses joined the trek to Asia.

A scant 450 years ago their domesticated scions were brought back to America, and some of these sired the wild horses of the west-ern plains. Today's steed (left) ranks as one of ev-olution's noblest works.

43

wore strange antlers and horns. Synthetoceras had a fork sprouting from its nose besides horns branching from its head. There was even a horned rodent.

How do we know such creatures existed? Tragedies millions of years old can be read in the fossil remains today. Take the ancient quicksands along Nebraska's Niobrara River, deathtrap in Miocene and Pliocene days. One section yielded some 17,000 skeletons. Many belonged to Moropus, weird, claw-hoofed relative of the horse. Most came from Diceratherium, a small edition of the rhinoceros. Perhaps, crazed with thirst after a trek across the dry plains, the little rhinos

André Durenceau

**Hunters ambush an enormous bison at a water hole**

*Bison antiquus,* the ancestor of today's bison, fed and clothed Americans in prehistoric times. Countless herds of these huge wild cattle roamed the plains, then died out mysteriously, as did other Ice Age giants.

Big as this ancient bison loomed, he was dwarfed by a predecessor, *Bison latifrons,* whose horns measured seven feet from tip to tip. Modern bison grow short, curved horns.

Like *banderilleros* in a bull ring, these bold Folsom hunters drive their darts into the bison. One launches his stone-tipped spear with an *atlatl,* a throwing stick believed older than the bow and arrow.

Capulin volcano erupts in the distance. Its extinct cone stands in northeastern New Mexico eight miles from the hunting site which gave Folsom man his name.

plunged into this river, then trampled each other. The sands snuffed out their lives.

Toward the end of the Pliocene, some two million years ago, life on this planet faced an incredible threat. Cool, damp weather, year after year, warned of a stupendous build-up of ice in polar regions. The great freeze drew so much water from the oceans that their levels dropped two to three hundred feet. Land bridges between the Americas and across Bering Strait were laid bare.

Then, four times the vast ice sheet—in some places two miles thick—ground southward, scouring the face of the earth, changing geography, driving animal life

*André Durenceau*

**Giant bear mauls hunters** who blundered into its lair. Lances are no match for daggerlike claws. True bears like this Ice Age ancestor of the 1,500-pound Alaska brown entered North America after short-faced bears had vanished.

46

**Saber-toothed cats,** terrors of the Ice Age, strike down mooselike Cervalces. Shape of the antlers sets him apart from the moose. Princeton University preserves the only known complete skeleton, found in a New Jersey bog.

before its inexorable march. The last ponderous withdrawal of the glaciers started as recently as 10,000 years ago, radiocarbon tests indicate, and is still going on.

Great migrations of animals took place during the Pleistocene, or Ice Age. Camels, except for the small variety that turned to South America and became the llama, took the bridge to Asia. So did horses, native Americans for 50 million years. The horse did not return to America until the days of the conquistadores. Cortés sent mounted men into battle against hordes of Indians, who broke and ran in terror, for they "thought that the horse and its rider were all one animal."

From South America came the armored Glyptodon, anticipating the day when his little relative, the nine-banded armadillo, would venture across the Rio Grande to United States soil. But whereas the armadillo can curl up in a tight defensive ball, Glyptodon's armor was unjointed. Another South American immigrant was the giant sloth Megatherium, probably outweighing an Indian elephant. He could rear 20 feet, stretching his coarse-haired body to strip leaves from trees with his long tongue. Swinging his great claws, he would try to fight off the saber-toothed cat, whose eight-inch fangs could rip the life out of him.

Smilodon, the sabertooth, we know best from the La Brea tar pits, today surrounded by Los Angeles. Here, oozing petroleum fashioned a deep, clinging quagmire, camouflaged beneath a film of water. Indians used the tar to seal baskets; Spanish settlers waterproofed adobe homes with it, little realizing what lay in the depths. In 1905, remains of extinct animals were found and the search was on. Scientists have since excavated hundreds of thousands of bones—skeletons of camels, dog-size antelopes, giant bison, and sabertooths that came to prey on the others and stayed to die. The extraordinarily well-preserved bones suggest a panorama of Ice Age mammals, bellowing and screaming, fighting and fleeing, perhaps on the very spot where Hollywood meets Vine today.

Moose, caribou, musk oxen, mountain sheep, true bears, and wolverines all came to America across the Bering land bridge—and flourished. But the mightiest immigrants of all, the mastodons and mammoths, were slated for extinction.

*Charles R. Knight, courtesy of Los Angeles County Museum*

## La Brea tar pits, deathtrap for Ice Age mammals, yield their bones to science

Saber-toothed Smilodon lowers his head and roars. The great cat is hungry, and here is a place where meat does not have to be chased. He glowers across the pool at a giant ground sloth that had come to drink and got mired. Springing, he stabs his helpless prey with eight-inch fangs. The sloth dies and Smilodon feasts. A paw slips, and the big cat struggles to free himself from the clinging tar. Overhead, a vulture soars on wings of 12-foot span. He waits for Smilodon to die, then swoops down to feast. But a wing-tip strikes the tar; La Brea claims another victim.

Lumbering mammoths, primitive bison, camels and horses come to drink. Dire wolves (right) and other predators throng to the banquet and are mired in turn. Bones sink into the blackness, layer upon layer, leaving a priceless record of extinct animals for 20th century scientists to dig out and study.

Today the black pond mirrors Los Angeles buildings, giving no sign of its history of death. But the tenacious tar still traps small animals.

The woolly mammoth, nine feet high at the shoulder, wore dense wool beneath coarse hair and roamed the very fringe of the great glaciers. Some must have bogged down in arctic swamps and frozen, for they turn up yet, perfectly preserved in nature's deep freeze, their meat still red. One was found in the Siberian tundra intact but for part of the trunk eaten by wolves. Falling into a crevasse thousands of years ago, it had fractured hip and foreleg and ruptured a blood vessel fighting to escape. Food was still clenched between its teeth. This Beresovska mammoth, mounted, remains in the U.S.S.R., but at the National Museum in Washington, D. C., we have samples of its skin, muscle tissue, 30-inch-long hair, and stomach contents.

**WHALES**

**GNAWING MAMMALS**

The mastodon, which preceded the woolly mammoth to this continent by millions of years, still thrived in North American forests perhaps as late as 5,000 years ago. Both were small compared to the imperial mammoth of the western plains—13 feet tall, with incurving 16-foot tusks.

One giant bison spread his horns seven feet. A smaller species sired the present bison. One other creation venturing out of Asia would have more impact than all the others. This was man.

Early hunters saw many fantastic American mammals. Men battled mammoth and mastodon, shied away from saber-toothed cats and dire wolves, met bear-size beavers. But these and other strange beasts soon vanished. Scientists can only speculate why.

Man spread over the continent, hunting wide, fashioning stone knives and tools, building fires and cooking meat. Near Lubbock, Texas, finely fashioned spear points have been found with the remains of an extinct bison. Charred bones have enabled scientists to date the site by the carbon 14 method. The reading: 9,883 years old, give or take 350 years.

The centuries slipped by. In 1519 a Spanish officer serving under Cortés found the leg bone of a mastodon and shipped it home. And in 1706 clergyman Cotton Mather corresponded with Governor Dudley of Massachusetts about some mastodon teeth and bones that had turned up in the Hudson River Valley. Thomas Jefferson, sending Lewis and Clark off to the Northwest a century later, told them to keep their eyes peeled for any mammoth that might still roam that wilderness.

Most pioneers would have dismissed such mammoth talk as simply another tall frontier tale—a case of "seeing the elephant," as they used to say of anything that stretched belief. Animals? Why, here were enough deer to suit a king. Here were untouchable porcupines and unapproachable skunks, shifting seas of bison, the flashing rumps of pronghorns. Here were beaver for a man to trap, and giant bears to challenge.

All these the settlers could see with their own eyes. And so can we, for they are still with us, as the following chapters reveal.

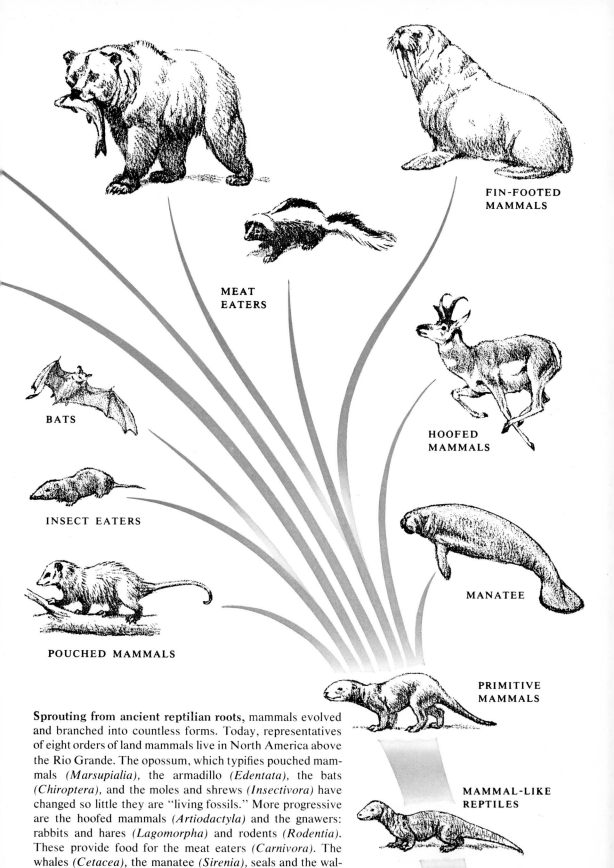

FIN-FOOTED
MAMMALS

MEAT
EATERS

BATS

HOOFED
MAMMALS

INSECT EATERS

MANATEE

POUCHED MAMMALS

PRIMITIVE
MAMMALS

**Sprouting from ancient reptilian roots,** mammals evolved and branched into countless forms. Today, representatives of eight orders of land mammals live in North America above the Rio Grande. The opossum, which typifies pouched mammals *(Marsupialia)*, the armadillo *(Edentata)*, the bats *(Chiroptera)*, and the moles and shrews *(Insectivora)* have changed so little they are "living fossils." More progressive are the hoofed mammals *(Artiodactyla)* and the gnawers: rabbits and hares *(Lagomorpha)* and rodents *(Rodentia)*. These provide food for the meat eaters *(Carnivora)*. The whales *(Cetacea)*, the manatee *(Sirenia)*, seals and the walrus *(Pinnipedia)* thrive in the adjacent seas.

MAMMAL-LIKE
REPTILES

*Walter A. Weber, National Geographic staff artist*

PART II

# The Hoofed Mammals

TEEMING HERDS dug their hoofs into rich soil and thundered
across America's unfenced plains. Forests and glens offered abundant
shelter, forage was everywhere. Eastern settlers found fat game
at their doorsteps. "Being in Want of Provisions," frontier scout
Christopher Gist "went out and killed a Deer." Out west a Sioux horseman
could spy a distant vapor cloud rising from a sea of panting bison.
Time and the conquering white man erased such visions. Pitifully few
horned creatures wandered the wild concourse where Meriwether Lewis
saw "immence herds of buffaloe, deer Elk and Antelopes." Falling
before hunters, they seemed doomed to extinction.
Thanks to game laws and sanctuaries the hoofed ones now have a chance.
Hope brightens for bighorn sheep, musk ox, and bison, for the
wily peccary of the Rio Grande, and the last few score dainty Key deer.

# CHAPTER 3

# Deer, the Antlered Tribe

By VICTOR H. CAHALANE

**Lordly bull elk,** aristocrats of the deer clan, parade towering racks of sharp-pronged antlers.

W HO'S THERE?
    Deep in the mashed potatoes and chicken of Sunday dinner in the
    Chiricahua Mountains of southeastern Arizona, I took a few moments to
reach the back door of my cabin.

The knock was repeated, this time more impatiently.

I opened the door to find an uninvited guest. Lowering his antlers, he advanced
to knock again. As I stepped back he peered into the room expectantly. Behind him
lay the wreckage of our Sunday dessert. Chunks of ice were scattered over the
ground, and lying in the dust was the empty ice cream freezer. This eager young

55

These wapiti high-step through Wyoming's valley of the Lamar in Yellowstone National Park.

ROSS HALL

buck had found a taste sensation unknown when his prehistoric ancestors
roamed the earth.

About 25 million years ago the predecessors of modern deer had no antlers,
and were neither so handsome nor so
large as their descendants are today.
No bigger than cats, they scurried
through the Oligocene forests of the Old
World, fighting their battles with long
saberlike teeth. Somewhere in those
lost mysterious centuries the deer's
structure changed. Most of them grew
larger and developed antlers.

During the thousands of years climates changed as mighty glaciers advanced and receded over the earth. A
land bridge rose out of the waters, joining Asia and Alaska, and over it deer
migrated to America. When the waters
again swept over the land bridge, the
isolated deer adapted themselves in form
and habit to their new environment.

Primitive man knew only a few kinds
of deer. Today mammalogists have dif-
ferentiated nearly 60 species around the
world. Seven species, with many times

**Yearling whitetail** wears his first pronged
spikes. Antlers grow larger, more branched
each year until the buck reaches his prime.

that number of races, roam America north of Mexico. These range in size from
the Alaska moose, seven feet at the shoulder, to Florida's dainty Key deer, sometimes less than two feet high.

The males of all American deer proudly display antlers. In the cooler regions
they fight bravely with these in the fall, lose them meekly in winter or early spring,
and in the next few months grow new ones for further conquests.

"What becomes of the antlers that deer cast off every year? Why don't we see
them?" everyone asks. The horns either provide calcium for millions of rodents
or rot into the ground.

A few European and Asiatic deer wear handsome spots throughout their lives.
The fawns of some North American deer are also spotted, but all adults are clad
in plain browns of various shades. They don new coats twice a year: heavy and
warm for winter, light and cool for summer. When time to change, they rip off the
old apparel in patches here and there on bushes and briers. At other times well
dressed, they appear badly moth-eaten by winter's end.

Deer ordinarily are vegetarians. Supposedly they confine themselves to browsing
and grazing, but I have seen them develop appetites for chewing gum, tobacco,
oranges, cantaloupes, fried eggs, bacon, tapioca pudding, chocolate bars, ice cream
—even wrapping paper. Virginia or white-tailed deer have been known to eat fish, and

57

**Mule deer in prime** sports many-forked antlers. This Idaho buck will
drop horns in midwinter, grow a new set before next breeding season.

KENNETH FINK AND (ABOVE) FREDERICK KENT TRUSLOW

Salt rubbed on chin coaxes a sticky kiss from a friend. Deer crave salt, and in the wild they get it from natural licks of salty clay or mud. Maine campers kept this pet whitetail under permit during the summer.

Winsome fawn (opposite) savors the milk of human kindness among Seminole Indians on Florida's Big Cypress Reservation. In the forest a whitetail fawn lies still and camouflaged when danger threatens, its white spots like flecks of filtered sunlight on the forest floor.

In the Canadian Rockies a bold buck mule deer sporting a handsome rack (lower) ventures into Banff, Alberta, for a handout. Keen eyesight, hearing, and smell keep deer alert to peril. Flying hoofs give speed for getaway.

B. ANTHONY STEWART, NATIONAL GEOGRAPHIC PHOTOGRAPHER

an elk has been seen gnawing a ham bone. But apparently they draw the line at onions. I remember seeing a deer, offered one, lift his hoof, slap the donor's wrist in sharp reproof, and walk disdainfully away.

All deer must have salt. They lick large holes in saline clay with their rough tongues. Imagine a deer's joy at finding this necessary item of diet rained like manna out of heaven. In vast game areas managers have dropped blocks of salt from airplanes, facetiously called "flying saltcellars."

Most deer love the water and are powerful swimmers. Gregarious species are often seen splashing one another and apparently playing water games. On land they delight in a game of tag and follow-the-leader. Some also indulge in a sort of dance. Keeping nose to the ground, wapiti and moose trot with occasional galloping steps in circles sometimes 30 feet in diameter.

Like white flags of distress, the upraised tails or hairs on the rumps of some species fly among the trees, communicating alarm. Many deer also have glands on their feet that leave a warning scent as they speed from danger.

Deer have a strong sense of curiosity and often investigate any unusual object. I saw this once on Mount Toby in Massachusetts. For a half hour I had been perfectly quiet. Then I heard a twig snap. I couldn't see anything through the brush,

WILLARD R. CULVER AND (BELOW) JAMES L. STANFIELD

ELK

but I realized that something was slowly circling me. Suddenly an ear-piercing whistle sounded just behind me. Practically jumping out of my shoes, I turned in time to see a whitetail leaping away through the tall brush. The doe evidently had been unable to tell what I was, for deer have trouble identifying motionless objects when there is no wind to carry scent. She had uttered that hair-raising shriek just to make me move —and she had succeeded!

Deer have other differently pitched cries for scolding their young, bugling a challenge to battle, bleating fright or pain, snorting rage or disgust, and calling their mates. Affectionate creatures, they often rub noses as if questioning and assuring each other of their mutual regard.

### Heads or tails, these deer present clues to their identity

New antlers are grown yearly by males of all American deer, as illustrated by the bull elk (left). First stage is a pair of simple budlike projections covered with velvet, which push out from bony pedicels on his head in late winter or early spring. The velvet—soft skin covered with fine hair—is laced with blood vessels. These carry nourishment and calcium to the rapidly growing antlers, which are true bone.

In early autumn antlers attain full growth. The blood supply is stopped and they harden. The bull rubs the velvet off against trees and rocks, then polishes his weapons for use against rivals. After the fall rut, antlers drop off.

A buck grows his first set of antlers when he is a yearling (page 57). These are straight spikes or single-forked weapons. With each suc-

60

MULE DEER

BLACK-TAILED
DEER

The buck is a polygamous creature. One species, like the whitetail, will take only a single mate at a time, but soon tire of her and rush off to seek a new one. Another, like the wapiti, will maintain a large harem during the mating season and stand ready to fight any male who attempts to steal one of his wives.

When fall dapples the North American landscape, the stag rubs his antlers free of velvet, then polishes and sharpens them for battle. Eyes bloodshot and neck swollen, he plunges through the forest challenging his fellows. Meeting a rival, he lowers his head and charges. The contestants collide with a crash. Antlers locked and heads down, they tear up the ground with their hoofs, trample bushes, uproot small trees. Again and again they break their lock and lunge at each other.

ceeding year the antlers become larger and heavier, with additional tines, until he reaches his prime. In old age his antlers are smaller, usually malformed.

**White-tailed deer** carries antlers with dominant main beams and unbranched rising tines. The large tail, white beneath, waves high as the deer bounds away. **Black-tailed deer** displays Y-branched antlers and a tail black on top frequently held erect but unwaving in flight. **Mule deer** has a dark horseshoe patch on the forehead and bears antlers similar to the blacktail's but larger and wider spreading. Its tail, white with black tip, is held down in running.

Glands on the hind legs secrete a musky substance; its function is not clearly understood.

Mule deer in velvet crowding a perch in the North Cascades (opposite) soon will scrape their horns smooth and go courting.

*Walter A. Weber, National Geographic staff artist*

WHITE-TAILED DEER

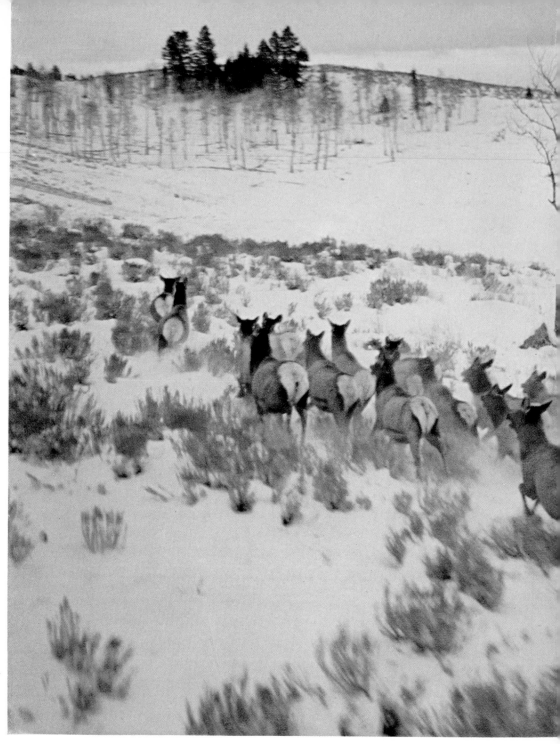

Ladies first! Bull elk and harem flee helicopter herders in Yellowstone. To prevent overgrazing,

Serious as these fights appear, few deer die from them. A losing stag often takes to the woods and the winner is usually content to let him go. If the loser battles on, his antlers may be broken—or he may be gored to death. Sometimes antlers become locked and the combatants face slow death together.

During the rutting period the males eat little, and by the end of the season they are gaunt and worn out. Rivalry ends, grievances are forgotten. Those species rangers round up excess animals in winter and ship many of them to other parks and ranches.

that live in herds often submit to a matriarchal system. Led by a wise old doe, they rest and restore their health for a new season. In late winter the bucks drop their antlers, and with the coming of spring the long, slow process of growing a new pair begins. At this time the does begin to drop their fawns.

Deer normally give birth to one or two fawns at a time, rarely triplets. Most fawns are spotted and do not have the strong odor of their parents to betray them.

63

The doe, leaving them hidden during the day while she browses, returns to nurse them. As they grow older, she takes them abroad at night for food. The fawn soon learns to drop in his tracks at the first sign of danger and stay still. Although fawns are usually well hidden, I once found one lying flat in the wheel rut of a road, blissfully unaware of how conspicuous he was.

Unlike bears, which are interested in no young except their own, deer mothers sometimes adopt orphans. A few years ago, an elk cow was seen running up a steep hill leading four calves. The youngsters floundered in deep snow, falling farther and farther behind. Looking back, the old elk saw their predicament. Despite the danger to herself, she retraced her steps. Pushing the youngsters with her forefeet, she forced them to turn back and take a less difficult route.

But this good neighbor policy does not always apply. In the mountains of Arizona I once watched a cocky fawn, evidently tired of the flavor of his mother's milk, edge up to his best friend's mother to try a new brand. With a swift, well-placed kick the doe sent him flying into the bushes. He bleated a sharp cry of surprise and scrambled back to his own mother. Thereafter he stayed home.

BEARS HAVE BEEN KNOWN TO KILL FAWNS, and many mother deer—especially elk—will not tolerate their presence. A ranger in Yellowstone National Park told me of seeing a mother elk charge into the woods after a black bear. Scrambling up a tree, the would-be assassin narrowly eluded her. Snorting with anger, she went back to feeding with her calf.

After a few minutes the bear descended cautiously to the ground and tried to sneak off. But the elk had seen him. She came at him with a rush, and the bear climbed back up. The elk shook her head menacingly and returned to her repast, casting an occasional stern eye toward the prisoner.

As the afternoon wore on, the bear made further efforts to escape but the elk would turn and with a threatening look send him back to the branches. At last the cow wearied of the sport and ambled off with her calf. Anyone who has been chased by a bear would have relished watching this rascal being treed by an elk.

Always suspicious of people, a mother moose grew angry when she found a park ranger trying to pull her calf from a quagmire. She charged the ranger up a tree and proceeded to rescue the youngster herself. Then she stalked off, snorting angrily at both man and calf.

Most male deer never recognize their own offspring. Even gregarious bucks who herd with the does and fawns show no concern for the young, letting them shift for themselves or run to their mothers. There are exceptions, however.

Toward the end of a long hard winter in Yosemite National Park a hungry coyote was seen slinking about the edge of a mule deer band, apparently trying to pick off one of the weakened fawns. Finally several anxious does ganged up on the marauder and trampled him to death. This over, a handsome buck appeared. With a lordly gesture of finishing a noble deed, he tossed the mangled corpse over his antlers and stalked away.

Coyotes, wolves, and other canines take their toll of deer, as do bears and

**Browsing moose** leaves a wake in a grass-choked pond in Wyoming's Grand Teton National Park. Bulbous nose and hump help distinguish him from other deer. Moose favor forest land with lakes and swamps; a calf only a few days old is an efficient swimmer and travels with its mother wherever she goes.

IAMES P. BLAIR, NATIONAL GEOGRAPHIC PHOTOGRAPHER

CANADIAN NATIONAL FILM BOARD

■ Winter Range of Caribou     ▨ Summer Range of Caribou

such cats as the puma, lynx, and jaguar. Besides these enemies, deer are subject to many diseases and parasites.

A deer's life expectancy ranges from three to 15 years, possibly longer, according to his species. Even if he survives disease and enemies' attacks, his life is threatened by one accident after another. Like a person, he can make a fatal slip in his bathtub. Many a moose has skidded and bogged down in a lily pond, never to rise again.

Northland deer sometimes break through the ice while crossing rivers, and drown or freeze to death. Snowslides may trap or bury them. They may leap from cliffs in terror-stricken flight and impale themselves on branches or sharp rocks.

OF ALL THE DEER, caribou are probably the most migratory. Like ghosts, they drift through the northern forests in their never-ending search for food, or wander over the scrub-covered tundra, where Eskimo hunters often lie in wait with guns.

The whole economy of many tribes of Eskimos and northern Indians has long been based on caribou hunting—just as the economy of the Plains Indians was based on the buffalo. As the caribou herds diminished, many Eskimos became impoverished. Around the turn of the century the U. S. Government brought reindeer from

67

A. W. F. BANFIELD, CANADIAN WILDLIFE SERVICE

**Caribou stampede** as a plane spotter tallies a herd (above). The Canadian Wildlife Service takes a census of the animals during spring migrations. Barren Ground caribou winter in forested areas shown in black on the map, then move north to summer on the lichen-rich Barren Grounds. Wanton slaughter and destructive fires have diminished their range and numbers.

Some years ago Old World **reindeer** were introduced as famine insurance for Eskimos dependent on dwindling caribou. A herd of these domestic deer (far left) holds aloft a thicket of branched velvet antlers.

Reindeer (right) thunders down the stretch in a Finnish race. The winning reindeer beat Finland's best racehorse, ran 2,000 meters in 2:56.8 minutes.

BERT PERSSON, ERWIN LÖWE

**Disguised in deerskins,** Indians approach their quarry undetected and shoot them easily, as depicted by Jacques le Moyne, artist with the French Huguenot settlers in Florida, 1564-5.

Siberia into Alaska to take the caribou's place. Their descendants were later introduced into Canada.

The reindeer is the only species of deer that has been successfully domesticated. For the Lapps and other inhabitants of northern Scandinavia and Finland, reindeer are the chief wealth and staff of life. The animals furnish meat, milk, clothing, and many other necessities. With no maintenance except herding, even a poor Lapp

**Deer antler tool** found in Alabama's Russell Cave was used by primitive man to chip flint arrowheads to a deadly point.

can afford a fair-sized herd. If he wants to go visiting, the Laplander harnesses a reindeer to his boatlike sleigh and rides merrily off at a nine- or ten-mile clip.

Many ancient remedies were made from the European elk, musk deer, and others. Most were worse than useless. The left hind foot removed from a living European elk was believed to cure epilepsy if part of it were worn, ground up in wine and drunk, or burned and inhaled. The antlers would do almost as well if taken the first of September. If gotten earlier, at a tender stage, the horns were sliced and steeped with herbs and spirits to treat snake bite. The animal's fat was made into an ointment. His heart, ground or burned, was considered a sure cure for heart trouble. The approved remedy for arthritis, rheumatism, and cramps was to wrap dried nerves about the afflicted limbs. If worn continuously, further attacks were prevented!

Deer fat is still rendered into grease and candles. Deer hides are in demand for fine leathers. Antlers go into umbrella and knife handles, furniture, chandeliers, glue, and cloth sizing.

Man has always hunted deer. Long before the dawn of history the American Indian stalked them with bows and arrows. He ate their flesh, warmed himself in their hides, wove ropes from their tendons, made harpoons, weapons, and tools from their antlers. European colonists pushing westward through the Appalachian forests depended on deer for food and clothing. When he needed meat, the pioneer hunted deer. When he needed a new outfit, he made it of tanned deer hide. Buckskins were the frontier fashion.

Today the sale of hunting licenses brings much revenue. Every fall, hundreds of thousands of eager hunters sally forth with the opening of deer season, armed with rifle, bow, or shotgun to get their buck.

Deer have even been hunted with music! Hunters in Europe have lured deer within shooting range by hiring violinists to play for them. Music indeed hath charms – if the animal is not a critic. In Sweden one moose became so enraged at what he heard that he charged into the blind and killed both hunter and musician.

69

## A Portfolio

Following are biographies of the principal species of North American deer, illustrated in full color by National Geographic Staff Artist Walter A. Weber and other noted wildlife artists. Heights and weights show the range between an average female of the smallest race and a large male of the largest race.

Wapiti bull bugles a challenge to a lucky rival. Winner's prize is the entourage of cows.

*Walter A. Weber, National Geographic staff artist*

WALTER A. WEBER

# AMERICAN ELK or WAPITI

*Cervus elaphus*

ASPENS FLAME GOLDEN in the crisp fall air as a great bull elk stalks proudly across the mountain meadow, his many-pointed antlers silhouetted against the sky. Behind come the cows of his harem. September is the beginning of the rut or mating season for elk in the northern Rockies and the bull is in his prime. Tossing his head, he bugles triumphantly.

Starting with a low hoarse bellow, his voice rises to a clear high tone, then explodes in a series of grunts. *A-a-a-a-ai-e-eeeee eough! e-uh! e-uh! e-uh!*

An answering bugle sounds nearby and another bull advances, stiff-legged, into the clearing. The master of the harem, dark mane bristling and swollen neck held high, strides forward to meet the challenge. Polished racks of sweeping antlers clash. Rugged, steel-sinewed bodies strain and shove against each other. Back and forth the struggle seesaws. Suddenly the interloper breaks off and retreats. Snorting, the victorious bull returns to his cows.

The elk or wapiti is the most polygamous deer of America, and perhaps of the world. The strongest and cleverest bull garners the largest harem, sometimes sixty or more cows.

The rutting season is over in late October or early November, and with the first heavy snows the elk bands descend to winter ranges in lower country, following well-defined migration routes. On their way, the bands merge into sizable herds.

Even in the rugged reaches of the Rockies, man has encroached on the wapiti's natural wintering grounds—the valley bottoms and foothill country where the snowfall is light enough for elk to reach the cured grasses beneath. He has fenced in fields, overstocked the land with cattle, or harvested the hay for his own livestock. Caught between the snow-locked mountains and the pre-empted valleys, many elk starved during severe seasons in years past. Today special feeding and refuge areas help provide for the herds.

Best known is the 24,000-acre National Elk Refuge in Jackson Hole, Wyoming, where each year as many as 9,000 elk find winter food on former farmlands. Licensed hunting keeps the animals from multiplying out of bounds.

In late winter the bulls lose their antlers. When spring comes, the big herds start to break up and scatter, drifting up the valleys toward the high country of their summer range. The bulls wander off alone or in small groups to grow new antlers and fatten on the lush alpine meadows. The cows begin to drop their calves.

Born in late May or early June, the spotted calf weighs 25 to 40 pounds. The enterprising little fellow begins to follow his mother when only three or four days old.

For the first few weeks the calf lives on milk alone, but gradually begins to nibble tender shoots of grass. By August he is partially weaned and has begun to lose his baby spots. It is hard to believe that the gawky bull calf will some day weigh 700 to 800 pounds, stand five feet tall at the shoulder, and brandish magnificent antlers that may spread another five feet.

Though he grows to be a huge, serious-minded creature, he still has his lighter moments. Wapiti that are not so old as to be overdignified or grumpy often have been seen playing tag and splashing one another in the water. Bulls can run an estimated 35 miles an hour. When necessary, they are strong long-distance swimmers.

When the English colonists first penetrated the eastern forests of America, they saw this magnificent animal, larger than their own European stag or red deer but closely resembling it. The Shawnee Indians called it *wapiti*. The English, however, named it elk, after yet another member of Europe's antlered tribe.

Originally the American elk ranged farthest of all our hoofed game animals. It flourished in the heart of the continent, from northern Canada to southern New Mexico, and from Massachusetts and

North Carolina to the California coast. Like the buffalo, the elk seemed equally at home in the forests east of the Mississippi River and on the plains flanking the Rocky Mountains. It ranged from sea level to above timber line on lofty mountain ranges. Advancing settlers, slaughtering for meat and hides, wiped out the eastern form *(C. e. canadensis)*. Records indicate that the last eastern elk was killed in 1867 in the mountains of central Pennsylvania.

The Rocky Mountain elk *(C. e. nelsoni)* is the most numerous of the surviving races. Coated in grayish brown, with darker legs and head, it has a straw-colored tail and rump patch. Small bands of this race have been transplanted to a few eastern wilderness areas in recent years.

The larger and darker Roosevelt or Olympic elk *(C. e. roosevelti)* inhabits the rain forest and redwood belt of the Pacific Northwest, while the much smaller, paler tule elk *(Cervus nannodes)* remains only in California's Kern and Inyo counties.

The Manitoba elk *(C. e. manitobensis)* is darker than the Rocky Mountain form and its antlers are usually smaller. It ranges throughout southern and central Canada.

*Shoulder height* 4–5 ft. *Weight* 450–800 lbs. *Range:* western U.S. and Canada. *Characteristics:* large size, pale rump and tail, maned neck in breeding male.

Walter A. Weber, National Geographic staff artist

**Enraged harem master** lunges at interloper, gores him with three-foot rack of polished antlers.

# WHITE-TAILED DEER
## *Odocoileus virginianus*

SHADOWS CREEP farther and farther out from the edge of the woods; in the distance a whippoorwill sounds its mournful cry, and deep in the forest a hermit thrush pours out its twilight song. Suddenly a twig snaps. Snorting, a startled deer takes off from her resting place in great soaring leaps, upright tail flashing behind like a waving white banner. A wandering black bear has flushed a whitetail doe.

For a moment the bear gazes after her. Then he lumbers on about his business, unaware that a tiny fawn is curled up nearby, hidden at the base of a giant beech tree.

The fawn lies motionless, its satiny spotted coat camouflaging it against the dappled background. Unlike its mother, it has no strong musky scent to give it away.

After all danger is past the doe returns to nurse the youngster, her first fawn. Hereafter she will usually have twins. Silent and alert she saunters through the June woods, sleek and shining in her reddish-tan summer coat, with spotless white muzzle, chin, throat, and underparts. From the end of her smooth black nose to the tips

**Snowy banners waving,** whitetails

bound down a New England hillside in autumn. Our most common deer, they favor open woodlands.

of her tapering black hoofs, she is a picture of grace and speed.

For several weeks after his birth the fawn stays concealed while his mother is away browsing. Soon he frisks along beside her on morning and evening rounds, samples the lush summer foliage, explores the shallow waters of ponds and streams for aquatic plants.

By September the fawn is completely weaned and has lost his dappled summer coat. As cold weather approaches, both adults and young grow winter coats that are thick and warm and brownish gray.

Now the eager buck stalks through the flame-colored woodlands looking for a mate. With swollen neck and temper at hair-trigger, he challenges any rival he meets. Unlike the elk, he usually contents himself with one mate at a time, although he may take several in succession during the season.

After the rut is over, the deer band together in family groups or small herds for the winter. In deep snow areas they break trails by force of numbers and constant moving about, forming what is called a deer yard. When too many gather in a small area, nourishing twigs and evergreen boughs within reach sometimes run short and deer may starve. In winter northern whitetails feel the pinch.

Best known of all North American game animals since colonial days, white-tailed

**Stop, look, and listen!** Doe in sleek red summer dress and her twin fawns freeze in mid-stride. Perhaps this is the youngsters' first sight of a muskrat.

*Walter A. Weber, National Geographic staff artist*

**The Arizona whitetail,** small and elusive, wears a coat of rusty brown in summer, gray in winter.

deer became scarce in many areas because of unreasoning slaughter. Through protective laws and their own adaptability whitetails have come back abundantly and are now a nuisance in many places, damaging orchards and gardens.

During a recent season hunters bagged more than 70,000 in New York State, and Pennsylvania harvested 105,000 from a deer population four times that many. Wildlife experts estimate that more than eight million roam the United States today.

Largest of the many races is the northern whitetail *(O. v. borealis)*. Record bucks from New York scale close to 400 pounds. Subspecies to the south are smaller. The Florida Key deer stands a mere two feet tall and weighs 50 to 80 pounds.

*Shoulder height 2−3¾ ft. Weight 50−350 lbs. Range:* S. Canada to Peru. *Characteristics:* bushy tail, white beneath; antlers with upright, unforked tines.

## ARIZONA WHITE-TAILED DEER

*(O. v. couesi).* This handsome race, also called Coues deer, Sonora deer, or fantail, is much smaller and paler than the northern whitetail. Rusty brown in summer, it changes to light brownish gray in winter. Common in many of the wooded areas of Arizona and New Mexico, it ranges southward in the Mexican highlands.

During summer and early fall, Arizona whitetails occupy high ranges, where they live among yellow pine forests and concealing growth about the heads of canyons and gulches. Winter snows send them down to the warmer canyon slopes, where they sometimes gather in bands of a score or more. Such a gathering, streaming in full flight along a steep slope, makes an exciting sight. More gregarious than other whitetails, they nevertheless scatter in early spring when the fawns are born.

## FLORIDA KEY DEER *(O. v. clavium).*

Shipwrecked on the Florida Keys in 1535, an adventurous Spanish youth with the resounding name of Hernando d'Escalante lived there for 17 years as a captive of the Calusa Indians. In his memoirs he noted that "a great wonder to the captives who were there, and to those of us from other places, was the existence of deer on the islands of Cuchiyaga [the lower Keys]."

These animals were the tiny Key deer.

Smallest of the whitetail clan, they also have the smallest range—fewer than a dozen islands about 115 miles southwest of Miami, keys with such picturesque names as Big Torch, Ramrod, Knockemdown, Cudgoe, and No Name.

Here, in an environment of coral reefs and sand bars, salt water marshes and scattered hummocks of tropical vegetation, they wander through mangrove flats, scattered stands of pine, and tangled thickets of scrub palmetto and cactus. Crocodiles, raccoons, and such birds as the great white heron, roseate spoonbill, and reddish egret are their wildlife neighbors.

Down to an estimated 40 or less in 1947, the Key deer have long been perilously close to extinction. Recent counts, indicating that they may now number more than 200, are encouraging.

Big Pine Key, eight miles long and two wide, is the center of the population. In 1954 a refuge of nearly a thousand acres was established for them here on land leased from private owners. Three years later Congress authorized the purchase of lands to establish a permanent National Key Deer Refuge.

With this done—and the deer protected from fires and dogs and speeding cars on U.S. 1—the future of this band of unique little animals looks bright.

**The Florida Key deer,** smallest of whitetail races, is making a comeback from near extinction.
*Walter A. Weber, National Geographic staff artist*

**Rocky Mountain mule deer,** ears spread like wings, stand ready to fly. The West's most abundant big-game animal, the mule deer thrives from Canada to Mexico.

# MULE DEER

## *Odocoileus hemionus*

BIG BLACK-FRINGED EARS, small white tail with a black tip, and antlers which fork then fork again distinguish the typical mule deer from the whitetail. Western hunters call him "muley" or "burro deer." His habit of bounding into the air and landing on all fours has earned him the name "jumping deer" in Manitoba.

Stockier than the whitetail, the mule deer sports a rusty yellowish-red summer coat which changes to warm brownish gray in winter. His legs and underparts are gray.

Ranging from the cold mountains of Alaska to the burning deserts of the Southwest, mule deer are exclusively western animals. Avoiding deep forest, they prefer a partly open, partly wooded habitat. In winter, when the snow becomes too deep at high elevations, they move down to lower country, sometimes banding in large numbers. The bucks meekly spend the winter in the herd, often led by a wise old doe.

With spring the deer scatter, moving singly or in little groups toward the summer range. As do other deer, the doe hides her fawns during the day and comes back to nurse them after feeding. When an enemy approaches, the mother stamps her feet in anger and her white rump patch bristles. Sometimes she tries to lure the intruder away by whistling and circling.

After the whitetail, the mule deer is our most abundant big-game animal. Some two million roam western North America.

*Shoulder height* 3–3½ ft. *Weight* 100–400 lbs. *Range:* Alaska to Mexico. *Characteristics:* large ears, multiforked antlers, black or black-tipped tail.

**BLACK-TAILED DEER** (*O. h. columbianus* and *O. h. sitkensis*) were once considered distinct species, but zoologists

"I'm boss here; stay away!" A buck **mule deer** confronts a presumptuous **blacktail**. Smaller buck shows now classify them as subspecies of the mule deer. Smaller and darker than the typical "muley," a blacktail seldom weighs more than 150 pounds. His black tail is white underneath.

Limited to the humid, heavily forested coastal area from Alaska to central California, blacktails slip like phantoms through the dark towering stands of northland cedar, spruce, and fir. In their southern range, they bed down under redwoods and giant ferns. The succulence of their food makes it unnecessary for them to drink for days at a time.

On the slopes of northwestern coastal islands the range of Sitka blacktails is often so restricted that many fall easy prey to hunters and such predators as mountain lions, lynxes, and wolves. Heavy snows force the deer down to the shores, but with warmer weather they scatter to higher pastures.

brushlike black badge which names him.
*Walter A. Weber, National Geographic staff artist*

81

**What deer goes there?** You can often tell by its hoofprints. The whitetail's prints are small and taper to the sharpest points. Caribou hoofs, round and blunt, spread to give a snowshoelike effect. Elk tracks are larger than whitetail's and not quite so pointed; moose prints are largest of all. Study of the track pattern tells whether the deer was walking, trotting, or running.

# AMERICAN MOOSE

## *Alces alces*

A LOON'S EERIE CRY shatters the wilderness silence as a moose cow and her gawky calf wade through the shallows of a remote northern lake. Mother and son stop to stare suspiciously at an old she-bear and her cub ambling along the opposite shore.

With their outrageously long muzzles, rubbery lips, humped backs, and clumsy gait, moose will never win any beauty prizes. They may appear awkward and grotesque, but they have the distinction of being the largest and most powerful deer in the world. A full grown bull slipping through the brush without cracking a twig is one of nature's most awesome sights. The tremendous palmate antlers, whiskered bell under the neck, short body, and disproportionately long front legs give the impression that here may be a survivor from remote geological time.

These huge creatures roam the northlands of Europe and Asia as well as North America. Britishers call Europe's moose an elk. But Americans give that name to another New World deer (page 72).

Most of the year the moose is a timid soul, but during and after the fall mating

83

*Walter A. Weber, National Geographic staff artist*

season the bull acts like the lord of all creation. He paces his domain, blood in his eye, clashing his great antlers against rocks, trampling saplings underfoot. Stalking along back roads, he barely deigns to step aside for onrushing cars. He evidently considers himself tough enough to tackle anything that comes along.

When he hears the grunting, blatting call of a cow, or another bull challenging his supremacy, he rumbles through the scrub like a light tank — crashing into trees, bulldozing through bushes. If he meets a rival he lowers his head in an earth-shaking charge. Flourishing their antlers, the two beasts try to outpush each other. Occasionally the antlers become permanently locked and slow death stalks the duelists.

The bull may take several mates, but keeps only one at a time. Taking advantage of his eagerness, hunters frequently decoy him into rifle range by imitating the call of the cow with a birch-bark trumpet. Wildlife authorities in Newfoundland report that moose mistake the moaning horn of diesel trains for the invitation of a lovesick cow. With romance their object, the bulls come a-running, sometimes collide with trains.

Moose calves, generally twins, are born in May and are dark brown. Unlike most other young deer, they have no spots. They stay with their mother until she drives them away the following spring, just before new babies arrive.

After the calf is born, it is the hornless mother moose who takes over in the terrible temper department. Momism runs rampant as over-protective females charge any real or fancied source of danger to junior. A hiker who once stumbled upon a moose cow with twin calves testified that the mother charged him without preliminaries. He dodged her once, but she caught up with him as he tried to scramble up a small spruce. The enraged moose reared, a murderous look in her eyes, and slashed out with sharp forefeet.

As a last resort the trapped hiker looked the moose straight in the eye and let out a yell. That did it. The startled cow took off.

When moose aren't worried about family matters, they're peaceable beasts that feed on leaves and juicy twigs, sometimes bending saplings down to a convenient height. They cherish water lilies and will wade far out into swampy north-country ponds, lipping plants from the surface or dipping their great heads completely under water to get at roots.

Four races of moose inhabit North America. The eastern moose (*A. a. americana*) is found from northern New England to Labrador, while the Manitoba moose (*A. a. andersoni*) ranges over most of the rest of Canada. The Shiras moose (*A. a. shirasi*) lives in the Rocky Mountains as far south as Colorado. It is named for the late George Shiras 3d, naturalist and long a trustee of the National Geographic Society. Bigger than all other races is the moose found in Alaska and Canada's Yukon Territory.

*Shoulder height* 5½–7½ ft. *Weight* 600 –1,800 lbs. *Range:* Canada, Alaska, also N. New England, Michigan, Minnesota, and Rockies. *Characteristics:* huge size, palmate antlers, bell.

**ALASKA MOOSE** (*A. a. gigas*) Weighing almost a ton, a bull Alaska moose may reach the record shoulder height of nearly eight feet! Towering over his massive head are antlers which may spread more than six feet and weigh 85 pounds — the most impressive big-game trophy in America.

This ponderous dark giant presents a magnificent picture of size and force as he trots effortlessly across alder swamps, crashes through windfalls, and plunges hip deep through heavy snow. Every year Alaskan railroads are bedeviled with moose that trot along plowed railroad tracks rather than flounder through the drifts.

When iron horse meets giant moose, railroad men try screeching whistles, flashing lights, flares, even snowballs to scare them off. Sometimes nothing works. A husky bull may even charge the engine. The result: a diet of mooseburger for some charitable institution.

Walter A. Weber, National Geographic staff artist

**The Alaska moose,** world's largest deer, browses and brawls in the vast wilderness areas of our 49th state. In autumn, northern forests ring with the clash of palmate antlers. One pair spread 77⅝ inches! Hunters sometimes lure bulls by imitating the cow's call.

# WOODLAND CARIBOU
## *Rangifer tarandus caribou*

SLOGGING through the snowdrifts of their northern wilderness home, caribou are well adapted to their environment.

Air-filled hair coats, worn over thick fat, provide extra warmth without extra weight. These built-in life jackets enable the caribou to swim faster and easier than other deer. Raised white tails and surrounding white patches signal alarm. Broad cleft hoofs function as snowshoes; stiff bristles below the fetlocks furnish a nonskid tread.

The clicking noise caribou make when walking or running can be heard a hundred feet away. Tendons rubbing tightly against foot bones produce the sound.

Caribou are the only deer whose females have antlers. Doe antlers are much smaller and slenderer than the buck's, which are flattened and have many branches. A broad vertical brow tine extends over the nose. Bucks drop their antlers after the fall rut, but females keep theirs until late spring.

Circumpolar in distribution, the genus *Rangifer* includes Old World reindeer and New World caribou. All members of the genus are so similar that scientists consider them a single species with numerous races. Caribou are commonly separated into three groups according to their habitat: Barren Ground caribou, mountain caribou, and the woodland species.

During the long Canadian winter small bands of woodland caribou wander through the northern forests, descending into tamarack and cedar swamps to avoid the coldest winds and heaviest snows. Trimmed with heavy, yellowish-white manes, their dull grayish-brown winter coats become a deeper brown in summer.

By June the bands have broken up and the does have their fawns in solitude. The youngsters match their mothers' color, with white spots barely visible. Caribou fawns, unlike most others, are never hidden, but precociously follow the doe in her wanderings a few hours after birth.

**Woodland caribou** falls to a Chipewyan

On hot days caribou often emerge from the woods and wallow in shallow lakes, trying to escape the black flies and mosquitoes. Rising, old bulls shake themselves like dogs after a bath.

Perhaps the abundant moss and lichens within its range explain why the woodland caribou bulks larger than the Barren Ground group or the closely related reindeer. Now comparatively scarce over most of its range, the woodland caribou once migrated into Maine, New Hampshire, and Vermont, as well as northern Michigan and Minnesota. Years ago, however, it was hunted out of these areas.

*Shoulder height* 3½–4 ft. *Weight* 150–400 lbs. *Range:* forested areas of Canada, Newfoundland to the Rockies. *Characteristics:* white-maned, both sexes antlered.

*Walter A. Weber, National Geographic staff artist*

arrow. Even today northern tribes use caribou for food, shelter, clothing, as Plains Indians used bison.

# BARREN GROUND CARIBOU
*Rangifer tarandus arcticus*

FROM LOOKOUTS on the ridges rolls the cry, "The deer are coming!" Downwind floats the clicking of caribou heel bones, the grunt of the loping herd, the rank distinctive odor. At defiles and oft-used crossings Eskimos and Indians wait with rifles, as their fathers did with bows.

Every April and May along the arctic tree line, Barren Ground caribou mass for their trek toward the lichen-rich tundra. Small bands emerging from the scrub join others in the northward march. First a trickle, then a stream, then a flood of dun-gray bodies moves over the ice.

Steel-jacketed bullets thud into flesh as the animals lumber into range. Pressed on by those behind, the caribou surge helplessly toward the guns. To the rear of the firing line women and children, eager for the season's first meat, heat kettles to boil the northland delicacy—caribou tongues. Later they cure the hides for clothing, dry the meat, remove sinews for sewing.

Now that the great buffalo herds are gone, this caribou migration is the one spectacle of its kind still to be seen in North America. It, too, may soon be a thing of the past, for wanton slaughter with the repeating rifle and destruction of ground forage by bush fires have drastically diminished caribou range and numbers.

An estimated two million caribou ranged the tundra between Hudson Bay and the

*Louis Agassiz Fuertes*

**A Peary caribou,** white as the wolves which attack him, blends with his far-northern setting.

Mackenzie Valley in 1900. In 1969 Canadian wildlife census takers estimated fewer than 400,000. Caribou are still plentiful in Alaska, but numbers have dwindled there, too, since gold-rush days, when vast herds fording the Yukon River held up paddlewheel steamers for hours at a time.

First to head north in spring are the does, heavy with fawns they are rushing to deliver on the Barren Grounds. The bucks follow a week or so later, coats patchy with molt, antlers still in velvet, flanks lean from winter fare. Wolves trail the bands, pick off aged stragglers, calves, or cripples.

All summer the caribou feed on lichens, moss, and shrubs of the treeless tundra. When fall comes they start south, but before they reach the tree line they turn briefly north again for the mating season. After the rut, they wander south to winter in the sheltering forest.

The typical Barren Ground caribou ranges the tundra from Labrador in the east to the Mackenzie River in the west. Next in abundance is the Stone caribou (*R. t. stonei*), the commonest big-game animal in Alaska. The mountain caribou (*R. t. montanus*) alone wanders south of the Canadian border. A few score still roam northern Idaho and Washington.

*Shoulder height* 3¾–4½ ft. *Weight* 200 –375 lbs. *Range:* Alaska, W. and N. Canada, arctic islands. *Characteristic:* generally paler than the woodland caribou.

**PEARY CARIBOU** (*R. t. pearyi*) is named in honor of explorer Robert E. Peary, who in 1909 was the first man to reach the North Pole. This splendid animal lives on Ellesmere and other Canadian islands, and in extreme northern Greenland, to 83° north latitude. Thriving on lichens and other scanty arctic vegetation, it holds its own against white arctic wolves.

Each winter the Peary caribou lives through three to five months of continuous night, its wanderings lighted only by moon, stars, and shimmering northern lights.

**GRANT CARIBOU** (*R. t. granti*) is found only on the Alaska Peninsula and Unimak Island. Slightly smaller and paler than the Stone caribou, which is found over the rest of Alaska, it does not make the spectacular migrations other races do.

**Grant caribou cows** warily follow a white-caped bull across barren lands of Alaska Peninsula.
*Carl Rungius, courtesy of New York Zoological Society*

CHAPTER 4

# Pronghorn, Speed Demon of the West

"HURRA FOR THE PRAIRIES and the swift antelope," Audubon wrote after seeing this swiftest of American mammals during a trip up the Missouri in 1843. ". . . they fleet by the hunter like flashes or meteors . . . they pass along, up or down hills, or

90

along the level plain with the same apparent ease, while so rapidly do their legs perform their graceful movements . . . that like the spokes of a fast turning wheel we can hardly see them, but instead, observe a gauzy or film-like appearance. . . ."

Their speed and wariness made them difficult to hunt, but when the easier-to-kill buffalo were scarce, Plains Indians shot pronghorns from rock blinds near desert waterholes, or slaughtered entire herds by the "surround" or stampede method. Spanish explorers were the first white men to see the pronghorn.

CHARLES J. BELDEN

*Walter A. Weber, National Geographic staff artist*

**Pronghorn mother** nuzzles newborn fawn; wary buck keeps an eye on a coyote prowling the sage.

# PRONGHORN

## *Antilocapra americana*

"LOOK OUT for that pronghorn!" Louis Schellbach and ranger-naturalist Joe Bryan were driving near Arizona's Grand Canyon National Park when a pronghorn suddenly took off, running straight for the road ahead of them.

"Joe stepped on the gas, hoping to avoid a collision," recalls the former chief naturalist. "But the pronghorn was faster than he figured. It got there a split second ahead of us and cleared the road with what looked like an 18-foot leap. Then it slammed on the brakes and whirled to stare at us as we breezed by."

"Never do it again," Schellbach advised Joe. "I'd rather try to beat an express train to a crossing!"

A short time later the two men met another pronghorn that seemed eager to test their speed. At 45 miles an hour it broke off the game by putting on an extra burst of energy and crossing in front of them.

Fleeter than any race horse, the pronghorn is America's swiftest mammal. With its graceful form and distinctive cinnamon-buff coat, it is also one of the most beautiful. The male has jaunty black sideburns on lower jaw, and both sexes have strong black and white markings elsewhere on head and neck. Underparts and rump are white.

In moments of excitement, the hairs of the huge rump patch rise on end to form two white rosettes. Flashing in the sunlight, they catch the eye for one or two miles as the animal runs away. When the pronghorn turns to look back at whatever frightened it, the pompon is hidden, and the animal seems to vanish.

But this curiosity which causes it to stop and look back sometimes causes its downfall. Theodore Roosevelt tells of luring antelope close in the hunt by waving a red cloth attached to a pole.

A peculiarity of the animal is its hollow horns, which grow over a bony core. Every fall the horns are shed and new ones form over this core. The male's horns are much bigger than those of the doe. Some females have none at all.

The young, usually twins, appear in May or June. Weighing four to six pounds apiece, they lie in separate hiding places the first few days, their soft color camouflaging them against the dusty background. If a coyote wanders too close, the mother pronghorn tries to lure him away.

Within a week the babies are able to run faster than a man, and begin to accompany their mother in her wanderings. Soon they band together with other females and kids for mutual safety and companionship.

The bucks fight in the fall, their curiously pronged weapons clashing furiously as each tries to collect and guard a harem. After the mating season all ages and sexes band together for the winter.

Speed and keen eyesight are their main defense against attack. Apart from man, the most feared enemies are probably coyotes and wolves. Generally running in a great circle, pronghorns easily outrun coyotes in the open. But sometimes the wily predators gang up on them, chasing in relays until one or more antelopes are exhausted and run down.

Despite its name, the pronghorn antelope is not a true antelope (like the many African species). It is the sole survivor of a unique American family, the *Antilocapridae,* which reached its heyday on the prairies in Miocene and Pliocene times.

Millions of pronghorns roamed the plains when covered wagons creaked and jolted westward over the Oregon Trail, but by 1908 the species had dwindled to fewer than 20,000 in all of America north of Mexico. Due to western settlement and excessive hunting, the pronghorn seemed doomed.

With protection, however, the species has come back strong. Nearly 250,000 pronghorns—half of them in Wyoming—now roam the western plains.

*Shoulder height* 3–3½ ft. *Weight* 80–140 lbs. *Range:* plains from S. Canada to Mexico. *Characteristics:* unique pronged horns, erectile white rump patch.

**Ground rumbles, dust swirls** as bison stampede across the prairie. This band, reminiscent

CHAPTER 5 # Bison, Monarch

**M**AJOR GENERAL Philip Sheridan, celebrated Union cavalry leader, now Indian fighter, halted his command on the divide between the Cimarron and Canadian Rivers in Oklahoma. It was the spring of 1869, and all day long his troops had been passing through herds of bison.

"How many buffalo have you seen today?" he asked his staff. Lt. Col. George Custer, whose name was to be immortalized seven years later at the Little Bighorn, gave his estimate. So did nine others, including Scout William F. Cody, who would soon be world-famous as "Buffalo Bill." The average came to 243,000—a quarter of a million buffalo.

This was not an unusual concentration for those days. In 1871 Col. R. I. Dodge

**Crescent horns** are worn by both sexes. Unpredictable, bison may attack without warning.

of thundering hordes of Wild West days, roams Wichita Mountains Wildlife Refuge in Oklahoma.

# of the Plains  By ROBERT M. McCLUNG

**Bison roamed North America** 2,000 centuries ago. Commonly called buffalo, the descendants of these immigrants from Asia once grazed by the millions; hunters all but exterminated them. This cow still sheds winter coat; calf sports baby wool.

RALPH GRAY AND (TOP) M. WOODBRIDGE WILLIAMS AND (LEFT) PAUL A. ZAHL, ALL NATIONAL GEOGRAPHIC STAFF

95

watched a herd passing through the valley of the Arkansas River. The black sea of animals took several days to pass; Dodge calculated it was 25 miles wide and 50 deep—at least four million in all. In their heyday buffalo roamed the western plains 60 million strong, the greatest spectacle of herd animals the world has ever seen. Yet in less than 20 years—from 1865 to 1884—the huge throngs were wiped out and the species almost became extinct.

Cortés and his conquistadores were probably the first white men to see the huge shaggy beasts, according to Antonio de Solís, a 17th century chronicler of the Mexican conquest. Visiting the menagerie of the Aztec ruler, Montezuma, in 1521, the Spaniards saw "the Mexican Bull; a wonderful composition of divers Animals. It has crooked shoulders, with a bunch on its Back like a Camel; its Flanks dry, its Tail large, and its Neck cover'd with Hair like a Lion."

In the early days bison ranged from the Mexican border far into Canada, and from Oregon almost to the eastern seaboard. "It is a fine place for Cattle and Hoggs," wrote William Byrd of his Virginia holdings in the 1730's, "and fortunately there is a large creature of the Beef kind, but much larger, called a Buffalo, which may be bred up tame and is good both for food and labour."

Pioneers pushing westward through the valleys of Pennsylvania, Kentucky, and Tennessee found many buffalo. By 1819 they had been killed off east of the Mississippi. But west of the great river

### Chants and dances invoke buffalo's return and success in the hunt

Traveling the upper Missouri in 1833, artist Karl Bodmer and Prince Maximilian of Wied witnessed the buffalo dance of the Mandan. ". . . they wear the skin of the upper part of the head, the mane of the buffalo, with its horns," wrote Maximilian. ". . . they have a woman, who during the dance, goes round with a dish of water, to refresh the dancers, but she must give this water only to the bravest, who wear the whole buffalo's head. . . ."

"The men have a piece of red cloth fastened behind, and a figure representing a buffalo's tail; they also carry arms in their hands. The men with the buffalo heads always keep in the dance at the outside of the group, imitate all the motions and voice of this animal, as it timidly and cautiously retreats, looking around in all directions. . . ."

97

**A Plains Indian rides circus style** as a charging bull gores his horse. George Catlin, the Pennsylvania artist who recorded this breakneck buffalo chase, lived among the Indians in the 1830's. Today range riders round up bison on Wichita Mountains Wildlife Refuge (right) and corral them for branding and vaccination.

the herds were as numerous as ever. For hundreds of years before the coming of the white man, Indians roamed this country of the big sky, following the buffalo herds, living as hunters and warriors. The way of life of the Sioux, Cheyennes, Comanches, Arikaras, Kiowas, and other Plains Indians depended on the buffalo. Because of its importance, the shaggy beast loomed large in their rituals and beliefs. It was "strong medicine," and each tribe did its best to propitiate the Great Spirit so the herds would always be plentiful.

The meat was eaten fresh, or dried in the sun, pounded, and mixed with berries to make pemmican. The tanned hides were fashioned into moccasins and leggings, dresses and shirts, and summer coverings for beds. The thick robes made snug blankets for winter, and the scraped hides were stitched together to cover tepees. Rawhide was used in trunks and containers, cooking pots, ropes, quivers and saddles. Warriors took the thick, tough hide from a bull's neck to make shields. Hoofs were boiled to obtain glue; horns provided spoons and ladles. Rib bones formed sled runners; other bones served as tools; sinew made bowstrings. Thick woolly bison hair stuffed medicine balls, and the beard decorated bows and lances. Nothing was wasted—even the tail found use as a whip or fly swatter.

Blizzards, ice-choked rivers, quicksands, prairie fires, droughts, and wolves took an enormous toll of the wild cattle year after year. But there were always plenty left for the redskins. Plenty, that is, until the white men came west in force after the Civil War, cultivating and fencing the land, building military posts, killing buffalo wherever they went.

The Plains Indians bitterly resented the slaughter of the buffalo and the invasion of land that the White Fathers had said was theirs "as long as grass shall grow and waters flow." They fought for their way of life in the great Indian Wars of the '70's and '80's. "Every buffalo dead is an Indian gone," General Sheridan had declared in 1869. How right events proved him to be!

Like slender steel ribbons the railroads crept westward through buffalo and Indian country. Professional hide hunters fanned out over the plains, killing buffalo literally by the millions. The carnage and waste were almost unbelievable.

Hides sold for $1.25 apiece. Tongues, the greatest delicacy, were 25¢, and hindquarters went begging at 1¢ a pound. In the years 1870-75 Dodge City, Kansas, was the buffalo capital of the world. By 1879 buffalo were gone from Kansas, and only scattered bands remained in the Southwest.

Railroads penetrated the Yellowstone region the next year, and the slaughter continued among the northern herds. By 1884 no more than several hundred wild and wary individuals survived in the entire world. Not even these few were safe. In 1893, more than a hundred were killed in the small band that had taken refuge in the Yellowstone wilderness.

Public feelings were outraged at last, and President Cleveland signed a bill protecting the 21 buffalo remaining in the park. Others were preserved in zoos and fenced areas. Slowly the bison began to increase under protection. But never again would the great herds roam the prairies as they once did.

On their reservations the Plains Indians dreamed of the old days, performed their ghost dances, and prayed in vain for the return of the vanished herds. The dread vision of the old Kiowa legend had finally come true.

As retold by Garretson in his book *The American Bison,* the Great Spirit descended to the Kiowas saying: "Here are the buffalo. They shall be your food and raiment, but in the day you shall see them perish from off the face of the Earth, then know that the end of the Kiowa is near — and the Sun set."

**Blackfoot hunters** stampede buffalo over a cliff by waving blankets and shouting. When the herd swept toward them, the Indians took refuge behind piles of rocks. Animals not killed by the fall were slain by hunters below. Blackfoot name for such a drive was *piskun*—"deep-blood-kettle."

LIBRARY OF CONGRESS

**1554**  **Earliest drawing** of the American bison appeared in *Historia General de las Indias* by the Spaniard Lopez de Gómara.

NEW YORK HISTORICAL SOCIETY

**1697**  **This oxlike bison** was portrayed in *Description de la Louisiane* by Father Hennepin, a Flemish Franciscan explorer.

"SPORT IN ART" BY WILLIAM BAILLIE-GROHMAN

**1768**  **"American Aurochs"** was pompadoured and seemingly wrapped in a shawl by imaginative Swiss artist J. I. Holzhalb.

Buffalo Bill does it again! An actual person as well as a legend, Buffalo Bill Cody fixed the image of the wild and woolly West in the world's mind as no one else has ever done. Dime novels made his name a household word in the '70s and '80s. Cody started his ride to fortune as a hunter for the Kansas Pacific Railroad, killing 4,120 buffalo in 18 months. Famed as a cavalry scout, he toured America and Europe with popular "Wild West" shows.

A great iron horse invades the buffalo's domain. Shooting stampeding beasts was a popular passenger "sport" depicted in *Frank Leslie's Illustrated Newspaper* for June 3, 1871. Great herds crossing the tracks stopped trains for hours at a time.

One pair of bulls turns to settle a personal feud.

The buffalo nickel,
a pocket reminder of
the monarch of the plains

"Black Diamond," an immense bull in Central Park Zoo, gave thousands of New Yorkers their first glimpse of a live buffalo. He also served as model for sculptor James Earl Frazer's design for a five-cent piece. First minted in 1913, Black Diamond's image supplanted the old Liberty head, in use since 1883. The Buffalo nickel was finally turned out to pasture when the Jefferson nickel was adopted in 1938.

# BISON

*Bison bison*

GREAT SIZE, dark shaggy coat, and hump single out the American bison among the big game of the world. Record bulls may weigh well over a ton, cows only half that much. The gregarious animals travel in family bands which sometimes unite to form large herds.

Yellowish-red calves are born from April to June, nine months after mating. Weighing 25 to 40 pounds, they resemble domestic calves, except for shorter necks and smaller ears. By fall they have brown coats and the beginnings of humps. Straight spike horns have started to grow.

In spring when they are shedding, bison scratch against trees, roll in wallows, and plaster themselves with mud as protection against insects. During the late summer rutting season, bulls bellow challenges and engage in mighty pushing duels for mastery of the bands. In their prime from six to ten, bison sometimes live 30 years or more.

Near extinction 80 years ago, bison in the United States now number close to 10,000. Some 600 of these roam Yellowstone National Park, about 1,000 thrive in Wichita Mountains Wildlife Refuge. Some years ago a small herd was successfully introduced into central Alaska.

*Shoulder height* 5–6 ft. *Weight* 1,000–2,000 lbs. *Original range:* Canada to Mexico, Oregon to Georgia. *Characteristics:* huge size, humped shoulders, shaggy brown coat.

**WOOD BISON** (*B. b. athabasca),* a slightly larger, darker form, roams Canada's Wood Buffalo National Park, south of Great Slave Lake. Plains bison were introduced years ago, so most of these animals—now nearly 15,000 strong—are intergrades between the two forms.

**Phalanx of determined musk oxen** presents a solid front of horns when danger threatens.

CHAPTER 6

# Musk Oxen, Wild Arctic Cattle

S HAGGY HORNED HEADS come up at the sound of wolves howling in the distance. The little band of musk oxen crowds together for protection, then breaks for the nearest hilltop as the wolf pack bursts into sight. Brought to bay, the adults form a defense ring around the calves. Heads lowered, they present an unbroken front of sharp horns. Glaring bulls snort defiance and make short charges at the wolves. As long as the circle remains unbroken, the stocky beasts will hold their own against the attackers.

With his thick body, short legs and tail, and long dark hair, the musk ox looks like a small, white-stockinged buffalo. But he is not really an ox, and has no musk glands. His name dates from the 17th century and reflects the wishful thinking of an era in which musk was a much-sought base for perfume. Perhaps the misnomer derived from the odor of the animal's droppings and urine.

The musk ox's generic name, *Ovibos moschatus,* bestowed in 1816, stems from another misconception, for ovibos implies the animal is part sheep, part cow. Actually, the musk ox's nearest living relatives are goats and, possibly, antelopes. The Eskimo name is probably best—*Oomingmak,* "the bearded one."

Gregarious, musk oxen usually live together in bands of five to 100 or more in arctic America and Greenland. Through the brief summer they roam the valleys, grazing or eating willow browse. Born in April or May and covered with short curly hair, the 20-pound calf huddles under its mother's long hair skirt for warmth and protection. In July the bulls fight one another for the cows, butting heads in skull-fracturing charges. Losers wander in grumpy isolation or form bachelor clubs with other frustrated males. In winter's blizzards and months of perpetual darkness, musk oxen paw for food on higher ground, where frigid winds sweep hillsides almost bare of snow. Their shaggy outer coats and shorter underwool protect them from temperatures plunging to 50° below zero.

Highly prized for their meat and robes, musk oxen were hunted relentlessly by Eskimos, whalers, and explorers. In recent decades their number dwindled almost to the vanishing point. They had disappeared from Alaska a hundred years ago, and only an estimated 500 remained on Canada's mainland by 1930. Protected, musk oxen have increased in total population to about 10,000. An experimental herd, brought from Greenland in the 1930's by the U. S. Fish and Wildlife Service, is thriving on Nunivak Island, Alaska.

In 1954-5, John J. Teal, Jr., of the Institute of Northern Agricultural Research captured seven musk ox calves and acclimated them to life on his Vermont farm. There, through selective breeding, they were fashioned into domestic animals for their *qiviut,* the fine, cashmerelike underwool, a pound of which can be converted into ten miles of yarn. Teal then established musk ox farms in Alaska, Quebec, and Norway, where the animal can serve a new textile industry.

*Shoulder height* 3½–5 ft. *Weight* 400–800 lbs. *Range:* arctic Canada, N. Greenland. *Characteristics:* long hair coat, dense underwool, down-curving horns.

Louis Agassiz Fuertes

**Thick blanket** of fine underwool, *qiviut,* enables musk ox to survive arctic winters.

Bighorn rams scan a mountain meadow for signs of danger. They can spot the gleam of a gun barrel several miles off. Lewis and Clark found bighorns "too shy to be shot." But this trio need fear no hunter's weapon; their sanctuary is Jasper National Park in the heart of the Canadian Rockies.

CANADIAN NATIONAL RAILWAYS

CHAPTER 7

# Mountain Sheep and Goats

By WAYNE BARRETT

BEFORE THE SEA washed over the land bridge spanning Bering Strait, sheep and goats streamed out of Asia and spilled into Alaska's teeming jungles. They grazed with camels, watched for saber-toothed cats, saw ponderous mammoths shake the forest floor. Then came the Ice Age, and great glaciers crept halfway down North America.

Nature decreed the most adaptable animals would survive, and buried many others in ice. Sheep and goats weathered the upheaval.

For the wild and whiskered goats the Ice Age never ended. Today they are found no farther south than the snow-capped Cascades. Wild sheep, however, with their graceful curving horns, have scattered from Alaska to Lower California and the arid Southwest. Adaptable? Desert bighorns scarcely touch water.

Few animals challenge the climbing skill of these robust ruminants. Even birds shun the wild goat's lofty retreat. Ernest Thompson

107

CHARLES T. HOTCHKISS AND (RIGHT) CLEVELAND P. GRANT

**A mountain goat** surveys his craggy domain in Montana's Glacier National Park. During the late fall mating season he'll bully other billies with his black-spiked weapons.

**Bighorn rams** (below) may batter each other senseless competing for a harem of ewes. Audubon reported one set of massive horns that weighed 44½ pounds!

Seton drew this analogy: "If, on some lowering morning when clouds and flying scud are drifting low over Manhattan, one could look from the Times Building, out and up to those higher peaks, the Equitable, the Metropolitan, and the Woolworth, and see white creatures—Goats, incredible Goats—crawling along the cornices, pulling themselves up on the turrets, or calmly chewing their cud as they lay looking down from the weather vanes, we should have much the same sensation as in watching the bearded mountaineer in his cloud-hung, perpendicular home."

The mountain goat is a careful climber. Stiffgaited, he plods up the scantiest ledge and hardly disturbs a pebble. The agile mountain sheep, on the other hand, seems to delight in displaying his audacious gymnastics. He skips up narrow canyon walls, bounding side to side, ricocheting to the top, and never comes close to falling. He balances on minute footholds, thinks nothing of broad jumping a chasm 15 feet wide. Even more daring, he leaps into space as though equipped with wings. John Muir tells of an entire band that plunged off a 150-foot cliff, "jumping down in perfect order. . . ."

The naturalist records that they avoided being dashed to death, "controlling the velocity of their half falling, half leaping movements by striking at short intervals, and holding back with their cushioned, rubber feet upon small ledges and roughened inclines until near the bottom, when they 'sailed off' into the free air and alighted on their feet, but with their bodies so nearly in a vertical position that they appeared to be diving."

Undaunted by treacherous footing, numbing cold, and sparse food, mountain sheep and goats survive nature's sternest tests. They live the Spartan life on barren peaks and toss their haughty heads at the lowland's plenty. Hardiest of North America's hoofed animals, they surrender to nothing; not to ice as did the lumbering mammoth, not to guns and arrows as did the bison and musk oxen. In majestic defiance they walk along the very edge of the world, at home among lofty horizons.

# BIGHORN SHEEP
## *Ovis canadensis*

NECK EXTENDED, nostrils aquiver, a ram sallies forth in December's crisp air to seek a mate. He spies six ewes, zealously guarded by a burly old bighorn. Undaunted, he slams into the harem master, knocks him sprawling. The offended ram scrambles to his feet and squares around to face his assailant.

Manes stand on end; eyes flash fire. The rivals back off, then halt — 40 feet apart. Suddenly they rear on stiffened hind legs, then charge. At the awful moment of impact the crash of their massive horns can be heard a mile away. Shock ripples the combatants' bodies.

They shake their dazed heads, walk away, and rush head on again like knights in a medieval arena. Chips and splinters fly from their horns; blood oozes from ears and noses; they reel drunkenly.

The battering rages more than an hour. A frenzied burst at last drops the older warrior to his knees. Struggling to rise, he meets a pile-driving blow. The victor glowers at the fallen, then strides away to claim his harem.

Except during the rut, a ram in his prime lives the bachelor's life. He bands with four or five other males and loafs all summer high in the mountains. Bringing up the lambs is ewe's work. Ewes, lambs, and young rams roam a different part of the range. They follow a wise old grandmother to alpine pastures deep in sweet grasses and flowers. Summer evenings — perhaps by moonlight — she cautiously leads her flock down to water and to clay banks rich with salt. In winter, snow quenches thirst.

Late spring ushers in the lambing season. An expectant ewe slips away from the band and climbs to a sheltered ledge to bear her young — usually a single lamb. "Owning the lamb," the mother's ritual of licking it fluff-dry, prevents blowflies from laying eggs. Ever alert for the golden eagle which might attack the lamb, she soon leads him down from the nursery to join the flock. Herds of as many as 60 sheep roam the green mountainside. Youngsters try the tender foliage and nurse less often. Wobbly legs gain strength. Playful butting matches test sprouting horns. While lambs feed and frolic, mother ewes watch for enemies. A snort signals danger.

Winter in the Rockies tries the bighorns' endurance. Heavy snow forces them to move. Risking attack by wolves and mountain lions, they shift to lower levels or to other mountains. They search for shrubby browse and paw the snow to reach short grass. Old sheep, teeth worn to the gums, slowly starve. Weakened, they become easy prey for hungry meat eaters.

Disease and parasites take heavy toll. Ticks, lice, and mites infest sheep hides, and worms cause diarrhea and weaken sheep against pneumonia. Blowflies lay clusters of eggs on a newborn sheep, and within hours armies of maggots overwhelm their host. But the bighorn's chief opponent has been man. The ram's grand curling horns make a handsome trophy.

Foremost among wild sheep races in the United States is the Rocky Mountain bighorn *(O. c. canadensis)*. In Nevada and the Southwest, smaller desert types live long periods without drinking. They get moisture from cactus.

More than a million bighorns ranged the West in prehistoric times, naturalists estimate. Today fewer than 20,000 survive. Human friends have come to the rescue, championed strict hunting controls, protected ranges, transplanted animals to less populous areas, even air-dropped feed during severe winters.

Though man has shrunk the sheep's domain, the bighorn still finds room to practice his famed acrobatics. In fact, in some remote ranges, mountain sheep abound as in primitive times.

*Shoulder height* 3–3½ ft. *Weight* 150– 300 lbs. *Range:* W. Canada to Mexico. *Characteristics:* brown coat, white rump patch, ram's massive curled horns.

**Snow buries alpine grasses,** drives rams and short-horned ewes to lower levels. Seeking forage, they risk attack from mountain lions.

*Walter A. Weber, National Geographic staff artist*

WALTER A. WEBER

# DALL SHEEP

## *Ovis dalli*

WINTER WINDS blast snow and ice against Alaska's barren mountains, enameling every rock crystalline white. Sub-zero cold binds the cover tight. In these bleak wilds Dall sheep huddle under ledges and poke through frozen crusts for grasses, shrubs, and willow tops. They outlast arctic rigors, see 18-hour days of sun peel back the icy glaze. Then they feast in green sky-meadows and fatten for another winter.

More northern in range and smaller than bighorns, Dall sheep differ little from their southern kin in habit. In December rams disturb the peace with head-on duels. A tough old warrior might amass a harem of 40 to 50 ewes. Mating enthusiasm spent, he joins a band of bucks and roams the high country. Lambs debut in May and June; in two weeks they can run. A wise matriarch leads the colony of ewes and lambs. Spike rams tag along, too young for the aloof bachelor clubs.

Born white, the northern race *(O. d. dalli)* at maturity appears yellow-tinged against the snow. Slender, dull amber horns show annual age rings. Golden eyes scan far horizons; sheep more often see than scent danger. Sharp-eyed ewes act as sentinels.

Wolves and lynxes sometimes outsmart white sheep. Naturalist Charles Sheldon saw a lynx crouching over a dead ram. Tracks in the snow told the story. "The lynx had waited on a rock, about 500 feet up, and as the ram (about two years old) crossed the slide, the lynx sprang on its back, and fastened its teeth in the left eye. Together they came down the slide, and at the bottom, a struggle ensued. The lynx lost its hold, and fastened again to the right eye. Not another tooth mark was on the sheep. Both eyes were completely gouged out."

Dall sheep turned the tables in another fight. A hunter describes what happened when five wolves trailed two Dalls to a canyon shelf: "The wolves came barking at every bound, and springing from ledge to ledge. The sheep stood perfectly motionless. The foremost wolf gained the shelf. Quick as a flash, the sheep struck him and hurled him off the cliff down to the depths below. The other four came dashing on. As they stepped on the fatal ledge, each was sent thundering down the same way."

Mountain sheep seldom migrate. They stick to the same range even when threatened with extermination, moving only when food runs short. Hoof trails cut 12 to

**Stone sheep,** despite his iron-gray color, is a blood brother to the white Dall of Alaska. The "black mountain sheep" lives in one of the most notable big-game regions of the continent, sharing British Columbia's rugged wilderness with mountain goats, caribou, and bears.

*Louis Agassiz Fuertes*

Walter A. Weber, National Geographic staff artist

**Dall sheep,** alert for wolves, venture across a rocky slope. White coats give no camouflage here.

18 inches deep in a mountainside attest to centuries of constant use.

Alaska's Mount McKinley National Park gives refuge to many Dall sheep. From the park road tourists glimpse the animals frisking along cliffs and ledges. Keep in full view when stalking sheep, naturalist Adolph Murie advises, and it's unlikely they will bolt. But disappear for a moment? Goodbye!

Murie once calmed an inquisitive bunch by imitating their call. As they headed into photography range he alerted his brother, hidden with a camera, by bleating: "Baa-a-a—they're moving to your right—baa-a-a—now they're coming straight up."

White sheep intergrade with the darker strains. In the Yukon they mingle with the gray Fannin sheep; farther south reigns the nearly black Stone race *(O. d. stonei)*. British Columbia yielded the world's record Stone ram. Some sportsmen say this massive head surpasses any other North American big-game trophy.

*Shoulder height* 2½–3⅓ ft. *Weight* 100–200 lbs. *Range:* Alaska to British Columbia. *Characteristics:* horns thinner, more flaring than bighorn; coat white to blackish.

WALTER A. WEBER

# MOUNTAIN GOAT

## Oreamnos americanus

Up the scarred face of a cliff the mountain goat fearlessly picks a path. Across the chasm four hunters gape in disbelief. "Stop, you idiot," one bursts out, "you can't climb that!" But he does. For this bearded beast of the northern Rockies is king of the high peaks.

Thickset and buffalo-shouldered, he looks clumsy; yet he is North America's surest-footed steeplejack. Digging non-skid hoofs into steep slopes, he scales dizzy heights seemingly for the fun of it. While tracking goats in the Washington Cascades, author Owen Wister wryly noted:

"They chose places to lie down where falling off was the easiest thing you could do. . . . The individual tracks we have passed always choose the inclined plane where they have a choice between that and the level. . . . If they play games together, it is probably to push each other over a precipice, and the goat that takes the longest to walk up again loses the game."

Old mountain men say a goat will look down from a cloud-scraping pinnacle and grin and waggle his whiskers. Cornered, he can impale hunting dogs with his horns and pitch them over a cliff.

Few predators seek the white goat in his high retreat. Aside from man's rifle, he fears mountain lion and lynx — and eagles that snatch unguarded kids. Only when he must descend into the valleys to mineral licks can bears, wolves, and coyotes prey on him. Lakes and bays pose no danger; he's a good swimmer. Along the Pacific coast between Puget Sound and the Kenai Peninsula in Alaska he fares well in wet, saline weather.

Cold can't chill the mountain goat. A heavy, shaggy coat protects him from the fiercest winter storms. His fleecy underwear, three to four inches deep, compares with fine merino and cashmere wool. He roams the same rocky ramparts all year, foraging on alpine plants, mosses, and scrub. This whiskered ascetic disdains the easy life of sheltered valleys.

A careful mountaineer, he looks before he leaps, rarely makes a misstep. Curiously, he pays little heed to avalanches — perhaps the chief threat to his life. Poor hearing may be the cause: gorged wood ticks sometimes plug his ears.

Mountain goats often travel in family bands, an old billy in the lead. At treacherous crossings they string out in single file, kids sandwiched between adults. A goat doesn't panic when his high ledge trails off into space, leaving him no room to turn on all fours. He rears and adroitly executes an about-face, or pulls himself up to another ledge. His concave suction-cup toes cling to precarious footholds.

During November's rutting season, billies get pugnacious as their mating ardor rises. They slash brush with their spikes, anointing these woody scent posts with musk from glands at the base of the horns. They square off against each other with a dignified air, maneuver stiff-leggedly, spar awkwardly. It looks comic but it's deadly — one thrust can disembowel an opponent.

In the spring, six months after mating, kids are dropped. Generally the nanny has one, but twins aren't uncommon. Ten minutes after birth the infant goat can stand; within 30 minutes he'll jump. He weighs about seven pounds at birth.

Unlike many game animals, mountain goats have not dwindled. Hunters bypass them because goat meat tastes strong, and the head does not make a striking trophy.

Observers have long disagreed on what to call the animal. Explorer Alexander MacKenzie decided it was a white buffalo; to Lewis and Clark it was a mountain sheep; today it's dubbed a goat. Actually it's an antelope related to the alpine chamois. Farthest afield was Captain Cook's remark when Indians brought him goat skins in 1778: "There is here the White Bear."

*Shoulder height* 2¾–3½ ft. *Weight* 125 –300 lbs. *Range:* S. Alaska to N. Idaho. *Characteristics:* whiskers, humped shoulders, shaggy white coat, black spike horns.

**Sure-footed mountain goats** follow the leader across a cliff face. Hunters sometimes lure them to the gun by waving something bright.

*Walter A. Weber, National Geographic staff artist*

Peccaries **swill** their fill at a desert waterhole. They forage in bands or family groups.

MARVIN H. FROST

CHAPTER 8

# The Peccary or Javelina

RESTLESS PECCARIES, scurrying through mesquite, suddenly freeze in their tracks. An ominous buzzing sounds from a clearing. Rattlesnake! Black manes bristle and heavy musk charges the air. The bold peccaries encircle the serpent, nimbly avoid his darting head. A crusty old boar, leader of the band, picks his moment and pounces on the writhing coil. The others spring into action and sharp hoofs rain down from every angle. The peccaries tear the rattler to bits and eat him on the spot.

Once in a while a dusky little peccary challenges man. "In the old days," Theodore Roosevelt observed, "it had been no uncommon thing for a big band to attack entirely of their own accord, and keep a hunter up a tree for hours at a time." Ordinarily the animal knows better; dogs and men send him scooting.

Far less familiar than the barnyard porker, which also falls in the superfamily *Suoidea,* the collared peccary *(Tayassu tajacu)* is the only native pig-like animal found in the United States. He roams foothills and desert country from southern Texas, Arizona, and New Mexico to South America. In tropical America he meets a larger relative—the white-lipped peccary. Naturalists named him the collared peccary because a white stripe circles his neck. But Southwesterners call him

116

America's **little peccary** grubs for food beneath the golden blossoms of a paloverde, Arizona's state tree.

*Walter A. Weber, National Geographic staff artist*

javelina or musk hog. Elusive, he's often smelled before he's seen. When startled, the scraggly animal emits pungent odors from musk glands buried in his back.

"It has one thing very strange that the Navel is not upon the Belly, but the back," reported buccaneer Lionel Wafer in 1681, mistaking the musk gland for the navel. "And what is more still, if upon killing a Pecary the Navel be not cut away from the Carcass within 3 or 4 hours after at the farthest, 'twill so taint all the flesh, as not only to render it unfit to be eaten, but make it stink insufferably."

Peccaries know no fixed mating season; they breed any time. After four months, the sow retires to a hollow log or den and bears two reddish-brown young, occasionally more. Within hours the spry infants can outrun a man. They tame easily, make amusing pets. One captive eight-pounder loved to have its head scratched and would run to its owner with the eagerness of a puppy.

Until hunting was regulated, men slaughtered javelinas by the drove for their hides. They make fine gloves and jackets. Many farmers favored complete extermination; when drought didn't ruin their crops, rooting peccaries did. These indiscriminate diners eat almost anything, from cactus to wild figs.

A host of animals relish javelina meat. Jaguar, bobcat, wolf, coyote, ocelot all prey on him. Plagued with poor eyesight, he depends on keen smell and hearing to detect enemies. He sniffs the air; if danger lurks, a loud grunt signals "Run for your life!" But the peccary fights when he must, and fights well. Sharp tusks in a single swipe can rip a dog from shoulder to hip.

*Shoulder height* 17–20 in. *Weight* 40–65 lbs. *Range:* southwestern U. S. to South America. *Characteristics:* grizzled coat, white collar, musk gland on back.

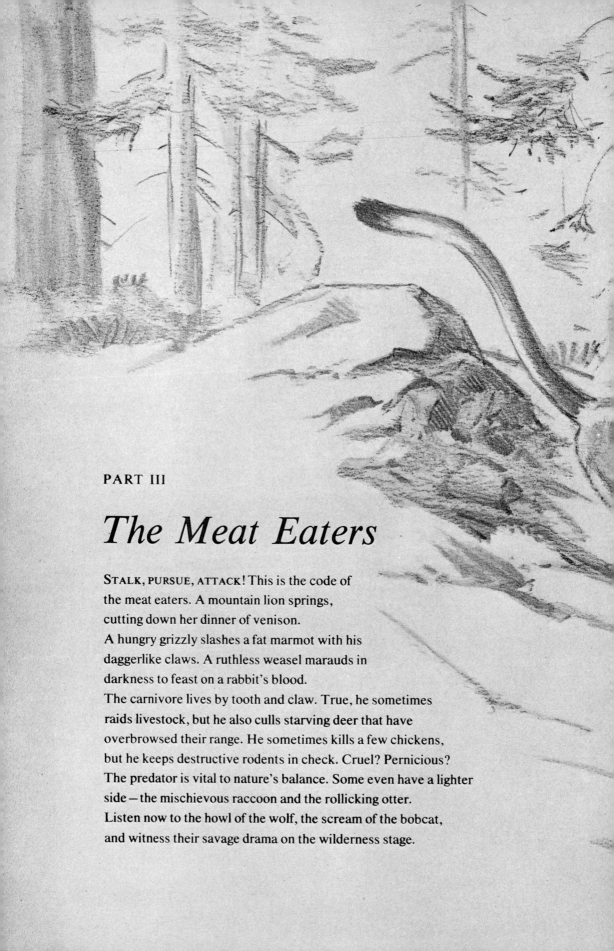

# PART III

# *The Meat Eaters*

STALK, PURSUE, ATTACK! This is the code of
the meat eaters. A mountain lion springs,
cutting down her dinner of venison.
A hungry grizzly slashes a fat marmot with his
daggerlike claws. A ruthless weasel marauds in
darkness to feast on a rabbit's blood.
The carnivore lives by tooth and claw. True, he sometimes
raids livestock, but he also culls starving deer that have
overbrowsed their range. He sometimes kills a few chickens,
but he keeps destructive rodents in check. Cruel? Pernicious?
The predator is vital to nature's balance. Some even have a lighter
side — the mischievous raccoon and the rollicking otter.
Listen now to the howl of the wolf, the scream of the bobcat,
and witness their savage drama on the wilderness stage.

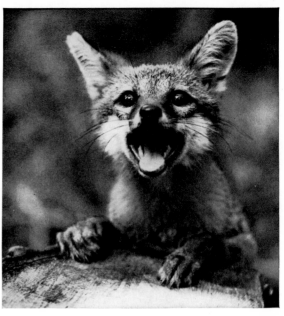

**A gray fox pup,** face to face with an intruder in Alabama, snaps defiance.

CHAPTER 9

# Wolves, Coyotes, and Foxes

By STANLEY P. YOUNG

K ILLERS OF LIVESTOCK, an old she-wolf and her whelps had been ravaging the farms around Pomfret, Connecticut, for several years. Now, in a single night they slaughtered 75 sheep and goats belonging to one young farmer. The year was 1739 and the farmer Israel Putnam, destined to become a famous Revolutionary War general. He wasn't one to take this lying down.

Organizing a hunt, Putnam and his neighbors caught up with the young wolves and killed them. They then tracked the old pirate to her den. Dogs, guns, fires, and brimstone failed to drive her out. Putnam, out of patience, grabbed a pine torch and crawled into the hole. He saw the wolf's eyes blaze in front of him, heard her growl. Retreating hurriedly, he took a gun loaded with buckshot, crawled back in, and fired away. Then he dragged out the dead wolf—one more casualty in man's unrelenting war against the wild canines.

We call the dog, our faithful household companion, "man's best friend." But through the ages man has feared and despised the dog's wild relatives, for they prey on his cattle, occasionally even attack man himself. Playing the role of villain in the drama of civilization, the wild canines have a bad name everywhere. From the werewolf of folklore to the "wicked wolf" who ate Red Riding Hood's grandmother, and the "big bad wolf" of Walt Disney's animated cartoon, the wolf has always been a symbol of evil and fear. Through the tales of Aesop and La Fontaine the fox has come down to us as a sly character, ever ready to pull a fast one. The coyote is branded a knave and coward, and the jackal spells treachery and

121

**Timber wolf,** standing beside his den, surveys a hostile world. Once common throughout North America, wolves are now scarce between Mexico and Canada.

TOM MCHUGH, NATIONAL AUDUBON SOCIETY AND (ABOVE) WIDE WORLD

avarice. But despite a bad press, the wild dogs have a few friends. Romulus and Remus, legendary founders of Rome, were suckled by a soft-hearted mother wolf. So was Mowgli, hero of Kipling's *Jungle Books*. In World War II the U. S. Army had a Timber Wolf Division (the 104th), named for the wolf's traits of courage, tenacity, and fighting ability.

Wolves, coyotes, and foxes—in fact all the wild dogs that make up the world-wide family *Canidae*—share common characteristics. All have long narrow muzzles, erect ears, slender limbs, and bushy tails. All have keen sight, hearing, and smell. All regulate body temperature by panting, moisture being passed off through the tongue. All evolved from the *Miacidae,* small, tree-climbing mammals that lived 50 million years ago. These primitive carnivores were also the progenitors of the bears and raccoons.

From the Miacidae came *Cynodesmus,* the type from which the dog family is believed to have developed into its varied offshoots. Many kinds of wild dogs evolved, but only the fittest survived. One that became extinct was the huge dire wolf, whose bones have been recovered from the La Brea tar pits in Los Angeles, California. These wolves attacked animals mired in the oil, only to be trapped themselves.

**Life-or-death drama** in the snows of Isle Royale pits 14 wolves against a lone but healthy moose. The hungry wolves close in warily, for slashing hoofs can take their toll. Flying biologists studying the wolf-moose relationship on this Lake Superior "laboratory" watched the pack give up after a five-minute skirmish and trot off to seek weaker quarry. Wolf predations help keep moose numbers in balance with the browse.

L. DAVID MECH

E. R. KALMBACH, U. S. FISH AND WILDLIFE SERVICE AND (RIGHT) WARREN F. STEENBERGH

SOMETIME, somewhere, primitive man began to make pets of wild dogs, and the first animal companions came to share his fireside. When men migrated from Asia across the land bridge to North America, they no doubt brought domesticated dogs with them. Coronado, exploring the Kansas plains in 1541, saw huge dogs probably descended from these, which the Indians used as beasts of burden. They also tamed the native wolf and coyote, and various breeds of Indian dogs appeared. No record exists of domestic dogs hybridizing with their cousins, the foxes; but wolves and coyotes will mate freely with dogs and have fertile offspring. After all, they are virtually the same species — one wild, one tame.

Both dogs and wolves establish runways, marked by scent posts on which they leave telltale messages for friend and foe. A family of wolves has been known to cover more than 100 miles on a single runway. Another runway, in southern Arizona, was about 70 miles long. Wolves made the circuit with clocklike regularity every nine days. The wolf runway, generally an ellipse, is a hunting route. It may consist in part of trails used by range cattle, sheep, or game; in part of wood roads, and dry washes and canyons, particularly with sandy bottoms. Its width may be but a few feet, as on a game trail, to more than a mile, where the wolves range out to hunt. Using scent posts and scratching near them is unquestionably the vestige of an ancestral habit of burying the urine or excreta.

Dog and wolf show their close relationship in many other ways as well. Each holds its tail straight up when playing, wags it to express pleasure, and tucks it between the hind legs when frightened. Both gorge food, often to stupefaction. Finally, both dog and wolf have the same gestation period—approximately 63 days.

Despite these qualities in common, man has taken the domesticated dog to his heart, but has extirpated wolves. He has placed a price on the wolf's head since the days of Solon, the Athenian lawgiver, 2,500 years ago. In North America, the first wolf bounty was declared only 10 years after the Pilgrims landed. Soon all the colonies passed similar laws. In 1663 the citizens of Jamaica, Long Island, agreed that "whosoever shall kill any wolf, the head being shown to the town or nailed upon a tree, shall have seven bushels of Indian corn."

**Resourceful coyote** in Colorado brings home a jack rabbit for dinner. Both parents help bring up young. Woolly **red fox** pups (below), alerted by a strange scent or sound, interrupt play near their den in Alaska's Mount McKinley National Park.

After settlement of the West, the Government and settlers waged all-out war against wolves and coyotes, hunting, trapping, and using poison. As late as 1913 a stock growers' association in Colorado paid $7,000 to one trapper for 140 wolves killed at $50 a head. The long campaign resulted in virtually exterminating the wolf south of Canada, but the wily, omnivorous coyote flourished in spite of it, and even extended his range into Alaska and the East. The fox has been warred against in various states in recent years because of the fear of rabies. Afflicted animals transmit the disease by biting.

The lure of the bounty is so powerful that many frauds have been practiced to collect it. William Cooper, writing in the early 1800's of western New York settlements, tells of a man who found a she-wolf and six whelps in a pitfall he had dug. Leaving them there, he hurried to town meeting and made a rousing speech advocating an increased bounty on wolves. "His eloquence was popular and successful," reports Cooper. "The bounty was doubled; next morning he went with a neighbor to examine his pitfall and taking the seven scalps claimed and received . . . the augmented recompence."

**A mushrooming cloud** of white fox fur envelops an Eskimo trader in the Canadian Arctic.

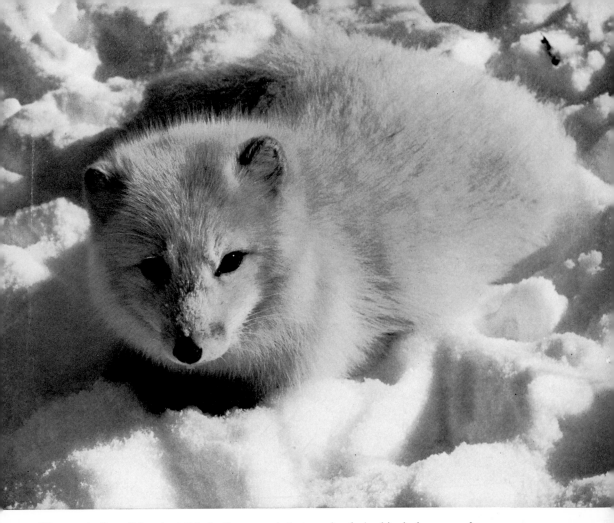

**The arctic fox,** all but invisible in the snow, is betrayed only by his dark eyes and nose.

There's no denying that wild dogs, when they live close to man and ravage his livestock, should be controlled. But the deep-rooted idea that all wolves, coyotes, and foxes should be exterminated is being disproved by modern wildlife research. More and more we are coming to realize that these predators, when kept within bounds, do more good than harm. They serve as a check on rodents, and cull surplus or weakened big-game animals that otherwise would die of starvation. They should be assured a place in the North American fauna, for they are one of nature's balances, useful and necessary. They are true symbols of the wild.

*A Portfolio*  Following are biographies of all the North American wolves, coyotes, and foxes, illustrated in full color by National Geographic Staff Artist Walter A. Weber and other noted wildlife artists. Heights and weights show the range between an average female and a large male.

# GRAY or TIMBER WOLF

## *Canis lupus*

A LONG LOW HOWL—tremulous, desolate—floats through the night air, and a shiver runs down the listener's spine. Few Americans today have heard the call of the wolf, but it was an all-too-familiar sound to our pioneer forefathers.

In colonial days hordes of wolves ranged North America. Everywhere man waged war on them, and slowly the fierce wild dogs retreated. They are among the most intelligent of carnivores, but the regularity of their habits, such as the use of runways, has helped man to destroy them.

Sole survivors between Mexico and the Canadian border today are a few hundred that linger on in the forests of northern Michigan, Minnesota, Wisconsin, and possibly Oregon. A few stray across the border from Mexico. But in the Canadian and Alaskan wilderness, wolves still abound.

Unlike the "human wolf," the four-footed variety is monogamous. He usually

**Scourge of the West** in days when bison roved by millions, the huge plains or buffalo wolf *(C. l. nubilis)*

mates for life and is a devoted parent and provider. In spring litters of six to twelve are born in dens among rocks, or in hillside burrows. The mother stays with the young while the male hunts or stands guard. At weaning time both parents disgorge predigested food for the pups to eat. Finally the young join their parents on hunting trips, and their long education begins.

The wolf can be domesticated if taken very young. A tame wolf generally becomes a one-man pet, savage and unapproachable to any stranger.

From Greenland to Mexico, 24 different races are recognized. Variously called American, gray, or timber wolf, all are the same species as the European wolf. Coats, varying from black to white, are usually grizzled. Different colors may occur in the same litter. The largest wolves, with record weights up to 175 pounds, roam the arctic coasts of Canada. Many of them wear white coats all year (page 88).

*Shoulder height 26–38 in. Weight 60–125 lbs. Range:* Greenland to Mexico. *Characteristic:* our largest wild dog.

129

shadowed the herds, picking off calves and stragglers.
*Walter A. Weber, courtesy of National Park Service*

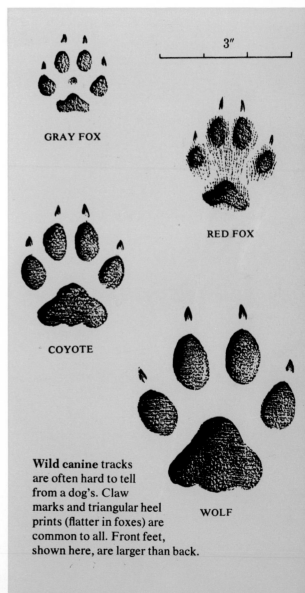

GRAY FOX

RED FOX

COYOTE

WOLF

**Wild canine** tracks are often hard to tell from a dog's. Claw marks and triangular heel prints (flatter in foxes) are common to all. Front feet, shown here, are larger than back.

WALTER A. WEBER

# RED WOLF

## *Canis rufus*

BESIDES A RED or tawny phase from which the red wolf gets its name, there is a black phase which once was common east of the Mississippi River.

"Wolves of this color were abundant near Henderson, Kentucky, when we removed to that place, and we saw them frequently during our rambles through the woods," wrote John James Audubon, the famous 19th century naturalist.

"Once when we were travelling on foot not far from the southern boundary of Kentucky, we fell in with a Black Wolf, following a man with a rifle on his shoulders. On speaking with him about this animal, he assured us that it was as tame and as gentle as any dog, and that he had never met with a dog that could trail a deer better. We were so much struck with . . . the noble appearance of the wolf, that we offered him one hundred dollars for it; but the owner would not part with him for any price."

Intermediate in size between the gray or timber wolf and the coyote or prairie wolf, the red wolf once ranged from Florida to Texas, and up the Mississippi Valley to Illinois and Indiana. Subject to the same persecution as its two close relatives, it is now fast disappearing, and is found only in a small area along the Texas coast.

William Bartram described this unique American species in 1791, after seeing examples of the now extinct Florida race.

"The wolves of Florida are larger than a dog," wrote the Philadelphia naturalist, "and are perfectly black, except the females, which have a white spot on the breast, but they are not so large as the wolves of Canada and Pennsylvania, which are a yellowish brown color."

Bartram further noted that the wolves "assemble in companies in the night time, howl and bark together, especially in cold winter nights, which is terrifying to the wandering bewildered traveller."

*Shoulder height* 24–30 in. *Weight* 50–80 lbs. *Range:* Brazoria, Galveston, Chambers, and Jefferson counties, Texas, and perhaps in adjacent Cameron Parish, Louisiana. *Characteristic:* red phase tawnier than gray wolf or coyote, especially on muzzle, ears, and legs.

131

**This sunset serenader,** the flourishing western coyote, is also called the brush or prairie wolf.

## COYOTE

*Canis latrans*

LOPING THROUGH THE SAGE or racing across the prairie, the coyote is a familiar sight. At night his high-pitched wail—"a prolonged howl which the animal let out and then ran after and bit into small pieces"—echoes across the plains. His scientific name means barking dog.

A cunning and resourceful hunter, the coyote seldom goes hungry. He'll eat carrion as well as fresh-killed meat. By helping to control rodents, his chief food, he probably does as much good as harm. But since he sometimes kills livestock, ranchmen have branded him public enemy No. 1, now that the wolf is scarce.

For a century man has campaigned against the coyote with guns, traps, and poison. But today his kind, numerous as ever, have even extended their range. Un-known in Alaska prior to the gold rush, coyotes now roam there by the thousands. Within the past 25 years they have invaded the east, appearing in at least 13 states from Maine to Florida. The brush wolf is now so well established in New York that the State Conservation Department is trapping and studying it in the Adirondacks. Some upstate counties post a $25 bounty. In 1958 they paid for 239.

In many areas the coyote has crossbred with dogs to produce a "coy-dog" that sometimes plays hob with sheep and deer.

The coyote's secret of survival? He's intelligent, omnivorous, prolific. He knows how to keep just out of gunshot, and it takes skill to poison or trap a region's last pair. Averaging seven pups to the litter, that last pair can soon repopulate the area. Record litters reach 19!

*Shoulder height* 23–26 in. *Weight* 20–50 lbs. *Range:* Alaska to Central America. *Characteristics:* wolflike, but smaller.

Walter A. Weber, National Geographic staff artist

**Alaska red fox,** largest of foxes, brings a ground squirrel to his hungry family. Both father and mother fox tenderly care for their young. When grown, the pups may be different colors, as their parents are.

# RED FOX

*Vulpes vulpes*

THE SLY RED FOX has led many a hunter and hound a merry chase. Once a 100-man posse, bent on avenging poultry losses, scoured the countryside for red-coated chicken thieves, The tally? Foxes: no casualties. Men: two hit. Another time a fleeing fox swerved sharply at cliff's edge, and seven hounds plummeted to death.

Reynard, as medieval poets named his European counterpart, is a past master at losing dogs. He doubles back, sidetracks, skips along fence tops, splashes through streams, dashes over thin ice. Sorely pressed, he will hide in a chimney or kitchen stove. One sought refuge in a church during morning worship.

Rust-red coat, white-tipped tail, black ears, legs, and nose mark him one of nature's handsomest. A litter may include other color phases: the cross fox with dark bands bisecting back and shoulders, the black fox, and the prized silver fox.

In January or February foxes mate, and 51 days later the vixen gives birth to four to ten pups. The den, often borrowed from a woodchuck, serves as nursery; the red fox usually sleeps in the open. The male helps raise the young, will risk death to divert enemies. In distress his bark may change to a "perfectly appalling scream."

Occasionally the fox falls prey to coyote, wolf, bobcat, lynx, or eagle; and rabies thins his ranks. But man and dog cause him most anxiety. He prefers farm land to wilderness, sometimes dwells in suburbs. He feeds mostly on field mice, cottontails, insects, berries, and fruits. Now and then he raids a hen house. But until man learns to outwit him, Reynard probably will consider the delicacy worth the gamble.

*Shoulder height* 15–16 in. *Weight* 6–15 lbs. *Range:* Alaska, Canada to southern U.S. except Pacific coast and central plains. *Characteristic:* white-tipped tail.

# KIT FOX

*Vulpes velox*

A NOCTURNAL HUNTER, the kit or swift fox is rarely seen by day. If surprised, he may hug the ground and lie still, hoping to escape notice. Frightened, he flashes away with his tail straight out behind, running with a smooth-flowing motion as effortless as thistledown floating on a breeze.

Pressed, he wheels suddenly and takes off in a new direction, throwing his pursuer off balance. Or he may disappear into a handy burrow.

Scarcely larger than a house cat, this little fox sports a black-tipped tail, and a dark spot on either side of his nose. He roams the western plains and foothills of the Rockies, from Texas to Alberta and Manitoba. A close relative, the desert swift fox *(V. macrotis)*, inhabits arid reaches from California, Nevada, and Utah south into Mexico. It has larger ears than the plains kit fox, and a somewhat paler coat. Otherwise the two can hardly be told apart.

Home may be an abandoned badger or prairie dog hole. Usually, however, the kit fox digs its own hole, taking care to make both a front and back entrance. Here four or five young are reared during the spring and summer.

Usual prey of the kit fox includes kangaroo rats, ground squirrels, and other small rodents, as well as rabbits, lizards, birds, beetles, and grasshoppers. It even eats grass and fruit.

Shy and guileless, this handsome little wild dog does not have the red fox's cunning or the coyote's sophistication. It has thinned out in many areas because it eats poison bait put out for the wary coyote.

*Shoulder height* 12 in. *Weight* 4–6 lbs. *Range:* plains and deserts, Canada to Mexico. *Characteristics:* small size, big ears, black-tipped tail, generally nocturnal.

**A kit fox pounces** on a meadow mouse; the swift end of a long hunt. Black markings on muzzle and brushy tail identify this little western fox.

*Walter A. Weber, National Geographic staff artist*

WALTER A. WEBER

Carl Rungius, courtesy of New York Zoological Society

**The gray fox** has a trick up his wily sleeve: he eludes pursuers by climbing trees.

# GRAY FOX

## *Urocyon cinereoargenteus*

BAYING HOUNDS, fox scent burning in their nostrils, pound across fields into the woods, pursuing a grizzled phantom with black-tipped tail. The hot trail fades out, and the bewildered dogs wander aimlessly, sniffing for a new sign. High in a tree the gray fox watches. Shaking them was easy.

He's the only fox that climbs; hence his nickname, tree fox. In the open he dives into a hole. But he's not always cunning: one hunter lured him to the gun with a crow call.

The gray fox usually hunts at night. He catches rabbits, mice, lizards, insects, sometimes nabs a squirrel or steals a chicken. His keen nose leads him to wild turkey and partridge;

he "winds them like a pointer dog," observed naturalist John Bachman. Shellfish, eggs, nuts, fruits, and berries round out the gray's diet.

Fierce battles between males often announce the January mating season. Two months later, in a hollow log or under a rock pile, mother fox bears four or five dark pups. The male brings food, helps care for the young.

Bobcat, coyote, wolf, and eagle harass the fox, and rabies sometimes plagues his kind. But sportsmen, farmers, and bounty hunters pose a greater threat. Yet the gray asks no quarter. Even when trapped, he "will growl, snap, and bark from the time he sees you till he is dispatched."

*Shoulder height* 14–15 in. *Weight* 4–13 lbs. *Range:* S. Canada to South America. *Characteristics:* gray coat with orange, black, white markings.

# ARCTIC FOX

## *Alopex lagopus*

THE GREAT WHITE BEAR eats his fill of the seal he has killed; from a discreet distance a little white fox watches. When the bear wanders off, the canine camp follower takes his turn at the banquet table. Arctic foxes are the scavengers of the polar wastes.

Sometimes they follow arctic wolves, cleaning up what is left of a caribou or reindeer. A stranded whale might provide a year-long feast for all the foxes in the area. Doglike, the white fox also follows man on his expeditions. Arctic travelers report its pestering tameness and curiosity, its shrill yapping bark, "like a bantam hen that has just laid an egg."

In summer the foxes feed on lemmings and other small rodents; also birds and eggs. When lemmings grow scarce — about every fourth or fifth year — the white foxes hunt far south of their usual range. In winter's season of scarcity they stalk the snow-white ptarmigan and arctic hare, sometimes venture over sea ice miles from shore in their endless search for food.

In April or May, four to seven young are born in hillside burrows. Each weighs but two ounces at birth and has a fuzzy brown coat. The adult molts in spring, growing a summer coat of dingy brown. Before winter comes, he replaces it with a coat of white or blue. The blue phase may occur anywhere in the range, or in the same litter. But blues are more common at the eastern and western edges of the fox's territory — in Iceland, and in the Pribilof Islands off Alaska.

*Shoulder height* 10–12 in. *Weight* 6–15 lbs. *Range:* the Arctic to beyond 83°N. *Characteristics:* rounded ears, short nose; white or bluish fur in winter.

**Prized for their soft fur,** arctic foxes don winter coats in two shades — white or smoky blue.
*Louis Agassiz Fuertes*

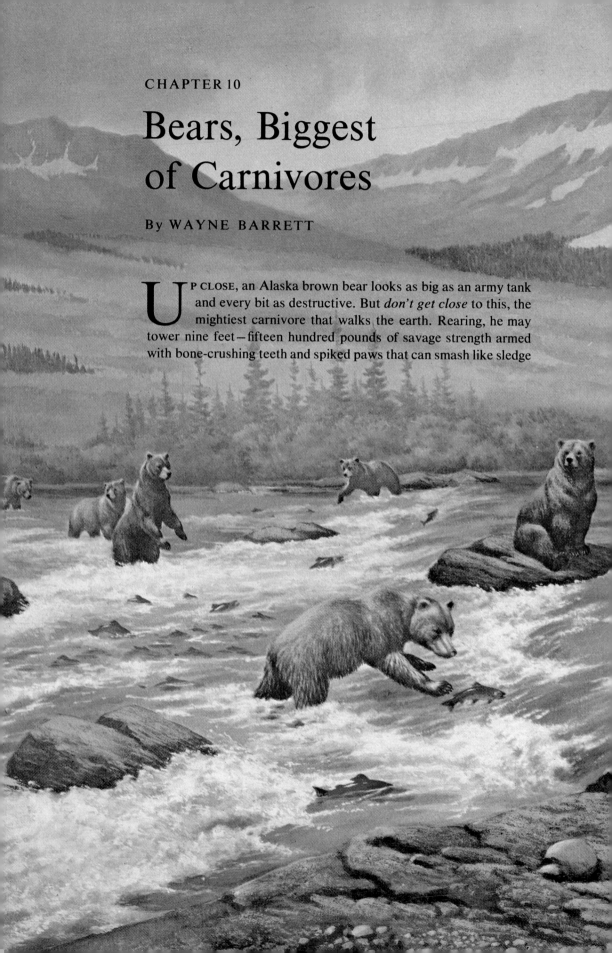

CHAPTER 10

# Bears, Biggest
of Carnivores

By WAYNE BARRETT

U P CLOSE, an Alaska brown bear looks as big as an army tank
and every bit as destructive. But *don't get close* to this, the
mightiest carnivore that walks the earth. Rearing, he may
tower nine feet—fifteen hundred pounds of savage strength armed
with bone-crushing teeth and spiked paws that can smash like sledge

hammers. "I have seen a wounded Bear strike a tough black alder four inches through, and break it as smoothly as though it had been shot off," reports an awed pioneer.

Big bear country is the length of the Alaska Peninsula from Cook Inlet to False Pass. Here snow-born streams cut through grasslands to Bristol Bay and Bering Sea, and when the salmon are running, the brown bear fishes amid the swirling waters, ducking his shaggy head, scooping with massive paws. Early one August, National Geographic artist Walter A. Weber squinted through his binoculars at 23 browns reveling in pools of red, or sockeye, salmon. Here he made his sketches.

Ever since Stone Age artists drew bears on the walls of caves, bruin has excited man's wonder. He bulks large in folklore, literature, and religion. The Old Testament tells how David slew a bear to save his flocks. Siberian nomads and ancient Japanese held the bear sacred: Chinese respectfully called him "man bear"; Cree Indians apologized to the bear for killing him, then hung his skull in a tree and offered up prayers. In Greek legend, Zeus transformed his mistress Callisto into a bear, then banished her to the heavens where she reigns as Ursa Major.

Plutarch recorded that bears brought from Britain to Rome were held "in great admiration." The beasts battled with armed men before cheering crowds in the Colosseum.

Pliny the Elder was fascinated by newborn cubs, "formless pieces of flesh, somewhat larger than mice." But the old Roman misled generations to come when he added: "By virtue of the mother's licking they gradually

**"Once upon a time there were three bears . . ."**

No bedtime stories for **black bear** triplets; they learn survival lessons like how to climb a tree. Mother calls them when they bawl to be nursed, and down they slide, braking with short claws. Seeing a cub, Theodore Roosevelt said, "I'll hold my fire for anything that cute." Clifford Berryman's cartoon of the incident in the Washington *Star* inspired the Teddy bear.

Adult **grizzly** (right) seldom climbs, but takes to water readily. So do **Alaska brown bears** (overleaf), catching sockeyes near Bristol Bay. These salmon, blue as they enter streams, turn bright red when spawning time approaches.

*Overleaf: Walter A. Weber,*
*National Geographic staff artist*

140

assume shape." An American settler revived the tale: "This rude Lump they fashion by degrees, by their constant licking."

White men met the bear in the New World and tasted its meat almost a century before the *Mayflower* dropped anchor off Plymouth Rock. In 1534 Jacques Cartier's expedition killed a polar bear near Newfoundland. "His flesh," remarked the French explorer, "was as good to eat as that of a two-year-old heifer." Two years later English navigators landed on a nearby island, finding "beares both blacke and white, of whome they killed some, and took them for no bad foode." Willem Barents's crew, exploring arctic waters in 1596, tried polar bear fare. The animal's liver "made us all sicke," logged the Dutch skipper, "specially 3 that were exceeding sicke . . . for all their skins came off from the foote to the head." The high concentration of vitamin A in the polar bear's liver can cause such symptoms.

American settlers praised bear fat, "incomparably milder than hogs-lard and near as sweet as oil of cloves." Bear pelts made fine rugs. Indians used them as robes and tepee doors. Napoleon's elite infantrymen looked fierce in tall bearskin hats. At Britain's Buckingham Palace Her Majesty's Brigade of Guards still parades in traditional busbies, towering helmets of Canadian black bear fur.

Bears have thrived in North America since Pliocene times. In arctic wastes the white-robed polar bear flourished on sea food; in Alaska the giant brown prospered on salmon and endless crops of berries. Farther south, pristine forests and meadowlands made a veritable Eden for thousands of black bears and grizzlies. Then civilization spread across the continent, and the first bear to feel its pressure was the one who fought back hardest—the ferocious, fabulous grizzly.

In his heyday "Old Ephraim"—as trappers dubbed the grizzly—was a spine-tingling symbol of the untamed wilderness. Lewis and Clark met this "most tremendious looking anamal" in 1805, and one promptly chased Lewis right into the

**Knife-against-claw** duels to the death, like this combat with a bear that Currier and Ives depicted in 1861, gave a mountain man a reputation for valor—if he survived. One mauled trapper vowed he'd "never fight narry 'nother grizzly without a good shootin-iron."

Missouri River. "There was no place by means of which I could conceal myself from this monster untill I could charge my rifle," wrote Lewis. "In this situation I thought of retreating in a brisk walk ... untill I could reach a tree about 300 yards below me, but I had no sooner terned myself about but he pitched at me, open mouthed and full speed. I ran ... into the water to such debth that I could stand and he would be obliged to swim, and that I could in that situation defend myself with my espontoon [pike]." Fortunately for Lewis, the bear quit the chase.

Henry Brackenridge, venturing up the Missouri soon after, concluded that the grizzly "thirsts for human blood." Kit Carson no doubt agreed as he sprinted for a tree with a pair of grizzlies tearing up the sod in pursuit, "flashing fiery passion, their pearly teeth glittering with eagerness to mangle his flesh."

Bears actually attack a man only if provoked or startled. But when one gets his dander up, watch out! He comes galloping on all fours, and slashes with teeth and claws. Legend has it different: the animal is said to stand on his hind legs and hug the life out of his victims. Thus an Indian girl supposedly thwarted a bear by clasping a knife in front of her breast. According to another belief, a bear won't hurt a man who plays dead—but who wants to test that theory?

Hot-blooded California gold seekers harnessed the grizzly bear's ferocity. Borrowing a page from the Spanish, they chained the bear to a stake, then loosed a maddened bull. Miners and Mexicans thundered approval as horns and head crashed into hairy hide. They roared again when the bear sank his teeth into the bull and ripped him to shreds. The fights drew big crowds. "The shelving bank of human beings which encircled the place was like a mass of bright flowers," recounted one observer. Such spectacles, it is said, induced Horace Greeley to coin "bull" and "bear" as Wall Street terms.

Californians, in time, sickened of their grisly sport, but the bear found fame from another source. Out of the east came a Massachusetts shoemaker, John Capen Adams, who set out to capture, train, and exhibit wild animals—particularly grizzly bears. "Grizzly" Adams became a legend. He rode grizzlies, wrestled them, used

**Lassoing a grizzly** tested the vaqueros of Old California. They'd lash him to a cart and drag him to the arena to battle a bull. On fiesta days spectators found it a "soul-refreshing sight to see the growling beasts of blood." Los Angeles banned the fights in 1860.

"ROPING OF THE BEAR" BY JAMES WALKER, CALIFORNIA HISTORICAL SOCIETY

143

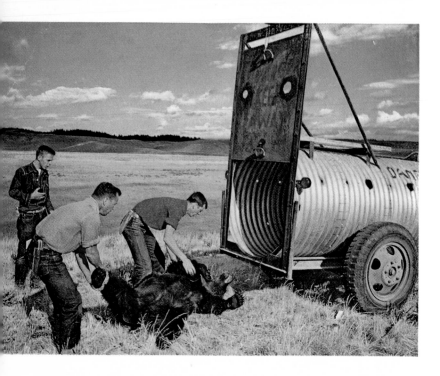

## A jolt of tranquilizer soothes the savage grizzly for the sake of science

To study the grizzly's range and habits and help insure his survival, naturalists John and Frank Craighead needed to tag bears with colored tabs.

But how to get close to 500-odd pounds of snarling fury? Thanks to immobilizing drugs, the brothers did it without getting bitten.

In Yellowstone National Park they baited their portable culvert (upper left) with bacon rind, bread, and honey, then jabbed captives through a porthole with a hypodermic syringe loaded with a muscle-relaxing drug. Doped bears took about a minute to crumple helplessly, though still conscious. Free-wandering bears were brought down with drug-filled darts fired from a rifle.

Dragging Old Ephraim from the trap, the men had precious little time to affix the ear tags (lower left). Sometimes a bear regained muscular control and started to bite before they could finish. The ungrateful "patient" at right charged the scientists, who discarded dignity and lit out for their truck.

Since 1961, the Craigheads have tracked grizzlies by radio. Strapping battery-powered transmitters to drugged animals, the brothers can follow the bears and learn more about their wintering habits, breeding, social behavior, and range.

144

them as pack animals, sometimes fought them hand to hand. Once a charging female bear nearly scalped him. While his dog and a pet grizzly bedeviled the intruder, Adams wiped the blood from his face, then fired a crippling shot into the bear.

In 1860 Adams and his menagerie embarked for New York City. There showman P. T. Barnum, who hired him, heard Adams confess: "I am not the man I was five years ago. Then I felt able to stand the hug of any grizzly living, and was always glad to encounter, single handed, any sort of an animal that dared present himself. But I have been beaten to a jelly, torn almost limb from limb, and nearly chawed up and spit out by these treacherous grizzly bears."

A few months later Adams died from bear wounds.

Today scientists have discovered how to get close to a grizzly without getting clawed. They drug, then study him. Brother naturalists John and Frank Craighead, by hanging radio transmitters on the animals, even get grizzlies to broadcast their life secrets. Backed by the National Geographic Society, the Montana Cooperative Wildlife Research Unit, and others, the brothers use rifles to shoot the bears with hypodermic darts. Frank describes the immobilizing effect on a 520-pound bear: "He went down in one minute, but regained the use of his muscles and was on his feet and chasing us seven minutes after being shot." Usually an anesthetized grizzly can be safely examined for 15 to 20 minutes.

FRANK AND JOHN CRAIGHEAD

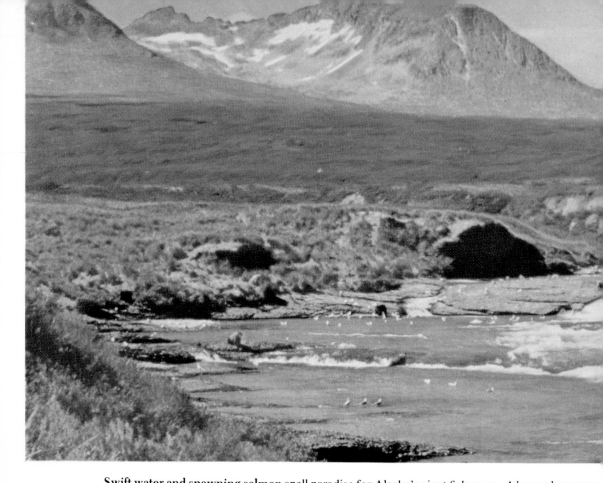

**Swift water and spawning salmon** spell paradise for Alaska's giant fishermen. A brown bear may

Conservationists deal similarly with the black bear. Portable culvert pipe traps baited with ripe garbage lure him. Once he enters, the trap door bangs shut and he gets a dose of ether. When asleep he's weighed, measured, and ear-tagged. Before he's hauled up into the hills and released, he's splashed with bright paint. This enables scientists to check his movements.

To determine the Alaska brown bear's wanderings along salmon streams, Fish and Wildlife personnel, using bows and blunt arrows, shoot him in the rump with vials of dye. A brightly stained stern shows up well from a safe distance. An estimated 20,000 browns and grizzlies inhabit Alaska, but no one counts noses — unless from an airplane. Bear tracks aid census takers. Rangers claim they reveal nearly as much individuality as human fingerprints.

PALEONTOLOGISTS TRACE BEARS to an early ancestor that had a long tail and looked mighty like a dog. Bears and dogs (and cats as well) evolved from one of the *Miacidae*, small, tree-climbing creatures that lived 50 million years ago. Down through the ages the bear family tree has sprouted many branches, and the new leaf looks nothing at all like the root. How did the bear lose his tail? A wily fox, says German folklore, persuaded him to fish with it through a hole in the ice; of course it froze off. One thing's sure. Bruin now has embarrassingly little to wag.

catch and devour six or eight big fish before knocking off for the day. Gulls clean up the leavings.

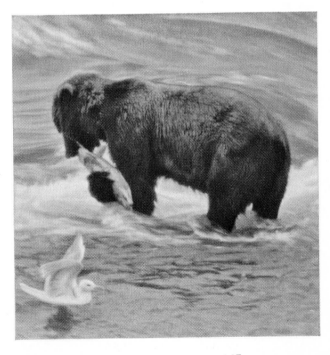

Today's bears, varying in size from Asia's 100-pound sun bear to Alaska's giant brown, range mostly in the Northern Hemisphere. Only the Andean spectacled bear lives south of the equator. Australia's koala looks like a bear, but isn't. He's a marsupial, related to the kangaroo.

Bears have thick, hairy coats, walk flat-footed, possess keen scent, strong claws, and shearing teeth. Though the largest of carnivores, they eat less flesh than wolves or foxes. In fact, except for the polar bear, they are vegetarians much of the time.

Indians thought there must be a relationship between bear and man since they eat the same foods. But

147

one wise redskin deemed bears the smarter "because a man does not know how to live all winter without eating anything." Bears usually sleep like drunken lords during the cold months, but they don't truly hibernate; pulse and respiration stay nearly normal, and in dead of winter bears have been seen shuffling grumpily through the forest.

"Bear trees"—those blazed with teeth and claws—long puzzled woodsmen. Some thought that in this fashion a bear marked off his property. Naturalist Ernest Thompson Seton termed the trees "bear signboards." He reasoned that a bear could read, "by touch and taint on the register trunk, that here there has recently been a bear of such sex and species." Many naturalists support this view.

Dissenters argued that such trees were measuring poles: the higher the mark, the taller and more formidable the bear.

One bear with no tree to mark is the polar bear. In his frigid retreat he always seemed secure from civilization's march. But now sportsmen, zooming low in airplanes, are blasting him off the ice. Hunting limits do not apply

**Mother polar bear** raises a warning paw in defense of her dripping cubs. A moment later she charged the schooner *Bowdoin,* biting futilely at its wooden hull.

Homeward bound from a Greenland voyage, crew members spotted the bears off Baffin Island. Rear Adm. Donald B. MacMillan, whose exploits are well known to National Geographic members, commanded this expedition to the Far North.

148     DONALD MACMILLAN

beyond three miles offshore, and white pelts are prized trophies. So for the first time since the Pleistocene, the polar bear faces extermination. He'll need an anti-aircraft gun to survive.

The black bear, still common in much of North America, has refused to follow the grizzly bear's vanishing trail. He has hung on civilization's fringes, clowned his way into woodland resorts, and become a friend—though an untrustworthy one—to camera-toting tourists. In the Adirondacks, Great Smokies, and Rockies he raids garbage dumps, begs for handouts, and sometimes gets so lazy he refuses to dig a den. A Yellowstone Park ranger reports that black bears "crawl under buildings rather than seek a place in the forest to spend the winter."

Theodore Roosevelt scorned black bears as big-game animals, but loved to watch them "jump about with grotesque agility." A dedicated conservationist, he would have applauded one black bear, the Forest Service's "Smokey," rated the Nation's most powerful force in preventing forest fires. Smokey Bear was only a cub when he was rescued from a New Mexico forest fire in 1951. Now full-grown, he draws admirers to the National Zoological Park in Washington, D.C., while his likeness, in a ranger hat, pleads from placards everywhere to "Be Careful." Children send him thousands of letters. One little girl wrote: "I have tried to break my daddy from throwing out cigarettes from the car."

Smokey is safe at the zoo. But the bears that once reigned supreme in the North American wilderness are fast dwindling. Man's resistless expansion of cities, suburbs, and farmlands doomed the grizzly and crowded the black. Now the polar

**An armful of twins** (opposite) explodes the theory that hybrid bears can't have babies. Parents of these six-week-old cubs were two of the National Zoological Park's famed hybrid bears, half polar, half Alaska brown. Geneticists felt sure the mixture would prove sterile.

**Alerted by man scent,** a grizzly sow rises to full height in a spring-bright meadow in Yellowstone. Fewer than one-third of the cubs in the national park survive as long as 18 months. These live an average of less than six years, a maximum of 30. Control measures within the park account for 18 percent of mortalities, but hunters take much heavier toll outside the preserve's boundaries.

FRANK AND JOHN CRAIGHEAD

150

bear and that titan of them all, the Alaska brown bear, find their secluded empires threatened. If bears are to escape annihilation they must have wilderness where they can hunt and fish, strip berry bushes, hole up in winter, and raise cubs without being molested. To get such reserves, they must look for mercy from their old enemy, man. It's a long shot, but bruin has no choice.

*A Portfolio*    Following are biographies of all the North American bears, illustrated in full color by noted wildlife artists. Heights and weights show the range between an average female and a large male.

In a slashing, snapping free-for-all, black bears of three color phases break the forest's peace.  ▶

*Walter A. Weber, National Geographic staff artist*

WALTER A. WEBER

**BLACK BEAR**

**GRIZZLY BEAR**

6"

**Long claw marks and hind prints "a good third of a yard long and a hand wide" tell that you're on the trail of a big grizzly bear. Also flat-footed, the black bear leaves a smaller track, and often his short nails and inside toes fail to register at all. Blacks and grizzlies, as well as Alaska's big browns, beat deep trails through their haunts.**

# AMERICAN BLACK BEAR
## *Ursus americanus*

THE PARK RANGER couldn't believe his eyes. He saw a man pushing a black bear into the front seat of a car. He raced to the scene, pulled the man away, then shooed the animal into the woods. The tourist wanted a photograph of the bear sitting behind the wheel—next to his wife!

Bruin affects people that way. Deceptively friendly, he reminds you of fun-loving Uncle Louie. But that's a guise—as many park visitors who poke him with sticks and ply him with sweets find to their dismay. Affable but unpredictable, he sometimes bites the hand that feeds him.

In the wild he gorges on berries, roots, grass, laps up ants, digs out rodents, eats bark, robs beehives—even devours the bees. He likes fresh meat, also carrion.

Stuffed and drowsy, the bear greets winter well insulated with fat and fur. In the north he usually snoozes in a cave or hollow log October to May. His sleep is deep, but he can be waked. Farther south he merely catnaps a few days at a time.

Half-pound cubs, usually twins, are born in midwinter. Eyes closed, the almost hairless babies huddle against the mother's warm fur and hum like bees while they nurse. Spring rouses the mother. She introduces her young to the forest, teaches them to climb, cuffs them when they disobey. If danger lurks, her woof sends them scampering up a tree; they stay put until she grunts an all clear.

Bears are mainly nocturnal, but in undisturbed districts wander widely by day.

Black bears come in assorted hues—cinnamon, dark brown, even white for the Kermode bear of British Columbia. An ebony cub may have a brown twin. Alaska's glacier bear appears bluish—making him "powerful medicine" to coastal tribes.

*Shoulder height* 2–3 1/3 ft. *Weight* 200–500 lbs. *Range:* Arctic to central Mexico. *Characteristics:* pale muzzle, straight facial profile, short curved claws, climbs trees.

154

**Hungry grizzly turns a rock, looking**

# GRIZZLY BEAR

## *Ursus arctos horribilis*

HALF A TON of sinew, bone, and muscle, the grizzly is a powerful brute. His long foreclaws, ill-suited for climbing, can deal destruction. He swims well, and runs like the wind in the open; he's been timed in 30-mile-an-hour bursts. Keen hearing and a superlative sense of smell compensate for poor eyesight. He coughs, grunts, sniffs, "growls like distant thunder."

*Ursus horribilis*—horrible bear—was the name that flashed through naturalist George Ord's mind when reading Lewis and Clark's descriptions of the grizzly. Lewis confessed that he would rather "fight two Indians than one bear."

The bear's common name, as well as his nickname "silvertip," refers to his grizzled coat. Light-tipped hairs give a frosty sheen to his deep fur. Usually brown, it may be yellowish, gray, or black.

Grizzlies mate in midsummer. Mother bear gives birth in her winter den to eight-inch-long cubs, generally twins. A bear reaches maturity in eight to ten years, and may live to 30. The grizzly's lifelong interest is his stomach. "To him almost everything is food, except granite," quipped naturalist John Muir. The bear stuffs himself with grass, roots, nuts, berries, fish, and small animals. He relishes carrion, delights in pilfering honey, occasionally catches a sheep, goat, or an elk.

Sometimes a frontier bear turned rustler. One Colorado renegade, "Old Mose," allegedly killed 800 steers and at least five men. Thousand-dollar rewards for such outlaws hastened the grizzly's doom. His hide was sought for rugs, his fat made cooking and hair oil. In gold-rush days bear steak and roasted paw were delicacies.

Indians revered the grizzly; some claimed him ancestor. He could stand on his hind legs like a man, but was mightier; arrows seldom felled him. Honor and glory came to the brave who killed one. A Sioux chief vowed he would sooner part with his wife than his necklace of grizzly claws.

Of the thousands of grizzlies that once roamed the West from Kansas to California, only a few hundred remain—some in Yellowstone, Glacier, and North Cascades National Parks.

Most scientists believe that the grizzly and Alaska brown bear are different races of the same species, *Ursus arctos.*

*Shoulder height* 3–4 ft. *Weight* 400–1,000 lbs. *Range:* Alaska and arctic Canada south to Colorado; mountains of northern Mexico. *Characteristics:* grizzled coat, shoulder hump, concave face, long claws.

for tasty insects, frogs, or snakes.

*Louis Agassiz Fuertes*

# ALASKA BROWN BEAR

## Ursus arctos gyas

THE ALASKA PENINSULA comes alive in July. Here brown bears, world's largest carnivores, picnic all summer long. They shuffle down age-old trails to treeless flats sprawled at the feet of volcanic hills, thread their way through tall grass and pink fireweed to salmon-choked streams. Converging at riffles and pools, they feast on the silver hordes migrating upstream to spawn.

Browns often quarrel over choice fishing sites. They box, push, feint like pugilists, bite and tear with sharp teeth. Most bears take their salmon ashore, but some sit in the water and eat, clutching the slippery morsels between huge paws. They down everything except heads and gills.

Browns differ on the best way to fish. Some favor the sit-and-wait method; when a salmon darts close to the bank, a paw shoots out and pins it down. Other bears wade out among the fish. Sometimes they squat, let the current boil up over their backs; an effortless nod produces a meal. Occasionally a lazy or inept fisherman sneaks off with his neighbor's catch.

A yearling cub learns the art of angling from his mother. He follows her to fast water, makes false passes with his fore-paws, ducks his head exactly as she does. His first catch, like as not, flaps out of his mouth back into the stream. He tries again and again until he gets the hang of it. Soon he is "flipping salmon from streams like a cat at a goldfish bowl."

In summer salmon rates as the brown's staff of life, but he does not disdain other fare. He hunts mice, marmots, ground squirrels, strips berry bushes, grubs roots, crops grass. If a dead whale or seal washes ashore he feasts on that.

When days grow short and winter's steely breath puts bite in the air, the brown holes up. If a hillside cave or lava tunnel isn't handy, he scoops out a den with pitchforklike claws. In January or Feb-ruary, seven months after mating, dozing mother bear gives birth to one to four tiny cubs. In April or May the bear ventures out, leaving hat-size tracks in the snow.

The Alaska brown bear dwarfs his Asian and European cousins. He is a direct descendant of the great cave bear that the earliest Americans battled in the Stone Age (page 46). Kodiak and Peninsula races produce giants that weigh three quarters of a ton and on hind legs dwarf the tallest man. Color usually ranges from dull yellow to dusky brown; the Shiras or Admiralty Island bear, however, is almost black. In all, eight different forms of big brown bears have been described.

The Alaska brown bear usually avoids man, his only enemy. He rarely attacks unless wounded or startled; instinct for self-defense triggers his fury. He champs his teeth, thunders a full-throated roar, and charges on all fours in great leaping bounds. Seldom does the hunter have time for more than one hurried shot.

Against the invasion of white men, the brown bear has so far held his own. His days, however, may be numbered. Southern coastal Alaska, his ancestral realm, ranks as one of the state's most rapidly developing areas. Canners complain that the bear consumes 30 per cent of the salmon run in some streams. Settlers claim he endangers families and livestock.

Dr. Alfred Brooks, the noted Alaskan geologist, prophesied "it is certain that so huge an animal cannot maintain itself in a settled region." Several refuges provide the bear with sanctuary, but as one Alaskan said: "You can't fence them in; not those babies."

The brown bear must retreat farther into Alaska's vast wilderness, stay a jump ahead of bulldozers and jackhammers. Not for generations, perhaps, will civilization doom the northland monarch. By then, man might have decided to let him live.

*Shoulder height* 3–4½ ft. *Weight* 600–1,500 lbs. *Range:* coast and islands, Alaska Peninsula to British Columbia. *Characteristics:* massive size, dished face.

**Thick hooks** hold fast Brownie's lunch. After gulping the salmon, he may loll on the bank awhile, then wade out for a second helping.

*Louis Agassiz Fuertes*

*Carl Rungius, courtesy of New York Zoological Society*

**Nomad of the Arctic,** the polar bear may rove as far south as Labrador in his search for food.

## POLAR BEAR

*Thalarctos maritimus*

THE ARCTIC SUN dawns in mid-March, hovers over polar islands like a cyclopean eye, then blinks out in September. During this long day of summer, the polar bear, most carnivorous of bears, eats well. His menu includes lemmings, nesting birds, fish, young walrus, perhaps a stranded whale. But seal ranks as the main course.

He spots his fin-footed prey dozing on the ice and stalks it with the stealth of a hungry tiger. Chest and forelegs hug the snow; hind legs inch him closer. Only black dots—eyes, nose, lips—can betray the creeping white ghost. The seal suddenly lifts his head and looks around. The bear freezes. The seal nods again. Now! White fury explodes from the snow; a trip-hammer blow crushes the seal's skull. The bear eats his fill and ambles off.

March heralds new life too. Mother bear breaks out of winter's ice-crusted den and leads three-month-old twins to coastal shallows. She introduces them to tasty mollusks, crabs, shrimps, seaweed. Eskimos call cubs *ah tik tok,* "those that go down to the sea." Man's scent rouses mother's protective instinct. Cubs clinging to her tail, she swims to an ice floe. "If perchance her offspring are tired," 18th century geographer Thomas Hutchins noted, "they ascend the back of the dam, where they ride secure either in water or ashore."

Young stay with mother the first winter. They do not den up, but wander in cold darkness broken only by flickering northern lights. When summer arrives the parent abandons her 200-pound babies and again accepts a mate.

Except for naps, the male knows no season for sleep. He prowls the long night searching for food. His radar nose, some authorities claim, can scent a whale carcass 20 miles away. He hears poorly, but has good vision and never suffers from snow blindness as does the grizzly. Nonskid soles enable him easily to outrun a man; he sprints 25 miles an hour.

Usually the bear steers clear of people. But when hungry he's a killer, and man is fair game. Naturalist Edward Nelson tells of a bear that approached two unarmed Eskimos tending seal nets near Point Hope, Alaska. The first man fell to the ice and held his breath. The bear sniffed him head to foot and "pressed his cold nose against the man's lips and nose." Then the bear spied the other hunter and lunged at him, "while the man he left sprang to his feet and ran for his life to the village." He brought help, only to find the beast devouring his partner.

Eskimos sometimes deliberately exposed themselves to the bear. Their dogs darted in and slashed his flanks, dancing away from swinging paws. The hunters closed in for the kill with short spears, and often gained ugly wounds for their courage. Custom decreed that whoever sighted the bear got the coat; the slayer received the flesh. Though a gun administers the coup de grâce today, a white pelt remains the badge of a mighty hunter.

*Shoulder height* 3–4½ ft. *Weight* 500–1,100 lbs. *Range:* arctic coasts and sea ice. *Characteristics:* dense white fur, small head, long neck, Roman nose.

**These tireless swimmers** sometimes venture far out to sea. Forelegs churn, hind legs trail.

MIRIAM MACMILLAN

CHAPTER 11

# The Raccoon
# and His Relatives

By MELVIN R. ELLIS

EXCEPT FOR BR'ER FOX, no scalawag with taking ways
has aroused as much favorable comment as the ring-
tailed raccoon. This bear-faced rascal, native only
to the Americas, gets away with just about everything. Even
in fable he usually comes out on top. Thus Br'er Coon advised the opossum to put its tail in the fire so it might be decorated with rings. The possum did as the coon said, and poof!
—now it goes through life with a naked tail.

To find out how the coon lives, go where the fields come
down to the forest, where the moon silvers the leaves of the
high trees, where the creek's white ribbon rolls through the
brown marsh. Here the cousin of the ringtail and coati shuffles
flat-footed like a bear.

Not that the forest is the only place to find raccoons. They
roam the beaches of both oceans, hide from the glare of the
desert sun in rock crevices, scamper along mangrove roots
in southern bayous. Practically every state has them. They
range in size from the little five-pound Florida subspecies to
breeds weighing thirty pounds. Texans claim the largest, but
Oregonians dispute this. Basically, what holds true of the
coon in Canada is true of one in Florida. A desert raccoon

160

**Amiable rogue in a black mask,** the tough,
curious raccoon is unawed by man or dog.

THOMAS J. ABERCROMBIE, NATIONAL GEOGRAPHIC STAFF

This **cornfield raider** dunks his meal, but would eat it wet or dry. Some scientists say the coon moistens his food because he has poor salivary glands. He usually forages at night.

**A raccoon swims** as readily as he climbs. He doesn't dive for fish like the otter or mink, but in shallows can catch crayfish, trout, and ducklings.

may eat a snake instead of a frog, but still ambles along like a contented dowager reared in Maine.

Study northern raccoons when cold winds whistle through bare branches, and February snow covers the ground. Then the female coons are waiting for males to come calling. Raccoons do not hibernate; during severe cold snaps they merely nap, tails curled over their sharp muzzles and black-button noses. Comes a warm spell and their paw marks show up in the sun-softened mud. The male, done with his courting, shows no further interest in the female or the kits soon to be born.

Since the roaring twenties when college boys sported coonskin coats, the raccoon population has spurted to a record high for this century. Even the Davy Crockett craze of 1955 didn't reduce the coons much; coonskin caps blossomed everywhere, but cheaper furs hogged the market. As raccoons continue to increase, some biologists claim that the animals must be harvested by man or suffer those ravages of overcrowding: hunger and disease. Whatever happens, I think Br'er Coon will take care of himself. Cut his den tree and he'll live in your

163

**Like a cat,** mother coon carries junior by the nape of the neck. She teaches him how to find food, avoid dogs. By late fall he's on his own.

**First come, first served.** Orphans of the wild line up for the breakfast bottle. Roaming the woods or exploring the house, *Procyon lotor* spends most waking hours in quest of food.

drain pipe. Guard the corn and he'll visit the house while you are away and pick the cherries from your pie.

Raccoons take civilization in stride. Caught young, they make reasonably affectionate pets; some have been housebroken, even have learned to tolerate a dog or a cat. But they thrive better outside in a hay-lined box with a covered wire runway. Coons seem to have a sense of humor, and young ones clown all the time. But you can't trust them completely; they may bite.

Suburban traffic noises don't seem to bother them. But let another coon start up their tree and the slightest scratching will make them investigate. Flashy objects fascinate raccoons. I once watched a pet trying for ten minutes to capture the gleam on an automobile bumper. Trappers sometimes hang tinfoil above traps to lure them.

Coons may be relatively easy to trap, but old ones know how to outsmart pursuing hounds. They scramble along the crests of windfalls and swim creeks to break the scent line; they "tap" trees with their forepaws, making the dogs think they climbed up. Raccoons usually avoid fights, but woe to the dog that meets a big male in the water. He will clamber on the dog's head, dig in his claws, and stick like a burr until the dog drowns.

I remember one October night's hunt on the Door Peninsula in Wisconsin. The hounds bayed far ahead of the hunters strung along a dim trail leading to a plateau—an enchanted place where tall, leafless hardwoods let the moonbeams through. City lights

**Anybody home?** Like a thief in the night, the raccoon deftly opens doors, turns on faucets, raids the sugar bowl. Full of mischief, young coons never tire of romping.

165

twinkled 16 miles across the water. I was delighting in the sights and sounds of the night when the dogs howled "treed." Flashlights found the coon high in a big maple. A boy shinnied up, but as he went to shake the limb, the coon leaped to the ground and fled.

The dogs raced across the white-frosted carpet of leaves. Soon they bayed again; the masked one was silhouetted in a small apple tree. A hunter grabbed for the coon, but the animal bit him. Someone else reached for a tail hold, and again teeth sank into human flesh. The man howled and spun away like a ballet dancer. Finally we got the coon into a gunny sack. The hounds quieted down, and the hunters sifted through the orchard toward the road.

Then a high, clear, excited note split the air — a hound had struck another trail.

**Frisky triplets join mother** on her rounds for food. Marsh rabbit

The nimble toes are long and narrow; otherwise a raccoon's track pattern resembles a bear's in miniature — reminding us that bears and coons have a common ancestry. Look for lotor's tracks along stream banks and beaches, which he patrols with flat-footed, shuffling gait.

3″

# RACCOON

## *Procyon lotor*

"WAHO-O-O-O," wails the raccoon, saluting the dying day. This evening cry fits his curious getup of black-brown tail rings, grizzled coat, and black mask. Perhaps nature decided the forests needed a highwayman—a furred Robin Hood. Coons rob nests, raid garbage pails, sleep in other animals' dens. Nosy? When police checked a lady's complaint of a masked windowpeeper, they found a raccoon.

The raccoon's talented hands rival the monkey's: he can twist doorknobs, even open refrigerators. He sits on a creek bank and deftly sorts crayfish and snails from stones. He eats anything, and loves honey. He often dunks food, but makes no distinction between muddy and clear water. *Lotor* means "a washer."

About nine weeks after the midwinter mating, three to six kits are born. Mother cuffs her young to instill discipline. She boosts them up a tree when coyotes, bobcats, or horned owls threaten. Cornered, she attacks ferociously. Coons have bested dogs twice their size. Said naturalist John Burroughs: "The Raccoon is clear grit."

*Length* 30–36 in. *Weight* 5–30 lbs. *Range:* S. Canada to South America, except N. Rockies and Great Basin. *Characteristics:* black mask, bushy tail.

167

watches with wary eye. Raccoons thrive in many environments, even where lampposts replace trees.

*Walter A. Weber, National Geographic staff artist*

# RINGTAIL or CACOMISTLE

## *Bassariscus astutus*

RAGGED SHADOWS of mesquite and chaparral melt into the night, and many creatures of the Southwest nod in their dens. But not the ringtail. He scampers from his hollow tree to find breakfast in the dark, savoring rodents, birds, insects, and fruits. In New Mexico, naturalist Olaus Murie found a cave where ringtails dined on bats.

Occasionally hunters glimpse the elusive animal sunbathing high in a tree. Half of what they see is bushy black and white tail. When alarmed, the ringtail arches his tail and barks a warning.

In spring the female bears three or four fuzzy white kits, each weighing about an ounce. Their eyes remain closed until they are nearly five weeks old. Horned owls and rattlesnakes prey on the young when they leave the nest.

The "miner's cat"—as prospectors call him—catches mice better than a cat. A forest-fire lookout left this word for his successor: "Treat the ringtail to scraps and he'll repay by destroying rats." Several years later he visited his old cabin and asked about his pet. A cardboard box held the answer—four dozing ringtails.

*Length* 25–32 in. *Weight* 2–2½ lbs. *Range:* southwestern U. S. and Mexico. *Characteristics:* foxlike face, ringed tail.

**Sharp-eyed ringtail** catches an unwary quail. He is sometimes called "civet cat" and "coon cat."
*Louis Agassiz Fuertes*

*Walter A. Weber, National Geographic staff artist*

**A band of young coatis** parades tall tails, handy balancing poles when venturing out on a limb.

# COATI

## Nasua narica

"THAT ANIMAL," the zoo visitor declares, "looks like a little bit of everything." He points to the rust-colored coati twitching its anteaterlike snout and holding aloft its barber-pole tail. Ernest Thompson Seton terms it "a mixture of Coon and Monkey, with not a little dash of Pig."

Coatis range the rocky areas and woodlands from southern Arizona and New Mexico to tropical America. Always hungry, this cousin of the raccoon grubs night and day for roots, fruit, insects, and lizards.

Females and offspring, dark-ringed tails held high, travel in troops of 10 to 20. Alarmed, they hiss, spit, lash their tails. Coatis shun trouble, but in a brawl their sharp teeth can punish larger animals.

In late spring, 11 weeks after mating, mother coati finds a rocky niche and bears her litter of four to six. The young have darker coats than grownups. The adult male, twice as large as his mate, shows little interest in home life. Latin Americans call him *gato solo* — lone cat. In 1948 the Canal Zone honored this low-slung Lothario, picturing him on a postage stamp.

The young coati makes a lovable pet. Sold in shops, he brings from $60 to $150. Though hard on china and drapes in his endless explorations, he washes after eating, is odorless and easily housebroken, and loves attention. Left by himself, he whimpers like a child. One owner hired a "coati sitter."

*Length* 30–50 in. (half is tail). *Weight* 10–25 lbs. *Range:* Mexican border to South America. *Characteristics:* long, slender tail; narrow, flexible snout.

# CHAPTER 12

# The Weasel Tribe

By ROBERT M. McCLUNG

FISH WERE JUMPING in the Canadian stream, and the angler was in luck. He glanced proudly at his catch lying on the bank, then snorted in surprise. A mink was brazenly eating one of his fish. Impressed by such boldness, the fisherman set a small steel trap. Slowly he raised the string of fish and drew it toward him. Ignoring the man, the mink followed the bait and was caught in the trap.

Audacity is the word for the deadly hunters of the weasel tribe. A ranger in California's Sequoia National Park reported that he had seen a wolverine bluff bears, even a mountain lion, away from fresh kills. And a three-inch-high weasel has actually attacked a man who blocked it from its prey!

The weasel, mink, marten, fisher, otter, skunk, badger, and wolverine are North American members of the widespread family *Mustelidae*. Many of them run down their prey with such skill and ferocity that they earned the superstitious reverence or dread of primitive peoples.

To Alaskan Eskimos, catching a weasel meant good luck. A father would often fasten the head and skin of a least weasel to his small son's belt, so that the youthful hunter might be filled with the "little chief's" fiery spirit. But the wolverine, biggest of the weasel family, was a different matter. They called him *Kee-wa-har-kess,* Evil One, because he plundered traplines with almost mystical cunning. Eskimos believed that his body housed the lost soul of a great hunter, whose only pleasure was to plague other hunters until they joined his company of the damned.

Naturalist Edward Nelson tells of an Indian who found a wolverine in one of his

171

**The lithe and lustrous mink** is aristocrat of the weasel tribe. A restless hunter in forest or stream, it is the easiest fur bearer to raise.

NEW YORK ZOOLOGICAL SOCIETY

lynx traps. The redskin suspected bad medicine: Who ever heard of a wolverine getting
caught in so simple a trap? Back he went to
consult with the village elders, who finally
decided he should take the beast from the
snare. But to avoid bad luck, he was told to
curse the white man all the time he was doing
it. Then the spirit of the wolverine would
think it was the fault of the whites that he
was trapped.

In North America the weasel family falls
into four main groups according to body structure: the typical slender mustelines like the
mink, marten, and short-tailed weasel; the
squat, bow-legged badger and wolverine; the
sinuous aquatic otters; and the confident
plume-tailed skunks. All eat flesh or fish. All
have insatiable appetites, yet often kill more
than they can eat. Sometimes they cache food
for future use.

With a macabre taste in interior decoration,
many weasels line their nests with bloody
fur, bones, and dried meat—trophies of the
hunt. Occasionally weasels play havoc in henhouses, slaughtering whole flocks, and thus
are denounced as vermin. Actually they help
farmers by destroying rodents and rabbits.

Eyes and ears alert, they track their quarry
by scent. Mad with the lust to kill, they close
in, heads swaying, beady eyes glittering, then
strike at a vital spot—the brain, the nape, the
jugular vein. Weasels are the most efficient
machines of destruction in the mammal world.

**Otters, clowns of the wild,** frolic in the water
like small dolphins playing follow-the-leader, then
pop to the surface to rub noses Eskimo style.

Streamlined shape, whiplike tail, short powerful
legs, and webbed feet make them champion swimmers among land mammals. Expert fishermen, they
sometimes team up, diving in a circle and driving
the fish toward one another's jaws. The puffy upper lip and cheeks hide strong muscles that clamp
down like a steel trap.

King James I of England kept a pack of tame
otters to catch fish for his table, even appointed
a "Keeper of the King's Otters" to tend them.

ROBERT J. SMITH, BLACK STAR, AND (ABOVE)
JOHN E. FLETCHER, NATIONAL GEOGRAPHIC PHOTOGRAPHER

All the weasel clan use potent musk glands if annoyed or attacked, but only skunks can spray their scent any distance. Powerful as it is, skunk odor is almost pleasant compared to the reek of an angry mink. Many also share a strange phenomenon—the growth of their embryos is delayed, for months in some species. The marten, for example, mates in July. But soon after fertilization, the egg stops developing. Not until the following February does the growth process of the embryo pick up where it left off, producing a litter of baby martens in April.

Scientists at a U. S. Fur Farm Experiment Station at Saratoga, New York, gave a mated female marten artificial light during the fall, simulating the lengthening days of spring. As a result, her young were born in December, four months before the usual time. Apparently spring's increased daylight stimulates embryonic development. Length of daylight also seems to affect the weasel's change from brown summer coat to white winter one. Studies show that as autumn days shorten, the little animal's pituitary gland stops making a certain hormone. Without it the weasel's hair lacks pigmentation, and a snowy coat grows in, called ermine.

In medieval times ermine was reserved for royalty. Now it adorns anyone who can afford it. Many of the world's luxury furs come from the weasel family. Marten is treasured the world over. And what woman doesn't hope for a mink coat? Wolverine fur is prized for trimming arctic garments because oils in the hair make it shed hoarfrost easily, even when the thermometer sinks out of sight. But the most valuable fur in the world is the dense, soft pelt of the sea otter.

Vitus Bering, explorer of Alaskan waters for Imperial Russia, began the sea otter trade in 1741 without realizing it. When his ship, the *St. Peter,* was wrecked on a lonely island at the southern edge of the sea that now bears his name, Bering's half-starved crew kept themselves alive through the winter by eating the flesh of the "sea apes" they found there. Bering died, but in the spring the survivors built

HUGO H. SCHRODER

NATIONAL AUDUBON SOCIETY AND (BELOW) JOHN E. FLETCHER, NATIONAL GEOGRAPHIC PHOTOGRAPHER

a ship from their wreckage and sailed to Kamchatka. With them they brought a fateful cargo—no fewer than 900 sea otter skins.

When the adventurous *promyshleniki,* fur hunters of Siberia, heard of the abundant sea otters, their pulses quickened. Reckoning the fortunes these pelts would bring in China, where mandarins fancied the lustrous fur for their gowns, they set

**Fierce wolverine** (top) is the largest and strongest of American weasels. The names man gives him— Indian devil, skunk-bear, glutton—reflect his formidable reputation.

**Friendly otter** (left) is "the only fur-bearing animal that makes a real pet," claims Emil Liers, famed Minnesota "otter man." Liers (right) has devoted a lifetime to raising and training more than 200 of what he calls the "smartest animal in the world."

175

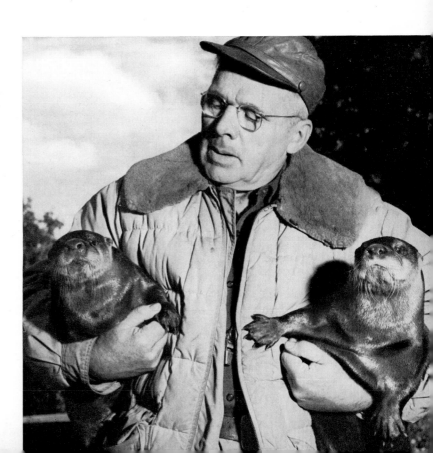

out in droves for America's northwest coast. For nearly 40 years they had a monopoly on the trade and killed sea otters by the hundreds of thousands.

Then in 1778 Captain James Cook, searching for the fabled Northwest Passage, dropped anchor in Nootka Sound on the west coast of Vancouver Island. Cook was an English explorer, not a fur hunter, but many of his sailors picked up sea otter pelts from the Indians in exchange for trinkets.

During the return voyage, Cook was killed in Hawaii. His two ships sailed on to China. When they put in at Macao for provisions, the crew discovered that their furs fetched fabulous prices. "The rage with which our seamen were possessed to return to Cook's River, and, by another cargo of skins, to make their fortunes, at one time, was not far short of mutiny," wrote Captain James King in the expedition's journal —"and I must own, I could not help indulging myself in a project . . . with the prospect of very considerable advantages."

The news spurred frantic trade. British and French vessels headed for the Northwest. Spaniards sailed up the coast from California. The Russians continued their ruthless slaughter. And that brash new nation, the United States, lost no time getting into the act.

A Boston skipper, Robert Gray, sailed his little 90-ton sloop *Lady Washington* into Nootka Sound in September, 1788, and quietly set about trading for sea otter skins. Many other American vessels soon followed in his wake. Thus the United States began a three-cornered trade that made the Stars and Stripes known around the world.

Rounding Cape Horn, the Yankee ships carried peddlers' wares to the Northwest, to be traded with the Indians for sea otter pelts. These were taken to Canton, China, and exchanged for silk, chinaware, and tea to delight the ladies of Boston and Salem— and enrich New England merchants. By 1805 the sea

"Isn't he a beauty!" Trappers

otter trade had started to decline. But the youthful nation had established itself as a trading power, and gained a foothold in the Oregon country.

The sea otter, which helped shape the course of history, has never been tamed. Yet its close cousin, the land otter, makes an affectionate pet. Playful, intelligent, and curious, land otters have been trained and pampered for centuries. In 1555 Olaus Magnus in Sweden reported "The cook in our inn has an otter that sleeps by the fire. When the cook gives him a sign, the otter runs to the fishpond, catches a fish, and brings it to him for cooking."

admire a mink taken from a deadfall. Today mink is in more demand than any other luxury fur.

*A Portfolio*

Following are biographies of the principal North American weasels, illustrated by National Geographic Staff Artist Walter A. Weber and Louis Agassiz Fuertes. Lengths (with tail) and weights show range between an average female and a large male. Skunks, also members of the weasel family, are quarantined in the next chapter.

WALTER A. WEBER

# MARTEN

## Martes americana

TWISTING, DODGING, scrambling desperately from branch to branch, the red squirrel tries to shake the sinuous enemy that matches its every turn. With a chitter of terror it leaps to a lower limb, but the hunter is close behind. It pounces! The victim's shriek is cut off by sudden death.

The marten crouches over her kill. Her underparts gleam pale orange, but lustrous brown fur covers the rest of her supple body. ". . . take a share of the cunning and sneaking character of the fox, as much of the wide-awake and cautious habits of the weasel, a similar proportion of the voracity (and a little of the fetid odour) of the mink, and add there-to some of the climbing propensities of the raccoon," and you have the marten, according to 19th century naturalists Audubon and Bachman.

After she has eaten her fill of the squirrel, she buries the rest for future use, then starts for her leaf-lined nest. Some martens live in hollow trees, a few in burrows.

She bears one to five babies in late March or early April, nearly nine months after mating. Their eyes stay shut six weeks. Soon she begins to teach her young the hunter's art. By fall, they are on their own.

Among the most solitary of animals, martens rub their groin glands on the ground during summer's mating season to leave a scent trail for mates. At other times they show fierce antagonism to one another.

A close relative of the Russian sable, the marten is prized for its fur. Good pelts bring $20 to $30 apiece. The inquisitive little predator is easy to trap. Some 65,000 are taken yearly in Canada, with about 6,500 caught in Alaska and the western states. In many places martens are in danger of extermination. A few, rigidly protected, still roam the Adirondacks.

*Length* 25 – 30 in. *Weight* 2 – 4 lbs. *Range:* forests of Canada, Alaska, Sierra Nevadas, Cascades, Rockies. *Characteristics:* weasel shape, agile tree climber.

179

**End of a treetop chase:** a marten (American sable) crouches over its red squirrel victim.

*Walter A. Weber, National Geographic staff artist*

WEASEL

MINK

OTTER

2"

**Members of the weasel tribe** have five toes on each foot, but the fifth toe does not always show. Front and hind prints are drawn above. Of all carnivores, weasels leave the smallest tracks. Bounding through snow, they often land hind feet in their front paw prints. Mink prints are larger editions of the weasel's. An otter trail often shows slide marks where the playful animal took a bellywhopper. Webs between its hind toes do not show in the tracks.

# FISHER

## *Martes pennanti*

THE FLEET MARTEN can overtake a red squirrel in his leafy backyard, but a fisher, though bigger and heavier, can make the marten run for his life. He moves like a dark streak through the treetops, and he's fast enough on the ground to dine on a hare occasionally. His legs are short, but he can cover 16 feet or more at one bound.

Powerful and courageous, this north woods predator can lick a coyote or bobcat in a fair fight, or kill a fox or deer for food. Man is his only formidable enemy, but the fisher often outwits him. Trappers complain that fishers follow their lines at night and make off with the bait or the catch.

The fisher appears to be the only animal that habitually dines on porcupine. Dodging the spiky armor, he flips porky over and bites into the unprotected throat or belly. The few barbed quills he may acquire in the scuffle generally work free in time. Wisconsin wildlife officials imported 13 fishers from New York State in 1957, hoping they will re-establish themselves after a 40-year absence and help reduce Wisconsin's porcupines.

Small game is the fisher's usual fare. Despite his name he rarely eats fish, except from traps. He is also known as black fox, black cat, pekan, Pennant's cat, and fisher marten. Chippewa Indians call him *tha-cho,* which means large marten. Like most of the weasel tribe, fishers are prized for their fur. Pelts of prime females bring the best prices—as much as $60 apiece.

In April three or four babies are born in a nest, often high in a hollow tree. Mother comes and goes like a squirrel, scuttling down the trunk head first. When the young are just a few days old she seeks a mate for next year's litter. The gestation period is more than 50 weeks, and she is receptive to a mate for only a day or two each year.

By winter the young are able to take care of themselves, and the family usually breaks up. Each animal establishes a hunting beat for himself, sometimes 10 or 20 miles in diameter. It takes the fisher a week or more to make the circuit.

*Length* 34–40 in. *Weight* 8–12 lbs. *Range:* N. New England, Adirondacks, Canada; Alaska panhandle to Yosemite. *Characteristics:* dark color, expert tree climber, looks like short-legged fox.

180

**Like black lightning,** an Adirondack fisher pounces on a snowshoe rabbit.

*Walter A. Weber, courtesy of National Park Service*

WALTER A. WEBER

# SHORT-TAILED WEASEL

## *Mustela erminea*

"SYMBOL OF SLAUGHTER, sleeplessness and tireless incredible activity," one noted naturalist has labeled the weasel. Ounce for ounce, tooth for tooth, it's about the bloodthirstiest of creatures. With reckless courage it fights animals many times its size, and often wins. The skull of one never-say-die weasel was found with teeth imbedded in the neck of an eagle.

More than thirty species of weasels pursue their prey in various parts of the world, but only three live in the United States. Largest is the common or long-tailed weasel *(M. frenata)*, up to two feet in length. Its southwestern form, with black and white facial markings, is called the bridled weasel. Smallest is *M. rixosa*, the least weasel, only seven to nine inches long. It is the world's tiniest carnivore.

Between these two in size, but the same in disposition and way of life, is the short-tailed weasel. About the size of a chipmunk, it lives in any ready-made cavity or den, often taking over a victim's burrow. Here as many as 13 young are born in spring, 10 months after the mating. Soon the youngsters follow their mother on the hunt, skirmishing on all sides like a pack of little hounds. They dart in and out of rodent holes, among rock crevices, through brush piles, pausing now and then to stand up and peer about. Squirrels, rabbits, birds, eggs, insects are eagerly devoured.

Expert ratters, weasels are the farmer's friends when checking rodents, but his enemies when loose in the henhouse.

The weasel's white winter coat, ermine, is the traditional badge of kings, nobles, and judges. The black tails symbolized the highest rank. More than 50,000 skins have gone into robes for a British coronation.

*Length* 7–14 in. *Weight* 2–5 oz. *Range:* arctic islands to northern and western states. *Characteristic:* black-tipped tail.

**Short-tailed weasel** in white winter fur is called ermine; farther south he stays brown all year.

*Walter A. Weber, National Geographic staff artist*

WALTER A WEBER

**The mink** is a solitary rover. Fiercely aggressive, it seeks its kind only during spring mating.

# MINK

## *Mustela vison*

A MINK COAT on a woman spells the height of luxury, but on the mink it identifies one of the most irascible creatures in the animal kingdom. Happily, the mink's disposition has no effect on the beauty of its fur, the most sought after in the world today.

From the Gulf of Mexico to the Arctic Circle, trappers tramp marshes and river-banks in quest of this lustrous and durable fur, which reaches its prime in November. About half a million wild mink are trapped each season, but they don't begin to fill the demand. America's 3,300 mink ranchers raise an additional 5,500,000 yearly.

Mink ranching was started back in 1866 by an enterprising New Yorker, who sold breeding animals at $30 a pair. The deepest browns brought the best prices until recently, when cross-breeding and mutations created pastel shades. "Silverblu," buff, pale lavender, even white mink now grace milady's coat, which takes 65 to 100 skins. Wisconsin leads the Nation in ranch pelts.

Active both day and night, the restless mink is equally at home in the forest or in the water. He trails prey by scent, captures small game and birds, raids henhouses, eats eggs. He varies this diet by devouring fish, frogs, crustaceans, and other aquatic life.

The mink's den may be a muskrat hole in a stream bank, a cavity under tree roots, a hollow log, a stump. Here in a nest of grass or leaves a litter of four to eight is born in the spring, some six weeks after mating.

Baby mink weigh about a fifth of an ounce apiece and have their eyes tightly closed for five weeks. The mother guards them well. She carries them by the scruff of the neck when they are too young to walk, at times hauls them pickaback in the water.

*Length* 20–28 in. *Weight* 1–3 lbs. *Range:* Florida to California, north to Alaska. *Characteristics:* weasel shape, uniform dark coat with white throat spot.

**Black mask, feet, and tail tip** mark the black-footed ferret, one of America's rarest mammals.

# BLACK-FOOTED FERRET
## *Mustela nigripes*

THE TRIM LITTLE FERRET stands like a totem pole on a prairie dog mound, then whisks below. Promptly a black-masked face glares out — a rare sight, for the species was unknown to science until 1851, when Audubon and Bachman described it from a skin obtained from a trapper.

Never numerous, ferrets now face extinction because of the drive to wipe out prairie dogs, their principal food. Recently the U. S. Fish and Wildlife Service has arranged to live-trap ferrets in dog towns slated for extermination and free them in national parks.

Mainly nocturnal, the bold, inquisitive, restless ferret fights viciously, hissing and spitting like a cat, when caught.

*Length* 20–24 in. *Weight* 1–1½ lbs. *Range:* plains, E. Rockies. *Characteristics:* buff-yellow coat, black markings.

184    MEAT EATERS

# WOLVERINE

*Gulo luscus*

"PICTURE A WEASEL," Ernest Thompson Seton said, "that scrap of demoniac fury, multiply that mite some fifty times, and you have the likeness of the wolverine."

Squat and heavy-bodied, with powerful teeth and claws, this giant weasel is notorious for its destructive ways. Bane of trappers, he follows trap lines, eats or destroys fur bearers that are caught, even hides the traps. Breaking into a cabin, he makes a shambles of its interior. Finding a hunter's food cache, he gorges himself, then sprays what is left with foul-smelling musk to mark it as his own. Anything—large or small, alive or dead—is fair game.

Not a speedy beast, the wolverine sometimes trails his victims relentlessly until they are exhausted. Or he climbs a tree and waits for prey to come to him. He often drives other animals from their kill. Incredibly strong, he can drag a carcass three times his size a mile or more.

Antisocial even with each other, adult wolverines live apart except during the brief spring mating period. The two or three woolly youngsters, born in May or June, stay with their mother until fall.

Once found in woods and mountains as far south as Pennsylvania, this brown-furred predator has long since disappeared from most states east of the Rockies. He has been extremely rare in Michigan, the Wolverine State, for at least a century. A few still range the Sierra Nevadas.

*Length* 36–44 in. *Weight* 20–50 lbs. *Range:* arctic islands, Canada, Alaska, western states. *Characteristics:* bearlike form, yellow bands on sides and rump.

**Wolverines wait in ambush** to pick off a calf or sick straggler from a caribou herd in Alaska.
*Walter A. Weber, National Geographic staff artist*

# BADGER

## *Taxidea taxus*

PIGEON-TOED, bowlegged, broad-shouldered, underslung—that's the badger. He wears a long grizzled coat of multicolored hair. Distinctive black and white markings decorate his head.

His favorite home is the plains country, where there are plenty of mice, pocket gophers, and other small mammals to eat. A hunter by night or day, he checks rodents, also kills poisonous snakes.

When his acute nose tells him a burrow is occupied, he tunnels down with two-inch front claws, showering dirt. If danger threatens, he can disappear into the earth and plug the hole behind him. Badger holes, hazards to men and livestock, make him an unwelcome neighbor. One pair burrowed under an airport runway and buckled the concrete.

The badger makes his cozy grass-lined nest in a chamber two to five feet underground, at the end of a tunnel up to 30 feet long. Here two to five blind and helpless babies are born in spring or early summer. Their eyes open at five weeks, and soon the young join mother on hunting trips.

Brought to bay, the slow-footed badger charges man or dog. It fights with such ferocity and desperation that nothing its size can overcome it.

*Length* 25−30 in. *Weight* 12−24 lbs. *Range:* dry open country, S Canada to Mexico. *Characteristics:* squat body, long digging claws, head markings.

An otter, sharp-toothed and web-footed,

*Louis Agassiz Fuertes*

**Strong-clawed badger,** excavating for food, is champion digger of the carnivores.

*Walter A. Weber, National Geographic staff artist*

vanquishes a water snake in the Everglades. Florida otters (*L. c. vaga*) are smaller than northern races.

# OTTER

## *Lutra canadensis*

A FAMILY of sleek otters climbs a steep snow slope above a stream; they tuck their forepaws close to their sides and bellyflop down the slide into the water. Then up the bank and gaily down again.

The playful otter is also a restless wanderer. He is more agile and graceful in water than on land, but sometimes travels far across country in search of fresh hunting grounds or a den beneath a riverbank. On level snow or ice he bounds, then slides as far as he can. Roving his range, he may cover 25 miles in a week.

The pups, one to five, arrive in early spring. For nearly three months mother guards them closely, driving even their father away. Later she takes them out to play, teaches them to swim and hunt. They eat almost anything they can find in the water — crayfish, clams, fish, frogs, insects.

Now the male joins his offspring and takes a hand in their upbringing. He romps with them, leads the way on family forays.

*Length* 38–55 in. *Weight* 10–30 lbs. *Range:* most of continent N. of Mexico. *Characteristics:* streamlined; webbed feet.

# SEA OTTER

*Enhydra lutris*

ONE DAY IN MARCH, 1938, strange animals were sighted bobbing in the ocean off Bixby Creek, south of Carmel, California. Wildlife experts, incredulous at first, identified the mysterious creatures as none other than sea otters—a whole herd of them! Here was a sight unknown in these waters for more than a hundred years.

Sea otters had flourished for countless centuries along the rock-bound coasts from southern California to the Aleutians and the Kuril Islands. Their downfall began in the 1740's, when Russian adventurers started to explore and exploit the northwestern reaches of North America.

No fur was ever more prized than the sea otter's—thick, lustrous, durable, soft as velvet. Slaughtered relentlessly for its pelt in the 18th and 19th centuries, the mammal had disappeared virtually every-

**In their element off stormy coasts,** sea otters swim with grace. Clumsy on land, they seldom venture

WALTER A. WEBER

where by 1911, when it was finally protected by international treaty. The sea otter was so rare that in the 1920's single skins sold for close to $2,500.

Conservationists sadly concluded that the species was doomed. But the drama at Bixby Creek was a hopeful sign. Maybe the sea otter would survive after all.

What kind of animal is this fabulous beast whose coat sparked Russia's dreams of empire in the New World, caused the subjugation and virtual annihilation of the

ashore. Here a female cuddles her nursing youngster.

Aleuts, and changed the course of history on North America's western rim?

*Amikuk,* as Eskimos call him, is long and heavy-bodied. He is flat-headed and has bulging dark eyes in a white-whiskered face. Equipped with webbed hind feet, he spends practically all his time at sea, living in herds or pods. His otter shape and forepaws distinguish him from a seal.

Active mainly by day, sea otters sleep in beds of kelp, wrapping strands of the seaweed about their bodies to anchor them. Forests of kelp also serve as hiding places from killer whales and sharks.

Off California, the otters feed mainly on abalone, but in arctic regions they relish sea urchins. They also hunt mussels and crabs, and snap up fish. The animal eats while floating on his back, often with a flat stone balanced on his chest. Using his paws like hands, he breaks up his food on this temporary lunch counter.

On their backs, sea otters scull with their tails. When they want to make time, they roll over on their stomachs and swim like a land otter, kicking with their feet and undulating their bodies. They can hit about 10 miles an hour, and often stay underwater four or five minutes.

In April or May the female otter gives birth to one pup, rarely twins. About 15 inches long and weighing three and a half pounds, the well-developed baby enters the world with teeth, fur, and wide-open eyes. The devoted mother cuddles the youngster as he nurses, plays with him, and tucks him under her arm and dives when danger threatens. She does not wean her pup for at least a year. Even then she continues to look after him. He reaches full growth when about four years old.

The sea otter has taken nearly 50 years to stage a comeback. Recent counts by the U. S. Fish and Wildlife Service show an estimated 30,000 sea otters in Alaskan waters, perhaps 1,000 off California.

*Length* 36–60 in. *Weight* 25–80 lbs. *Range:* coastal waters, California to Kuril Islands. *Characteristics:* smaller than seal, webbed feet, forepaws instead of flippers.

**Flat-footed** like a bear, the little skunk ambles along with short, deliberate steps.

⊢——3″——⊣

# CHAPTER 13

# Skunks, Experts in Chemical Warfare

By MELVIN R. ELLIS

WHEN THEODORE ROOSEVELT recommended that the United States speak softly but carry a big stick, he might well have been describing the attitude of skunks instead of outlining a foreign policy. If ever an animal served as an example of how to live in peace by being perpetually prepared for massive retaliation, it is the striped or common skunk.

Yet a truly ornery "polecat" probably never lived. And to shout "Skunk!" at contemptible people is to slander one of nature's least offensive creatures. Practically all animals — except man and sometimes foolish dogs — respect the skunk's desire to avoid trouble.

Despite its desire to go its way in peace, the skunk is not a true isolationist. It has only minor objections to sharing its burrow with a fleeing rabbit and will tolerate an itinerant woodchuck. It will stroll of a summer evening alongside the opossum, or it may bed down in the lower flat of a raccoon's apartment — or in just about any animal's burrow. But threaten it, force a fight, and the consequences are terrible. In a flash the skunk discharges, through twin nozzles just inside the anal tract, a spray of stinging, acrid, yellowish liquid. Almost from birth it is "loaded for bear." Each mature skunk's gas gun is capable of from four to six successive discharges, accurate up to 15 feet.

Chemists know the skunk's secretion as *n*-butyl mercaptan. Sulphur, an important component, helps give the fluid an evil odor. On damp nights weeks later the aroma hangs like an invisible mist to remind all who pass that here someone

190

"**Not one step closer!**" A skunk hoists his warning flag. If the signal is ignored, he will whirl and give it to the intruder with both barrels.

made the mistake of challenging *Mephitis mephitis*, the common skunk. The skunk's scientific name refers to its powerful weapon of defense. The Latin *mephitis* means "a noxious or pestilential exhalation from the ground."

STRIPED SKUNKS EVERYWHERE lead somewhat similar lives. About nine weeks after the male goes courting, four to six young arrive—nearly naked, blind, and helpless. Birth usually occurs during the latter part of April or the first two weeks in May. In rare instances a litter may number as high as ten. Though there is but a hint of fuzz on the newborn, less than on a peach, the white stripes are discernible as if tattooed into black skin.

The youngsters chirp constantly, like a nest full of ever-hungry baby sparrows. Within a week the fuzz clearly shows on their bodies, and a week later they have grown a silken coat of very short hair. At the age of three or four weeks they start exploratory trips to the spot of sunshine at the mouth of the burrow. The mother skunk seizes by the scruff of the neck any youngster that tries to leave the den prematurely and promptly hauls him back home.

The young soon require meat, and Mrs. Skunk is hard put to keep their stomachs filled. Snakes, grasshoppers, crayfish, beetles—an endless variety is presented to the little skunks. At six weeks they start making short forays with their mother and their education begins.

They make trips to the marsh for frogs and leave their naked paw prints where minnows have been trapped by receding waters. They learn how to smell out turtle eggs and to dig them up with their stubby, powerful front paws. They begin to recognize which stumps are rotten enough to house beetles and insect larvae. They discover how to lurk among the rushes where the blackbird has its nest. Perhaps that is the reason you heard a bird cry out one night last summer.

From kindergarten in late spring to college in the autumn, the mother skunk teaches the youngsters everything she knows. After the first snow falls, when beetles become scarce and frogs have hibernated, the family may raid a hen-house or even move in beneath the floor of the roost. But count every chicken or chicken egg as a bonus well deserved for the constant pressure the skunk keeps on rat, mouse, and insect populations.

As the temperature dips in northern states, the skunks make fewer forays. When winter closes in, they go below and sleep. But comes a southern breeze and its warmth edges down into the den below the frost line; then the skunks venture to tramp old trails and perhaps eat a snack before going back to sleep for another month.

My personal experience with skunks during these brief winter expeditions indicates that they are not as alert or indignant at being accosted then as they are during the warmer months.

My young Labrador retriever Ace scooped up a black skunk one January thaw and insisted on bringing it to me. Instead of spraying, the skunk fastened its teeth into Ace's upper lip. Nothing the dog had ever retrieved had bitten him, so he dropped the skunk and retreated—for which I was immeasurably grateful.

My Irish setter Patsy, wise in the ways of skunks, barged within two feet of one before either was aware of the other. She froze on point, and the skunk did likewise. Finally, as if by agreement, they inched

**By the scruff of the neck,** mother skunk retrieves a month-old baby that wandered from the den on a premature sight-seeing safari.

At nine weeks, the little stinkers (right), with glossy fur and bushy tails like their mother, are ready to face the world. At dusk they trail behind her in search of insects, rodents, and other food. The rising sun will find the brood back in their burrow, where they sleep by day.

193

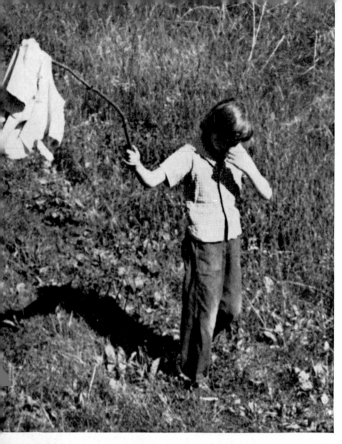

back cautiously until five feet separated them, then turned and went about their business.

But as a small boy I learned the hard way just how aggressive skunks can be in spring. Evening shadows were on the pasture when another boy and I vaulted a stone fence into the middle of a family of skunks.

Time stood still. A meadow lark on a near fence post stopped singing. The cows we had come to bring in lifted their heads as if in anticipation. It was a moment of decision — and we made the wrong one.

Instead of remaining motionless and allowing the skunks to amble off, we turned to flee. We might have come out all right if only we hadn't turned in upon each other, smacking our heads together. Down we went. The six skunks, a mother and five half-grown youngsters, swung their sterns about, and all 12 guns belched salvo after salvo of malodorous fluid over our inert forms.

Like cubs being dive-bombed by hornets, we went scrambling and bellowing, sobbing and retching, for the creek. Water helped some, but time was to be our only salvation.

Mortified, we crept home and were immediately banished to the barn. The horses stomped in their stalls as we passed. The bull rattled his chain and rolled his eyes. While the calves in the next stall stared wide-eyed, we were stripped and scrubbed with lye soap strong enough

**A chastened victim** of skunk chemical warfare attends the funeral of his shirt and pants. His sister (above) holds her nose as she brings the foul-smelling clothes for burial. The next step for the boy is a brisk scrubbing with strong soap.

194

to blister the shell off a turtle. Today we'd probably have gotten a tomato-juice rubdown or an ammonia rinse; both are considerably more effective, but still not completely purifying in cases of extreme saturation like this. After our clothes had been buried and we'd been dressed in ragged overalls, we sat downwind of the house and picked listlessly at plates of beans and pork chops. That evening we bedded down on the porch with burlap for covering.

This assault, which we considered unprovoked, turned us into vengeful hunters of the skunk. We located the den, consulted old-timers, and after the first cold snap sent the skunks into their burrow, we dug down to the master bedroom. Cautiously we covered the half-sleeping skunks with loose earth. As each poked its nose up through the loam, we shot it with a .22-caliber rifle. There were eight, and at $3 per skin, they made us $24 richer. Then there was the skunk fat, to be rendered as "cold medicine." Today we'd be hard put to get $5 for the eight skins. As for the cold remedy, we'd sooner tar and feather our chests.

If taken and tamed at an early age, skunks rarely get belligerent later. To be on the safe side, George Speidel, director of Milwaukee's zoo, usually keeps his resident skunks deodorized. He still remembers the day one broke faith during its first appearance on television, leveled off, and let go. The deodorizing operation is a simple one which any veterinarian can perform, preferably while the animal is very young. But if the skunk is allowed to wander off to become wild again, bereft of his spray guns, he is as helpless as a soldier sent unarmed into battle.

In his natural state Mephitis, resourceful as the white-tailed deer, unabashed as the porcupine, and prolific, has a better chance than many other animals for survival. That's just fine with me. Because every time I see a skunk or get a whiff of one, I'm reminded to mind my own business—a sure way to keep out of trouble.

**The victor shows** how it's done! Irritated skunk raises tail, triggers its atomizers, and sprays victim from head to foot with potent amber fluid. Salvos are fired by muscular contraction.

195

The skunk as pet? Trained early, he makes an engaging one. A simple operation by a veterinarian removes scent sacs. Some pet shops sell skunks—guaranteed safe.

The young skunk is inexpensive to feed, housebreaks easily, keeps himself clean, is an excellent mouser. Playful and affectionate, he can be taught to walk on a leash. One New Yorker takes his de-scented pet on the subway; he always gets a seat.

"Move along, chum, I got here first!" An egg strains a friendship between pets (left). The skunk outglared his raccoon rival and lapped up the prize by himself.

197

# STRIPED SKUNK

## *Mephitis mephitis*

ENFANT DU DIABLE—child of the devil—French-Canadian trappers used to call this four-legged fumigator. Today he's often dubbed "wood pussy" or "polecat," a name proper to several Old World weasels.

Making his presence known from Atlantic to Pacific, and from Hudson Bay to south of the Rio Grande, the striped or common skunk most often dwells in woodland mixed with fields—sometimes under the doorstep of civilization where insects,

his principal fare, abound. He is generally nocturnal and his typical pattern is black with a white nape and two broad white stripes down the back.

Not a tree climber, he ambles along without fear of having his dignity assailed. That's why so many get hit on the highways. Mephitis can't conceive of anything deliberately attacking him. But when starvation stalks the land, the coyote, cougar, and mink will risk his noxious barrage, just as animals sometimes dare the rattlesnake's fangs and the porcupine's quills. Great horned owls dine on skunks whenever they can and often get sprayed.

198

**Striped skunk signals** her ultimatum, and the badger decides discretion is the better part of valor.

"It is tonic and bracing," said naturalist John Burroughs of the skunk's odor. Explorer Samuel Hearne was less enthusiastic. "I cannot help observing that the foetid smell . . . has not been much exaggerated by any Author," he wrote.

Operators of one western mine use skunk oil as an alarm; they pour it into the air system. One whiff of that and the miners come up on the double. But skunk musk can be put to pleasing use too — refined into a fixative for making milady's perfume.

*Length* 24–30 in. *Weight* 4–10 lbs. *Range:* Canada to Mexico. *Characteristics:* stripes, plumed tail, gas defense.

**Hooded skunk** (right) flaunts larger plume.

*Walter A. Weber, National Geographic staff artist*

## HOODED SKUNK
### *Mephitis macroura*

DESERT COUSIN of the striped skunk, this night prowler brandishes a tail longer than his body and wears the ruff, usually white, that inspired his name.

Photographing Arizona wildlife one night, naturalist Lewis Walker played grudging host to two hooded skunks that met at the meat dispenser and took up battle stations. Facing opposite directions, they leaned against each other and went into a tight pinwheel. If one let up, the other bit savagely. Startled by wild pigs, the skunks brushed by Walker and resumed battle inside the blind.

Petrified, he waited for them to open fire. Agonizing minutes later the loser scampered out, the other in hot pursuit.

*Length* 24–32 in. *Weight* 4–10 lbs. *Range:* S. Arizona, New Mexico to Nicaragua. *Characteristics:* hood, long tail.

199

**A sporty zigzag of spots and stripes** decorates the glossy coat of *Spilogale*, smallest of skunks.

# SPOTTED SKUNK

### *Spilogale putorius* and its relatives

"WE WERE CAMPING OUT. I must have been asleep several hours when something tickled my nose, waking me. Opening my eyes, I stiffened. A small spotted skunk was sitting on my chest licking the salty perspiration from my face. I didn't even dare twitch my nose. After what seemed an eternity the skunk stepped daintily from my chest and walked away. I could breathe again!"

Many campers have had a similar experience, some without the happy ending. Besides a possible gas attack, at times there is more serious danger. Like other mammals, the spotted skunk is subject to rabies. Infected, it has bitten persons sleeping on the ground—hence its nickname "hydrophobia skunk" or "phoby cat."

You can tell a spotted skunk by its curious markings. No other North American mammal has this pattern of white on black, breaking into spots on the rump. And no two spotted skunks are the same. They tend to be larger and blacker in their northern range, smaller and lighter to the south. Those found on the western coast of Mexico from Rosario, Sinaloa, to the isthmus of Tehuantepec are considered a distinct species (*S. pygmaea*).

If threatened, the spotted skunk may do a handstand, throwing body and hind legs into the air and bristling its tail. But it usually sprays with all four feet on the ground. Most agile of skunks, it climbs trees like a squirrel if hounded.

The graceful little animal often dwells around farm buildings and does a service killing rats, mice, and insects injurious to crops. But one cunning rascal was seen removing downy chicks from under a brooding hen without her knowing it!

*Length* 12−22 in. *Weight* 1−3 lbs. *Range:* northern U.S. to Costa Rica. *Characteristics:* small size, unique coat.

**Hallmark of the hog-nosed skunk** is white top, black bottom. He digs for food with long claws.

# HOG-NOSED SKUNK

## *Conepatus mesoleucus*

LOOKING AS IF he had been put together out of spare parts of other animals, this most unskunklike of the tribe has a long, flexible muzzle similar to the snout of a hog. It uses this to root for insects, hence the nickname "rooter skunk."

Prey that retreats deeper underground brings out the badger in him. Strongly muscled shoulders and long, heavy front claws make this squat and sluggish creature an expert digger—hence another label "badger skunk."

He differs further from other skunks in his coat pattern; his tail is not as plumelike, and his hair is short and harsh. Coats and muffs made from the soft, glossy pelts of the common striped skunk once sold under such fancy aliases as Alaska sable or black marten; and more recently, many a Davy Crockett "coonskin" cap was dyed skunk. But not hog-nosed skunk; his coarse fur finds no market here, although Patagonian tribesmen at the bleak extremity of South America used to make cloaks of it.

South America actually is the center of origin of the hog-nosed skunk. Many species live there, but only one ranges as far north as the United States. Usually nocturnal, it is rarely seen. This hog-nosed skunk bears one to four young each year in the den it has dug or borrowed. It seems quite resistant to snake venom. A whiff of skunk scent triggers alarm in rattlesnakes—indicating that they fear skunks.

Mainly an insect eater, the hog-nosed skunk also relishes rodents, eggs, and prickly pears. Some have odd tastes. A Texas naturalist reported the strange death of a number of young goats. Their noses had been bitten off, and he caught a hog-nosed skunk in the act.

*Length* 25–33 in. *Weight* 5–10 lbs. *Range:* southwestern U.S. to Nicaragua. *Characteristics:* bare snout, long claws.

# CHAPTER 14

# The American Cats

## By VICTOR H. CAHALANE

A CALIFORNIA FOREST RANGER was sleeping in his tent one night when something touched his lips softly. Smiling in his sleep, he brushed it aside. He was dreaming of a girl back in town. He hadn't seen her for two months.

The caress was repeated—not like his girl's at all. It felt cold and a bit prickly. The ranger opened his eyes in pitch-darkness. Reaching for his flashlight, he flooded the tent with light. There, looking wistfully down on him, were two mountain lions!

No one will ever know who got out of the tent first, the lions or the ranger—but the ranger kept on going.

America's wild felines seldom act like those bold tent visitors. Perhaps the pumas were hungry; perhaps just curious. Ordinarily wary of man, the mountain lion, bobcat, and jaguar are seldom seen outside a zoo. Walking on toes with soft fleshy cushions,

202

**Fangs bared, a bobcat spits a challenge.**

N. PAUL KENWORTHY, JR.,
WALT DISNEY PRODUCTIONS

**Mountain lion springs,** a tawny streak of death. Prowling Washington's Olympic wilderness, it

these cats pad through the forests so quietly nobody can hear them coming. Their coats blend with the surroundings, and they usually prowl under cover of night.

Their whiskers are much more useful than man's: equipped with sensitive nerves at each root, they measure the width of tight places and tell when there is room to pass. As for weapons, the cat is armed with one of nature's most ingenious and murderous inventions, the retracting claw. He wears five on each front foot, four on each hind foot. He needs only to lift a paw and twitch a muscle and these glittering claws flick from their soft padding. When the cat goes into action with all 18 of his switchblades slashing and flaying, his prey is done for. After feasting on the kill, the feline licks his knives clean and folds them back into their fur-lined sheaths to save them the wear and tear of constant travel.

No wonder the cat is credited with nine lives, outfitted as he is with foot pads, warm camouflaging coat, antennalike whiskers, and automatic cutlasses. He can see in the dark too. We have all been startled by a cat's eyes moving in the night with apparently neither face nor body. During the day the pupils are scarcely more than slits. As light ebbs, the irises open until the pupils almost fill the eyes. A substance in the back of the eyes absorbs the faintest light, enabling the cat to track down quarry in almost total darkness. Unless teaching their young, cats hunt in the stalks with endless patience, then crouches, twitching, muscles like coiled steel, and leaps to kill.

daytime only when very hungry or bored. The larger cats knock small animals flat with a mighty paw and occasionally hamstring a big one. Sometimes they seize their victim by the throat and sink their teeth into its neck. Ordinarily they leap at its flank or shoulder, which throws the prey and even breaks its neck, then plunge eager fangs into the throat.

Some cats occasionally go mad with the lust for killing. A bloodthirsty puma has been known to kill as many as 30 sheep in one night. Ordinarily the puma's big game kill doesn't amount to more than two or three deer a month. After eating his fill, he frugally covers the carcass with brush and returns every day or so for a meal, unless he runs across something more tasty in the meantime.

EVERY CAT HAS SURPRISES in his bag of hunting tricks. The ocelot stretches out on a jungle branch and stays quiet. His tail hangs limp, and he doesn't move a muscle as chattering monkeys gather curiously. They call excitedly to their relatives to come and see the "body." They scream insulting epithets, but the ocelot stays dead. At last a monkey gathers enough courage to approach and tweak its hair. And that is the end of the monk!

The jaguar has an ingenious way of getting food, say Brazilian Indians. He catches fish by drooling over a limpid pool. Splash goes the saliva. Up leaps the fish. Down dips the jaguar. A tasty meal is caught with little effort.

Most cats dislike water and detest getting their feet wet. Few besides the jaguar and tiger enjoy a swim. Even so, they keep themselves fastidiously clean. They scrub themselves and their cubs for hours with tongues covered with sharp, hooklike projections which point toward the throat. These washboards facilitate eating as well. Any cat can strip a bone clean in a few minutes with its tongue.

Usually cats live alone and like it—except at mating season. As we all know from the tabbies on our back fence, the courting period of a cat's life is lusty and loud. The wild felines are even more vocal when they get to feeling that way. Two amorous lynxes shriek duets that would turn a house cat green with envy. Most dramatic of all is the puma's mating cry. It sounds like the scream of a woman being murdered. But to the lady pumas this nocturnal serenade must be pleasant indeed.

Most cats are born blind and helpless. All require a long period of education in contrast to their prey, who come into the world with their eyes open and begin running from their enemies almost immediately. The appealing, cuddlesome little kittens show no signs that they will grow up to be sinister night prowlers.

The mother cat does most of the work rearing the young. She brings food to the youngsters, boxes with them, smacks them hard when necessary, and takes them out on practice hunting trips.

Some wild kittens enter the world with coats quite different from their parents'. Baby mountain lions, for example, are spotted. The birth coat is soon shed, and the cubs don the plain coats of their elders. The distinctive pattern of the baby fur is apparently an evolutionary throwback to remote ancestors.

Fifty million years ago the predecessors of modern cats prowled the Eocene forests, but they left no trace until the Oligocene epoch, some twenty million years later. Spreading out from Asia, they stalked their prey all over the world, except in Australia and New Zealand, Madagascar, and the polar regions. During the Oligocene or a little before, the catlike carnivores separated into two main branches—the forerunners of the true cats, and the sabertooths (pages 47, 48).

**Arizona bobcat** in a prickly situation poses atop a saguaro. The bobcat is at home in both desert and forest.

N. PAUL KENWORTHY, JR., WALT DISNEY PRODUCTIONS

The mouth of the sabertooth was obstructed by monstrous upper canine teeth—curved eight-inch-long sabers with saw-toothed edges. Thus armed, these odd-faced, stubby-tailed beasts could slice and stab thick-hided mastodons, elephants, and giant ground sloths until they bled to death. But when these huge, slow-moving creatures began to die out during the Ice Age, the overspecialized saber-toothed cats disappeared too. Their long weapons, blocking their mouths for any other type of attack, had become obsolete. With no such encumbrances, the true cats survived and flourish today.

BESIDES OTHER CATS, the only wild animal which can really annoy any of the American *Felidae* is the slow-moving little porcupine. A lynx or a mountain lion may come home with his face and paws sore and festering, as full of quills as a cushion of pins.

A far deadlier enemy is man. Cats, especially the big ones, are too much of a threat to livestock—and humans—to be considered safe neighbors. So for thousands of years man has hunted them, improving his weapons and techniques as the centuries passed.

Cats seem to recognize this enmity. They usually fear man and avoid him whenever possible. Even in captivity they remain aloof and independent. Jaguars, among the most difficult of animals to train for acts, almost never abandon their efforts to kill their trainer. But sometimes a big cat forms a strange attachment.

One April morning Walt Weber, who painted the following color portraits of the American cats, was watching a bored and indifferent puma sunning itself at the zoo. Walt spoke to it persuasively, but the cat didn't blink an eyelash.

Suddenly the puma came to life. His ears twitched. He sniffed. His body quivered as he looked up the path. Weber looked too. There wasn't a soul in sight.

The cat became jubilant. He bounded excitedly around the cage and peered expectantly up the path again and again. At last a pretty girl came into view. As she approached the cage, the mountain lion pressed eagerly against the bars.

*"Mon ami, mon ami!"* exclaimed the girl affectionately. The mountain lion went into an ecstasy of contortions and gymnastics. The visitor put her hand into the cage, and the animal pressed his face against it

207

Canada bobcat, spellbound by jack light, sits for lakeside portrait by pioneer wildlife photographer George Shiras 3d.

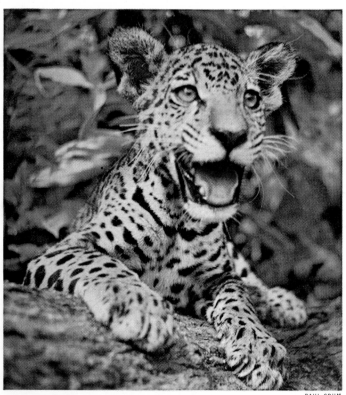

## Elegant coats, jaunty whiskers are standard style for cats

Cats are constant groomers. Some wear plain fur, others have developed camouflage to match their environment. Loud coats shrieking with design and color, as worn by **margay** (top left) and **jaguar** cub (left), dissolve into the lights and shadows of the tropical forest.

Both species usually live south of the border. Only U.S. record of a margay is from Eagle Pass, Texas, on the Rio Grande.

Dully mottled or plain coats like those of **Canada lynx** (above) and **mountain lion** (right) blend into open country. Desert bobcats and pumas are generally paler than those that live in forests. Sideburns, "lynx eyes" give Canada lynx a disdainful look. He and look-alike bobcat are the only New World cats with short tails.

JACK FIELDS

happily. For most people the result would have been a severe mauling, or worse.

"Did you raise and train him?" asked Weber.

"*Non! Non!* But he is a good friend. Always he is very glad to see me." She scratched the puma under the chin and around the ears. Rapturously he rolled over and purred in perfect contentment.

"*Mon Dieu!*" looking at her watch. "I go at once!" The cat tried to detain her, thrusting his paws through the bars. Not once were his claws unsheathed. She patted his head affectionately. "*Au revoir, mon ami!* Be good!"

The cat pressed his face against the bars, watching long after she had gone.

Mountain lions, however, are not recommended as house pets. Apparently one must be *sympathique* like this big cat and the girl with the French accent!

## A Portfolio

Following are biographies of the principal species of North American cats, illustrated in full color by National Geographic Staff Artist Walter A. Weber. Heights and weights show the range between an average female and a large male.

209

*Walter A. Weber, National Geographic staff artist*
**The lynx** bounds on snowshoe pads; slim-legged red fox flounders in drifts.

# CANADA LYNX

*Lynx canadensis*

STIFF BLACK TUFTS of hair rise from sharp-pointed ears like feathers in a war bonnet. Hard yellow eyes peer malevolently from gray cheeks between imposing side ruffs. This is the Canada lynx, who rarely leaves the deep north woods. One was shot in New York's Adirondack Mountains in 1951, the first in many years.

The lynx prowls stealthily at night. But like any cat, he meows if lonely. Making love, he yowls his affection with hair-raising volume. One to five kittens are born in spring, eyes open. In two hours they can stand, and soon after stagger about the den—a hollow log or rock cavity. Weaned at three months, they pad after mother on her hunting forays. Birth spots and bands give way to long gray fur, mixed with brown and black. After nearly a year, the young are on their own.

French Canadians call the lynx *loup-cervier* (wolf which attacks deer). Yet cautiously he keeps claws off any prey he cannot conquer. He'll sometimes jump a fawn, perhaps catch a fox. But the varying hare is his main dish. When it suffers periodic declines, so does the lynx.

*Shoulder height* 22–24 in. *Weight* 15–40 lbs. *Range:* northern half of the continent. *Characteristics:* ear tufts, short black-tipped tail.

# BOBCAT or WILDCAT
## *Lynx rufus*

"HE CAN LICK his weight in wildcats" was no mean compliment to a frontier scrapper. For a cornered wildcat—a hissing, spitting, snarling bundle of claws and fangs—fights like a demon. But left alone, he is wary of man. This cat is seldom tamed.

Looking like an oversized tomcat, he gets the name bobcat from his absurdly short tail, which twitches with excitement, hangs inert, or sticks impudently straight out. Because of the reddish tone of his coat, some tag him with a third name—bay lynx.

Unlike the nonconforming Canada lynx, the adaptable bobcat lives wherever there is enough forest or brushland to provide adequate cover and food. Dark-shaded races live in northern forests, while paler cats match the sun-baked sand and chaparral of the Southwest. Home is usually an underground den in a thicket, or in a hollow log. There in a nest of dry leaves, two to four blind, helpless kittens are born in spring. The father takes no part in rearing the family. Male bobcats are normally solitary.

The bobcat is an expert tree climber, but hunts mostly on the ground, stalking small prey at night. Especially in the Southwest, where he is common, he checks rabbits and destructive rodents. But since he also takes a toll of game birds, fawns, and lambs, he's not welcome near settled areas.

Many states put a price on his head as a harmful predator. In Michigan, however, he's a favorite game animal, protected except during hunting season.

*Shoulder height* 20–23 in. *Weight* 15–30 lbs. *Range:* S. Canada to Mexico. *Characteristics:* coat redder, more mottled than Canada lynx; short white-tipped tail.

**The bobcat,** a smaller, southern edition of the Canada lynx, agilely carries its prey, a spruce grouse.

**A devoted mother,** the mountain lion or puma guards her playful kittens. Unlike the leopard, these cubs

## MOUNTAIN LION

*Felis concolor*

LISTENING TO YARNS of old-timers, or reading chronicles of the frontier, you might think that America once teemed with many predators now extinct. Nineteen of these fierce beasts were actually the one we know today as the mountain lion or puma.

He has also been called cougar, panther, painter, catamount, brown tiger, red tiger, purple panther, silver lion, American lion, deer killer, Indian devil, mountain devil, mountain demon, mountain screamer, varmint, sneak cat, and king cat!

His blood-curdling scream in the evening gloom of the forest and his size (second only to the jaguar among American cats) no doubt contribute to his fearsome repu-

tation. And there are records of unprovoked attacks on humans — several on children. But the 175-pound, 7½-foot carnivore usually avoids man.

Lean and lithe, with short tawny coat, clear yellow eyes, and dignified mien, this American lion drags his long tail like the African lion. But he's not as big and lacks the heavy mane and coughing roar.

No other American mammal has so great a range. Distributed from Peace River, Canada, to the Strait of Magellan, the puma lives on cold mountaintops as well as in deserts and steaming jungles. Wherever he roams, the puma likes plenty of cover.

For her den the female selects a cavern or sheltered ledge. Here she bears one to five spotted cubs — usually in late winter or early spring, three months after mating.

Until they are several months old, the

BOBCAT

3"

LYNX

MOUNTAIN LION

**Mark of the feline hunter.** Cat tracks are broader and show larger heel pads than wild dog prints; claws are usually sheathed. Furry feet of the lynx spread more than the bobcat's. Mountain lion and jaguar tracks are almost identical. Forefoot prints are shown.

will soon change their spots for solid tan.

kittens feed only on their mother's milk. When they venture outside the den, she brings home bones and meat for them to chew. Soon the youngsters tag along on hunting forays, learn how to stalk and run down game. They sometimes stay with their mother for two years. Father puma lives and hunts alone, except during the brief mating period.

Deer are favored victims, but pumas prey on many other animals, including sheep, cattle, and horses. Because they kill his stock, man is the big cat's one deadly enemy. Over vast areas he has exterminated the tawny predator. In pioneer days mountain lions roamed the forests of eastern North America, but by 1900 they had vanished from practically all this region. A few, however, still hold out in the Florida Everglades. Lions today inhabit Missouri,

Arkansas, Louisiana, and New Brunswick; also there are persistent reports of the species in Maine and northern New York. And scattered news stories tell of big long-tailed cats glimpsed in the southern Appalachian wilderness. Perhaps the eastern puma's day is not yet done.

In the West, where bounty hunters take their toll, the puma has received help; since 1965 Colorado, Washington, Utah, Nevada, and Oregon have offered it protection as a game animal.

Stockmen are happy at the puma's decline, but not conservationists. When predators like this are eliminated, deer populations often expand beyond control. Then disease and starvation take heavy tolls.

*Shoulder height* 26−30 in. *Weight* 100−225 lbs. *Range:* Canada to Patagonia. *Characteristics:* large, tawny, long-tailed.

213

Walter A. Weber, National Geographic staff artist

**Crouching jaguar,** gorgeous but lethal, surveys a Mexican jungle stream with hungry eyes. Ignoring the egrets, he may want a crocodile. Unlike most cats, the jaguar is an avid swimmer.

# JAGUAR

*Felis onca*

A COW AND CALF were found slain and partially eaten on a ranch in Arizona. Trailing the culprit to a cave in the Chiricahua Mountains, rancher John Hand crept inside, clutching his rifle and knife. He heard ominous growls, saw two eyes glowing in the darkness. Backing out, he fired, killing a big jaguar. That was in 1912.

Such incidents now are rare, for the present haunt of *el tigre* is south of the border. A century ago it ranged from Texas to California as well. California's last recorded jaguar was killed at Palm Springs in 1860 when it attacked an Indian wearing antlers and deerskin as a decoy. Today only an occasional jaguar wanders north of the Rio Grande. One was killed in Texas in 1946, another in Arizona in 1949. Soon the Southwest's jaguar may have coughed his last series of powerful grunts.

Mightiest of American cats, the jaguar sometimes measures nearly eight feet from nose to tip of tail. He closely resembles the leopard of Asia and Africa, but has a heavier chest and legs, a larger head, and shorter tail. The cubs, usually two to four in a litter, are spotted at birth. There is no definite mating season.

At home in forests, on treeless pampas, in semidesert, and on cold mountains, the adaptable jaguar seemingly prefers to rove along jungle streams, where he can swim to cool off on hot nights and escape flies and gnats. Here he preys on deer, peccaries, tapirs, and smaller game; digs up leathery-shelled turtle eggs; or, says folklore, lures fish within range of his claws by twitching his tail above the water.

In cattle country he often dines on beef. Amazingly strong, he can easily break the neck of a full-grown horse, mule, or ox. In Brazil, Theodore Roosevelt was told of a jaguar that dragged a horse a mile from the scene of the kill. Little wonder that natives in the tropics fear el tigre; to ancient Mexicans the powerful beast was sacred. From frontier South America come dread tales of ravenous jaguars invading villages along the great rivers at floodtime. One hungry cat even swam out to an anchored boat and attacked the cattle aboard.

Brazilian cattle ranches used to lose as many as 6,000 head a year from jaguar raids. To combat this ferocious predator, ranchers hire professional hunters. Best known is the adventurous Sasha Siemel. Often armed only with spear or bow and arrow, he has killed more than 230, most in the Mato Grosso, where the biggest cats roam. Siemel makes it sound simple. Track a jaguar with dogs; when the cornered 250-pounder charges, impale it with a spear!

*Shoulder height* 27–30 in. *Weight* 125–250 lbs. *Range:* U.S.-Mexican border to Argentina. *Characteristics:* largest American cat, rosettes with black spots in center.

**A dashing figure** in his tight-fitting coat of yellow and black, the jaguar has fewer but larger rosettes than his more streamlined cousin, the Old World leopard. Seldom seen is the black jaguar; on its velvet coat the spots are only faintly outlined.

The tail, held high, beats a restless accompaniment to nervous movements of the sinewy body.

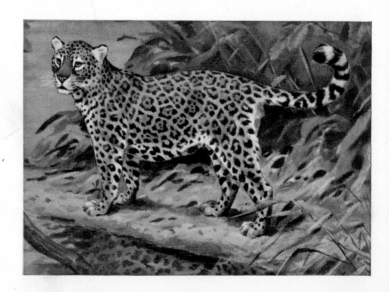

# OCELOT

*Felis pardalis*

OFTEN CALLED TIGER CAT or leopard cat, the ocelot has a smooth buff or grayish coat dizzily splashed with black spots, blotches, rings, bars, and stripes. No two have the same pattern. In fact, the cat's right side doesn't even match his left. His huge, reddish-brown eyes—all iris and no white—glow like living coals in his pointed little face.

Unlike most other wild felines, this debonair man-about-forest tames easily, often makes a good pet if taken as a cub. The handsome spotted animal, about twice a house cat's size, has become such a vogue that fanciers form clubs just to talk about ocelots. The Long Island Ocelot Club holds annual banquets and a good time is had by all, even the ocelots. The pampered pets sit down to feasts featuring hors d'oeuvres of chicken heads and beef hearts.

But affectionate as they may be, ocelots are too exotic to be taken in stride by the public. Taking French leave from a pet shop in Washington, D.C., one caused almost as much excitement as a man-eating tiger!

At home in the tropical forest, the ocelot dines on small mammals, birds, even snakes and other reptiles. Naturalist Edward Nelson tells of surprising one in Mexico eating a seven-foot boa. They hunt mainly at night. Good climbers, they steal up on monkeys asleep in the treetops.

The young, generally twins, may be born at any season, in a rocky den or hollow log.

The margay *(F. wiedii)*, a small, longer-tailed relative of the ocelot, is found over much the same range (page 208).

*Shoulder height* 16–18 in. *Weight* 25–35 lbs. *Range:* Texas, Arizona to Paraguay. *Characteristics:* small size, long tail, spots.

**A Texas ocelot,** like an overgrown tabby in fancy dress, tests an armadillo's scaly ball of armor.

Walter A. Weber, National Geographic staff artist

**Sleek jaguarundis**, red and gray, stalk a wary tree duck. "Otter cat" is their popular name.

# JAGUARUNDI

## *Felis yagouaroundi*

LEAST KNOWN of the American cats, the secretive jaguarundi reminds one of an otter. He has a small flattened head, short legs, and long tail. He's adept in the water, too, swimming rivers when necessary.

Like the black bear, red fox, and screech owl, the jaguarundi comes in two color phases—red and dark gray. Both occur in the same areas, even in the same litter. At one time the rusty red animal was thought to be a distinct species called the eyra. His back has a spattering of black-tipped hairs. Lips and throat are white.

The short fur of the gray jaguarundi seems sprinkled with pepper and salt. Many of the dark-tipped hairs are lighter next to the skin. When the jaguarundi bristles, the lighter parts come into view and he "pales with anger."

The jaguarundi occupies the same range and habitat as the ocelot, but is smaller and roams such dense undergrowth that he is less often seen. In southern Texas he lives in thorny thickets. King of his stunted forest with its network of tortuous byways, he dines on mice, wood rats, and rabbits. For dessert he goes into the mesquite and cat's-claw shrubs for birds. In Paraguay he is said to kill deer by biting the neck, but this is probably true only of fawns and small species.

Although most cats are active only by night, the jaguarundi frequently seeks water or hunts in daylight. Young have been seen both summer and winter, indicating that breeding may occur at any season.

One naturalist who had a jaguarundi kitten as a pet reports that it purred, was friendly and playful, and often chased its tail. Active at night, it chirped like a bird.

*Shoulder height* 10–12 in. *Weight* 10–20 lbs. *Range:* S. Texas and Arizona to Paraguay. *Characteristics:* small size, long tail, unspotted coat of red or dark gray.

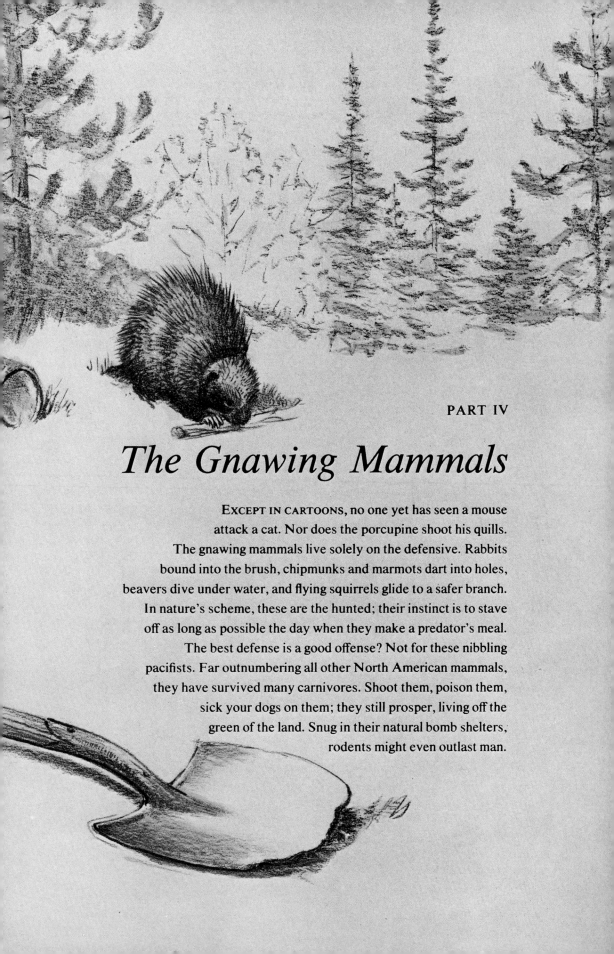

# The Gnawing Mammals

EXCEPT IN CARTOONS, no one yet has seen a mouse
attack a cat. Nor does the porcupine shoot his quills.
The gnawing mammals live solely on the defensive. Rabbits
bound into the brush, chipmunks and marmots dart into holes,
beavers dive under water, and flying squirrels glide to a safer branch.
In nature's scheme, these are the hunted; their instinct is to stave
off as long as possible the day when they make a predator's meal.
The best defense is a good offense? Not for these nibbling
pacifists. Far outnumbering all other North American mammals,
they have survived many carnivores. Shoot them, poison them,
sick your dogs on them; they still prosper, living off the
green of the land. Snug in their natural bomb shelters,
rodents might even outlast man.

CHAPTER 15

# Beaver, Master Dam Builder

By WILLIS PETERSON

CONSTRUCTION GANGS working on a dam raced against winter's deadline. Some felled trees. Others dug a canal to float logs to the site. Divers fitted timbers into a stream-bed foundation, filling the chinks with mud and stone. No signboard advertised that this dam was being built by small brown animals under the auspices of the Arizona Game and Fish Department. Yet tireless beavers were working for conservation as surely as if they had been on the payroll.

221

**Busy beavers** dammed the infant Rio Grande in Colorado to make this pond for their lodge.

LUIS MARDEN, NATIONAL GEOGRAPHIC STAFF

These particular beavers were transplanted to Arizona's rugged Mogollon Rim country by the State's wildlife commission. Operation Beaver Lift, executed in the field by veteran wildlife worker Howard Borneman, was spurred by demands of irate farmers in the valleys. For the beaver will dam an irrigation ditch as quickly as a stream, and is capable of chopping down half a dozen young fruit trees in a single night. Once he sets up housekeeping, only death can stop his building.

I had met "Barney" Borneman in the foothills of Arizona's White Mountains. He was trapping a "nuisance" beaver, using what appeared to be two hinged wire baskets. When sprung, the halves snap together, enclosing the animal without harm. As bait, Barney offered tempting aspen bark slivers. Tearing a hole in a nearby beaver dam, he placed the trap about eight inches deep in the water—"Put it any deeper and the beaver'll drown." When the amphibious rodent discovers the break, his hind foot usually springs the trap.

Beavers have prospered in the Mogollon Rim wilds. Where seeps trickled in springtime, beaver dams now store water. Where topsoil formerly washed away, lush meadows now grow. Where grass previously withered in midsummer heat, the water table has risen and keeps the soil wet. Where wildlife and livestock once watered at stagnant pools, they now drink from fresh streams.

To see how all this works, I joined Barney on a beaver lift high into the evergreen-clad White Mountains. Pack sacks, bedrolls, and five pairs of 35- to 40-pound adult beavers squirming in soaked gunny sacks were loaded aboard pack horses. The lift was not a long one, but steep terrain slowed our progress. Spread out beneath us like silver coins on a green rug glis-

**Wildlife workers** live-trap "nuisance" beavers in Arizona's irrigated valleys and pack them into uplands where beaver dams and ponds will check erosion. Freed captives (right) explore their new home.

WILLIS PETERSON

222

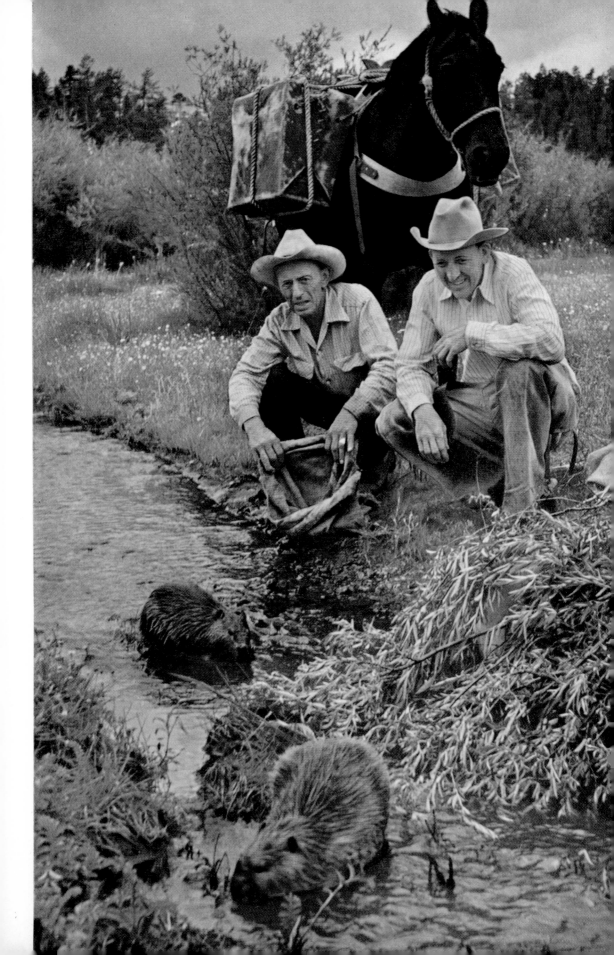

tened strings of beaver ponds. Aspens quivered white and green at water's edge. At intervals Barney halted the pack train to pour water over the sacks. "Beavers have a lot of fat under their heavy fur, and it's hard for them to stay cool," he explained. "Besides you've got to keep a beaver's hind feet wet. Otherwise the webbed tissue between the toes gets dry and chapped."

Nine miles into the mountains, we reached a stream that crept through a small flat. Deciduous groves promised many a meal for our bark-loving passengers. Barney's sigh of satisfaction told me that this was the end of the trail. Now he applied wildlife psychology. He piled brush alongside the stream, then released the beavers. Sure enough, they scrambled for the shelter. When we returned a week later, the new settlers had begun construction. The colony was off to a good start.

THE BEAVER SWARMED in streams almost everywhere in North America when white men first came. Woodsmen thought him a weather prophet extraordinary, and settlers credited him with fabulous cures. Castoreum, a secretion of the perineal glands, was a cure-all for every ailment from colic to sciatica. One writer endorsed the substance for deafness, pleurisy, and apoplexy, and said it would strengthen sight and stop hiccoughs. Another favorite remedy called for powdered beaver teeth in soup. Prescribed for epilepsy was a night's snooze on a beaver's furry pelt. This sleek fur coat almost caused the creature's undoing.

The demand for beaver fur, especially for export to Europe's hatmakers, sent trappers ranging across the continent. Beaver pelts became a widely recognized standard of exchange. In the 1780's, 12 skins bought a gun, and six furs paid for a red Hudson's Bay Company blanket. The fickleness of fashion alone saved the beaver. Around 1840, silk hats moved ahead in popularity, and the rodent

224

## Fur traders, seeking fortunes in beaver, pushed into an untamed continent

*. . . once 'twas Fame that led thee forth*
*To brave the Tropick Heat, the Frozen North,*
*Late it was Gold, then Beauty was the spur;*
*But now our Gallants venture but for fur.*

So wrote a 17th century English poet of the Hudson's Bay Company adventurers.

French voyageurs (right) snowshoed lonely miles across Canada's white wilderness; brawny American flatboatmen later fought their way past redskins on the Missouri (left). Through forest and swamp, trappers blazed trails that settlers would follow. They bartered with Indians (above) and built trading posts that would become great cities — Quebec, Detroit, St. Louis.

Beaver was the coin of the times, the basis for far-flung trading empires. The quest for it spanned three centuries, from Jacques Cartier to Kit Carson. It led trappers to the shores of the Pacific and helped open a continent to civilization.

FROM "HISTOIRE DE L'AMERIQUE SEPTENTRIONALE" BY
CLAUDE CHARLES LEROY BACQUEVILLE DE LA POTHERIE,
PARIS, 1722, CULVER SERVICE AND (ABOVE) "TRAPPEUR,"
LITHOGRAPH BY LEMERCIER, THE OLD PRINT SHOP

gained a new lease on life. Now he thrives, thanks to protective laws and beaver lifts.

Arizona game authorities did not originate the idea of "planting" beavers. A generation ago Federal conservation agencies transported them from one stream to another with beneficial results. Idaho gave the plan a new twist in 1948: it literally bombed the forest with beavers. Pilots, experienced in dropping fire-fighting "smoke jumpers," parachuted specially crated animals into the wilderness near streams. The boxes broke open when they hit, and the beavers, with nothing injured but their dignity, soon started to work.

Considering the animal's works, "busy as a beaver" ranks as an understatement. As woodcutter, hauler, architect, and mason, he has no four-footed peer. Building his house in the pond created by his dam, he gathers sticks and brush and forms them into a rough circular platform extending a few inches above water. Stones, boughs, and slender poles, chinked with mud, form walls and roof. Rising three or four feet high, the cone-shaped structure resembles a crude moated castle.

Passageways all lead downward. Thus the beaver must dive under water to enter his home, but this offers protection from wolverine, coyote, lynx, and bear. To ward off flash floods, the beaver often builds a diversion dam, causing angry water to fan out and lose its force. I have found three of these loosely knit barriers before coming upon the builder's home dam and lodge. Beavers living on larger and swifter watercourses burrow in the banks. Their tunnels begin under water, then turn upward to a hollowed-out nest above waterline.

In water the beaver is hard to beat. Nose valves shut automatically when he submerges, and oversized lungs permit him to stay under sometimes 10 or 15 minutes. Away from the safety of the pond, he fashions logging trails. Graded and smoothed, these direct routes provide for quick escape, and also make it easy to

226

**Nature's lumberjack,** graceful in water, clumsy on land, scouts for juicy aspen near shore. He usually works alone, but two may team up on a large pull logs to his wood yard. In the logging area the beaver becomes a gourmet, choosing only trees with the best bark. Bracing himself on hind legs and tail, he grasps the sapling with his forepaws and cuts a notch with his lower incisors. Lowering his head, he chisels again, then twists away bark and wood between the cuts. When the trunk creaks, he rushes to safety. Despite popular notions, he cannot control the direction of the tree's fall.

Because beavers do not hibernate, they must lay in winter food supplies. They wedge short tree limbs in the stream's muddy bottom, weighting them down with mud and stones. This fresh food locker can be reached even though the pond freezes over. If provisions run short, the beaver must break through the ice and flounder through snow to find a meal.

Though the beaver is primarily nocturnal, you can find him abroad in daytime. Once I saw two brown noses break the water, and a pair of young beavers clambered onto their brushy lodge. In mock battle they charged each other, whacking tails on the mud-covered sticks. They wrestled with handlike forepaws, tumbling over and over, then dived into the water to play tag.

When the young are two or three months old, the family usually junkets up and down its stream for several weeks. If the aspens are giving out at home, the beavers may start work on a new dam and lodge. When spring comes, the new dam will conserve the rains that precede the dry season. Trout may prosper in the new pond and waterfowl breed in new nesting sites. Muskrat, mink, and raccoon will flourish in an improved habitat. In summer the impounded water will quench the thirst of stock and give farmers a much needed supply for their irrigation ditches.

As Barney Borneman puts it, "The Arizona game department relocates many forms of wildlife, but beavers are the only ones that return work for our efforts."

227

tree. With wrenching bites he tapers the trunk until it snaps. He must wear down his ever-growing incisors by gnawing, else they prop his mouth open.

WALTER A. WEBER

# BEAVER
## *Castor canadensis*

"SUMMER IS HERE TO STAY!" the green marshland seems to shout. But the beaver knows better. He puts in long hours toting armloads of mud and sticks to repair his dam and lodge. To guard against lean winters, he fells trees, gnaws them into portable lengths, then floats this food supply down ingenious canals, or drags it over trails and anchors it in his pond.

His underwater food pile may grow to be 25 feet long, nine wide, and four deep. "The Indians observe the quantity which the beavers lay in their magazine at the approach of winter," recorded 18th century naturalist Thomas Pennant. "It is the Almanack of the Savages; who judge from the greater or less stock, of the mildness or severity of the approaching season."

Ice may seal the beaver's pond, but snug in his shelter of sticks and mud plaster, he sleeps and eats all winter. When hungry, he slips down the underwater entrance of his lodge and selects a tasty branch. If he chooses to dally in the pond, he breathes air bubbles trapped under the ice.

Even in cold water the beaver keeps warm. Oil secreted from two large glands under his tail waterproofs his coat, and long guard hairs that flatten when wet shield his fine underfur. The beaver grooms his coat with his hind feet's inner claws.

His fur in prime condition, the animal cuts a handsome figure as the January-February mating season nears. About three months later he and yearling beavers leave the den to the expectant mother. On a soft mattress of twigs and shredded bark she gives birth to three or four young.

Weighing up to a pound or more, a kit comes into the world cloaked in soft, brown fur and with his eyes open. He walks readily and soon learns to swim. At year's end he is half-grown; when two years old he mates and establishes a lodge of his own.

Largest of North American rodents, the beaver has short legs, webbed hind feet,

WILLIAM VANDIVERT

**Nibbling** a poplar twig like an ear of corn, a weaned baby beaver tastes succulent bark, his first adult food.

and a flat, scaly tail that's a rudder when he swims, a brace when he stands. He slaps it on the water to signal danger. By the time a predator reaches the pond, only ripples remain.

The beaver's enemies no longer threaten in many areas, for man has cleaned them out. He nearly exterminated the beaver too. In days when European markets clamored for the beaver's pelt, trappers literally made killings. Now conservation practices save his hide.

The beaver also served as food. A 17th century gourmet said boiled beaver tail was "exceeding good meat," and Meriwether Lewis in 1806 agreed: "the beaver was large and fat we have therefore fared sumptuously today." But a latter-day diner — Dr. Remington Kellogg, Director of the U. S. National Museum — found it "far from my idea of a tidbit."

*Length* 3–4 ft. *Weight* 30–70 lbs. *Range:* N. Mexico to Alaska. *Characteristics:* stocky; chestnut fur; flat, naked tail.

229

**Vegetarian beavers** prefer the soft bark of aspens, willows, and cottonwoods, but also eat aquatic plants. Peeled limbs go into dams. Paddlelike tail serves as rudder.

*Walter A. Weber, National Geographic staff artist*

**Nesting gray squirrel** cocks a curious eye at the outside world.

# Squirrels, Marmots, and Prairie Dogs

By ROBERT M. McCLUNG

HIGH IN A MAPLE TREE, the gray squirrel took aim on his target and launched into space, his tail spread like a sail. Destination: a well-filled bird feeder swinging from a metal clothesline far below. It was supposedly squirrel-proof, but bannertail couldn't be expected to know that. Startled birds scattered as the daredevil landed on the feeder roof. Then, hanging upside down like a trapeze artist, he began to stuff himself greedily, all the while chittering insults at the couple watching from a window.

"You've got to admit that squirrels are cute," laughed the housewife.

"Cute, nothing!" snorted her husband, who had put up the feeder only that morning. "They're just smart alecks!"

Bright-eyed and bushy-tailed, squirrels and their relatives are some people's favorite animals. To others, they're merely nuisances. Abundant, sprightly, active by day, they are certainly our most familiar wild mammals. The *Sciuridae* live practically everywhere man does except Australia and Madagascar. Resourceful and adaptable, they even flourish where man finds it hard going; in arctic wastes and

231

**Thirteen-lined ground squirrel** wears jazzy camouflage that deceives prairie birds of prey. He's nicknamed "picket pin" for the way he sits erect.

LEONARD LEE RUE III AND (ABOVE) H. A. THORNHILL, BOTH NATIONAL AUDUBON SOCIETY

## Not mumps but greed gives ground squirrels a bulgy look

When a visitor to Glacier National Park, Montana, sounds chow call, **Columbian ground squirrels** come a-running to fill their cheek pouches. These panhandlers gorge all summer to put on fat for seven or eight months' dormancy.

Craving overcomes caution as the **chipmunk** (right) hops on a human perch to cram his cheeks with nuts. Mother **gray squirrel** (left) has no built-in shopping bags, yet is an expert shoplifter, especially at bird feeders.

F. RICHARD BAXTER, NATIONAL GEOGRAPHIC STAFF, AND (ABOVE) GEORGE W. LONG

232

in steamy jungles; in burning deserts at sea level and on slopes of lofty mountains.

*Sciurus* means "shadetail," and the true aristocrats of the clan are the tree squirrels with their long, elegant tails. The fluffy banner curves gracefully over a squirrel's back while it sits, curls about its body like a blanket while it sleeps, acts as a rudder when it leaps, as a parachute if it falls. Shadetail has a host of ground-dwelling relatives: the stolid marmots, biggest of the tribe; gregarious prairie dogs, yapping from their doorways; and appealing little chipmunks and ground squirrels, gathering nerve to accept a tidbit, then darting for their holes, overcome by their own daring.

The chipmunks and ground squirrels have internal cheek pouches where they carry seeds or nuts to store against winter. A chipmunk can pack 15 corn kernels in each pocket, or two hickory nuts, first carefully nipping off the sharp points. Other species, carrying morsels one at a time in their mouths, make trip after trip to hide prodigious amounts of food. As summer wanes, red squirrels even work night shifts in bright moonlight to lay in supplies.

Champion harvesters are probably the pine squirrels, the Douglas and the red. A naturalist at Grand Teton National Park once found 10 bushels of lodgepole pine cones stored in one shed by these busy little critters. Canadian foresters find it easier to plunder squirrel caches than to pick pine seed by hand for reforestation projects. Gray squirrels seldom store much in one place, but they bury nuts in innumerable holes. Some sprout to grow into trees.

While squirrels, marmots, and prairie dogs vary widely in looks, practically all move in the same quick, nervous way. They appear suddenly, and are gone in a flash. Early Scandinavians thought squirrels messengers of the gods, carrying news to animals in distant lands. One thing for sure—they all "talk" and "gossip" endlessly. Marmots whistle, ground squirrels trill and chirp, while the tree squirrels chatter and harangue, sometimes even sing. John Muir called the Douglas squirrel "the mockingbird of squirrels, pouring forth chatter and song like a perennial fountain; barking like a dog, screaming like a hawk, chirping like a blackbird or sparrow; while in bluff audacious noisiness he is a very jay.''

Despite their gay personalities, squirrels can be destructive pests. In 1749 gray squirrels ruined so many crops in Pennsylvania that the colony offered threepence bounty and paid out £8,000 for 640,000 squirrels. So many concentrated in certain areas that hordes would emigrate to new territories. In 1842 an estimated 450,000 were on the move in Wisconsin. "Onward they come," intoned the Reverend John Bachman, "devouring on their way everything that is suited to their taste, laying waste the corn and wheat-fields of the farmer." In recent years, smaller emigrations have been observed in New York and Connecticut.

But even the teeming gray squirrels pale into insignificance compared to the prairie dogs that inhabited the West. Ernest Thompson Seton calculated that at least *five billion* of these perky little beasts scampered over the plains a hundred years ago. At the turn of the century a single dog town in Texas covered 25,000 square miles and housed an estimated 400 million prairie dogs. These rodents consumed enough grass to feed one and a half million head of cattle. Stock farming couldn't compete, so prairie dogs were exterminated practically everywhere.

Many of the ground squirrels also live in colonies and are injurious to crops.

234    GNAWING MAMMALS

**Short on size, long on courage, a prairie dog will even snap at a coyote if cornered**

The house-proud prairie dog (left) constantly tends his mound, tamping it with his nose. Members of his own select circle are welcome, but outsiders he briskly ejects if he can. At Wind Cave National Park, South Dakota, bison roll on prairie dog hummocks and flatten them. Patiently the rodents rebuild—and, unable to kick out the buffalo, graze good-naturedly beside them.

Cross-section of a nursery deep underground (below) shows a well-upholstered chamber off the main tunnel. Babies are fully furred a month after birth. Eyes open at about five weeks, and the youngsters begin to explore their burrow. At six weeks they venture outside to forage and soon move to homes of their own, up to 10 miles off.

**The woodchuck** eats "to give him strength to dig holes," said a farmer, "then digs holes to give him an appetite." Excavating with front claws, he flings dirt out of the tunnel with his hind feet. Here he backs out rolling a stone that blocked his way. In winter he hibernates in an underground nest, as does the ground squirrel curled in a ball below. In this death-like sleep, respiration and heartbeat all but stop; body temperature may drop below 40°.

A few carry disease as well. But ounce for ounce, tree squirrels can be the most destructive of the lot. They often dig up bulbs and ruin plants and fruit. They seem to take special delight in gnawing through the lead sheathing of telephone and telegraph cables. And if they invade your attic — look out! "When permitted to have the freedom of the house," commented Dr. Bachman, the gray squirrel "excites the displeasure of the notable housewife by its habits of gnawing chairs, tables and books."

Yet many communities take pride in the squirrels that frisk about their lawns and parks. Olney, Illinois, is the "Home of the White Squirrel." The town boasts a colony of about 700 pampered white squirrels, all descended, says local legend, from a pair of albino grays released in 1902 after entertaining the patrons of a saloon. Devils Tower National Monument in Wyoming, Wind Cave National Park in South Dakota, and Mackenzie State Park near Lubbock, Texas, safeguard flourishing prairie dog towns. Each year, thousands come to feed the little animals and delight in their antics.

**When gray squirrel runs,** five-toed hind feet land ahead. Heel pads often show, tail marks never.

The tree squirrels live in hollow trees or construct bulky leaf nests. All other members of the family are expert burrowers. They dig their own homes, some with many corridors and rooms. In Liberty, Kentucky, a woodchuck drilled up through 20 inches of roadbed and blacktop to open a doorway right in the middle of Main Street. A tiny ground squirrel dug 38 feet of tunnel in less than 24 hours. Another made one of the world's greatest ore strikes. In 1859, Nevada prospectors panned dirt brought up by the rodent and found gold. Digging soon uncovered a rich vein of silver. The resulting bonanza — the Comstock Lode.

When not eating or digging, squirrels are generally sleeping. Among them are some of nature's most enthusiastic hibernators. The Columbian ground squirrel says good night as early as July or August and often doesn't reappear until the next March or April. The woodchuck slumbers almost as much. Chipmunks sleep lightly. Wake one up in the middle of winter and he'll totter around drowsily until, left to himself, he can drop off again.

What greater boon could such creatures have, asked one naturalist, than this "sleep of insensibility, free from all cravings of hunger and all danger of perishing with cold, till the warm sun of spring once more calls them into life and activity?"

*A Portfolio*   Following are biographies of principal North American squirrels, marmots, and prairie dogs, illustrated in full color by National Geographic Staff Artist Walter A. Weber and noted wildlife artist Louis Agassiz Fuertes. Lengths (with tail) and weights show range between an average female and a large male.

237

**Pudgy woodchuck**, best known of the marmots, is content in a pasture downing a pound of green food a day. Cornered by a farmer's dog, he will fight savagely.

# WOODCHUCK

## *Marmota monax*

FEBRUARY SECOND is the day when the ground hog rises from his hole to look at the weather. If he sees his shadow, down he goes for six more weeks of winter. If not, spring is on the way, says the legend. But don't count on it. Five days after a shadowless ground-hog day, Bismarck, North Dakota, shivered at 38° below zero.

Farmers forgive the woodchuck's faulty forecasting, but not his other sins. He plunders gardens and hayfields, digs holes that cattle may stumble in. At his burrow exits he heaps mounds of earth that can wreck farm machinery. In 1883 New Hampshire pronounced the woodchuck "destitute of any interesting qualities" and slapped a 10¢ bounty on him.

Despite his critics, the gritty rodent persists in open woodlands and meadows over much of North America. He sits like a sentinel, alert to all within sight and earshot. Sensing danger, he whistles a warning, chatters his teeth, then disappears under the sod—safe from coyotes, dogs, and bullets. True, the red fox digs him out and man corrupts his chambers with gas and poison. Still he flourishes, every spring siring four or five heirs.

Unlike many rodents, the woodchuck does not lay up stores for winter. Instead he gorges on greens all summer. Usually he feeds close by one of several entrances to his underground home. In branching tunnels that may total 40 feet, he makes his bed of grass.

Increasingly fat and lethargic, he finally turns in about September and rarely awakens by the time tradition decrees the ground hog has his day.

*Length* 18–26 in. *Weight* 4–10 lbs. *Range:* eastern U.S., Canada. *Characteristics:* heavy-set, grizzled, white on nose.

# YELLOW-BELLIED MARMOT

*Marmota flaviventris*

Color, not cowardice, gives the yellow-bellied marmot his name. But Westerners know him as "rockchuck." A creature of the mountains, he maintains a grass-lined apartment under a ledge or amid a jumble of slide-rock. There he can rest secure from coyote, wolf, fox, lynx, and eagle. The grizzly bear might dig him out, although naturalist Ernest Thompson Seton couldn't "imagine anything less than a big charge of dynamite" opening a rockchuck den.

**Typical yellow-bellied marmot** and melanistic brother compare coats in Wyoming's Teton Range.
*Walter A. Weber, National Geographic staff artist*

The yellow marmot can't whistle as loud as his hoary cousin. Just the same, fellow cliff dwellers get the message when they hear his short, sharp notes. "Take cover!" he chirps. "Enemy in sight!"

The chisel-toothed vegetarian minces leaves and stalks of many wild plants. Occasionally he invades a garden and gets a taste of buckshot as well. Plump and sluggish, he sleeps most of his life away. If the weather gets too warm, he takes a midsummer nap (estivation), and in early autumn he goes into deathlike hibernation.

He returns to the living in spring and almost immediately sets out to replenish his race. Babies, as many as eight in a litter, are born in May.

*Length* 19–28 in. *Weight* 4–12 lbs. *Range:* western states, S. British Columbia. *Characteristics:* coat yellowish brown or black; dark face, white band on nose.

# HOARY MARMOT
## *Marmota caligata*

STATIONED ON A ROCKY LOOKOUT, the hoary marmot scans his domain. Sharp eyes detect an enemy! He pipes a warning to his brothers, and they relay the shrill, staccato call. A mile or more away, mountain sheep grazing the high slopes and deer in the valley perk up their ears and sniff the wind. French-Canadian voyageurs rightly named the rodent *siffleur*—whistler.

Wolf, coyote, fox, and lynx all stalk the marmot; he often escapes them by darting into a hillside hide-out. A grizzly may dig him out. But the golden eagle probably kills the greatest number.

The marmot feeds abundantly on flowering plants, berries, roots, and grasses; so much that by midsummer his bulging belly

**Archenemy** of the hoary marmot, the golden eagle sinks its talons into a victim's flesh. Torment also comes on smaller wings. On warm, still days mosquitoes drive the rodent underground.

*Walter A. Weber, National Geographic staff artist*

**The vigilant hoary marmot** signals danger with high-pitched whistles; low notes mean all's well.

may rub the ground. After a big meal he likes to sprawl on a sunny ledge.

The first frost signals bedtime for the whistler. He curls up underground—and how he snoozes! In the Arctic he hibernates from September to May.

Leaving his den in spring, the marmot often has to tunnel through several feet of snow. Soon he finds a mate; in about six weeks two to five young are born. They remain with their mother throughout the summer and may winter in the home den.

The hoary marmot usually lives near timber line, though in Alaska he also homesteads at lower levels. From a distance he looks silvery. Actually his coat is gray-black "tipped with white," as 18th century naturalist Thomas Pennant noted, "so as to spread a hoariness over the whole."

*Length* 25–31 in. *Weight* 5–15 lbs. *Range:* Idaho to arctic Alaska. *Characteristics:* largest American marmot, grizzled coat, black feet, black streak from head to each shoulder.

**Black-tailed prairie dogs** keep lawns short for unobstructed view, fix front porches after a rain.

# BLACK-TAILED PRAIRIE DOG

## *Cynomys ludovicianus*

As DAWN BRIGHTENS the Great Plains, the prairie dog town awakens. Blunt noses thrust from burrows; portly little citizens greet the morning and one another.

Their doorways resemble craters of tiny volcanoes, for the blacktails dike them with mounds of earth one or two feet high to prevent flooding. Any danger signal sends each rodent scampering to his hillock. There he sits, joining in the high-pitched barking that explains his name. Should the alarm prove real, down he goes.

Before turning horizontal, the burrow drops like a mine shaft eight to 16 feet. But a handy niche near the entrance gives the prairie dog a listening post where he can wait for the coyote to lope away, the hawk to soar off, or the man to drive on. Rattlesnakes often slither into vacant homes and settle down to feast on their furry neighbors. Burrowing owls also nest in empty holes, and prairie dogs steal their eggs.

The rodent's dread foes are the badger, who digs him out, and the ferret, who pursues him underground. To foil them, he often pushes an escape tunnel close to the surface, a hatchway through which he can claw free. If rain swamps the burrow, he sits high and dry in this air lock.

At protected prairie dog towns such as that at Lubbock, Texas, people can watch the friendly little villagers and study their social system. Within every town, groups rule their own precincts. Members kiss and groom each other, share grazing rights, help dig homes. Trespassers are tossed out.

Each day brings crises, but there's always time to sun-bathe, to roll in the dust, to play and squabble, even to yap an alarm when there really isn't any danger in sight.

*Length* 14–17 in. *Weight* 1½–3 lbs. *Range:* plains, Canada to Mexico. *Characteristics:* black-tipped tail; mounded den.

# WHITE-TAILED PRAIRIE DOG
## *Cynomys leucurus*

SLIGHTLY SMALLER than his black-tailed cousin, this prairie dog is a mountaineer instead of a plainsman and not so gregarious. In his upland meadows the slope of the ground eliminates flood danger. So his doorway has no dike, though he may pile bushels of dirt beside it.

While the black-tailed species often stays active all year, white-tailed prairie dogs usually hibernate when winter comes. To both, spring brings a litter of about five naked, blind babies who stay in their grass-lined nursery for about six weeks.

Emerging at last, the youngsters tumble and play in the bright beauty of the outside world. Mother schools them too, and butts them into the hole when an alarm sounds.

Prairie dogs are tolerated outside their precinct while too young to know better; later they're sternly chased off. Soon they set up housekeeping in vacant holes, staking claims with much yipping. Standing up to declaim territorial rights, they jerk with the vehemence of their barks. Sometimes they knock themselves over!

Two similar white-tailed species, the Utah *(C. parvidens)* and the Gunnison *(C. gunnisoni),* are included below.

*Length* 12–15 in. *Weight* 1–3 lbs. *Range:* Wyoming to Arizona, New Mexico. *Characteristics:* white-tailed; upland habitat.

**White-tailed prairie dogs** nibble most of the day on weeds and grasses, nap during midday heat.
*Walter A. Weber, National Geographic staff artist*

# WHITE-TAILED ANTELOPE SQUIRREL
## Ammospermophilus leucurus

A PERKY WHITE TAIL curled over his back is the badge of this little ground squirrel. It flicks jauntily as he scuttles across a canyon or skirmishes among the brush. He has a prolonged twitter, also a shrill chirp when on lookout in a bush top.

Hibernating only in higher, cooler parts of his range, this desert fancier usually keeps active all year. When temperatures soar to 125°, he takes a siesta in his den, away from the blazing sun. Morning and late afternoon he's out foraging for seeds, fruits, and insects in season.

In April or May, anywhere from four to 14 young are born underground. Big families are needed for survival; bobcats, badgers, foxes, and hawks attack the rodent on sight, while snakes and weasels pursue him right into his burrow.

Two antelope squirrel relatives, the Yuma (*A. harrisi*) and the San Joaquin (*A. nelsoni*), also inhabit the Southwest.

*Length 9–12 in. Weight 3–5 oz. Range:* Idaho to New Mexico, Lower California. *Characteristics:* recurved tail, white stripes.


# THIRTEEN-LINED GROUND SQUIRREL
## Spermophilus tridecemlineatus

KNOWN AS THE "STRIPED GOPHER" to many Midwesterners, this distinctively marked ground squirrel is destructive to grain in some areas. But it also benefits the farmer by devouring grasshoppers, caterpillars, grubs, even mice.

Moving abroad with watchful hesitation, the little critter often stands bolt upright, motionless as a statue, until satisfied there is nothing to fear. He calls to his brothers with a chirping note or shrill whistle. At the slightest suspicious sound, he retreats to his burrow. This descends vertically for several inches, then winds horizontally, with side branches and storage rooms as well as the nesting chamber.

Striped ground squirrels hibernate throughout their range, entering the long sleep very fat. Males are first to reappear in the spring. Females follow several weeks later, and soon the breeding season is in full swing. Five to 13 blind, hairless young are born four weeks later. When six weeks old they're ready to strike out on their own.

*Length 8–11 in. Weight 5–9 oz. Range:* plains, Canada to Mexico. *Characteristics:* unique pattern, light and dark stripes.


# CALIFORNIA GROUND SQUIRREL
## Spermophilus beecheyi

SEEING THIS MOTTLED FELLOW for the first time, you'd be forgiven if you took him for a heavy-bodied tree squirrel. He has the same bushy, gracefully curving tail. But the "digger," as Californians call him, is a close cousin to the marmot. He dwells underground, mounts a stump or boulder to sun himself and keep watch, whistles if he spots a foe. At his signal the colony scurries. The meadow is suddenly deserted and the golden eagle sails off with empty talons.

Once this species overran grain fields and orchards, causing an annual loss of $20,000,000 to the state's farmers. It also carries tularemia and bubonic plague. Trapping and fumigation help control it.

The digger's tunnels may extend 140 feet, with as many as 20 entrances. Holes sometimes pierce irrigation ditches, which doesn't improve the squirrel's popularity. In the spring, four to 11 young are born in a deeply cupped nest.

*Length 15–20 in. Weight 1–1½ lbs. Range:* S. Washington to Lower California. *Characteristic:* mottled brown coat.

*Louis Agassiz Fuertes*

Richardson ground squirrel faces swift death in the tightening coils of a bull snake. Another of these rodent grain thieves (right) keeps the vigil of the hunted, ready to pop down his hole.

# RICHARDSON GROUND SQUIRREL

## *Spermophilus richardsonii*

COMPARED WITH the three preceding ground squirrels, the Richardson is a plain Jane. Its smoky-gray coat blends with its northern prairie home. In rolling fields of grain it digs its long tunnels well below the scratch of a prairie plough.

A patient mammalogist counted 240 grains of wheat and 1,000 wild buckwheat seeds in one squirrel's cheek pouches—a diet that often gets the Richardson in trouble with farmers. Standing erect to spot danger, it whistles if alarmed, then dives into its burrow with a flick of its tail.

Curiosity is sometimes its undoing. Boys will set a noose at the entrance and nab the squirrel when it peeks out.

About a month after spring's mating, the female goes to a softly lined nest and bears six to 11 young. Though adults start their prolonged siesta in the dry spell of July and early August, the youngsters stay up late, until September, eating and growing. Then they too go to sleep and not a nose appears above ground until the next spring.

Naturalists recognize 27 ground squirrel species in North America—all have habits much like the Richardson.

*Length* 10–14 in. *Weight* 11–18 oz. *Range:* central Canada and the Dakotas to Colorado and Nevada. *Characteristics:* dark crown, white-edged tail, gray coat.

# EASTERN CHIPMUNK ▶
## *Tamias striatus*

THE LATIN NAME means "striped steward," and it aptly describes this familiar little squirrel. For he is a compulsive provider: his many cupboards are never bare.

All summer long, except on the hottest days, the chipmunk is up early harvesting nuts, grain, and seeds, cramming them into his bulging cheek pouches. He can carry a heaping tablespoonful of seeds or four acorns in each cheek. Eventually these supplies will fill his pantries. Now, to save time, he buries them in a shallow hole, replacing the dead leaves on top. When he wants the trove his nose will find it.

If he is a youngster, fresh from the nest, he must excavate his own home. Scratching under a stone wall or the roots of a tree, he extends his corridor below the frost line, adding branches and storerooms, then digs up to pierce a tiny hidden opening. This becomes the entrance. He fills in the original shaft and scatters the left-over dirt.

Darting in and out of rock piles and brush,

*Walter A. Weber, National Geographic staff artist*

*Louis Agassiz Fuertes*

**Eastern chipmunk's** love of seeds evoked wrath of colonial farmers; they put a price on his head.

dashing home when danger threatens, the chipmunk is a fur ball of vigor. Varying his diet, he pounces on insects, climbs trees to sample spruce cones or raid a bird's nest. He swims if he must, bushy tail sticking up like a sail. He chatters and sings, likes company, even makes friends with humans.

With the nip of the first frosts he slows his pace, rising late and dawdling away the chilly daylight hours. Soon he is curled in his nest, heart barely beating. Sleeping on his food supply, he need only nibble at his mattress when he wakes. Warm weather, even in midwinter, brings him out to frisk across the snow.

Five babies on the average, tiny and pink, arrive in spring, 32 days after the mating. But not until summer, when they gain permanent teeth, do the young venture out.

*Length* 9–11 in. *Weight* 3–5 oz. *Range:* U.S. and Canada, E. of plains. *Characteristics:* 5 dark, 4 light stripes, chestnut rump.

*Walter A. Weber, National Geographic staff artist (also right)*

WALTER A. WEBER

Least chipmunk pounces on a Montana grasshopper; cousin **yellow pine chipmunk** watches.

# GOLDEN-MANTLED GROUND SQUIRREL

## *Spermophilus lateralis*

A CHESTNUT MANTLE and single broad white stripe on each side distinguish this handsome species from all others of his tribe. Some people call him "calico squirrel." Others know him as "golden chipmunk." But he is larger, stouter, and slower than the chipmunks and has a different facial pattern. His home is the foothill country and mountain slopes of the West.

A true ground squirrel, he nevertheless often climbs trees in search of seeds or fruit. Frequently he digs his burrows near camps. Here he becomes quite tame, boldly cadging handouts from amused vacationers or slyly filching their food.

Cheeks stuffed with booty, he scampers home and unloads in his storerooms.

Retiring to his den in the fall, the golden-mantled ground squirrel hibernates through the long cold months. Soon after he emerges in the spring he mates, and four to seven young are born in May or June.

*Length* 9–12½ in. *Weight* 6–10 oz. *Range:* Canadian Rockies to California. *Characteristics:* bright hood, white stripes.

# LEAST CHIPMUNK

## *Eutamias minimus*

WITH A SHRILL CHIPPER-R-R of fear, the least chipmunk streaks for its burrow, tail erect. It pauses at the entrance a moment, then whisks out of sight with a saucy flick

Golden-mantled ground squirrels look like oversized chipmunks with unstriped faces.

of its tail. Overhead soars a hungry hawk.

Smallest of chipmunks, this tiny rodent also varies most in color—from pale buff in some forms to dark gray in others. A distinctive denizen of the sagebrush flats, it also thrives in open woods and rocky areas to above 11,000 feet elevation.

The yellow pine chipmunk *(E. amoenus)*, its relative in the Northwest's forests, is slightly larger and wears brighter colors.

In all, there are 16 species of western chipmunks in the genus *Eutamias*. They range from Alaska to Mexico in a variety of habitats—peaks to valleys, cool moist forests to sizzling deserts. Markings and colors are so similar it's hard to tell them apart. In general, their habits correspond to the eastern chipmunk's, and as with all their kind, the world is filled with peril of sudden death. Not only birds of prey, but snakes, weasels, badgers, bobcats, foxes, and coyotes are ever hunting them.

*Length* 7–9 in. *Weight* 1–2½ oz. *Range:* Yukon Territory to Great Lakes, south to New Mexico. *Characteristics:* smallest chipmunk; five dark, four light stripes.

# FOX SQUIRREL
## *Sciurus niger*

HE'S A CLUMSY GIANT beside the lithe gray squirrel. Scrambling along a branch, he slips, twists through the air, and plops on all fours. Unhurt, he scampers back up.

The fox squirrel, largest North American species, is a late riser. Not until the sun stands high does he stir from his hollow log or leafy tree nest. During cold spells he may sleep several days at a stretch.

Out and about, he stays on the ground much of the time, particularly when nuts ripen and fall. He digs shallow pits by the hundred and plants his hoard, usually one nut to a hole. In lean winter months his sensitive nose leads him to the buried treasure. He also samples roots, fruits, corn, and insects, even taps maple trees.

Fox squirrels range in open hardwood groves and cypress swamps; color can be rusty yellow, grizzled, or black with white ears and nose. They mate in midwinter. Feathery tail curled over his back, the male

**In fox squirrel circles** fashions vary. Black fur is the vogue down South, rust in the Ohio Valley.
*Louis Agassiz Fuertes*

**Gray squirrel's fur** is typically black and tan tipped in white, but all-black coats are often seen.

perches on a woodland balcony and serenades his love with deep chucking notes. In early spring, two to four young arrive. Two-thirds of an ounce at birth, they crack nuts in ten weeks, may live six years if a fox, bobcat, or hunter doesn't kill them.

*Length* 19–28 in. *Weight* 1½–3 lbs. *Range:* eastern U.S. except New England. *Characteristics:* large size, slow-moving.

# EASTERN GRAY SQUIRREL

## *Sciurus carolinensis*

THE GRAY SQUIRREL takes to city life as if designed for New York's Central Park. When bread crumbs and peanuts are scattered, he's right on hand, competing angrily with pigeons, grabbing his share, and scuttling off with never a thank you.

It's hard to believe that this brash urbanite could be the same elusive creature that flicks ghostlike through a secluded wood.

But his natural home is the hardwood forest that once matted much of the East.

Pioneers collided with about a billion of these graceful garden and orchard raiders. Long-barreled "squirrel" rifles barked away; axes hacked down their homes. By the late 1800's bannertail was rare in many areas. Game laws saved him.

Walk through a hardwood stand today, and high in a tree bright eyes follow your every move. Search for the squirrel, and he slithers behind the trunk. Only when you leave will he resume clipping acorns or hickory nuts, chattering defiantly.

In early spring, a litter of about five helpless babies is born in a bulky leaf-and-twig nest high in a tree. At six weeks, the youngsters venture from the nest. In the South, a second litter usually follows.

The western gray squirrel *(S. griseus),* of Pacific Coast states, is slightly larger.

*Length* 16–21 in. *Weight* 1–1½ lbs. *Range:* eastern U.S., southeastern Canada. *Characteristic:* bushy, white-laced tail.

Walter A. Weber, National Geographic staff artist

**Egg-stealing Abert squirrel**, ear tufts flying, retires in haste before the magpies' stabbing beaks.

## TASSEL-EARED SQUIRRELS

*Sciurus aberti* and *S. kaibabensis*

THE GRAND CANYON cleaves a wilderness realm. Hundreds of thousands of years ago the Colorado River cut a mile-deep gorge that isolated the tassel-eared squirrels on one side from those on the other. Time and separation made them distinct forms.

Hemmed in by desert and chasm, the Kaibab squirrel inherited little more than elbowroom in his 40-by-50-mile island

forest on the canyon's north rim in Arizona. The Abert, found on the southern rim, ranges to Colorado and New Mexico, with isolated groups south of the border.

Garbed in gray with rich chestnut saddles, the squirrels differ mainly in tail and underside coloring. The Abert wears a white vest and gray-topped tail. The Kaibab has a black chest and snowy tail. Both flaunt long ear tufts in winter.

Though nature has made them strangers, both thrive on mountain slopes and high plateaus thick with yellow pine, fir, and aspen. Both eat the same foods: pine seeds, acorns, roots, mushrooms, and young birds. They store little if anything, often dieting in winter on bark from pine twigs.

Babies, usually three or four to a litter, arrive as early as April or as late as September. Sometimes the young dwell in their parents' bushel-sized tree nest of pine needles and twigs until full-grown.

Tassel-eared squirrels have a throaty churring call, but rival the red squirrel's chattering if excited. Protected in Grand Canyon National Park, they fear only hawks and four-legged hunters. Threatened, one may freeze an hour or more.

The stoutly built rodents leap with abandon. One Abert squirrel plunged 50 feet when a bullet slammed into his perch. Legs spread like a flying squirrel's, he landed flat on his belly, but came up running.

*Length* 19–21 in. *Weight* 1½–2 lbs. *Range:* Colorado to Mexico. *Characteristics:* plumelike tail, chunky build, ear tufts.

**Tassel-eared cousins** show the contrasts isolation has wrought. Trademark of the **Abert squirrel** (upper) is his white belly, gray tail; the **Kaibab squirrel** (lower) has a dark belly, white tail.

*Louis Agassiz Fuertes*

**The red squirrel** will tongue-lash a mighty bear, but a weasel or marten may paralyze him with fear.

## RED SQUIRREL

*Tamiasciurus hudsonicus*

"THE RED SQUIRREL is a veritable Puck-o'-the-Pines—an embodiment of merriment, birdlike activity and saucy roguery," rhapsodized Ernest Thompson Seton. If man or beast, even another squirrel trespasses on his half acre of forest, he stamps his feet, flicks his tail, chatters, barks, and sputters. A coyote triggered such a tirade and the squirrel "cussed the coyote as far as he could see him."

The rust-colored tree climber knows every branch in his domain. But when he ventures into unfamiliar woods, he's an easy mark for marten, weasel, mink, and hawk. Though an able swimmer, he's vulnerable in open water to attacks from gulls, occasionally lake trout and pike.

The squirrel will live in a hollow oak, squeeze his half-pound frame into a woodpecker hole, or build a cocoonlike tree nest of twigs and leaves. Sometimes he burrows under roots. Untidy, plagued with fleas and mites, he moves frequently.

In the fall he harvests bushels of spruce and pine cones, hoards acorns, and piles mushrooms on branches to cure. When snow falls he digs out buried stores. At spring's mating time he dines—too often, say critics—on birds' eggs and fledglings.

Six weeks after breeding, the female bears four or five young; she may have a second litter in September. The newborn weigh less than half an ounce. Soon they're climbing, even if not yet weaned.

Dubbed "chickaree" by New England colonists, known as "boomer" in the Appalachians, the red squirrel proves his right to such titles as he rolls out pleasant churring notes, or explodes with raucous scolding. Shakespeare's words suit him: "What a spendthrift is he of his tongue."

*Length* 11–14 in. *Weight* 5–11 oz. *Range:* Alaska, Canada to Appalachians, S. Rockies. *Characteristics:* red coat, white vest.

**The Douglas squirrel** lives amid towering evergreens and harvests cones from dawn till dusk.

# DOUGLAS SQUIRREL

## *Tamiasciurus douglasii*

"CHEE CHEE CHEE CHEE-E-E-E-E!" Trilling birdlike notes shatter the hush of the forest. High in a sugar pine the Douglas squirrel sits erect like a choirboy and warbles woodland music. His red cousin is not the only troubadour in the family.

The olive-brown sprite with an orange belly owes his name to David Douglas, the botanist who discovered the species near the mouth of the Columbia River about 1825. Some 60 years later another Scot, John Muir, acclaimed him "squirrel of squirrels" while studying his ways in the Sierra Nevadas.

At home among branches 200 feet high, the chickaree of the West visits the forest floor sparingly—to drink, to store cones he has scissored from lofty moorings, or to reach trees too distant for his Olympian leaps. "Give him wings," said Muir, "and

he would outfly any bird in the woods."

The Douglas hoards his cones in hollow logs, under leaves, and in springs where they stay fresh several years. Foresters sometimes sell these cone caches to nurseries; one man scattered grain beneath the trees as "conscience money." Husking the cones for seeds, the rodent often gums his facial fur with pitch; he rounds out his diet with nuts, fruits, and fungi. His turpentine-flavored flesh—appetizing to marten, fisher, fox, and coyote—doesn't tempt man.

A hollow stump, burrow, or tree-top home of twigs and moss houses three to seven young, born in spring or summer.

Rising with the sun to harvest cones, pausing on a limb to try a high note or scold an intruder, *douglasii* sets a madcap pace the year round. To John Muir he was "the wildest animal I ever saw—a fiery, sputtering little bolt of fire."

*Length* 12–14 in. *Weight* 5–11 oz. *Range:* British Columbia to California. *Characteristics:* rusty underparts, yellow-fringed tail.

255

# The

WHEN I WAS A BOY, I climbed a big beech tree, its dead top full of woodpecker holes. I pounded it with my fist. Instantly little gray faces with big eyes peered out of almost every hole. Then flying squirrels leaped out in all directions and glided to adjacent trees—like the shower effect of a lawn sprinkler. Looking back, I realize that this glimpse was far more than most people ever see of flying squirrels, though they are plentiful in the eastern United States.

# Flying Squirrel, Nature's Glider

## By ERNEST P. WALKER

Strictly nocturnal, these highly specialized little squirrels usually live in trees, but may nest in a bird box or an attic. Sometimes they come down a chimney and meet a sad fate at the hands of someone who does not realize what gentle, lovable creatures they are. Gray above, white underneath with delicate buff on the flanks, the flying squirrel's fur is soft and fine. Sitting with arms and legs enclosed in the loose skin and gliding membrane, he looks pudgy and as if his coat were much too

257

ERNEST P. WALKER AND (ABOVE) EDWIN L. WISHERD, NATIONAL GEOGRAPHIC STAFF

**Flaps down,** the flying squirrel comes in for a landing. Tail drops, he swings up to check speed, extends legs to absorb the shock. Alighting, he darts around to the other side of the trunk to elude any pursuer.

large. But when he extends his limbs, stretching the membrane in flight, he flattens almost into a square. He steers by raising or lowering his arms to warp his flattened form. The feather-shaped tail acts as a stabilizer and helps make the upward swing on landing.

I have known flying squirrels since boyhood, but never raised any until friends gave me a five-month-old pair. They sleep all day. Awakening in the evening, they sit and dreamily groom themselves, sometimes for half an hour. Then they dash about their cage, eager to be released. They seek human companionship, are as curious and free with strangers as the friendliest dog, and show affection in many ways. One will stand on my shoulder and gently bite the rim of my ear or put his nose into my ear and sniff rapidly. They enjoy having me stroke behind their ears and on cheeks and chin, and rub their backs.

Usually I can call them by rattling nuts in my hand, or by making a scratching sound like a squirrel gnawing. Sometimes they come when I say "nuts"—coincidence, maybe, but I believe they know the word. They are fond of pecans, about the hardest nuts my pets can open. They will work on one at intervals for several days and finally find a weak place in the shell, through which they cut.

They also like other nuts; acorns are doubtless their principal food in the wild. I offer them fruits and berries, vegetables and leaves, but they are indifferent. Their meat diet is mainly insects. They particularly like white grubs and select wormy acorns to get them. My pets cache food in many places—in the folds of a shower curtain, in my pockets, or in the angle of my elbow. Some of my human friends develop remark-

259

**Tiny teeth** chisel through nutshell to the flying squirrel's favorite food. Whiskers brush obstacles in the dark, signal danger.

able agility when the playful squirrels get inside their clothes. On bare skin the tiny needle-sharp claws tickle.

The squirrels' fondness for people made it easy to induce them to leap to me. I pat my chest as a signal, and they almost invariably land smack on the spot. They look before they leap, leaning far to one side, then to the other, finally rising high on their arms. Are they measuring the distance by triangulation?

When danger threatens, they usually leap to me or take refuge in the highest nook they can find. Crumpling of paper alarms them; perhaps it suggests an enemy rustling through dry leaves. When at ease the squirrels utter a low chuckling note; sharp chucks mean displeasure, and high-pitched barks signal danger. When annoyed they stamp their feet.

After our pair had lived with us about seven months, I suspected that Beautiful, the female, was going to have young. I became certain of it when she began to pluck the fur from around her eight nipples. Eleven days later she gave birth to two babies: naked, pink, blind, and weighing 88 grains (about one fifth of an ounce) each. She was an ideal mother and never left the little ones for more than a few moments. She wouldn't allow the father to come near his children until they were practically full-grown.

I photographed the babies every few days and made notes on their progress. A parent could hardly have felt prouder. Two women in a gift shop exchanged significant looks when I asked for cards announcing the birth of twins.

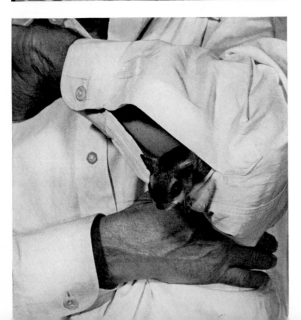

**Leaping** with gay abandon, the pet stuffs an acorn inside its master's collar, peeks out his sleeve. Daylight hurts its sensitive eyes, but it will tolerate dim blue light. "I am trying to become more nocturnal," quipped the author.

ERNEST P. WALKER

**Gliding membranes** folded, a flying squirrel sights his course. Air-borne, he flattens into a furry kite.

# SOUTHERN FLYING SQUIRREL

## *Glaucomys volans*

FIND A GLEN where acorns abound and a few dead trees stand; then sit on a log and wait. When twilight comes, if you're in luck, you'll hear scurrying feet on the branches and the squeaks of these pint-sized Tarzans playing aerial tag among the trees. "Wings" extended, whiskers aquiver, they soar through space, then land above you with soft thumps.

Cousin to the red and gray squirrels, "that Remarkable Creature the Flying Squirrel" fascinated early colonists. They reported it could "flie thirtie or fortie yards" and imagined it had "Skinny wings, almost like those of a Batt."

Smaller than the northern species, *G. sabrinus*, who haunts the tall timber in Canada and the western states, *volans* is a tasty tidbit for cats and owls, who snare him at night. During the day he curls up, hidden in a hollow tree. He does not hibernate, but stays in his hole during cold or wet weather. He usually has acorns laid aside for a rainy day and eats meat when he can get it, whether carrion, insects, or a fledgling bird. Sometimes he eats upside down, hanging by his toenails.

Flying squirrels mate in late winter, and 40 days later the female whelps two to six young. They develop slowly and may nurse two months or longer. If alarmed, the mother may grasp a baby with her teeth and glide to safety. Southern forms, usually browner, often bear a second litter in fall.

"A more gentle, docile, and graceful animal than the flying squirrel does not exist," said naturalist C. Hart Merriam. It does make a charming pet, but never grab one by the tail. One lady did, and the tail fur slipped off the bone like a glove!

*Length* 8–11 in. *Weight* 2–5 oz. *Range:* eastern U. S., Mexico. *Characteristics:* gliding membranes, flat furry tail, big eyes.

GNAWING MAMMALS 261

*Louis Agassiz Fuertes*

**Mountain beaver's** long whiskers help guide him through his dark tunnels.

CHAPTER 18

# Two Unique Rodents

NONE OF THE FLYING SQUIRREL'S HIGH JINKS for this down-to-earth pair. Mountain beaver and pocket gopher prefer a somber, solitary life in the long, dark tunnels created by their enormous industry. And master miners they are, with their long claws, heavy shoulders, and thickly muscled forelegs. Many species of pocket gophers make up the family *Geomyidae*, but the mountain beaver alone represents the family *Aplodontiidae*. Both of these animals are native only to North America.

**Pocket gopher** bulldozes dirt out his door, feels way back through burrow with naked tail.

# MOUNTAIN BEAVER

## *Aplodontia rufa*

CHINOOK INDIANS of the Pacific Northwest once wore robes of mountain beaver. Their name for the garment was sewellel, but fur traders misunderstood and applied it to the animal. Yet calling this chunky, hard-muscled little tunneler a sewellel is no worse than dubbing it mountain beaver, a misnomer if ever there was one. He's far more like a gopher than a beaver, and much prefers damp glens to lofty peaks — though he will excavate as high as 9,000 feet in the Cascades and Sierras.

About the size of a muskrat but lacking all but a vestige of tail, the aplodontia may dig his tunnel several hundred feet long. Painstakingly he keeps this four- to eight-inch corridor clear, pushing dirt and waste into short spurs off the main track. Where ground cover is thickest, the tunnel may come to the surface and become a path, roofed by tangled vegetation or the underside of a fallen tree. If rain floods his tunnel system, he swims through it.

Above ground in his verdant domain, the aplodontia moves with creeping gait, harvesting grasses, ferns, and small saplings, and stacking them neatly, butts all in a row, outside his home. After curing in the sun a day or more, this food and bedding is carried below. Should a predator appear, the mountain beaver breaks into a lumbering gallop toward his nearest entrance. In winter he burrows through snow, undeterred by cold.

Mating in March, the female a month later bears two or three babies in her clay-roofed bedroom. Weaned in two to three months, the young immediately set out to dig their own burrows.

*Length* 13–18 in. *Weight* 2–3 lbs. *Range:* British Columbia to California. *Characteristics:* brown fur, stub tail, long front claws.


# POCKET GOPHER

## *Geomys bursarius* and its relatives

ONE OF NATURE'S most efficient digging machines, this busy bundle of fur can tunnel two or three hundred feet in a night. The pocket gopher abounds over most of the continent, yet plays the hermit in his maze of corridors, seldom venturing out.

He scratches the soil with long claws, using sharp upper teeth like mattocks to shear away a clay bank. He shoves the dirt out side exits with hefty forelegs and blunt head. These mounds indicate the course of his two- to five-inch tunnels.

Spring breeding season brings him out on folded claws to shamble through the night seeking a mate. At other times gophers fight on meeting. Indians would put a leashed gopher down a burrow. When intruder and resident locked in combat, the hunters would extract them, kill the second gopher, and pop the bait down another hole.

If a snake or weasel pursues the little miner, he slams the door, plugging it with dirt. But a badger can dig him out.

When weaned, the half-grown young, one to seven in a litter, dig their own burrows. Cutting through roots and tubers, they pause to eat. On the surface they clip plants and grasses, eating some and storing the rest in cheek pouches. The pocket gopher gets his name from these reversible, fur-lined sacks outside his cheeks. Sitting up, he stuffs them with rapid motions of his paws, empties them by squeezing forward.

Gophers damage crops, irrigation ditches, and earth dams. But like giant earthworms, they churn and aerate the soil, making humus. There are many species and forms, some so similar only an expert can identify them. Data below includes all.

*Length* 6½–13 in. *Weight* 5–16 oz. *Range:* S. Canada to Panama, Pacific to southeastern states. *Characteristics:* external cheek pouches, large front claws.

CHAPTER 19

# Rats, Mice, and Lemmings

By GOODE P. DAVIS, JR.

LIKE WHITE GHOSTS haunting a silent world, snowy owls drift across the arctic tundra. Golden eyes sweep the ground. Suddenly one of the big birds of prey dives into a clump of moss. Pinned by cruel talons, a stubby, six-inch-long lemming wriggles futilely, then dies. He had gambled his life on a dash in the open—and lost.

On Florida's warm east coast, the sun sets behind wide beaches. Surf foams beneath brightening stars. Well above high-tide line, a twitching nose framed by long whiskers emerges from a hole under a fallen palmetto frond. The coast is clear, so the beach mouse darts to a patch of sea oats to forage for supper. Behind him he leaves a tracery of tiny tracks.

Moonlight silvers the leaves of live oaks in California's Coast Range. Fog rolls in from the Pacific and spills into brushy canyons. Moving with the mist, a wood rat scurries along a branch toward his favorite acorn tree. He spots a white object shining on the ground. Intrigued, he descends to investigate. This bleached bone would make a fine addition to his collection of trinkets. But didn't a shadow just move? The rat flees—and a gray fox trots off in search of better hunting.

The night is quiet beside a Maryland stream, though not far beyond the horizon great cities throb with life. On the bank a muskrat noses along one of his well-marked paths, sniffing for plants to eat. He freezes at the sound of voices. A canoe glides toward him. He leaps for the water, his loud splash startling the intruders.

Under the mantle of darkness covering the continent, the vast tribe of rats, mice,

265

"Wee, sleekit, cow'rin', tim'rous beastie, Oh, what a panic's in thy breastie!" penned Robert Burns. For a' that, the **house mouse** (left) dares to raid corncrib and pantry. The **deer mouse** (above)—there's a bonny lad!—usually eats out.

H. A. THORNHILL AND (ABOVE) STEPHEN COLLINS, BOTH NATIONAL AUDUBON SOCIETY and lemmings stirs to nervous activity. From arctic islands to the jungles of Panama, countless little dramas are being played out — and many a performer will perish this night. With dawn, survivors will start to sleep the day through in retreats, or beget offspring to fill the gaps made by a host of hungry enemies. Or, like field mice and lemmings, keep active round the clock, eating their weight every 24 hours.

Few regions are inhospitable to these small rodents. They flourish at Rocky Mountain timber lines and on hot Sonoran deserts; on Florida sands and in rain forests of the Pacific Northwest.

Most native rats and mice belong to the *Cricetidae,* the largest family of North American mammals, with more than 300 forms. And a varied group it is. Some, like deer mice, have large eyes and ears, and long, sparsely haired tails. Others, like the field mice or voles, have short tails, small eyes, and ears concealed in shaggy fur. The family includes the three-inch pygmy mouse — also the 24-inch muskrat.

The family *Heteromyidae* boasts the kangaroo rats and pocket mice, uniquely adapted to the arid West. They rarely drink. Digesting, they

**White-footed mouse** lives comfortably in any old shoe, but prefers a remodeled bird or squirrel nest in a tree. House mouse (right) climbs too, even walks a "high wire." Another tightrope artist is the ship's rat scampering up a hawser.

IRVING GALINSKY FROM "POSSUMS" BY CARL G. HARTMAN AND (LEFT) UNITED PRESS INTERNATIONAL

manufacture water from starch in the seeds they transport in cheek pouches. Retiring for the day, they plug their burrows, keeping them cool though outside temperatures soar. Push open a door, and the occupant, with little jets of dirt, promptly kicks it shut. Masters of camouflage, pocket mice usually blend with dun-colored desert. But one New Mexico mouse is as black as its lava bed home, while a neighbor, the white Apache mouse, matches the snowy waste of White Sands.

The small family *Zapodidae* includes the jumping mice. These beautiful but seldom seen rodents abound in certain meadows and damp woods of the northern United States and Canada.

The *Muridae* are represented in North America by three undesirable immigrants: the Norway rat, the black rat, and the house mouse. These enormously destructive spreaders of filth and disease have followed man wherever he has settled. They have even been accorded a firm, if grudging place in literature and folklore. Mice play the hero in many of Aesop's fables. Plautus, the Roman dramatist, enjoins us to "consider the little mouse, how sagacious an animal it is which never entrusts its life to one hole only." Pliny the Elder noted, "When a building is about to fall down, all the mice desert it." Rats inspired "The Pied Piper of Hamelin."

Vermin? Yes—but their domesticated brethren in research laboratories partially compensate for the family's misdeeds. And mice enjoy this distinction: they were the first earthlings to survive a rocket trip into space.

The elfin hordes of these four wide-ranging families will eat almost anything. Seeds, nuts, roots, tubers, greens. cactus pulp, fruit, bark, and pine needles figure

on their menu. In warm months they devour insects. They relish any meat they can get and don't even stop at cannibalism.

Many stock-pile plant foods to sustain them in times of scarcity. In 1804, Lewis and Clark took note of a large nutritious bean which Arikara Indians gathered from caches stored underground in autumn by field mice. Squaws sometimes replaced the beans with grains of corn to compensate the little harvesters.

Female rats and mice prepare for the birth of their young by lining a nest chamber with soft, dry plant material. Depending on the species, the nursery may be high in a tree, hidden in a tuft of grass, or underground in a burrow. The newborn are blind, naked, and helpless. If danger threatens, the female often flees with the youngsters firmly attached to her teats. Usually weaned in two weeks, the brood is on its own within a month. By then, mother may be nursing a new litter. In a world fraught with peril, small rodents seldom live more than a few months. High birth rates guarantee racial survival.

Some species of mice reach fantastic peaks about every four years. Abundant food and good weather lead to larger, more frequent litters until the tattered vegetation can no longer support the hordes. Such irruptions of small rodents cause millions of dollars' damage. Field mice riddle alfalfa crops and kill orchards by girdling trees.

3"

LEONARD LEE RUE III, THREE LIONS, AND (BELOW LEFT) A. AUBREY BODINE

**A lowly marsh dweller, the muskrat is prominent in fur-fashion circles**

America's No. 1 fur bearer, this amphibious rodent supplies more than five million pelts annually. Louisiana tops all states in number trapped, but the finest furs come from marshes farther north.

Chesapeake Bay trapper (left) takes a muskrat from steel jaws set outside its door. A prime skin may fetch to $2, and the meat, a delicacy to gourmets, 40¢. Marylanders trap about 200,000 "marsh rabbits" yearly.

Like the beaver, a diving muskrat (right) slaps the water with its tail to warn neighbors. It can stay down several minutes. Dense underfur keeps dry, holds body heat in coldest weather.

Muskrat tracks (upper right) include drag mark of tail between pairs of footprints.

269

Pocket mice destroy livestock range. White-footed mice devour vast quantities of seeds used in reforestation. In 1927, naturalists estimated that house mice in one section of Kern County, California, averaged 17 to the square yard—a horrendous 82,000 per acre!

At the peak of its cycle, the lemming of the Far North presents one of nature's most awesome dramas. Quite suddenly, as though each had heard a warning, they burst from their complex subterranean cities and swarm over the tundra in unbelievable millions, devouring every plant they come to. A Siberian village once had to radio for help as lemmings flooded inexorably toward it. Townsfolk were airlifted out.

Scandinavian migrations are even more spectacular. Pouring down from the mountains, the beady-eyed lemmings eat their way across rich coastal lands like a scourge of locusts. They lay waste every crop, pass right through haystacks, consuming every stalk. Reaching the sea, they plunge in as if it were a stream or lake. Vast "rafts" of lemmings have been seen swimming forlornly off the Norwegian coast. Behind them—desolation. Before them—death.

In the North American Arctic, such huge migrations are sporadic. But when they do occur, entire populations of lemmings advance like tidal waves, devastating all vegetation in their path.

As the lemmings boom, birds of prey, bears, wolves, foxes, and weasels increase with them. Caribou abandon their normal diet of lichens to munch lemmings crushed beneath their broad hoofs. Even trout grow fat on small victims trying to swim streams.

Eventually the burgeoning rodents "crash." Predation, disease, and sheer exhaustion all but wipe them out overnight. Starvation then stalks the predators. Snowy owls, rough-legged hawks, and northern shrikes head south. The little arctic fox follows the polar bear, hoping for a leftover scrap of seal. Fur bearers dwindle and traps go empty. Caribou vanish from stripped ranges, so Eskimos face disaster.

But always a few surviving lemmings rebuild their shattered numbers. And in several years the whole incredible business starts all over again.

"Vermin? Who, me?" protests a white-footed mouse from his woodland pulpit. He meant no harm, it's just that your camp larder was so tempting, and "the best-laid schemes o' mice an' men. . . ." As calling card, he leaves these tracks.

KARL MASLOWSKI, NATIONAL AUDUBON SOCIETY

1"

*A Portfolio* Following are biographies of representative North American rats, mice, and lemmings, illustrated in full color by noted wildlife artists Louis Agassiz Fuertes and Walter A. Weber. Lengths (tail sometimes more than half) and weights show range between average and large individuals of this wee tribe.

# HOUSE MOUSE
## *Mus musculus*

GNAWING SOUNDS in the wall and black pellets in the pantry are usual signs of this unwelcome boarder. A hole in the cereal package, a corner missing off a loaf of bread —*Mus musculus,* "the little thief," lives up to his name. Long ago the house mouse found out that the easiest way of making a living was to move in with man.

American mice descend from mice that left southwestern Persia centuries ago. Following caravans to Italy and Spain, they stowed away on ships bound for the New World. Later immigrants embarked from ports in northern Europe.

Moving indoors from the fields in fall, the little parasites invade any building where they can find food. They vary their wide-ranging diet with paste, glue, soap, and leather. They are excellent climbers, jumpers, and swimmers, active at any hour. Eyes are poor; keen ears warn of danger.

Who would think that mice can sing? Many have performed for their hosts, chirping and trilling like canaries.

Each mouse in a colony establishes squatter's rights to his territory. Any sheltered nook serves as nursery, which the female vigorously defends. For bedding she may steal stuffing from the sofa.

A graybeard by the time he's 18 months old, a mouse starts breeding at two months. In a warm climate a female may have eight litters a year, each with four to 11 blind, pink babies. No wonder house mice have populated the earth!

*Length* 6–8 in. *Weight* ½–1 oz. *Range:* wherever man has settled. *Characteristics:* gray or brown underparts, long scaly tail.

# NORWAY RAT
## *Rattus norvegicus*

A HORDE OF SAVAGE INVADERS swept into eastern Europe from Asia in 1727, crossing rivers and occupying towns. Soon after, they landed in Britain. Paris fell about 1750, despite the frantic resistance of her populace. By the outbreak of the American Revolution, the conquerors had reached the New World and were penetrating every

**Norway rat and house mouse,** the world's most destructive rodents, scavenge in a garbage dump.
*Louis Agassiz Fuertes*

corner of the globe. They crossed North America in covered wagons and trains, and spread from grimy cities to villages, farms, and salt marshes. By 1910, Norway rats outnumbered humans.

Consuming about 50 pounds of food a year, the freebooter includes on his menu vegetables, meats, grains, packaged goods, and eggs. He even samples paint, cloth, and books. Overcome with blood lust, he'll slaughter hundreds of chicks in a single raid. Gangs of rats overpower and kill young pigs and lambs. And that isn't all. They gnaw through lead pipes to get at water and strip insulation from wires, causing short circuits, fires, and once plunging much of New York City in darkness. Rats have cost Americans $200 million a year.

The rat's talents as saboteur are equaled by his menace as disease carrier. His lethal cargoes include typhus, rabies, and bubonic plague—Black Death. Carried by fleas of the black rat (*R. rattus*), this scourge slashed medieval Europe's population in half, changing history. Rat-spread diseases have killed more people than all man's wars.

Rats often live in colonies, infesting trash dumps, warehouses, tenements, stores, ships, and docks. At home in hollow walls and sewers, they also dig burrows in open fields. Males stake out territorial claims and fight off newcomers. They battle over food, also females, far scarcer than males. Some three weeks after mating, the female bears about eight young; litters of 20 have been reported. In mild climes breeding goes on all year. Old at three years, rats can reproduce at four months.

Cunning, tough, and aggressive, the Norway rat withstands ingenious poisons and traps. He will even attack man. Destroy 95 per cent of a rat population, and the prolific survivors quickly restore ranks.

*Length* 13–18 in. *Weight* ½–1½ lbs. *Range:* wherever man has settled. *Characteristics:* coarse brown fur, long scaly tail.

**Young Norway rat** exposes himself to bright-scaled death. A taste for rodents makes the corn snake a staunch friend of the farmer.
*Walter A. Weber, National Geographic staff artist*

Walter A. Weber, National Geographic staff artist

**Racing for safety, Alaskan vole** *(M. miurus)* is home by a nose, barely eluding his archenemy, the hawk owl. Predators make life a series of narrow squeaks for this northern field mouse.

# FIELD MOUSE or VOLE

## *Microtus pennsylvanicus*
and its relatives

A BUSY ANT, struggling through the dense grass-roots forest, comes abruptly to a smooth avenue roofed by arching grass. No sooner does he start across than a stocky mammal, bigger than a house mouse, bustles around a bend and bowls the ant over. This is the field mouse or vole, dynamo of energy and builder of inch-wide highways.

Eating his own weight every 24 hours, the field mouse chews out his network of paths, clipping grass, eating the seed heads, neatly piling the stems beside the road, tamping the surface with his busy feet. On the move day and night, this dense-haired mouse may die of exhaustion before his first birthday, if he hasn't already furnished a meal for a predator.

Snakes and shrews invade his burrow in warm months when he goes below to dodge the heat. Hawks, owls, crows, herons, and gulls attack from the air. Bullfrogs, trout, and turtles snap him up when he takes to water, and he is a good swimmer. Skunks, foxes, and bobcats sometimes feed on nothing else. One least weasel can wipe out the mice of an entire meadow. Even the grizzly and the giant Alaska brown bear dig him out as a tasty hors d'oeuvre.

Yet the genus *Microtus* thrives in meadows and marshes, on plains and cold peaks, reproducing at a staggering rate. A vole could bring forth 17 litters in a year.

Young mice are born in a globe-shaped grass nest inside a burrow or in a tuft of weeds. The five to nine young are weaned at two weeks and go their way at three. They are tough—one resumed breathing after half an hour underwater—and precocious. Fully grown by three months, they may already be parents several times.

Once on his own, the male digs his burrow and clears his paths. Side spurs lead to toilets and escape tunnels. Females seldom wander beyond 20 or 30 feet from their birthplace. They quickly settle down

*Louis Agassiz Fuertes*

**Field mouse,** ever vigilant, furtively surveys his highway through a tangled forest of grass.

to raising the babies that cease coming only in extreme cold.

Sitting up like squirrels, holding grass blades in their forepaws, field mice nibble furiously. In winter they forage under cover of snow. Some store berries, bulbs, roots, and seeds along tunnels up to 350 feet long. One larder yielded 24 pounds. Eskimo women in Alaska probe with sticks to find field mouse pantries packed with bulbous grass roots, delicious when boiled.

In farm land, field mice are as thick as 50 to the acre. And like many other mammals, their numbers may suddenly increase. Some 12,000 mice per acre once smothered Humboldt Valley, Nevada, laying waste 18,000 acres of alfalfa. Even normal numbers of mice destroy orchards by girdling trees for winter food.

*Length* 5½–7½ in. *Weight* 1–2½ oz. *Range:* Alaska to Labrador, south to New Mexico and Georgia. *Characteristics:* stocky; short tail, small ears, beady eyes.

# BROWN LEMMING
## *Lemmus trimucronatus*

DURING PEAKS, when breeding may continue all year, this stocky rodent bursts from his honeycomb of tunnels and runways and swarms over the tundra in incredible numbers (page 271). Other years females produce litters of three to 11 month after month, April to September. The nursery is a grass ball, lined with moss, fox molt, or feathers. Home is preferably a lowland where snow insulates the active colony. *Length* 5–6½ in. *Weight* 1½–4 oz. *Range:* Alaska, N. and W. Canada. *Characteristics:* long brown fur, stub tail.

# COLLARED LEMMING
## *Dicrostonyx groenlandicus*

IN WINTER, say the Eskimos, this lemming swirls to earth with snowflakes from a land beyond the stars. It's the only mouse in America that dons a white winter coat, and Eskimo children prize its fluffy fur as robes for their walrus ivory dolls.

In summer the collared lemming wears a handsome mixture of chestnut, browns, and grays. Weaned in two weeks, gray-clad youngsters with a black stripe down the spine join their elders foraging. At the end of the brief northern summer the energetic rodents stack grasses, sedges, willow catkins, and moss underground. In winter they sometimes dig up through the snow, aided by horny growths on front claws. These claw-pads are shed in spring. *Length* 5–6 in. *Weight* 1½–3½ oz. *Range:* Alaska, arctic Canada, Greenland. *Characteristic:* coat white in winter.

Louis Agassiz Fuertes

# RED TREE MOUSE

## Phenacomys longicaudus

HIGH IN THE MISTS that caress the tops of Pacific Coast forests dwell about half of the red tree mice. For the female has lofty tendencies. Her down-to-earth mate usually is content to rummage under the debris on the forest floor. In a romantic mood, he ventures a few feet up the trees, builds a temporary nest, and goes courting.

His mate constructs her own twig and needle apartment sometimes at the 100-foot level. Or she may remodel an abandoned squirrel nest. In these snug quarters, her one to three infants spend a month maturing. Some will never touch ground.

Needles and bark of young Douglas firs are their favorite food. Enemies include loggers who send their forest worlds crashing to the ground, and jays which tear open the nest to get at the mice.

*Length* 6¼–7 in. *Weight* 1–1½ oz. *Range:* N. California, Oregon. *Characteristics:* red coat, long black tail.

# RED-BACKED MOUSE

## Clethrionomys gapperi

FOREST COUNTERPART of the field mouse, this two-toned forager is seldom seen, though often abundant. Darting through the leaf mold on the floor of cool northern woods, or haunting spruce and sphagnum bogs, he is active both day and night.

His hearty appetite takes him into mole burrows, windfalls, and the lower branches of trees in search of seeds, nuts, berries, bark, lichens, fungi, and insects. He industriously stores food for winter.

He breeds almost any time of the year. About 18 days after the mating, three to eight young are born in a grass-lined nursery tucked in a stump or under a log or rock. Gray, occasionally black mice occur in the same litter with red-backed brothers.

Owls, weasels, and other predators take heavy toll of these little woodland mice.

*Length* 5–6 in. *Weight* 1–1½ oz. *Range:* N. Canada to New Mexico, N. Carolina. *Characteristics:* reddish back, light sides.

# PINE MOUSE

## Pitymys pinetorum

FOR THIS SECRETIVE, nearsighted fellow, life is good where the digging is easy. He patters through tunnels just under the leaves in open woods or clearings. If a mole subway is handy, he'll gladly use it.

Like the mole's, his velvety fur lies flat forward or back, so he can back up in a hole with ease. He surfaces only to dash from one burrow to another, or to make furtive forays for seeds and berries.

If a fierce shrew follows him below, *Pitymys* may fight it to a standstill. But a snake can slither through the earthen corridors to the spherical nest where baby mice are born. Preyed on far less than his field mouse cousin, the pine mouse can afford smaller families. Two to four young suffice.

These gregarious mice chitter when they meet. Alarmed, they pipe a thrushlike note. They relish roots and tubers and can ruin orchards and potato fields. They store food in larders with dirt doors kept shut.

*Length* 4–5¾ in. *Weight* 1–1½ oz. *Range:* Maine to Georgia, west to plains. *Characteristics:* small eyes, ears, stub tail.

# MEADOW JUMPING MOUSE

## Zapus hudsonius

AS THE MOWING MACHINE clatters through a stand of hay, a tiny brown shape rockets from its path with prodigious eight-foot leaps, long tail streaming. The mother mouse may drag her nursing young with her on her bounding flight. If she jars a baby loose, don't worry. She'll return for it.

Normally *Zapus* emerges only after dark to feed on seeds, insects, even daisies. To get at seed heads, he clips the stalks, leaving telltale patches of cut grass. Nicknamed "kangaroo mouse" because of his hops, he can also swim underwater, hind legs kicking. Daylight finds him asleep in a globular grass nest hidden in a tussock or in a shallow burrow.

June brings three to six young; a second brood often follows in September. In the fall young and old put on fat, then hibernate. Below frost line they curl in their nests, noses on bellies, hind feet behind ears, and wrap themselves in their tails.

*Length* 7¾–9 in. *Weight* ⅖–1 oz. *Range:* Alaska to Labrador, S. to Colorado, Alabama. *Characteristics:* long hind legs, tail.

# MUSKRAT

## Ondatra zibethica

WHERE CATTAILS rustle in the breeze that carries the song of the red-winged blackbird, the muskrat builds her dome-shaped house of rushes. Underwater entrances lead to a spacious chamber where she will bear up to 11 young a month after mating.

If spring floods threaten her offspring, the female picks them up with her teeth and carries them through the water to safety. In a month they will run a gantlet of enemies—snapping turtles, pike, mink, otters, foxes, great horned owls, and trappers seeking dense, glistening pelts. But the hardy rodent multiplies in the face of adversity, with several litters each season.

With webbed hind feet acting as built-in oars and a tail flattened to serve as rudder, this overgrown field mouse patrols swamps, lakes, rivers, and salt marshes from the Arctic Circle to the Rio Grande. Introduced abroad, it thrives in Europe and parts of Asia. Overcrowded, muskrats fight and emigrate. Sometimes they wander miles from water.

Active day and night, the muskrat, named for musk glands in the groin, dines on woody plants, pond weeds, cattails, water lilies, fish, and mussels. He may eat his own house, if it's built of tasty roots.

*Length* 16–24 in. *Weight* 1½–3½ lbs. *Range:* Alaska to Labrador, south to Mexico. *Characteristics:* brown fur, scaly tail.

Louis Agassiz Fuertes

**Adult whitefoot** in a fawn coat watches a gray-hued youngster come skittering around the trunk.

## WHITE-FOOTED MOUSE

*Peromyscus leucopus* and relatives

WHEN THE FLUTED VESPER SONG of the wood thrush heralds first starlight, forest sprites emerge from hollow log and stump, tree cavity, and old squirrel nest. Immaculate in white vests and fawn coats, black eyes shining, they explore the secrets of the sleeping woods.

Whitefoot inhabits eastern woodlands. Including the deer mouse *(P. maniculatus)* and other kin, his tribe covers the continent, holding the altitude record for North American mammals—16,000 feet on Mount Orizaba, Mexico. Some burrow; others play 50 feet high in trees. Fleshy footpads give them a grip.

At mating time, lady whitefoot stays properly at home while amorous males wander to seek her. Discovered, the female forsakes coyness and chases her suitor enthusiastically. Settling down, the pair defends their territory. Usually he leaves before she bears one to nine infants in a soft nest—perhaps last year's bird nest roofed over. The gray-coated young start their own families before ten weeks.

White-footed mice garner fruit, seeds, nuts, and insects. They often eat each other. Snakes, birds, carnivores prey on them.

*Length 6–8 in. Weight ½–1 oz. Range:* U.S. east of Rockies; Mexico. *Characteristics:* white belly; long, short-haired tail.

## PIÑON MOUSE

*Peromyscus truei*

THIS NIMBLE HIGHLANDER, with ears almost an inch high, most often dwells in cliff crevices and caves amid dry mesas. With other whitefeet of the canyon country, this alert Mickey Mouse delights in piñon nuts and juniper seeds. Loading his cheek pouches, he lays up stores for winter.

"I was in my sleeping bag near a dying fire," reported a New Mexico camper, "when one of the whitefeet boldly crossed my face. Finding a tidbit on the ground, the little freebooter chose my chest as dining table. His furtive meal over, he washed his face, then vanished."

*Length 7–9 in. Weight ⅓–1 oz. Range:* southwestern states and Mexico. *Characteristics:* big ears; long, well-haired tail.

# OLDFIELD or BEACH MOUSE
## *Peromyscus polionotus*

SMALLEST of the white-footed clan, this dainty little Southerner inhabits fields and shores from northern Alabama to Miami. In porous earth he digs a burrow — marked by a mound at its entrance — that slopes sharply for a foot or so, then levels off and leads to a round nest chamber. An escape route stops just beneath the surface; he can quickly pierce an exit if needed. A dirt plug keeps rain from flooding his basement apartment and disturbing his daytime sleep.

The beach mouse offers a striking example of a mammal's adaptation to its environment. In the cotton fields of Georgia and Alabama its coat is dark grayish brown, matching the soil. On the lighter soil of Florida the velvety fur is lighter. And along the beaches it's bleached even more. One race is almost pure white, matching the quartz sand of its island home off Florida.

Wherever sea oats grow, this chameleon

**Beach mouse** blends with his sandy habitat.

of the mice harvests his crops, digs his hole, and traces tiny tracks on the sand.

*Length* 5–6 in. *Weight* 1/3–1/2 oz. *Range:* southeastern states. *Characteristics:* tail short, bicolored; coat brown to near white.

**Big-eared piñon mouse** represents the white-footed clan in the rugged canyons of the Southwest.

Louis Agassiz Fuertes

**White-throated wood rat** vibrates his tail when alarmed, likes to sun-bathe after a rainy spell.

# WHITE-THROATED WOOD RAT

## *Neotoma albigula*

NATURE'S BARBED WIRE rings the fortress-home of this rodent engineer. Beneath a paloverde or in a clump of prickly pear, he builds a lodge of sticks and stalks, spiking it with cactus. This deters most enemies except a snake, the red racer. But the wood rat scampers about his spiny roof with impunity, constantly adding to his home until it may grow five feet high.

Some wood rats of the western forests build tree houses; the eastern wood rat often nests in a cave (page 24). Kleptomaniacs all, they steal anything that takes their fancy. They sneak into camp and lug off a watch, a spoon, a set of false teeth, perhaps leaving a pebble in exchange. Thus the name "pack rat" or "trade rat."

*Neotoma* is a sober, hard-working thief, foraging at night for berries, seeds, bark, and greens. Plants supply his moisture, so he seldom takes a drink. Even so, his married life is stormy. Once he moves in with his mate, the couple scraps incessantly, standing on hind legs to slug it out.

Divorce is inevitable, and the rat walks out, leaving his mate to support the young. When they are about 60 days old, she kicks them out. The doleful adolescents may hang around until the next of their mother's two or three yearly broods arrives, then set up their own establishments. Sometimes they rout an old gentleman rat from his improved mansion and move in, while he starts all over in a little trash shack.

Many predators relish wood rat meat; southwestern Indians also considered it a delicacy. Naturalist Edward Nelson tells of Mexican vendors who used to shout: "Country rats, very delicious, very cheap!" He tried one. It tasted like young rabbit.

*Length* 13–16 in. *Weight* 6–8 oz. *Range:* southwestern states, Mexico. *Characteristics:* white throat, feet; well-haired tail.

# NORTHERN GRASSHOPPER MOUSE

## *Onychomys leucogaster*

A LION AMONG MICE, *Onychomys* rules the world beneath the grassheads of the Great Plains. In winter he eats seeds, but meat is his dish. He sallies forth at night, piping hunting cries like a peanut-size hound, and relentlessly tracks by scent. Creeping up, he rushes his victim and sinks his teeth into the skull.

He devours field, harvest, deer, and pocket mice; his brethren taste just as good. He bites grasshoppers' heads off, then sits up munching away. He relishes lizards, spiders, scorpions, but seems scared to death of ants. Owls, badgers, snakes, coyotes stalk the velvet-furred killer in turn.

In spring and summer, litters of two to six are born, perhaps in a borrowed den. A longer-tailed cousin (*O. torridus*) ranges from California and Nevada into Mexico.

Strange to say, the ferocious midget makes a friendly, even-tempered pet.

*Length* 5–7½ in. *Weight* 1½–2½ oz. *Range:* plains, Canada to Mexican border. *Characteristics:* stocky; clublike tail.

**Grasshopper mouse,** underworld terrorist of the plains, dines on any creature he can kill. The peaceful **harvest mouse** of field, meadow, and marsh dwells in a baseball-size globe of grass, lashed to weeds or slung in a bush or tree.

# WESTERN HARVEST MOUSE

## *Reithrodontomys megalotis*

HE'S LIKE the house mouse in size and color, but he's no bold pantry-raider. Retiring and inoffensive, he lives inconspicuously amid tangled greenery. In a grassy nest he sires several broods. At three months offspring find mates of their own.

Most active at night, this little pacifist dines on seeds and tender grass tips, and falls victim to carnivores, snakes, and owls. More than a dozen related species live from southern Canada to Central America.

*Length* 5–6½ in. *Weight* ½ oz. *Range:* Wisconsin to Pacific, S. into Mexico. *Characteristics:* large ears, scantily haired tail.

283

Louis Agassiz Fuertes

The **silky pocket mouse** scouts for seeds. His larger, bristly cousin is the **hispid pocket mouse.**

## SILKY POCKET MOUSE

### Perognathus flavus

THIS TINY SEED HUNTER lives like a hermit in his closed-off network of shallow tunnels. So prodigious is his appetite and so slim the pickings, he's loath to share his territory. But he'll sire litters of two to six.

Like all pocket mice, he carries seeds by the thousands in fur-lined cheek pouches to fill his larders. He empties his pockets if pursued, sometimes loses his tail.

*Length* 4–4¾ in. *Weight* ¼–⅓ oz. *Range:* plains, Wyoming to Mexico. *Characteristics:* soft, pale fur; underparts white.

## HISPID POCKET MOUSE

### Perognathus hispidus

A DESERT DWELLER, hispid rarely drinks. His metabolism, like that of other pocket mice, converts seed starches to water.

He nests under a rock or in a burrow screened by vegetation. If his chambers are invaded, he'll scurry into a side tunnel and plug it with dirt so the predator will think no one's home. Similar stoppers at the several entrances prevent loss of moisture during the heat of day.

*Length* 8–9 in. *Weight* 1–2½ oz. *Range:* South Dakota to Mexico. *Characteristics:* harsh brown hair, bristly on rump and tail.

## BANNER-TAILED KANGAROO RAT

### Dipodomys spectabilis

BOLD STRIPES and an elegant white-tipped tail make bannertail the handsomest of kangaroo rats. This big cousin of the pocket mice lives in the arid Southwest, manufacturing water from seeds. Outsize hind legs enable him to escape foes by leaping like a tiny, erratic kangaroo. The tail, longer than his body, props him when resting and stabilizes him when he hops.

The solitary kangaroo rat digs elaborate tunnels capped by a broad mound with perhaps a dozen entrances. He clears away vegetation so he can scout for danger before emerging to hunt seeds. He crams his external cheek pouches, empties them into temporary caches, and when the sun has

284

**The banner-tailed kangaroo rat dwells in an air-conditioned desert apartment.**

cured the seeds he stores them underground. He's quick to fight over a pile of food, grunting and growling as he delivers battering-ram kicks with his hind feet. A little pocket mouse that got belted for butting in was heard to cry with pain. Bannertail hates to be disturbed. At home he'll thump angrily, ordering the intruder away.

Meeting a suspicious object during his nocturnal foraging, the rat kicks sand over it, then whirls around to see what happens. This often exposes the ambush of a sidewinder rattlesnake who, like the fox, coyote, badger, and owl, is a deadly foe.

Two or more times a year, bannertail's home becomes a nursery for two to six infants, mewling like puppies.

*Length* 12–14 in. *Weight* 3½–4⅔ oz. *Range:* southwestern U.S., Mexico. *Characteristics:* white stripes, tuft on long tail.

Louis Agassiz Fuertes

**Stout chisel-teeth** chip away outer bark to reach succulent inner layers, the porcupine's favorite food. Gnawing keeps his orange-enameled incisors from growing too long. Porky also chews anything salty: antlers, sweaty saddles, ax handles. He even tries automobile tires.

DONALD A. SPENCER

**This albino porcupine,** one in 50,000, was delivered by the author in a Caesarean operation.

CHAPTER 20

# Porcupine, Nature's Pincushion

By DONALD A. SPENCER

I HAD CAMPED in the mountains of the West many years, but never before had I been startled from a sound sleep by such a weird cry. Note by note the wail ascended until quite shrill, then dwindled away. It set my scalp to prickling. Cautiously I felt under the bed for flashlight and pistol, then set out to locate the ghostly vocalist.

Imagine my chagrin when I found a pint-sized baby porcupine under the cabin floor! I had believed the porcupine to be practically voiceless. Since that night I've learned a great deal about the fascinating pincushion-on-legs.

Porcupine pets of ours have repeated that cry many a night during the first months of their lives. Adults are quieter, but in the fall breeding season you may hear porky's call drift down from some distant tree. One mid-November a young forester and I, cruising a timber stand in northern Wisconsin, spotted a porcupine high in a large hemlock. Standing perfectly still, I began calling him in the language I had learned from my pets. Presently he started down, and we could hear his low, continuous back talk. Several times he stopped as if not quite sure my "porky talk" was all it should be. Reaching the ground, he ambled in our direction, talking all the while. At last he stood beside my leg and sniffed. My first movement set him off at an awkward gallop.

Calling a porcupine down is one thing, climbing up for him quite another. I have done it hundreds of times, occasionally with near-disastrous consequences.

Near Brattleboro, Vermont, a co-worker and I spotted a porcupine in the top of a 40-foot spruce. I went up after him. Since four feet of snow covered the ground, I planned to push the animal out of the tree for my partner to retrieve. I dared not go high enough to grab him by hand, for the tree was dying at the top. The trick was to reach up with a stick and rap him on the nose, being careful not to touch his back. After several raps he began to back down. I slid out on branches, so that he passed between me and the trunk—inches from my face. Then I put my foot on his head and shoved. Alas! While I was dislodging him, a branch snapped and sent me backward out of the tree into the snow. Luckily, I didn't land on the porcupine. My partner upended a pail over him.

I recall a less lucky night in the Colorado Rockies. Three of us were intent on capturing a big porcupine, aided only by car lights beamed into the willow scrub. Porky came out unexpectedly, right at our feet. Startled, my brother stepped back, bumped into me, and fell across the animal. We spent the next hour jerking out the maze of quills that nailed his trousers to his thigh. A painful operation!

Porky's armor of some 30,000 multibarbed quills is formidable, especially when you consider that they are replaced when lost or broken. Only the face, legs, belly, and undersurface of the tail are free of them. Quills embedded in flesh tend to

## Grab a porcupine barehanded? Author's wife does it often

She feints at a yellow-haired pincushion (lower left) to make it present its lashing tail. Then she grasps the tail from beneath, folding the quills back, as demonstrated (lower right). Though the rodent's teeth can sever a finger, it tries to pull away, not bite.

Dr. Spencer often turns lumberjack to capture a porcupine, sometimes descends holding it by the tail. Here (left) he stuffs one into a wire cone and lowers away from 50 feet up.

Porky spends almost half his life in trees, for winter's frosts and snows destroy or cover plant food on the forest floor. He often returns to feed on the same tree. On one 8-inch maple the original feeding scar had been enlarged upward on each of 11 successive years. Removal of the cambium layer impedes flow of the tree's nourishment, and sugars manufactured by the leaves accumulate above the wound. So the porcupine instinctively takes his second meal from above the first.

289

DONALD A. SPENCER

## Porky can't "shoot" his quills, but his tail packs a prickly wallop

"Ouch!" A sharp yank rids a dog of another quill—painful treatment for getting nosy with a porcupine. Quills are not poisonous and rarely carry infection, but can kill if not extracted. Tipped with microscopic scales that act like barbs (below), they work into the victim's throat and mouth and prevent his eating.

A ranger (lower left) explains the porcupine's thorny armor. The rodent can erect or flatten quills at will. "Held by the tail he's harmless, but free he can drive those needles clean through a heavy glove."

Many are the home remedies for removing quills. "Cut the shaft to let out the air, a collapsed quill pulls easily," folks say. Some claim that swabbing with vinegar or sweet oil softens barbs. Others counsel twirling, to twist barbs out.

A quick jerk works best. The pithy shaft is not hollow, does not collapse, nor will any solvent soften embedded barbs.

work deep because of the victim's muscle action. Imagine the plight of a coyote foolish enough to tackle a porcupine and get his muzzle and tongue filled with quills. The truncated points work into his mouth and throat until, unable to eat, he dies of starvation. Hunting dogs often fall victim, and cattle pay dearly for nuzzling the prickly creature.

In days gone by, quills were widely used to decorate garments, weapons, and implements. The antennalike guard hairs were fashioned into cockscomb head-dresses. In Longfellow's *Song of Hiawatha,* Kagh, the hedgehog, offered his quills to decorate a birchbark canoe: "Take my quills, O Hiawatha!" Some Indian tribes of the Southwest considered the porcupine a semideity; today he's more often considered an economic pest, because of his damage to forests, crops, and stock.

Equipped with four remarkable wood chisels, he chips off a tree's outer bark and feeds on the inner layers. If the incision encircles the trunk, the tree dies; even spot damage weakens it. In parts of southwestern Colorado 85 per cent of the pine trees more than four inches in diameter show scars from porcupine feed-ing. Years after teeth marks have weathered away or been covered with new growth, scientists can study the scars and tell when porky dined, thus determining population cycles for the past 150 years or more.

In the spring he abandons bark for the flowers, catkins, and leaves of willow, maple, and cottonwood. As the countryside comes into bloom he may forsake the forest for gardens, orchards, and hayfields. In settled areas his craving for salt gets

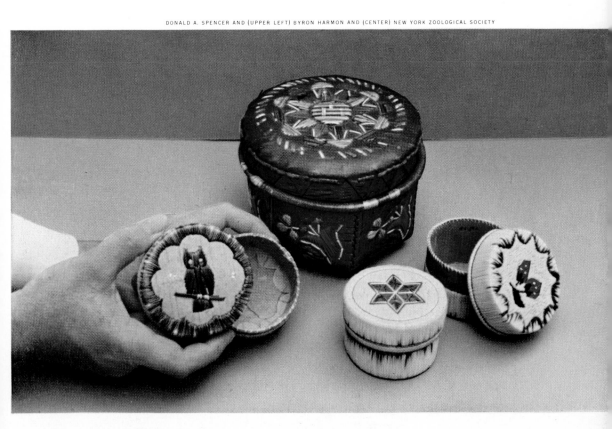

**Featherweight quills** (about 4,000 to the ounce!) adorn boxes made by Ottawa Indians. The Sioux stitched brightly stained quills into deerskin shirts and moccasins, and Crow Indians fashioned combs from porcupine tails. The white man has also used porky's spines — as phonograph needles.

291

him into trouble. Anything human hands have touched is apt to be impregnated with salt from perspiration, enough to whet his appetite. How often I have walked into an abandoned farmhouse or miner's shack to find great holes eaten in the floor. Where the cellar stairs had been, only the stringers and a fragment of one or two steps remained. There's a saying in the north woods: "No need to move a lumber camp—the porkies will eat it down."

The porcupine is commonly abroad at night. During the day he hides in a rock crevice, a thicket, or a hollow log. There are no comforts of home in his den—no nest, no bed of leaves, no stored food. In fact, porky may be sitting unconcernedly on a cake of ice, for the den serves only as protection against predators and weather. In the Rocky Mountains and the Southwest, the yellow-haired porcupine uses a "rest tree" instead of a den. On high limbs he sprawls asleep, all four feet dangling overside.

For animals so solitary in habit, porcupines as pets exhibit an unusual desire for man's company. Hilarious times are in store, especially if two or three little fellows grow up together. They are as playful as puppies and fully as noisy. We start them on diluted cow's milk, feeding them at first from a syringe, graduating to bread and milk in a saucer. Before long they nibble on fruits, vegetables, and greens. It's comical to watch one holding a slice of orange in his forepaws, trying to bend his head so as not to lose the sweet drops.

About dusk the pets become most active. They follow you about like shadows, keeping up a low-pitched, plaintive cry. They even like to be picked up; only if you pet "against the grain" will you be pricked. They enjoy a romp on the lawn, being tumbled over backward and roughed upside down like a puppy. Understand that porky initiates this play; you don't. When he finishes, any insistence on your part results in raised quills—as emphatic a "No" as you will ever experience.

**Bristling in alarm,** porky paddles for shore. Buoyant quills normally lie flat when he swims.

FRANCIS HARPER, U. S. FISH AND WILDLIFE SERVICE

Walter A. Weber, National Geographic staff artist

**Spiked back and tail** are roused porcupine's "business end." Blazed tree shows where he dined.

# PORCUPINE

## *Erethizon dorsatum*

SPINES ERECT, the porcupine turns his back and thrashes his tail. The wolf pounces and instantly regrets it. Nose, mouth, tongue burning with quills up to four inches long, he retreats howling in agony.

Few predators that raid this walking arsenal of 30,000 spears escape the barbs. Only the fisher, bobcat, and puma manage a meal without injury; they flip the squat rodent over, attack his unprotected belly. Sensitive touch and hearing may warn the "quill pig" of danger, but his beady eyes often deceive him. One animal waddled up to a ranger and began gnawing his boots!

The porcupine moves slowly, but for a short way can gallop as fast as a man can run. In winter he seldom strays far from his favorite clump of trees; the rest of the year he may wander wide. In fall he courts his love with high-pitched calls and nuzzles her nose. Breeding, the female controls her quills so as not to spear her mate. In seven months she has her baby, weighing about a pound and covered with soft quills that quickly harden.

Within 15 minutes of birth the baby can walk and lash his tail. He climbs in several weeks, stops nursing in a month or so. By autumn young porky cuts family ties. In his second year he may mate. Captives have lived 10 years.

*Length* 26–34 in. *Weight* 10–25 lbs. *Range:* N. E. and W. states, Canada, Alaska. *Characteristics:* quills, chunky build.

CHAPTER 21

# Rabbits, Hares, and the Pika

By EDWARDS PARK

WHAT WILD ANIMAL more surely owns the hearts of children than the rabbit? Hairbreadth adventures of this diminutive hero enliven fables, fantasies, and animated cartoons. Like Alice, youngsters the world over have followed him into Wonderland. In harsh reality, the long-eared, bright-eyed bunny is little concerned with heroics; he's far too busy just surviving. His short life—rabbits seldom last more than a year—is one long narrow escape.

For the rabbit is a tasty morsel, and every carnivore knows it. From birth he is hunted by birds, beasts, and snakes. Man joins the chase enthusiastically; rabbits rank as the world's most popular small game. To fill the demand, nature made them prolific, able under ideal conditions to raise litter after litter. Where predators have been killed off, as in western farm areas, rabbits sometimes destroy whole fields of grain, nibbling through acre after acre. Facing ruin, farmers fight back, organizing jack rabbit drives that kill thousands in a day.

Introduced into Australia, where they do not occur naturally, rabbits proved what disasters may result from throwing nature off balance. With few predators or parasites to bother them, the two dozen European rabbits that were turned loose multiplied to an estimated two billion. They turned pastures into dusty craters. Sheep starved and the entire economy of this wool-growing nation was threatened. Scientists resorted to germ warfare. They inoculated trapped rabbits with myxomatosis, a disease that attacks the mucous membranes yet does not spoil the meat or pelt, both useful products. Ninety per cent of Australia's hordes were wiped out. And the rest? They're multiplying all over again at a hare-raising pace.

294

Black-tailed jack rabbit, huge ears cocked for danger, visits an Arizona pool. This lanky sprinter seldom drinks; moist plants quench his thirst.

"I AM AT A LOSS to know whether it be my hare's foot which is my preservative, or my taking of a pill of turpentine every morning," wrote Samuel Pepys in 1665.

Lucky or not, the hare's foot does wonders for the hare. The white-tailed jack rabbit, for example, can hit close to 45 miles an hour when pressed. Soaring through the air in 20-foot leaps, this speediest of hares almost seems to enjoy pursuit. His great ears twist like twin radars, picking up sounds of the enemy. Like all hares, this jack leaps high in the air so he can look back at his foe.

The smaller varying hare or snowshoe rabbit has a coarse growth of hair on his big hind feet to keep him from sinking into deep snow. When winter shrouds northern forests, the varying hare turns into a white ghost, almost invisible as he crouches in his nest or "form." But when the plodding hound approaches, the snowshoe explodes from hiding and skips over the snow like a ricocheting bullet.

Having left the hound far behind, the hare usually circles back to his starting place and tangles his own trail. One was known to backtrack in his own prints, then jump far to one side and sit like a statue while the eagerly caroling dog followed the scent to its dead end, then howled in frustration. Bugs Bunny could hardly have planned it better.

Though no hare ever raced a tortoise, it's true that the varying hare cannot maintain full speed for more than a few minutes. To escape the scurrying weasel, most savage of his enemies, the hare needs only a short burst of speed—and the chance to wind his trail into such a mystifying web that even the tenacious weasel gives up in disgust.

"The blood more stirs to rouse a lion than to start a hare," says Will Shakespeare in a slur on rabbit courage. Yet naturalists record many a case of bravery. Stalked by the deadly weasel, a little cottontail may turn on the

**Peter Rabbit,** Pierre Lapin, or Peterchen Hase —in eight languages Beatrix Potter's tale of the bunny in Mr. McGregor's garden patch has sent generations of youngsters happily off to bed.

## Easter bunnies, symbol of spring, recall ancient legends

One tells of Eostre, Teutonic goddess of spring, who fashioned the first hare from a bird. Grateful for this honor, the hare laid eggs once a year at the festival to its patron goddess. At the season of rebirth, folklore still clings to symbolic eggs and rabbits, signifying fertility.

Cottontails, ill-equipped for winter foraging, greet spring zestfully and soon have litters. Noses twitching, the babies below make an appealing double handful. But they are too high-strung to make good pets.

F. RICHARD BAXTER,
NATIONAL GEOGRAPHIC STAFF

297

killer and run straight over him, kicking him head over heels. A cottontail mother was seen attacking a black snake that was after her babies. And a pet Belgian hare is reported to have beaten up a neighborhood dog and to have protested vigorously when dragged away from television, which it loved to watch.

Rabbits and hares were once classified as rodents because of their strong gnawing front teeth. Now, with the pika, they form their own order, the *Lagomorpha,* distinguished by a second pair of upper incisors hidden behind the visible pair. Rabbit and hare are terms often interchanged. What distinctions do biologists make?

The hares, genus *Lepus,* are bigger and have longer hind legs developed for leaping, and taller, broader ears. They favor the wide-open spaces. Their young are born furred and open-eyed. Thus the jack rabbit is biologically a hare.

The cottontail, marsh, and other true rabbits, genus *Sylvilagus,* generally prefer plenty of cover. At birth they are blind and naked, with undeveloped ears.

**Rabbit pie for supper!** Garb has changed in a century, but box trap still catches cottontails.

"CATCHING RABBITS," LITHOGRAPH, 1850, FROM A PAINTING BY WILLIAM SIDNEY MOUNT, THE OLD PRINT SHOP

**Crop raiders bite the dust** as Paiutes wind up a jack rabbit drive. Homesteaders adopted this technique. Besides destroying grain, rabbits can carry tularemia, an acute disease which ticks, lice, flies, and other insects transmit to small mammals. Hares and rabbits, particularly the cottontail, are responsible for nearly every occurrence in humans.

*Warning—steer clear of any rabbit that seems sick or slow afoot.* Wear rubber gloves to skin a rabbit or hare, and cook the meat well.

American rabbits even belong to a separate genus from European rabbits. Unlike European rabbits, cottontails seldom live underground. As any student of Uncle Remus knows, they are generally "bred en bawn in a brier-patch," or a brush pile or thicket. Newborn rabbits are helpless, while baby hares scamper from danger.

The smallest and least known member of the order is the mouselike pika, scratching a living high up on western mountains. While most lagomorphs are silent except when hurt or badly frightened, the pika calls and whistles all day, for he has little to fear. He bustles about rock-slide areas where few would care to hunt him. Wise in aspect and safe in habitat, the pika is called "little chief hare." Sad to relate, he's not really very bright.

*A Portfolio*     Following are biographies of the principal species of North American rabbits and hares, and the pika, illustrated in full color by National Geographic Staff Artist Walter A. Weber and noted wildlife artist Louis Agassiz Fuertes. Lengths, weights show range between an average male and a large female (females are bigger).

299

WALTER A. WEBER

Darting cottontails circle to keep within the few acres that form their whole world. High-crying beagles

## EASTERN COTTONTAIL

### *Sylvilagus floridanus*

IN A WHIRLWIND of snow, brown shapes blast from cover, zigzagging crazily. Trailing beagles sight the powderpuff rumps and break into song, heads up, feet flying. For these are cottontails, their favorite prey.

In deep snow the chase may prove short and brutal—the cottontail is no snowshoe rabbit. If he is caught in the open, fast dogs can run him down, for he lacks endurance. But in his home, a brushy clearing or the edge of a wood, Peter Cottontail knows plenty of tricks to confound pursuit. He may double back, jump on a fallen log, and freeze into a lump. He may swim

*Walter A. Weber, National Geographic staff artist*
bore in to add this snow-hindered pair to the millions of rabbits taken each year by American sportsmen.

an icy stream. Almost always he will bend his course into a circle, for he is lost outside his own small patch.

Finally shaking off the hounds, he slips into his nest well hidden under a brush pile or deep in a clump of bushes that conceals his network of little paths. He sprawls on his side, heart slowing to normal. Once again he has saved his warm hide.

But he lives all his life in peril. Next day it may be a fox that gives chase, or a bobcat, or worst of all, a weasel that will follow those runways to the thickest corner of brambles. These predators, plus a host of parasites, keep the cottontail population fairly constant. Without them, Americans would be wading in a sea of rabbits.

Of all this fecund clan, the cottontail is

301

Louis Agassiz Fuertes

**Wary cottontail** scouts the snowscape. Uneasy in winter, he sticks close to the "brier-patch."

the most enthusiastic reproducer. With a mating season limited only by cold weather, the doe has several litters a year, four or five babies each. When six months old, the young can breed, but usually a winter passes before the cottontail settles down to his lifework. In early spring courtship flourishes. Bucks battle, sending fur flying with powerful kicks. Once her affection is won, the doe, larger than her mate, literally boots him out.

The babies take about a month to arrive. Shortly beforehand, Molly Cottontail scratches out a shallow depression hidden by tall grass or bushes, or appropriates diggings left by another animal. She lines the nest or form with grass and tufts of fur pulled from her abdomen. By the time the

litter is born she not only has a warm nursery, but has exposed her nipples for her pink, blind, helpless brood. Nursing them at night, she keeps her distance in daylight so she won't draw attention to the young. She pulls a warming blanket of grass and fur over them, then scratches leaves over the nest to hide it.

Only about a third of all cottontail babies live long enough to leave the nest. Cold or rain may kill them. A skunk or cat may spot them. A snake or owl may raid the nest. With luck the bunnies open their eyes about the eighth day, squeal for food, and finally leave home when some two weeks old. By then they have grown from thumb- to fist-size and are perfect miniatures of their mother, with fur coats and long ears. At five months they reach full weight.

The cottontail eats almost every kind of vegetation, whether prize chrysanthemums or the twigs and bark of apple trees. At twilight he browses close to cover, along a fence or at the forest's edge. Ears cocked, nose twitching to catch alien scent, he hops to a patch of clover, nibbles, sits up to scan the landscape, nibbles some more. Surprised, he freezes, ears laid back. Approached, he catapults into dazzling speed, dodging so sharply that hunters suspect he can see a bullet on its way. Darting under a brush heap, he's apt to stay put even if a man jumps on top to flush him out.

Life is short for this bright-eyed bunny. A Michigan survey showed only seven per cent of a marked group passed the first birthday. But without cottontails woods and hedgerows would lose their magic for many Americans. So when rabbits dwindle (fire or drought cuts cover) man often comes to the rescue, restocking the area.

*Length* 15–18 in. *Weight* 2–4 lbs. *Range:* eastern states to Manitoba and New Mexico, south to Costa Rica. *Characteristics:* brown coat; white belly, underside of tail.

3"

**Hopping leisurely,** cottontail leaves typical rabbit tracks. Big hind feet thump down ahead of forepaws. Top speed widens the gap between sets of prints.

# PYGMY RABBIT

## *Sylvilagus idahoensis*

SMALLEST OF COTTONTAILS, this sprite haunts dry plateaus just west of the Rockies. Ride through the sun-baked flats of northern Utah or Nevada and keep your eyes peeled for rabbit brush. You can spot it easily in September, when its blossoms glint yellow among the gray sage.

Dismount and walk slowly amid the clumps. Suddenly something erupts almost under your feet, and a grayish form scuttles for a hole, or failing that, a thicket.

The pygmy is hard to see because its dusty color matches the soil of its habitat. And it flashes no white signal with its rump, for its tiny tail is colored the same below as above. But if you see one, watch for others. They seem to like company.

The nickname "burrowing rabbit" tells much of his story. He is America's only rabbit or hare known to share the European rabbit's habit of excavating a warren. He digs a shallow home, with several four-inch entrances usually hidden by brush, or converts the vacant den of a badger. The young, about six to the litter, are born underground between May and August.

The pygmy rabbit dons a winter coat of pale gray, as if starting to turn white like the varying hare.

*Length* 9–12 in. *Weight* ½–1 lb. *Range:* Great Basin. *Characteristics:* small, grayish; dusky stub tail; nests underground.

303

**Short-legged pygmy rabbit** scurries rather than bounds, rarely ventures away from brush canopy.
*Walter A. Weber, National Geographic staff artist*

*Louis Agassiz Fuertes*

**Marsh rabbit,** slow on land, swims fast with spread toes. Nickname: "pontoon."

# MARSH RABBIT
## *Sylvilagus palustris*

ANY RABBIT WILL SWIM if it has to. The marsh rabbit dives in for the fun of it. Naturalist John Bachman kept one as a pet: "In warm weather it was fond of lying for hours in a trough of water, and seemed restless and uneasy when it was removed. . . ."

This southeastern marsh dweller nests its two to six young in the rushes, often on tussocks. Through thick cover it steps like a cat along beaten paths, nibbling at reeds, digging up wild potato and amaryllis. Startled, it takes off for the water. One was seen going strong 700 yards from shore.

Bachman noted that marsh rabbits also hide amid water plants, floating with just faces showing. "On touching them with a stick, they seemed unwilling to move until they perceived that they were observed, when they swam off with great celerity."

*Length* 14–17 in. *Weight* 2–3 lbs. *Range:*

Virginia to Florida, Alabama. *Characteristics:* dark brown, aquatic. Larger kin, swamp rabbit *(S. aquaticus)*, lives farther west.

# VARYING HARE
## *Lepus americanus*

EVEN IF YOU KEEP a varying hare in a heated room, he will doff summer brown and change into his warm, white winter coat in autumn just as if he were in the wilds.

Changing clothes by the calendar, this north woods hare faces deep snow superbly equipped. Only his black eyes and dark ear tips spoil his camouflage. His big matted feet give him the run of the forest when most animals bog down in drifts. Hence his alternate name, snowshoe rabbit.

He greets the first blush of spring with wild courtship rites that are "mad as a March hare." Males battle furiously and pursue females in riotous chases. About

Here's how the varying hare got his name; in summer he's brown, in winter white.

Arctic hares often crouch in groups, alert for fox or wolf, on slopes where wind exposes dwarf plants.

36 days after mating, the female bears two to seven furry, open-eyed babies. In two weeks they're foraging, though mother supplements their grassy "formula."

Nibbling life away within less than 100 acres, this hare circles if chased, thumps warnings, takes dust baths, and grooms like a cat. Indians snare him along his beaten runways; he supplies them food and blanket-fur. Varying hares fluctuate in cycles. One fall western Manitoba held an estimated 5,000 per square mile. By spring a mysterious plague had wiped them out.

*Length* 17–21 in. *Weight* 2–5 lbs. *Range:* Alaska, Canada, N. and W. states. *Characteristic:* hair always dark at base.

# ARCTIC HARE
## *Lepus arcticus*

IN POLAR WASTES where all is featureless white, the Arctic hare can sit in plain sight with little to fear. Except for eyes and black ear tips, he's invisible.

This far north, hares stay pure white the year round. Farther south they switch to summer coats of brownish gray. Nature fits them with strong foreclaws so they can dig down to a willow twig through two feet of snow. Protruding, tweezerlike teeth enable hares of Ellesmere Island and north Greenland to glean bits of vegetation from

**Black-tailed jack rabbits,** plague of western farmers, grow less wary as their numbers increase.

cracks in rocks. Arctic hares seldom tunnel in snow, but simply wait out blizzards.

Spring mating may bring great gatherings that sit in solemn formation. Males sometimes box with each other, hopping upright on snowshoe hind feet. Litters as large as eight arrive in June or July.

Man and many predators feed on the big white hare. Eskimos make robes of its delicate, fleecy fur.

*Length* 18–28 in. *Weight* 5–12 lbs. *Range:* N. Canada, arctic islands. *Characteristics:* winter fur white to skin, tail always white. The Alaskan hare *(L. othus)* is almost identical.

# BLACK-TAILED JACK RABBIT
## *Lepus californicus*

TEXANS coined the name "jackass rabbit" for the long-eared hares that hopped about the prairie. Shortened to jack rabbit, it has become a name as closely associated with the West as the word cowboy. Of all the big, rangy, long-legged jack rabbits, the blacktail is the best known.

Settlers opening the West took pains to kill off every predator that showed its head around ranch and homestead. As a result jack rabbits flourished. Swarming through planted fields, they sometimes brought ruin to "sod-busters" and forced them to pack up and move.

Farmers retaliated by building corrals of wire fencing, then joining forces to beat the bushes and drive thousands of jacks into these slaughter pens. One drive in California netted more than 20,000 blacktails.

Still they thrived. At Los Angeles International Airport, thronging jack rabbits created a nuisance and got run over by landing aircraft—until runway construction reduced ground cover.

Roundly cursed by many humans, the blacktail makes a surprisingly nice pet. He can even be housebroken, says one owner. Given a pillow to sleep on, he will scratch out a "form" on it before settling down.

*Length* 19–25 in. *Weight* 4–8 lbs. *Range:* W. Missouri to Pacific, Columbia River to central Mexico. *Characteristics:* gray sides, black-tipped ears, tail black above.

# WHITE-TAILED JACK RABBIT
## *Lepus townsendii*

MEET THE CHAMPION SPRINTER of the tribe. When danger nears, the white-tailed jack twitches his great ears around to focus on the slightest sound. Uneasy, he rises to peer over the tall grass, then may make a few hops on hind legs alone. Pushed hard by a hopeful coyote, he lays his ears back, digs in with those slim, powerful hind legs, and rockets off, sailing close to the ground, yet effortlessly clearing a five-foot obstruction if he has to.

Whitetails range farther north than blacktails, and at their northern limits change to a winter coat nearly as white as the varying hare's. Farther south they replace their normal summer brown with pale gray. Again like varying hares, all the jacks tend to increase and decrease in cycles. Para-

**Whitetails** in their northern range change to winter coats, may burrow into snowbanks for shelter.

WALTER A. WEBER

sites plague them; diseases take heavy toll. Tularemia, or rabbit fever, threatens all lagomorphs and is transmitted to man.

During the spring mating season, jack rabbit males often stand toe to toe and slug it out with their forefeet, biting each other as well. Tattered ears may result.

Preparing for her family, the female makes a real nest instead of the usual scratched-out sleeping depression, and lines it with fur from her belly. White-tailed jacks bear an average of four babies — one or two more than blacktails — after a gestation of more than 40 days. Within moments of birth the little fur balls are able to hop, running and dodging frantically if something frightens them. Soon they learn to freeze, baffling pursuers by blending with the surroundings.

Owls, coyotes, foxes, snakes, and other predators hunt these dwellers of the tree-less plains. One of the prairie sounds that lingers in the minds of Westerners is the scream of a wounded jack rabbit — eerie, piercing, a chilling wail of despair.

*Length* 22–26 in. *Weight* 5–8 lbs. *Range:* Iowa to the Cascades and Sierras, S. Canada to New Mexico. *Characteristics:* tail all white, winter coat white or pale gray.

# ANTELOPE JACK RABBIT
## *Lepus alleni*

JOGGING THROUGH MESQUITE in the southern Arizona desert, a horseman is apt to rouse an antelope jack rabbit from a shady resting place. The big, long-eared animal takes off in low-flying leaps, veering from side to side. And as he flees, amazingly he changes from drab to blazing white.

At rest, the antelope jack is well enough camouflaged. But he wears a pure white vest that stretches around his belly and up the sides. With a twitch of his back muscles, he can move this white patch to cover one whole flank. Changing direction, he rolls the patch around to face the foe.

As if this weren't drawing enough attention to himself, the rabbit raises and lowers the white area to make himself look a little like a flapping pillowcase. Why? Naturalists don't know for sure. Seton suggests, tongue in cheek, that the big jack rabbit flashes his colors to warn pursuers that they are in for a hopeless chase, so why not forget it and save a lot of effort!

The antelope jack's extraordinary ears measure up to nine inches from skull to tip. Marvelous organs, delicately veined, they pick up the slightest vibration.

A creature of the cactus country, the big hare sometimes darts into a burrow to escape the swoop of an eagle. Perhaps he dug it himself. Litter size is usually two.

*Length* 20–24 in. *Weight* 4–6 lbs. *Range:* N.W. Mexico and S. Arizona. *Characteristics:* white sides, underparts; huge ears.

**Antelope jack,** boasting the biggest ears of all his clan, was named for his habit of flashing white like the pronghorn when in flight. Few of his kind remain north of Mexico.

*Louis Agassiz Fuertes*

# PIKA

## *Ochotona princeps*

CLIMBERS HIGH IN THE ROCKIES think twice about traversing a talus slope. But to the little gray-brown pika such a jumble of rock makes an ideal home. If an eagle or hawk threatens, he has a thousand holes to dive into. And in this labyrinth even a weasel is apt to give up.

Roughly guinea pig size and shape, the round-eared pika—inaccurately called cony—has little in common with other lagomorphs except a double set of upper incisors. His hind legs are no longer than his front, so he scurries rather than hops.

He's up and about at dawn, for the pika is a hard-working hay farmer. Venturing from a chink in the rocks, he scouts for danger, then scuttles nimbly on hair-soled feet to the nearest grass patch. Briskly he clips all he can carry crosswise in his mouth, then scrambles home, at times tripping because he can't see over his load. He spreads it to dry in the sun, on a slab outside his door, then hurries back for more.

Should rain fall, he rouses his fellows with curious flat bleats, and they bustle about getting their crop under cover. By summer's end he may boast a 50-pound hay mow—150 times his weight—to feed on in the long months ahead. Well-nourished and warm in his fluffy fur, the little alpinist moseys under or over the snow all winter. His three or four offspring arrive in early summer and are soon out foraging.

*Length* 6–8½ in. *Weight* 4–6 oz. *Range:* S.W. Canada to California, New Mexico. The collared pika *(O. collaris)* inhabits N.W. Canada and Alaska. *Characteristics:* short rounded ears, almost tailless.

309

**Mountain-dwelling pikas** make hay while the sun shines, stacking harvest from glacial meadows.

*Walter A. Weber, National Geographic staff artist*

PART V

# *Survivors of Ancient Orders*

BLACK FORMS hang stiffly from cavern walls. Then twilight
signals. Cries, inaudible to humans, bounce like radar beams;
the flutter of wings becomes a tornadic roar as, wing to wing,
a cloud of bats spirals into the dusk.
The rising moon outlines an opossum in a tree. She yawns,
scratches, climbs down and saunters off, her family on her back.
Evening breezes cool the valley floor. Now promenades that
ancient knight in coat of mail, the armadillo. A tiny shrew darts
across a moon-washed clearing and vanishes into an island of leaves.
A mole squints at a world of shadows, then ducks back
in his burrow where he sees no less.
These primitive Americans have haunted the night for millions of years,
have outlasted animal kingdoms that flourished, then fell.
Theirs were old established families when upstart man still lived in caves.
Altered little by time, they prosper today, living relics of the past.

CHAPTER 22

# The Opossum, America's Only Pouched Mammal

By AGNES AKIN ATKINSON

THE SLOW-MOVING OPOSSUM, hermit of the lowlands, is a fine example of relaxation and lack of push. His very ability to take it easy may account for the fact that his is one of the oldest living families of mammals. His ancestors roamed cheek by jowl with the dinosaur some 70 million years ago. Though the dinosaur was unable to survive the march of progress, the opossum has lived on little changed. Finding life easy in warm climates, this relic of the ancient order of marsupials survived from year to year, century to century, age to age. How did the placid creature manage so well? Observing him in our own side yard has given us some answers.

Near our home in Pasadena, California, where the earth drops off into a brush-covered canyon, we built a rock wall, leaving a large flat rock for an animal banquet table. Every evening we serve food to our wild friends: gray foxes, ringtails, raccoons, skunks, coyotes, and opossums.

"Old Poss" became one of our favorites. We first spotted him in a hole in our wall, looking as if he were asleep standing up. His body was about the size of a large house cat's, his snout was much like a pig's, his tail was scaly like a rat's. But he wore his own coat, cream at his throat and face, fawn-colored on his belly; the tips of the long hairs on his back were deep brown. His pink toes extended like fingers from black lace mitts. His hairless ears looked as if the wind had tossed them, one on each side of his face, where they had stuck. His large shoe-button eyes were black and glossy. Now and then his eyelids slid shut, only to open again.

**Popeyed, toothy opossum** wins no beauty prize; he also has a low IQ. But don't belittle him; his ancestors saw the dinosaurs quit the earth.

He opened his long slit of a mouth and yawned; then, as is the way of opossums, he yawned some more. Finally Old Poss climbed to the table and began eating.

One night an unusually heavy possum waddled to our rock table. Not until the creature sat back on its hind legs did we discover it was Mrs. Possum. She is different from any other animal in North America because on her belly she has a pouch—an incubator for her prematurely born young.

The bundles of pink flesh and pliable bone, scarcely bigger than navy beans, come into the world in a most immature form. A new-born opossum does not have honest-to-goodness feet and legs. Only nubbins. The front ones have tiny yet efficient claws. With these a baby pulls itself up through the mother's hair to the warm pouch. It attaches to one of the 11 to 17 nipples and hangs on, literally for dear life. For if it loses its hold, another baby may squeeze in.

Sometimes there are as many as 21 young in a litter, and the weakest are doomed to die.

A baby remains attached to the

**Built-in incubator** carries the blind and naked brood. After 11 to 13 days' gestation opossums bear bean-sized babies. A human mother in the same proportion to her six-pound infant would weigh 42 tons! In four days, nursing young (top) scale several times birth weight. Two weeks later (center) eye sockets show, and in a month (bottom) traces of hair appear.

Wide-eyed 11-week-olds (right) crowd the vertical pocket, which differs from a kangaroo's crosswise slit.

CHARLES PHILIP FOX

314

**Feeding antics** on the window ledge amuse the author and a young friend. The opossum relishes almost any food, including carrion, and helps man by destroying mice and insects.

nipple for 60 to 70 days; for another 30 it stays close to the pouch, nursing when hungry. When the young are about the size of full-grown mice, they leave their upside-down home and pull themselves up on mother's back. Each day the youngsters gain strength, become less timid. When their legs are strong enough to hold up their fat bodies, they wobble to the ground and toddle alongside mother. They don't play as other young animals do, but are even-tempered and docile.

Once we had a fine opportunity to get acquainted with a possum family. A friend found an opossum under his house and brought her to us. Her pouch was filled with babies almost ready for weaning. The mother was most cooperative. Though she hissed, sometimes snorted, she allowed us to handle her children. They curled in our hands, spat a little, then settled down with poker faces.

At three months, the youngsters are weaned and taught to eat solid foods— beetles, roots, and other goodies. When they are well into the yearling stage, their eyes seem to stand right on top of their ugly little faces. They begin to wander away from their mother, returning less and less frequently. Finally they do not come back at all. They have become hermits like their parents.

Mrs. Possum usually has one litter a year, but in warm climates she may have two. Almost always she has some sort of family. Either she is pregnant or has a pocketful, or a dozen little creatures are trailing her. She may even have a family in her pouch and one at her heels.

Mr. Possum walks alone, his gait slow, deliberate, heavy. His entire foot rests on the ground, making a track like a baby's footprint. He can hurry if he has to, although he trots awkwardly. Once we saw a full-grown animal going lickety-split. He climbs well, aided by thumbs and claws and a suction pad on each foot. He can also hang by his tail, but the most remarkable use he makes of it is to carry nesting materials. He gathers leaves with his forepaws, passes them back under his belly, and with hind feet slides them along to a loop he has made in his tail. When the loop is filled, he carries the load to his hole.

The female is an indifferent housekeeper. Possibly this is because her mate is a polygamist and no amount of careful homemaking could keep him true to her. Probably, like the old woman in the shoe, she has so many children she doesn't know what to do. Until she is about to give birth, any place that is dry and warm will serve for sleeping quarters. But when a litter is imminent, she appropriates an owl's deserted nest in a hollow tree, or perhaps even a skunk's den. She almost never makes a home of her own.

Mr. and Mrs. Possum keep their private lives private. Except for the large litters there is no evidence of any love life. Never have we seen two grown opossums side by side. Once we got a picture of two on the same negative, but they gave no sign of being acquainted or even remotely interested in each other. Unless the mother's pouch is full of children, it's almost impossible to tell male from female.

Though the opossum is thought to be stupid, he sometimes shows what looks like sense. He has been known to hitch a ride by automobile. Motorists have found him curled up under the hood, keeping warm from the engine. Vernon Bailey, long a naturalist with the Fish and Wildlife Service, told me that the brain cavity of an adult male opossum's skull will hold 25 small beans; the skull of a raccoon the same size will hold 150. If ideas were beans, it's plain that the possum's brain couldn't hold many.

And there never seems to be room in this small cavity for any idea of danger. In the South, where the opossum is hunted with dogs, he will climb a tree. If shaken down, he will play dead. You can twist him, kick him, swish him by the tail; he will just lie there on his side, body limp, mouth open in a silly grin.

When I was about 10 years old I went on my first possum

**Dragging his tail,** the flat-footed opossum leaves an unmistakable track. Clawless big toe on his handlike hind foot can touch the opposing digits—like the opposable thumb of man and apes.

3"

hunt. We shook from a small tree what looked like the great-granddad of all possums. The animal plopped to the ground and slumped. We thought he was killed. We picked him up by the tail and, taking turns, lugged him to grandmother's. It was miles too! He grew mighty heavy by the time we got him there and dumped him by the spring. Tearing into the house, we excitedly proclaimed our hunting success. Grandmother advised us to run quickly and bring the possum to her. When we returned to the spring, there was no sign of our prize. He had come alive and left for parts unknown.

Another time one of my friends reached into a box in the garage where he had stored some stuffed toys. One of the animals moved! The sight was one of the most fearsome things he had ever seen — an ugly gaping mouth with 50 gleaming white teeth, some as sharp as needles. The opossum has a larger mouth than man and more teeth than any other of our land mammals. With his four tusks he can tear meat, crack bones, and gnaw boards. When carrying one by the tail, remember that the supple animal can climb it and may bite. He also uses his teeth to chew his way out of a pen or cage and almost any kind of trap.

Even if a possum is caught in a steel-jawed trap, he will often free himself. He watches and waits while the trapped foot becomes numb; then he gnaws it off and limps away to a warm hideout to let nature heal the injury. In our yard we have had three-footed opossums to dinner.

Hunters and trappers are constantly after the animal. "Possum and taters" is a popular dish in many parts of the South. And opossum fur has long been used in inexpensive garments. Even though trapping is forbidden in our own canyon, we are constantly on the lookout for lawbreakers and their gear. We would rather see the gleaming fur on Mr. and Mrs. Possum than on anybody else.

"Playing possum" is how the slow-moving opossum meets danger. Slumped on his side, he feigns death, hoping the hand will leave him alone. Nothing disturbs his shocklike trance.

# OPOSSUM
## *Didelphis marsupialis*

SPANISH EXPLORERS probing Florida's woods and swamps in the 1520's marveled at a creature "with a pocket on its belly, in which it carries its young." A century later Capt. John Smith borrowed an Algonquian word to name it "Opassom." The term stuck, but it might not have if the French had had their way in the New World. To them the homely beast was *rat de bois*—rat of the woods.

Br'er Possum has long inspired song and lore in the South. His tail is bare because a raccoon tricked him into poking it into the fire, and his mouth is wide because he stretched it laughing at a deer that was trying to shake a persimmon tree!

> *'Possum am a cunnin' thing*
> *He rambles in the dark*
> *Nothin' 'tall disturb his min'*
> *'Cept to hyah ma bulldog bark.*

A barking dog *will* alert the marsupial. He can't see very well, but has good hearing and a keen sense of smell. Touch his sensitive whiskers and he snaps with teeth-studded jaws. Otherwise he's passive. He will feign death rather than run, take a beating rather than fight. Even when he's left for dead with his ribs caved in, like as not the hardy creature will survive.

Even so, few opossums live to the ripe age of seven. Hawks, owls, foxes, bobcats, coyotes, wolves all hunt them. Man takes several million a year for fur and countless more for food. Yet these prolific scavengers thrive, are even extending their range into Canada, and have been introduced into western states.

Born as early as January in the South, possums are apt to have a dozen new brothers and sisters by midsummer. They mature rapidly; females may breed before a year old. The animal's scientific name, *Didelphis,* refers to the double womb peculiar to the marsupial order.

The solitary opossum may prowl the night a mile or more for small rodents, in-

FREDERICK KENT TRUSLOW

**Prehensile tail** serves as a "behind hand," freeing forepaws to pluck fruit or pilfer eggs.

sects, frogs, berries, fruits, a chicken, or a nest full of eggs. After a meal he sits on hind legs and tail and washes like a cat. He doesn't hibernate, but may hole up in a hollow tree several days at a time. Hungry, out he comes, even in zero weather, risking frostbite on naked ears and tail.

*Length* 24–34 in. *Weight* 4–12 lbs. *Range:* eastern half of U.S. to South America. *Characteristics:* white pointed face, prehensile tail, pouch on female's belly.

**Star-nosed mole,** with outsize claws and 22 nose tentacles, looks like a prehistoric monster close up (left). But he's just a handful.

CHAPTER 23

# Moles and Shrews

By WAYNE BARRETT

ENORMOUS APPETITES packed into tiny bodies make life one meal after another in the nether world of moles and shrews. Considered enemies by gardeners, these ravenous insectivores are really allies in controlling Japanese beetles and cutworms. A mole may stow away his weight in insects every 24 hours. The smaller, more voracious shrew can do the same in three hours. Deprived of food for a day, he may starve to death.

The mole works incessantly, "spring-cleaning his little home." Digging 100 yards of tunnel is all in a day's work for him. With powerful shovel-like hands, he burrows through moist loam like a swimmer stroking through water. Seldom seen above ground, seldom pausing to listen to the wind in the willows, he lets people know he's about by the ridges and molehills he leaves on their lawns.

SURVIVORS OF ANCIENT ORDERS    321

The shrew, more streamlined than the mole, does not have spadelike forefeet, and is not so ambitious a digger. He often uses other animals' subways. His family boasts not only the world's tiniest mammals, weighing but a fraction of an ounce, but some of the fiercest. The short-tailed shrew, slashing lightning-fast, can paralyze a mouse with venomous bites. Most shrews have poison glands in their lower jaws. But the venom is secreted in such minute quantities that it has little effect on humans.

Nonetheless, some Eskimos fear the shrew, believing it can pierce a man's skin and enter his heart. One hunter told his tribesmen of a lucky escape. Meeting a shrew, he froze in his tracks until the tiny animal passed! The shrew's ferocious appetite, probably the source of this dread, knows no bounds. Put three together and what happens? Naturalist C. Hart Merriam found out. "Almost immediately they commenced fighting, and in a few minutes one was slaughtered and eaten by the other two. . . ." Eight hours later only one shrew remained and "its abdomen was much extended."

Feuding or feeding, the high-strung shrew leads a fast life. When excited, his heart beats 1,200 times a minute, and he may die of shock if picked up and handled. Solitary and quarrelsome, only when he mates does he live in peace. He fathers two or three broods a year, totaling as many as 20 honeybee-size young. Such prolificity insures his kind, for even if he escapes larger meat eaters, he may die of old age within a year and a half.

The mole, with a life expectancy twice the shrew's, sires about half as many offspring per year. Hard at work in the mines by two months of age, a mole seldom comes topside to tempt hawks and owls. Snakes, of course, are a threat any time, and if his lowlands flood, he may drown. The star-nosed species, however, takes readily to water, probing murky depths with his sensitive nose tentacles. But for real aquatic talent, consider the water shrew. He runs on water! Little pockets of air held in his feet enable him to sprint short distances on a calm surface.

Such feats, perhaps, help explain why moles and shrews have led charmed lives since the days of dinosaurs. Time has changed them little. They sleep sparingly, see practically nothing with their pinpoint eyes, and have precious little in the way of brains. Despite these handicaps, they keep right on burrowing. And unless man builds a better trap, they promise to be underfoot for a long while to come.

322

**Week-old least shrews** *(Cryptotis parva)* find two to a teaspoon roomy. Three inches long full-grown, these mobile peanuts, among the smallest of mammals, measure up when eating.

### The mole follows his nose grubbing for food

The sensitive pointed snout homes in on subterranean prey that broad hands unearth. Finding an insect, the mole often blocks escape by piling dirt on the victim, then tears it to bits. Or he may grab a worm and down it spaghetti-style.

His tunnel may meander half a mile, scarring lawns. Many home-owners, making mountains out of these molehills and ridges, combat the little hunter with traps and poison. Sometimes a dog digs him out.

# TOWNSEND MOLE

## Scapanus townsendii

POINTED NOSE, compact body braced with stout ribs, and flipperlike hands armed with strong claws all fit the Townsend mole for his main activity: digging. Undermining lush meadows in search of earthworms, grubs, and insects, he pushes up scores of mounds that mark the course of his tunnels at grass-root depth. Lower runways lead to chambers where three or four young are born in March. They develop rapidly and by June can make their own molehills.

The Townsend is North America's largest, handsomest species. In black plush fur, sought by trappers, he outshines the mousy eastern mole *(Scalopus aquaticus)*.

*Length* 7–9 in. *Weight* 4–6 oz. *Range:* Pacific Coast states. *Characteristics:* big out-turned hands, tapered snout.

# STAR-NOSED MOLE

## Condylura cristata

THIS MOLE has a face only a mother could love, and even she not for long. Born hairless, helpless, and with rose-colored tentacles blossoming on his snout, this child of spring can count on maternal care for no more than three weeks. Then, furred and self-sustaining, he and four or five litter mates leave their grass-lined nest and go their solitary ways.

Look for starnose in swamps and low meadows, where he'll risk capture to forage above ground. He eats worms, insects, crustaceans, even catches fish. He sculls in pools with his scaly tail. Active all year, he burrows in snow as readily as earth.

*Length* 7–8 in. *Weight* 2–3 oz. *Range:* Labrador to Georgia, west to N. Dakota. *Characteristics:* blackish fur, 22 tentacles.

# SHORT-TAILED SHREW

## Blarina brevicauda

"IT IS A RAVENING BEAST . . . it biteth deep, and poysoneth deadly," says a 17th century account of the shrew. Salivary glands of this savage little species contain enough cobralike venom to kill 200 mice! To fuel the ever-hungry machine of destruction, his sensitive, flexible nose is constantly probing for bugs, worms, and mice. Venturing above ground, the shrew becomes the hunted. Many birds and beasts—including other shrews—find him toothsome; others can't stomach the musky creature. Abroad all year, he reproduces fast enough to offset losses. In fact, he's one of the most plentiful mammals east of the Mississippi.

*Length* 3½–5 in. *Weight* ½–1 oz. *Range:* eastern states, S.E. Canada. *Characteristics:* pointed nose, short tail, thick gray fur.

# COMMON SHREW

## Sorex cinereus

FROM ARCTIC TO TROPICS, from lowland bogs to timber line, the common shrew displays uncommon adaptability. This fierce, sharp-nosed scamp has never submitted to taming. He pays little heed to hour, season, or climate in his quest for insects or mice. To keep pace, a man would have to consume 500 pounds of food a day.

No heavier than a penny, the shrew spends most of his life in dark tunnels or matted vegetation. In leafy mold or under a stump four to ten young, each weighing about 1/200 of an ounce, are born any time from spring to fall. Often the female becomes pregnant while still nursing a litter.

*Length* 3–4½ in. *Weight* to ⅕ oz. *Range:* Alaska south to New Mexico, North Carolina. *Characteristics:* slender, gray-brown.

325

**Four of North America's most skilled miners** pass in review: top, Townsend mole; center, star-nosed mole; bottom, short-tailed shrew (foreground) and common or masked shrew.

*Louis Agassiz Fuertes*

APELT ARMADILLO FARM, COURTESY OF "PEOPLE AND PLACES," AND (BELOW) LEONARD LEE RUE III, THREE LIONS

CHAPTER 24

# Armadillo, Mammal in Armor

NORTH AMERICA's oddest mammal has a scaled head like a lizard's, ears like a mule's, claws like a bear's, and a tail shaped like a rat's. He also wears a bony coat of mail like a conquistadore's. When the Spanish conquerors of Mexico saw him, they dubbed him armadillo—"little fellow in armor."

Related to sloths and anteaters, armadillos come in several sizes—five inches to five feet long—and are common in South and Central America. One species alone,

**Soft baby skin** hardens to a shell as the quadruplets (above) grow up. Threatened, the self-centered armadillo may curl into defensive ball.

the nine-banded armadillo (*Dasypus novemcinctus*), has invaded the United States. Until about 1870 this curiosity had appeared only in the Rio Grande country in Texas, where he is still known as "poor man's pig" because of his tasty flesh. From this foothold he has spread north to Kansas and Missouri and east into Louisiana and Mississippi. Introduced into Florida about 1920, he now flourishes there too.

His armor plate allows him to slip unscratched through the thorniest thickets of his scrubland haunts. He depends on it to protect him only as a last resort, preferring to take to the nearest burrow or even dig a fast foxhole (page 33). Though his armor is articulated — the nine "bands" are telescoping joints — it gives him a stiff gait and a clumsy gallop when alarmed. A man can overtake an armadillo, even creep close while the animal feeds, for eyesight and hearing are poor. He's an easy mark for the coyote, who flips him over and attacks the soft belly.

Foraging mostly at night, he dines on fire ants, roaches, tarantulas, and scorpions, and for a blander course, grubs, grasshoppers, and worms. Searching for insects, he may root up a garden, grunting and snuffling as he flicks out his sticky anteater tongue at savory morsels. To cross a creek, the armadillo gulps quantities of air, inflating his intestines so he can float like an airtight, ironclad *Monitor*. If the stream is small, he simply walks across on the bottom!

Quadruplets are customary, for the egg cell, when fertilized, splits four ways. The babies, born underground, are identical in every respect. The young nurse about two months, but are out foraging with their mother long before that. Their soft shell soon hardens, but bony plates come only with adulthood.

*Dasypus* sometimes has strange den mates. Side chambers of one armadillo's home were found occupied by a four-foot rattlesnake and a cottontail rabbit!

*Length* 2–2²/₃ ft. *Weight* 9–17 lbs. *Range:* central U. S. south to Panama. *Characteristics:* nine-banded shell, long claws, tapering plated tail, simplified teeth.

327

**Nine-banded armadillo** is named for overlapping plates at midriff, not joints of the tail.

*Louis Agassiz Fuertes*

# Bats,

**Frozen in mid-flight** by exposures
of a hundred-thousandth of a second,
the bat's flutter proves to be
a sweeping wing stroke. Ears cocked,
mouth agape, the little brown bat
guides himself by echoes of his
own supersonic cries.

HAROLD E. EDGERTON

**B**ATS! THE VERY WORD sends womenfolk scurrying for cover, hands clutching
their hair. Centuries of superstition, hair-raising stories of vampires, and a
few glimpses of elusive shapes darting through the evening sky—these make
up the average person's impressions of bats. Yet those we see in the United States
are beneficial, interesting, and usually harmless little mouse-size creatures, the
only vertebrates other than birds that can really fly.

Misconceptions? Bats do *not* get in women's hair. An animal that can wing its
tortuous way through pitch-black caves and thick forests is far too clever to get
tangled in anything as obvious as hair. Bats are *not* blind, nor are they birds. They
are mammals like ourselves, bearing live young that nurse at the breast.

Their wings are supported by greatly elongated finger bones. Skin stretches
between these bones, forming an exaggerated "webbed foot," the wing membrane.

CHAPTER 25

# Mystery Mammals of the Twilight

By DONALD R. GRIFFIN

329

**Free-tailed bats stream like smoke** from Ney Cave, Texas, summer home of millions. Last to leave meet the first returning. Such a sight led to discovery of Carlsbad Caverns, New Mexico.     331

**Tiny ogre's** teeth spell quick death to insects. Voracious bats subsist on moths, mosquitoes, fruit flies, and other insect enemies of man. No species found in the United States bites humans except in self-defense; most have teeth too small to puncture the skin. *Myotis velifer,* shown three times life size (left), weighs ¼ ounce.

HOWARD N. SLOANE AND (OPPOSITE) ROBERT W. MITCHELL

**Mysterious homing instinct** sends bats back, year after year, to winter in the same cave. There they squeeze together, like the disturbed freetails staring from the wall of Ney Cave (left) or the social bats of *Myotis sodalis* clustered in Kentucky's Bat Cave (above). During winter's long sleep, the mammals become stiff and cold; breathing almost stops. Here in Bat Cave a speleologist seeks banded specimens among the colony of some 5,000.

Bats are furred and have well-developed teeth which they use if picked up or frightened. Small bats only prick the skin, and bats are *not* poisonous. The legendary vampire that bites sleeping animals and men and laps their blood is found only in the tropics. But any bat or small mammal can transmit rabies, so its bite should be avoided.

Most bats in the United States belong to the family *Vespertilionidae,* which feeds exclusively on insects. Those in the north, lacking winter food, must hibernate or migrate. Cave bats, including little brown bats, pipistrels, and big brown bats, flock by thousands to the same caves each winter. I have seen hundreds hanging on a few square feet of rock, packed as tight as they can squeeze.

The less abundant tree bats — red bats, hoary bats, and silver-haired bats — do not gather in large colonies and seldom enter buildings. They spend the day in trees, apart from one another, and migrate south for the winter. Late summer finds them at Mount Desert Rock, 30 miles off the Maine coast, and at the barren tip of Cape Cod, where bats usually aren't seen. They alight on ships 200 miles at sea, and some show up in Bermuda in autumn—a flight of more than 600 miles over open ocean.

Cave bats migrate too; for example, from caveless areas in eastern New England to the limestone caves farther west. Interest in these migrations led me to band cave bats on weekends. More than 30 of us made winter trips from Harvard to distant caves, often doing the last lap on snowshoes. Disappointments came when some "enormous cavern" turned out to be a measly porcupine lair.

Most New England caves are hard to squeeze into. Exploring them often meant a belly crawl through water and mud to reach higher rooms with their clusters of bats, mostly little brown bats. Once I asked a fellow bat hunter to explore a narrow side passage. As his feet disappeared I heard a muffled remark. A porcupine was just ahead of him! Another zealous assistant remained at his post in an old mine, plucking bats from the wall even after rocks began falling from the roof. Rotting timbers make abandoned mines especially hazardous.

## Camera reveals how bats snare dinner on the wing

An old-world species, the horseshoe bat, scoops up a moth in his wingtip. One-fifth of a second later, in this double-exposure picture, the bat has the moth clenched in his jaws. White marker on background shows how far the bat has moved to the right.

Other high-speed photographs, made during studies by the Lincoln Laboratory of the Massachusetts Institute of Technology, show brown bats fielding meal worms with their tail structures. Scientists once assumed that the prey was caught in the bat's mouth.

Bats used in the project found their food by flying an orbit above a special gun that popped a worm into the air. As the bat swooped, a sequence camera caught the action and a super-high-fidelity tape recorder registered each beep.

Scientists hope someday to learn how the bat recognizes his own echo in a cave teeming with thousands of other bats, and how he distinguishes food from obstacles.

FREDERIC WEBSTER AND DONALD R. GRIFFIN

In a cave where the air is 33° F., body temperature of hibernating bats may be 33.5°. They feel cold and are stiff and unresponsive; it takes a close look to tell they aren't dead. But if handled or even disturbed by lights and talking, they awaken and soon are as lively as ever, with temperature, circulation, and respiration back to normal.

In fair weather we banded the bats outside, then released them in the cave. After flying around a few minutes they hung up again and relapsed into torpor. On later visits we'd find them in different places. Probably they wake up from time to time, fly about a bit, and perhaps venture out to see if spring has come.

If the cave is too warm, metabolism speeds up, they use stored fat too fast and starve to death. But temperatures mustn't fall below freezing. One November I found three or four hundred bats in a Vermont cave with a large entrance that let cold in. When I returned in February, many bats hung dead from the icy roof. Others were entombed in icicles. Most had awakened and left for another cave.

Bats mate in both spring and fall, even in the caves in winter. After fall matings the sperm stay alive in the female's uterus and resume activity in spring when

LINCOLN LABORATORY, M.I.T., AND (INSET AND OPPOSITE) W. E. GARRETT, NATIONAL GEOGRAPHIC STAFF

actual fertilization occurs. With warm weather, bats begin to leave the caves. Females take off first and assemble in "maternity wards," breeding colonies secluded in old buildings or hollow trees. Here each bears one or two young around the middle of June. Weighing a fourth to a fifth as much as the mother, the baby bat clings firmly to her fur and to a nipple.

Owls, hawks, perhaps a cat or snake may catch a few of the young. But on the whole, bats live remarkably free from the threat of sudden death. I recaptured one that had been banded 19½ years before. Since young are born in summer, this Methuselah must have been more than 20 years old.

MANY SCIENTISTS have sought to explain the bat's uncanny ability to fly in darkness, avoiding trees and telegraph wires, threading narrow, winding cave passages, even locating flying insects to feed on. In the 18th century the

Italian scientist Lazaro Spallanzani wrote that bats which had been blinded could fly about a room, missing walls, furniture, and silk threads stretched in their path. His Swiss friend Louis Jurine discovered that bats lost this ability when their hearing was impaired. Somehow, then, their ears helped guide them. Incredulous zoologists quipped: "Since bats see with their ears, do they hear with their eyes?"

Solution to Spallanzani's "bat problem" came at long last when Harvard physicist G. W. Pierce developed an electronic device to detect sounds of higher pitch than the human ear can hear. Holding a bat before this apparatus, we discovered it was emitting loud supersonic cries which the detector could translate into sounds audible to us. It seemed feasible that the echoes of these sounds, bouncing off obstacles ahead, enabled bats to dodge them.

Dr. Robert Galambos and I repeated Spallanzani's and Jurine's experiments. With black collodion we blindfolded our bats. They flew quite as well as ever. But lightly plugging both ears caused them to strike wire obstacles. We tied the jaws of several and sealed their lips with collodion. They blundered helplessly into wires, furniture, walls, even into us. If a bat recovered its orientation, we would turn the microphone toward it and invariably find that it had managed to crack the collodion and was again crying its ultrasonic signals.

Bats fly, then, by echolocation, picking up echoes of their own high-frequency sounds. Blindfolded, they can fly full speed between vertical 16-gauge wires 12, even 10 inches apart. As they hear echoes from the wires, they bank or pull in their wings to pass through.

The tapping of a blind man's cane is a form of echolocation. Many blind persons can move freely without striking obstacles. Most have no clear idea how they do this, but studies at Cornell University have shown that they lose the ability if their ears are plugged. In fog, ship captains use echolocation to detect cliffs or rocks. They give a blast on the whistle and listen for the echo. The sonic depth finder or fathometer sends sound waves through water and times the interval between sound and echo. The Navy's sonar similarly spots submarines, icebergs, or rocks.

You'll often hear that "bats have radar." This isn't strictly true. Radar uses radio waves, not sound waves as does the bat.

Next time you see a fluttering, shadowy bat erratically chasing insects in the summer twilight, don't shudder. If one flies in a window, don't belabor him with brooms and tennis rackets. This is no leather-winged dragon, but a harmless, intriguing little beast with a long evolutionary history of instrument flying.

**On target!** A brown bat emits beeps as he closes on his prey; big ears pick up echoes from the insect (opposite). The hunter's tiny brain computes the data and controls his speed and direction. To trace the beeps, pitched too high for human ears, a specialist adjusts an oscilloscope (inset).

Macbeth, a star performer, gets a drink of water (right).

# FREE-TAILED BAT
## *Tadarida brasiliensis*

AT CARLSBAD CAVERNS National Park the sky darkens each summer evening with a stream of bats pouring from the cave mouth.

"At the rate of 300 a second, the bats take four hours to clear the exit," reports a park naturalist. Of these four million-odd, the majority are free-tailed bats, most abundant species of the South and Southwest.

Membrane encloses the tail on most bats. *Tadarida*'s tail extends free about an inch. Head and body are flat, ears cock forward like twin visors. Free-tailed bats can squeeze into the slightest crevice. Many an old adobe building reeks with their musky odor and may hold a profitable cache of their guano, valuable for fertilizer.

Some 100,000 tons of Carlsbad Caverns' guano sold for up to $90 a ton. One Mexican earned more keeping bats in his two extra rooms than he could get in rent.

*Wingspan* about 12 in. *Weight* ⅓–½ oz. *Range:* Oregon to S. Carolina, south to S. America. *Characteristic:* free, hairless tail.

# LITTLE BROWN BAT
## *Myotis lucifugus*

WHO HAS NOT SEEN a pair of little brown bats flitting about the yard on a summer evening? They are abundant throughout the United States and hibernate in any cave with the right winter temperature.

About mid-May females leave caves and cluster in old buildings where they can bear young in safety. Bats in the belfry? Of course. It's a perfect place. The mother prepares no nest, but hangs by wing hooks as well as feet, curls her tail up to form an apron, and delivers her enormous, naked baby. (Imagine a woman bearing a 30-pound child!) She suckles her infant a few days, even while hunting, then hangs it up.

Her flight is fast and erratic. Sometimes she lowers her tail membrane like a net and scoops up an insect in mid-air. She grooms like a cat, even moistens the "thumb" of a wing and twiddles it inside her ear.

*Wingspan* about 10 in. *Weight* ¼–⅓ oz. *Range:* Alaska to Labrador, south to California, Georgia. *Characteristic:* round ears.

# RED BAT

## *Lasiurus borealis*

A BOY WALKING through a city square found a young red bat and took it home to feed. Later he carried it across the same square and was spotted by the mother bat. Circling, she finally dared to land on his chest. Maternal love overruled fear.

The devoted mother red bat clasps her two to four babies to her bosom and flies off to hunt, though their combined weight may approach hers. Narrow, tapered wings give the species speed and endurance.

Our most familiar tree bat, the red prefers twilight to full darkness for hunting. It sleeps on the sunny side of a tree and generally keeps to itself. But at autumn's first nip the reds join in small flocks and head south. Forsaking the typical swoops and darts of insect-hunting, they settle down to a steady, mile-eating pace that takes them far over open ocean.

*Wingspread* about 12 in. *Weight* $1/4-1/2$ oz. *Range:* Canada to Panama, except Rockies. *Characteristic:* frosted red fur.

# PALLID BAT

## *Antrozous pallidus*

BIG-EARED BAT is an apt alternate name for the pallid. Like radar screens, its $1\frac{1}{2}$-inch ears pick up and filter the echoing signals that pinpoint a hapless insect.

Swooping low, it plumps to the ground to seize a cricket and have a leisurely meal. The pallid bat has this distinction: it has been caught in mouse traps!

This cave bat holes up by day, squeaking and scrambling around its perch before settling down. But when evening falls, those big wings and remarkable ears go to work. The pallid beats its wings slower than many other bats, but still makes 10 or 11 thrusting strokes per second. At dusk it is sometimes seen at desert pools, scooping up a drink on the fly.

Its young, one or two, arrive in early June. In fall some northern bats migrate south. Others have been found dormant.

*Wingspread* about 14 in. *Weight* $2/3$ oz. *Range:* Pacific Northwest south into Mexico. *Characteristics:* big ears, pale fur.

# The Ocean Dwellers

MASQUERADING in sporty black and white, the killer whale
shows his true colors when his cavernous belly clamors for food.
He hurtles into a herd of seals, downing one after another.
A school of killers, ravenous as any wolf pack, will
overpower a giant gray whale and tear its tongue out.
Yankee whalemen in their puny boats proved deadlier still.
Armed with harpoon and lance, they scorned Leviathan's
awesome bulk and took his measure in barrels of oil.
A 45-barrel sperm whale was average; 80 was "greasy luck."
Seals and walruses also yielded blubber, but it was the
fur seal's lustrous pelt that lured ruthless fortune hunters.
Their greed transformed the fog-shrouded Pribilof
breeding grounds into islands of reeking death.
International law at long last came to govern the harvest
of ocean mammals. Too late was this protection to save
the sea cow that once grazed in the Bering Sea.
Its relative, the manatee, survives off
Florida's coasts and, though lacking golden
tresses, keeps alive the mermaid myth.

**Steller sea lions,** hot bodies steaming in icy Bering Sea waters, frolic at Sealion Rock, a rookery

FISHERMEN'S WHARF in Monterey, California, seemed strangely deserted for such a balmy September Sunday. Missing were the camera-laden visitors, the window-shoppers, the fair-weather promenaders; their absence puzzled me. Then two youngsters dashed past. "Hurry up!" one implored. I watched them race to the end of the boardwalk—and the mystery was solved. There, jammed against the guardrail, were the pier's patrons. My first thought was that some unfortunate had toppled into the harbor, but cheers and laughter spelled frivolity. Curious, I wedged forward.

Like torpedoes flashing through the water, a pod of sea lions was treating spectators to an amazing aquacade. In a wild game of dive and glide, they leaped clear of the surface, rolled atop one wave and under the next, into a sun splash and out of it. What zest! The show was more spectacular than any I had witnessed in circus or zoo. Suddenly the streamlined bodies streaked toward a breakwater. Puffing and snorting, they clambered atop tumbled boulders. The metamorphosis was startling; superbly graceful in the sea, they emerged as the most awkward where thousands mass in summer.

CHAPTER 26

# Seals, Sea Lions, and Walruses

By JAY JOHNSTON

pedestrians imaginable. It was like watching a ballerina do a pirouette, then fall on her face. But such a contrast is characteristic of all the "finfeet" — the sea lions, walruses, and hair seals that make up the order *Pinnipedia*.

Eons ago the ancestors of these warm-blooded mammals were land rovers. Little by little, through countless millenniums, their physical structure became fashioned for a life in the sea, the element where few learn from experience because few earn a second chance. Seals spend most of their lives there: they find their food there, sometimes sleep there. Yet the land still claims them, for they must leave the water to bear and suckle their young.

The sea is the pinniped's playground, and he revels in it. His whole anatomy is designed for underwater excursions. When diving, his heart may beat only one-tenth its regular rate, yet pumps a normal supply of blood to brain and other vital organs. His big veins and arteries carry more blood, weight for weight, than a man's. His red blood cells store enough oxygen to let him stay under 20 minutes or more. Rapid blood-clotting, as fast as five seconds in the northern fur seal, may spell the

343

## Cyrano of seals, the elephant seal sports a monstrous nose

Guarding his bevy of cows, he keeps a wary eye on the intruder. If cornered, he roars, huge snout swelling, and brandishes big canine teeth that can inflict ugly wounds.

Hunted almost to extinction in the 19th century, this 2½-ton giant among seals is staging a comeback on California's coastal islands. Like heaps of fat sausages, these elephant seals sprawl on the sands of San Miguel. Stains and battle scars blemish their rough hides.

A harem member (left) is blessed with a neater nose than her mate's. "Mermaids with tennis-ball eyes," one observer dubbed the cows. Those big, banjo eyes help the elephant seal find much of its food at night.

ED N. HARRISON AND (ABOVE) BATES LITTLEHALES, NATIONAL GEOGRAPHIC PHOTOGRAPHER difference between life and death when a seal is wounded in a mating battle or by shark or killer whale.

Five-toed, webbed hind limbs, clumsiest of appendages on land or ice, convert to powerful paddles in the waves. Foreflippers fit snugly against the body or move out to correct steering and balance. Such equipment serves seals well, for they are migratory animals. Northern fur seals journey as much as 3,000 miles through the Pacific to reach their breeding grounds; some Atlantic seals travel upwards of 2,000 miles a year.

An estimated 12 to 26 million pinnipeds, representing 31 species, inhabit the world's seas. Science divides them into three groups. The hair seal family, *Phocidae*, is perhaps best adapted for marine living. Known also as the earless seals, the sleek-headed creatures maneuver effortlessly in the water. But on land they hump along like outsize caterpillars, dragging hind limbs which cannot turn forward. Shorter forefeet and necks distinguish hair seals from *Otariidae*, the sea lions and fur seals.

These are the eared seals. They can rotate their hind limbs forward, enabling them to travel better on land. Their long necks taper to a spray of whiskers. But

**Harp seal pup,** trusting as any newborn babe, wears his finest fur as swaddling clothes. In a month he'll get a gray coat.

no seal looks so venerable as the mustachioed walrus. The walrus's family name, *Odobenidae*, means literally that tusks help him walk. His long ivories do come in handy when he climbs aboard a floe, but he uses his flippers for walking.

Structurally, the finfeet have much in common with land carnivores. German naturalist Georg Steller, when sailing the Bering Sea in 1741, described fur seals as "sea bears." Like bears and other carnivores, seals and walruses have claws, generally smaller than those of land mammals, and teeth which grasp and tear. Strictly flesh eaters, they feed on squid, fish, crustaceans, and mollusks.

The richest milk in all mammaldom—up to 53 per cent fat in the gray seal—nourishes young pinnipeds. Born after eight to 12 months' gestation, they usually stay close to their food supply, although they can swim and move about on land from the first. They grow rapidly; many double their weight the first two weeks. A 100-pound elephant seal infant may balloon into a 400-pounder in less than a month! Young pinnipeds love to play. They frolic in the surf, play king-of-the-hill, engage in mock battle. Only after two to five years do they become sexually mature.

**Snorting, bellowing walruses** churn toward Twin Islet in the bleak Bering Sea. Eskimos esteem

North America's coastal waters harbor 14 species of finfeet, ranging in size from the lithe, 100-pound ringed seal to the hulking elephant seal, weighing as much as 8,000 pounds. Pinnipeds boast impressive census figures, bolstered chiefly by the harp, ringed, and fur seal hordes. Nevertheless, the population has steadily decreased over the last 200 years. In fact, the Caribbean monk seal, now perhaps extinct, began its decline when Columbus paid his second visit to the New World in 1494; his crewmen found the unwary creature easy prey in Haitian waters.

Fast disappearing from Newfoundland's shores is the curious hooded or bladdernose seal, so named because of the pouch on top of the adult male's snout, "which it can inflate and draw down like a cap." Other species, such as the stocky gray seal found from the Gulf of St. Lawrence to northern Europe, have dwindled to a few hundreds or thousands in American waters. Ever since prehistoric man discovered that the seal's fur provided warm clothing and its meat filled empty bellies, human hunters have stalked the finfeet relentlessly.

Early each summer northern fur seals converge on the bleak Pribilof Islands in the Bering Sea. These are the isles of their birth, and here they return each year to breed. When Russian explorers first occupied the Pribilofs in 1786, an estimated five million seals swarmed over the islands. Fortune hunters thronged to the rookeries; soon rotting carcasses, stripped of their hides, were piled high on the beaches. Orphaned young died by the thousands. Eventually the Russian government halted the animal's dark flesh, carve curios from the ivory tusks, and cover boats with the split hide.

this ruthless waste of a valuable source of fur. But when the United States gained control of the islands with the purchase of Alaska in 1867, Americans copied the tactics of early sealers. Schooner after schooner prowled the Bering, killing animals at sea as well as in their rookeries. Some ships garnered many thousands of skins on a single voyage. Within half a century the Pribilof herd had shrunk to little more than 100,000. The fur seal faced almost certain extinction.

Top-hatted diplomats of the United States, Russia, Japan, and Great Britain finally took the fur seal's plight to heart. Their four-power agreement, signed in 1911, put an end to the mass slaughter. Today U. S. wildlife officials zealously guard the Pribilof seals, permitting an annual harvest of some 40,000 skins from the herd of about 1,500,000. Recently some females were taken to reduce the herd. Ordinarily, Aleuts employed by the government move into the "hauling grounds" of the islands, a sort of bachelors' quarters apart from the rookeries, and kill only young, unattached males. Pelts are soaked in cold sea water, scraped free of blubber, and cured in brine, then shipped to fur processors where they will emerge as sealskin coats—the soft, sleek, expensive wraps made fashionable by Russia's Catherine the Great. Processors remove the coarse outer hair, leaving the silky plush of the inner coat, tan the pelts, and brush in vegetable dye. A single skin requires more than 100 manipulations or treatments.

Each spring along the ice-crusted top of North America, from Baffin Island to

**A provoked walrus** is a ton and a half of fury—as arctic explorer Willem Barents's crew learned off Novaya Zemlya in 1596. The bull defied boathooks, oars, axes to sink his tusks into the gunwale. Old Norse sailors called the ungainly mammal *hvalross,* or whale horse.

eastern Greenland, the yapping and crying of seal pups swell to a throaty chorus, marking the end of the long arctic night. The vast icefields break up into creaking rafts that drift southward, carrying colonies of harp seals and the rarer hooded seals within reach of the hunter. The harp, unlike the fur seal of the Pacific, is valued more for its oil and leather than for its fur. A century ago as many as 600 vessels, manned by 20,000 hunters, took part in the harvest. The tall-masted ships, built of greenheart and oak, massively timbered and with iron-sheathed bows, sailed

348   OCEAN DWELLERS

in stately procession out of St. John's, Newfoundland, and Halifax, Nova Scotia. Day after day, week after week, they smashed and shuddered through the ice pans. In good years the fleet brought in more than half a million seals, and crews split earnings in excess of a million dollars. But tumbling market prices for the oil and skins have wrecked the industry. In recent years few Canadian ships have participated in the hunt, and their annual catch averages under 100,000 seals.

Biggest finfoot of northern waters is the walrus. This giant of the polar seas is to the Eskimo what the bison was to the plains Indian. Virtually every part of the walrus finds a use. The meat and blubber yield food and oil; the tough brown hide makes harnesses, rope, and shelters; the ivory tusks are carved into tools and ornaments.

But the very existence of the species is threatened by those most dependent on it. Once hunting the walrus by stealth and cunning, Eskimos have grown trigger-happy since discarding harpoons for rifles. In Pacific waters they probably kill more walruses each year than are born. With the harpoon line, few that were killed were lost. Today, of some 2,000 shot off Alaska each year, only half are recovered. Two centuries ago the Atlantic walrus frequented the Gulf of St. Lawrence; now it's no longer seen south of Hudson Strait.

I N THE EYES OF THE HUNTER the seal represents a wealth of oil-rich blubber encased in a glossy pelt. But to nonhunters the world over he's an entertainer—the clown with whiskers who can play catch, do handstands, or balance a glass of water on the tip of his snout. He's the California sea lion, that streak of black lightning zipping back and forth in a pool, the sad-faced trencherman who sits up and begs another scrap of fish.

Trainers who have worked with this sea lion, famous to audiences as the trained "seal" of the circus, rank him one of our most intelligent animals. "His bag of tricks is limited

**Fur seal, sea lion, and Steller sea cow** embellish the chart of a Russian officer who sailed with Vitus Bering in 1741. The first two are still plentiful in arctic waters. The 30-foot, 6,000-pound sea cow, slaughtered for its meat, became extinct near the end of the 18th century.

**Northern fur seals,** docile as sheep, go to their last roundup in the Pribilofs, five tiny islands some 300 miles off Alaska's mainland. Aleut sealers have sorted these surplus three-year-old bachelors from herds that crowd the breeding beaches each summer. Protection plus scientific harvesting maintains the fur seal's ranks. The Pribilof seals have repaid Alaska's purchase price nearly twice over. Aleut boy (left) cradles a sick pup.

VICTOR B. SCHEFFER, U. S. FISH AND WILDLIFE SERVICE, AND (BELOW LEFT) KARL W. KENYON

only by the instructor's ability to make him understand what he wants," says a sea lion trainer who puts his troupe through its lively paces at Marineland of the Pacific near Los Angeles.

Young males between one and two years old and not too heavy (under 200 pounds) prove the best pupils. After hearing certain commands repeated over and over, the animal recognizes the words and associates them with specific actions. Once it can do the simpler tricks—shaking hands, applauding with flippers—the more complicated routines come easier. At the San Diego Zoo, 130 miles south

JAY JOHNSTON, NATIONAL GEOGRAPHIC STAFF

of Marineland, Capt. Benny Kirkbride and his sea lions perform daily in a sunny amphitheater known as Wegeforth Bowl. Like any household, his menagerie has its outbursts of temperament. "If I had a dime for every time I've been bitten, I'd be rich," he said. "When a sea lion bites," he cautions, "don't jerk your hand away or you'll get a bad gash. I simply leave my hand in his mouth until he decides to let go. He always does — eventually."

If tempers get out of control, so does the fun. Kirkbride wryly recalls the time he stepped back too far and fell into the pool. "Of course the audience roared. And when I came up sputtering I could swear those clowns of mine were laughing too."

Sometimes pinnipeds outsmart humans. In World War II the Swedish Navy conceived a unique method of submarine warfare. Bomb-toting seals were trained to hunt down submarines girdled with gobs

352

"Hold it, hold it!" Jerry, a California sea lion, performs at the San Diego Zoo. A diet of fish supplemented by vitamins keeps him sleek and fit — though sea lions can get ulcers. Fur seals (below), returned from a fishing trip in the Bering Sea, listen for their bleating pups. Even among tens of thousands, a mother unerringly singles out her youngster.

KARL W. KENYON AND (RIGHT) NEW YORK ZOOLOGICAL SOCIETY

of fresh herring. Intensive tests proved the system perfect—except for one flaw. The seals looked with disdain upon any submarine *not* garnished with herring.

Nowadays, whenever I see a seal in a zoo or on a stage, I recall the carefree creatures gamboling in Monterey harbor. And the age-old question again comes to mind: Is it fair to capture these happy-go-lucky animals? Capt. Richard Headley, of Santa Barbara, one of the few California fishermen licensed to catch seals and sea lions, argues "Yes."

While aboard his trawler, appropriately named *Seal,* I watched him net and crate three sea lions in a rock-walled cove on Santa Cruz Island, 30 miles off the coast.

"I don't feel sorry for my captives," he said. "I've seen bulls with eyes ripped out and lips torn to shreds after a battle in the breeding grounds. I've seen disease wipe out an entire herd. Killer whales and white sharks patrol the waters about the rookeries and take their toll too."

Captives have an easy time, he concluded. "They live in style with big swimming pools, plenty of food, and no battles. And above all, their human visitors wear smiles instead of guns."

Olaf, a 3,000-pound Atlantic walrus, leads the life of Riley in the New York Aquarium at Coney Island. If he had to grub in the sea, he'd ruin his elegant mustache.

*A Portfolio*

Following are biographies of the major North American seals and sea lions, and the walrus, illustrated in full color with paintings by Walter A. Weber, Carl Rungius, and Louis Agassiz Fuertes, and with photographs. Lengths and weights show the range (sometimes great) between average female and large male.

**California sea lions** cram an oceanside tenement washed by Pacific swells. Atop

*Walter A. Weber, National Geographic staff artist*

each tablelike rock a lordly bull guards his harem while the cows attend their pups.

355

# CALIFORNIA SEA LION

## *Zalophus californianus*

"BIGGEST SHOW-OFF in the animal kingdom," a noted sea lion trainer says of this energetic mammal. Playful and gregarious even in the wild, it is the trained "seal" of stage, zoo, and circus.

Its coat ranges from buff to sepia, but glistens black when wet. Ashore the bulky yet agile animal can run almost as fast as a man. Larger than any of the earless seals, an adult male sea lion may measure eight feet long and exceed 600 pounds. The female, far shorter, rarely tops 300.

An estimated 16,000 California sea lions bask and breed on remote islands and rocks along the Californian and Mexican coasts. They feed on squid, octopus, deepwater crabs, and a variety of fishes. Sharp, interlocking teeth clinch the slippery morsels. Sometimes the animals swallow pebbles; science is not sure why. Yarning sealers say they're ballast! A more likely theory: the stones function as food grinders, since the animals bolt food without chewing.

With summer's approach, cows and young bulls raft together off the rookeries.

Mature males usually arrive in early July. Old patriarchs maintain harems and vigorously defend chosen bits of beach as their territories. A cow, fertile at three years, whelps a single pup a year; within days after giving birth she mates again.

Like the young of other eared seals, the pup tests his swimming prowess in tidal pools before venturing to sea. Blue eyes darken, blackish coat lightens as he matures. He will stick close to mother perhaps the rest of the year. Some sea lions wander hundreds of miles between breeding seasons; older bulls are more sedentary. Captives may live 20 years. In the wild, sharks and killer whales cut life short.

Despite its leonine label, the sea lion doesn't roar; it honks or barks. Its name has long puzzled etymologists. Some see its origin in the lionlike face. And naturalist Thomas Pennant had observed: "Along the neck of the male is a mane of stiff curled hair . . . such as distinguish a Lion." Actually, face and head resemble a dog's more than a cat's.

*Length* 5½–8 ft. *Weight* 175–600 lbs. *Range:* S. British Columbia to Lower California. *Characteristics:* pointed head, external ears; bull has mane, high forehead.

**Sleepy-eyed sea lion** idles below a Monterey, California, pier and begs handouts from visitors.

**Barrel-chested Steller bull** stays proudly aloof from the gossip of one of his slender wives.

# STELLER SEA LION

## *Eumetopias jubata*

SEEK THE STELLER SEA LION on bleak headlands where chill seas crash against the cliffs. This is the favored habitat of the largest of eared seals, named for Georg Wilhelm Steller, the German naturalist who first described the species in 1741. He called it "lion of the sea," noting the male's swollen neck and leonine eyes, with their golden pupils and white irises. This robust, bellowing beast can outswim any of the hair seals, and its high-diving would shame an Olympic champion. Captive specimens are rare, for the belligerent behemoth is hard to train.

Badge of a big bull is his scarred hide. Veteran of many mating battles, he takes no food while he guards his harem of about a dozen cows. Hunters respect his angry charges, yet claim that suddenly opening and closing an umbrella will drive him back! At sea he fears only the killer whale.

In the Barren Islands in the Gulf of Alaska some 15,000 Stellers mass in spring and summer. Smaller herds frequent the Pribilofs and the Aleutians, and one herd of about 1,000 breeds on the Oregon coast.

A pup weighs perhaps 30 or 40 pounds at birth, and its slate-gray coat blends with its rock-bound nursery. At two it gets the adult's thick yellow-gold back fur and red-brown belly. A grown bull may weigh a ton, a cow only a quarter as much.

Aleut hunters ate the Steller's flesh, burned its oil in lamps, made thread from its sinews. Today fishermen pose a greater threat, for man and sea lion compete for salmon. Though Stellers subsist largely on scrap fish, diving 400 or 500 feet for food, state laws permit killing them whenever they interfere with commercial fishing.

*Length* 7–12 ft. *Weight* 400–2,200 lbs. *Range:* California coast to north Pacific islands. *Characteristics:* larger than California sea lion, head less pointed, no crest.

*Carl Rungius, courtesy of New York Zoological Society*

**Guadalupe Island's** handsome namesakes today find sanctuary on its dark and rocky headlands.

## GUADALUPE FUR SEAL

*Arctophoca townsendi*

THIS THICK-NECKED, dusky fur seal has shown its foxlike profile to few humans in the last 150 years. Many summers ago Guadalupe Island off Lower California teemed with breeding herds and bleating young. The surf was alive with animals that rolled in the water and tousled their fur. But by 1830 they were gone; not one hoarse growl could be heard on the island. Sealers had slaughtered so many that the species was believed extinct.

Forty years later small herds appeared; again hunters wiped them out. Biologist Charles H. Townsend, whence the breed gets its scientific name, found only bleached bones on Guadalupe's beaches in 1892.

The fur bearer did not reappear until 1928, when a fisherman sold two young males to the San Diego Zoo. Reports trickled in of other sightings, but few were verified. Then in 1954 an expedition discovered a small breeding colony on Guadalupe. Today the herd numbers a thousand. Scientists hope the seal is here to stay.

*Length* 4–6 ft. *Weight* 150–300 lbs. *Range:* off southern California and Lower California. *Characteristics:* pointed nose, grizzled on head and neck.

358

**Burly sultan of the Pribilofs, a fur seal awaits his harem.**

# NORTHERN FUR SEAL

## *Callorhinus ursinus*

BREEDING BULLS, fat and strong from a winter of ease and feasting, wallow ashore on the Pribilof rookeries early in May. To the victors in fierce battles go choice stations near the water. In late June females inundate the beaches. Promenading the shore, burly 600-pound beachmasters coax the newcomers to their harems, which may include 100 cows. Any female that plays coy is bitten, mauled, and dragged until she obeys the suitor, six times her size.

Soon after already pregnant cows give birth to single pups, they are ready to conceive next year's brood. At the height of the season, in mid-July, a pup is born every five seconds! Jet black, eyes open, the 10- to 12-pound infant downs nearly a gallon of milk at a meal. He's not weaned for three or four months and will starve if orphaned, for no cow adopts another's young.

During the summer-long breeding season, bulls dare not go near the water to feed, lest covetous neighbors kidnap their mates. When winter gales strike, females and pups head south. Rib-lean and scarred, the exhausted bulls quit their posts.

*Length* 4½ – 8 ft. *Weight* 100 – 700 lbs. *Range:* breed on Bering Sea islands, winter south to California and Japan. *Characteristics:* blunt face, short pointed nose.

HARRY W. MAY, FOUKE FUR COMPANY

Louis Agassiz Fuertes

**Harbor seals**, nicknamed leopard for their spots, loll with **harp seals**, unaware hunters are near.

# HARBOR SEAL
## *Phoca vitulina*

NOSING INTO INLETS and rivers along both coasts, this intelligent, attractive animal is North America's most familiar seal. Yet he never fails to excite bathers as he bobs offshore or basks on a ledge.

Many a yachtsman in Puget Sound or on the Maine coast has met a harbor seal — suddenly there he is, peering intently at the boat with big, dewy eyes; then he slips underwater as quietly as he surfaced. What a shock to meet one in Lake Champlain! Yet harbor seals have been captured there, after coming up the St. Lawrence.

Disdaining large colonies and harems, harbor seals form small family bands and stay close to shore. Pups arrive in spring, white and woolly. In northern waters they keep this baby fur a week or two; farther south they shed it immediately to grow their typical coarse coats, ranging from yellowish gray with dark spots to near-black with light spots.

The devoted mother shields her pup from danger and offers it a broad back to rest on when it tires of swimming. As soon as she weans it, she may mate again. Gestation is 9½ months.

Harbor seals have doglike faces, ears that are mere openings in the head, and hind flippers that serve when swimming but are useless on land. Though shy, they make affectionate pets and can be taught to do tricks. Eskimos value their flesh and blubber and consider the liver a delicacy.

*Length* 4½–5½ ft. *Weight* 100–250 lbs. *Range:* Atlantic and Pacific, south to North Carolina and California. *Characteristics:* small size; spotted; doglike face.

# HARP SEAL
## *Phoca groenlandica*

A MARCH BLIZZARD HOWLS across the drift ice off Labrador, blanketing close-packed herds of harp seals. Newborn pups wail for attention as their mothers pop through holes in the ice. The baby lumps of snowy wool are known as "white-coats" to sealers, who prize the fur. The piebald adults, named for their harplike markings, are also called "saddle-backs."

For a couple of weeks the nursing mother builds up her pup from 12 to 60 or 70 pounds — then simply abandons it. For a week or two the youngster lives off its blubber, shedding baby fur for a gray coat. Finally it musters up courage to flop off the ice and try a new diet of crustaceans and fish. Later it joins the adults on the long trip north to summer hunting areas.

With three main breeding grounds — off Newfoundland, Iceland, and in the White Sea — these migratory seals total four or five million. Valued for hides, fur, and oil, hundreds of thousands are taken every year.

*Length* 5–7 ft. *Weight* 200–500 lbs. *Range:* Nova Scotia to Baffin Bay and Barents Sea. *Characteristic:* harplike band.

# RIBBON SEAL
## *Phoca fasciata*

ANTISOCIABILITY proves a boon to this rare hair seal. Traveling singly or in small groups on pack ice, it foils mass slaughter. Eskimos prize the hide, which makes decorative waterproof bags. The male, with dark brown coat and distinct yellowish bands, outshines his paler, grayer mate.

*Length* 4½–6 ft. *Weight* 100–200 lbs. *Range:* Bering Strait to Aleutians and Sea of Okhotsk. *Characteristic:* banded coat.

**A ribbon seal meets white death** on the ice, falling victim to the stealthy, savage polar bear.

# WALRUS

## *Odobenus rosmarus*

MONARCH OF THE POLAR SEAS, the walrus doesn't flinch at raging storms and bitter cold. He will sleep on a floe, pack ice grinding in his ears. Hungry, he'll dive as deep as 300 feet to the ocean floor and stand on his head to dig clams and other mollusks with his long tusks. He scoops in food with spikelike bristles on his muzzle. Powerful back teeth crack the shells.

Walruses drift south with the ice into the Bering Sea in autumn and swim back to the Arctic Ocean in spring. Although a strong and fairly rapid swimmer, the walrus cannot swim indefinitely. When tired he must find ice or land or drown. Calves, cows, and bulls travel together, bellowing and trumpeting like a herd of elephants.

Mating and calving take place on the ice in spring. Bulls, although polygamous, do not collect harems, but broken ivories attest to many a courtship battle. The female, unlike her seal relatives, does not mate in the same year that she calves; every second year she gives birth to a single four-foot youngster weighing at least 100 pounds. Holding with front flippers, he may ride mother's back as she swims. The first year or two he subsists on milk, then tusks sprout and junior grubs for himself.

A cow will often sacrifice her safety to defend her calf. Normally passive, she charges furiously and may even force a polar bear to retreat.

*Length* 8–12 ft. *Weight* 1,500–3,000 lbs. *Range:* Arctic Ocean south to Hudson Bay and Bering Sea. *Characteristics:* thick hide, small head, bristly muzzle; bull's tusks sometimes 3 ft. long, female's shorter.

**Blubber by the ton** flops ashore as wrinkled, warty walruses haul up on a Bering Sea beach.

MAC'S FOTO, ANCHORAGE

*Carl Rungius, courtesy of New York Zoological Society*

**Sluggish elephant seals,** world's homeliest sun bathers, bask on Guadalupe's somber sands.

# NORTHERN ELEPHANT SEAL

## *Mirounga angustirostris*

THIS GIANT AMONG SEALS quivers like gelatin as he shuffles on land. Tiring quickly, he slumps down like a gargantuan slug. But he swims with ease. Only his antarctic cousin *(M. leonina)* bulks as large.

When he's alarmed, his elephantine snout —absent on the female—puffs up as he thunders a protest; the longer the snout, the louder the roar. Relaxed, the leathery proboscis droops below his muzzle.

Sharing the Guadalupe Island rookery with fur seals (page 358), elephant seal cows bear single black 90-pound pups in spring after 50 weeks' gestation. These "rock seals" may nurse a year. As summer nears, shedding young and adults root in the beach, covering up with sand to escape the sun. After dark they waddle down to the ocean and dive deep for fish and squid.

Sealers had nearly wiped them out by the 1890's, but under protection the species has come back 20,000 strong.

*Length* 9−16 ft. *Weight* 1,000−8,000 lbs. *Range:* off California, Lower California. *Characteristics:* big; male's snout inflates.

*I'd hate to be kissed by a manatee,*
*The prospect's too much for my vanity,*
*Her bristly mustache*
*Would give me a rash*
*And destroy my last vestige of sanity.*

# Manatee, the Original Mermaid

L INNAEUS, natural history's great classifier, noted that the manatee "is delighted by music." If true, this only adds to the many strange features of the ungainly aquatic mammal. Because its sparsely haired, sacklike body tapers to a pancake tail, and because in legend the female clasps her young to her breast, impressionable sailors were convinced that here was a mermaid. Science went so far as to place the manatees and their cousins from Africa and Australia, the dugongs, in the order *Sirenia,* or sirens. But it's a safe assumption that after one close look no 20th century mariner, however susceptible, could confuse a half-ton manatee with the delectable fish-tailed maiden of his dreams.

Once there was a giant sea cow in north Pacific waters. This, the Steller sea cow (page 349), was wiped out by Russian hunters in the Bering Sea two centuries ago. The American species, *Trichechus manatus,* the manatee or sea cow, lolls in warm, shallow bays and brackish river mouths along the Florida coast. It browses on aquatic vegetation, helping keep fast-spreading underwater plants from choking canals and waterways. With its cleft, flexible lips it tweaks plants below the surface, sometimes stuffs them into its mouth with a paddlelike flipper. Hungering for riverside grass, it may rise partly out of the water to crop, then subside and munch contentedly. It has been timed at nearly 13 minutes submerged without a breath.

Rising for air, a manatee sometimes confronts a Florida boatman with a real-life nightmare—an earless, massive gray head often barnacle-encrusted, drooping lips with bristly whiskers, big wet nostrils

364

**Scientist** with a plastic chart studies the manatee in Florida's Crystal River.

exhaling mightily, and solemn eyes half-lidded in ponderous coyness. Usually the manatee feeds at night. It swims sluggishly with vertical sweeps of its tail that send the water boiling up in its wake. It can't stand cold water and will migrate down the coast to avoid it. On cold days manatees gather under the Miami Avenue Bridge where a factory discharges warm water into the Miami River. They cluster around the current like cracker barrel pundits about a pot-bellied stove.

Mother manatee gives birth to her yard-long infant (rarely twins) underwater. She slides it onto her back and holds it above water for about 45 minutes. Then she dunks the baby up to his nose, finally submerging him for increasing spans. In half a day all memories of the ancient ties with land have been washed away and the youngster is adjusted to his environment. Like mother, he'll rest with head and tail under, lifting his face to breathe between naps.

Once hunted for meat and oil, Florida's manatees are now protected. They are gentle, easily tamed, but shy of humans. Netted by accident, one panicky sea cow dragged a fisherman 50 feet through the water before it broke loose!

*Length* 8–15 ft. *Weight* 500–1,200 lbs. *Range:* Florida, east coast of Mexico and Central America, and West Indies to E. South America. *Characteristics:* paddlelike forelimbs, flattened tail in place of hind limbs.

JAMES A. SUGAR

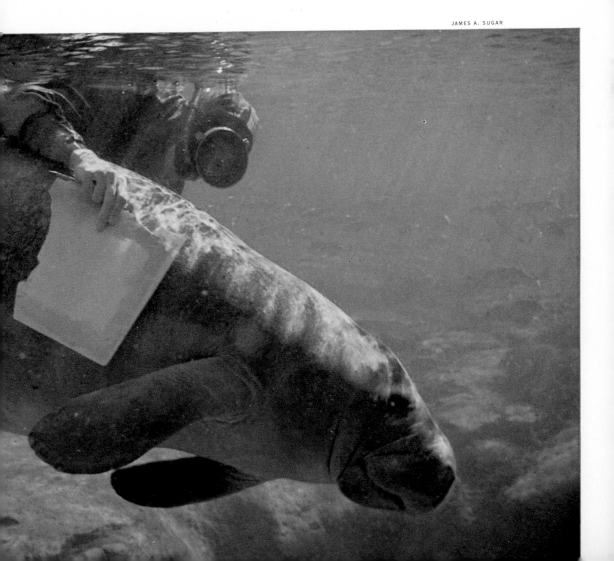

# Whales, Giants of the Sea

By A. REMINGTON KELLOGG

T HERE SHE BLOWS!"

"Where away? Sing out, lad! Sing out every time!"

"Ay ay, sir! She's three points off the lee bow, sir! There—there—*thar* she blows! She bl-o-o-o-w-s...."

Whaleboats smack the water, and oarsmen strain to press close—"wood to blackskin." The harpooner cocks his arm, heaves the iron. Strike! Recoiling at the sting, the sperm whale thrashes like some monstrous devil; his flailing flukes smash a boat to smithereens. Then he sounds, reeling out the leash of hemp. The calm that follows is shattered when his tremendous square head climbs out of the water, streaming waterfalls as he rises. The whalemen spring to their oars and close the gap. Now! A second harpoon sinks to the hilt. Crazed with pain, the whale pulls men and boat over the waves in a shower of spray—a "Nantucket sleigh ride." At last he tires, and the lance is readied. Six feet of steel thrusts deep into blubber, probing for the vitals. Blood spurts and a voice rings out, "There's the flag!" With a mighty shudder leviathan rolls fin out in the reddened sea.

"A dead whale or a stove boat!" was the battle cry in the days of Herman Melville. From New Bedford, Nantucket, Mystic, and other New England ports Yankee square-riggers scoured the seas for the kin of Moby Dick. Such adventure fired young imaginations, set sober minds reeling, held promise of fortunes in whalebone, oil, and ambergris. It was something to chant about:

*"Oh, the rare old Whale, mid storm and gale, in his ocean home will be*
*A giant in might, where might is right, and King of the boundless sea."*

Whales have been hunted for more than a thousand years. When they were pursued in small ships and killed with hand harpoons, whaling was limited to animals that floated when dead, such as the right whale (the "right one" for whalers), the bowhead, and later the sperm whale. The larger "finner" whales, including the finback, blue whale, sei whale, and humpback, sank when killed. And these animals were too speedy and dangerous to be hunted successfully until the harpoon gun was perfected in the mid-19th century. Whalers could now use a heavier harpoon line and haul whales to the surface, then pump them full of air.

◀ **Smashing a boat in the agony of death,** a sperm whale feels the deep stab of Yankee iron. The crew has already killed one whale. Its blubber is being peeled off and rendered into oil. The captain keeps the ship downwind so reeking smoke from the try-pots won't blow aft.

"CAPTURING A SPERM WHALE," FROM A PAINTING BY WILLIAM PAGE, PEABODY MUSEUM OF SALEM

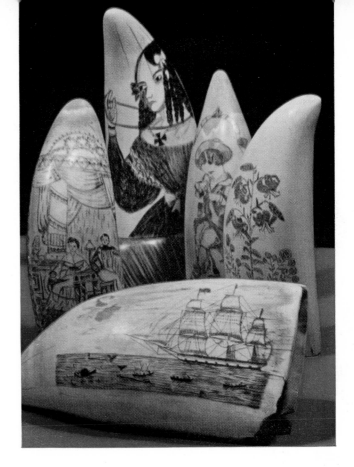

"Hold fast, John Tabor! Hold on like grim death!" cried the whiskered stranger, and off they went like lightning from the tropic isle. All night they sped over the sea, the old man gripping his harpoon, Tabor clinging to the old man's pants. "Land ho!" shouted the stranger next morning as they raced past Nantucket. Entering Buzzards Bay, the whale hit the beach at Tabor's home town and plowed right up Main Street to the town pump, scattering women and children. The old man went flying, and Tabor never saw him again. Or so the fable goes.

**Scrimshaw**, the whaleman's art, produced carved bone trinkets and etchings on sperm whale teeth (above). Sperm cow defending her calf inspired the forecastle art below.

369

Today's harpoon, fired from a swivel cannon at the bow of a catcher boat, has strong barbs that open once it enters the whale. It contains a bomb that kills or fatally wounds. It takes nine or more whale-catcher boats to keep a factory ship operating full blast. Winched up the stern ramp of this seagoing processing plant, a carcass is swarmed over by flensers in spiked boots. Their curved knives carve a gridwork stripping pattern into which they insert hooks. Then slabs of blubber are peeled off and fed through manholes to giant pressure cookers which convert fat to oil. Knives and power saws further reduce the whale to meat, waste, and bone.

The demand for whalebone — horny flexible strips growing from the upper jaws

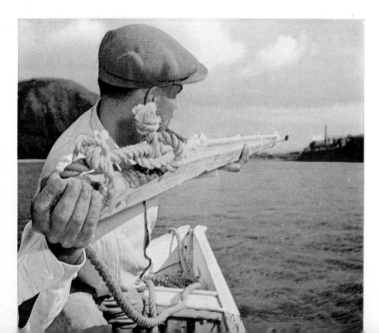

### Whaling in the Azores recalls Nantucket days

Portuguese whalemen still fight Moby Dick the way Captain Ahab did. Closing in, brawny islanders pit their courage against leviathan's bulk. Spurning explosives, the harpooner heaves a nine-foot dart. The wooden shaft breaks free when the pronged steel head buries itself. The men must be expert swimmers; thrashing flukes can splinter a boat.

ROBERT F. SISSON, NATIONAL GEOGRAPHIC PHOTOGRAPHER, AND (BELOW RIGHT) CARLETON MITCHELL

**A harpoon drives to its mark!** When steel sinks into blubber, oarsmen back water furiously. Smoking line snakes out after the sounding whale, then slackens; men haul it in and wait. Spouting, the monster breaches. The men row near and a lance cuts deep into the sperm whale's lungs. A motor launch tows the vanquished titan to shore for processing.

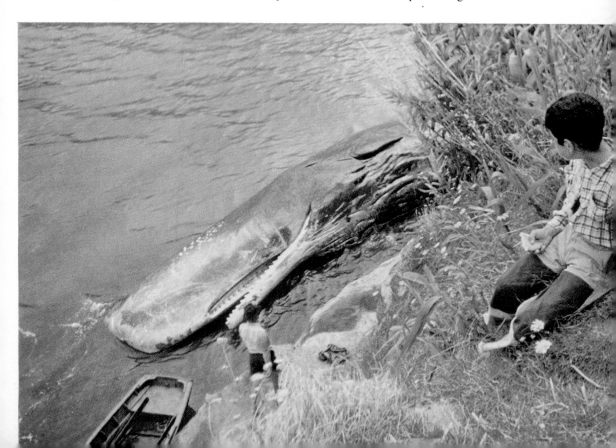

of baleen whales — led to an amazing expansion of the whale fishery. Fashionable ladies of the 19th century strait-laced themselves in garments braced with whale-bone. It stiffened bustles, bodices, collars; and without it the billowy hoop skirt literally would have been a flop. Whalebone sold for up to $7 a pound, and a single bowhead whale might yield a ton and a half. But when steel corset stays came into vogue many whalebone dealers went broke.

Whale oil went into soaps, varnishes, and paints, and was used to treat leather. Homes were lighted with whale oil lamps or candles of spermaceti — the clear oil from a sperm whale's head. The advent of the kerosene lamp, the gas mantle, and the electric light, plus the change in women's fashions, gave the whale a respite. But with World War I, munitions makers needed glycerin, obtainable from whale oil. Since then, the oil has found use in margarine, face creams, and ointments.

The most precious whale product was ambergris, a grayish, spongy substance from the intestines of sick sperm whales. As a fixative it commanded high prices on the perfume market; even now it brings up to $12 an ounce.

T HE WHALE is the mightiest mammal that ever lived. Even a dinosaur would be dwarfed by a blue whale, which may weigh 150 tons or more. A 92-foot model of this giant among whales towers over the Hall of Oceanic Life at the Smithsonian Institution in Washington, D. C. Only about 300 years ago did naturalists

**Rapid rendering marks modern whaling**

Skilled hands dismember a gigantic blue whale in an hour on a dock in Iceland. Flensers strip off tons of blubber (left), then lemmers cut up the mountain of meat.

The whale yields many oil and bone products. Its meat contains more protein than choice beef. Vitamins are extracted from the liver, insulin and other hormones from the glands; glue comes from flippers and tendons.

Old Nantucket whale-men would rub their eyes in disbelief at today's high-geared operations. Even with hunting regulated, far more whale oil is produced than in days when Yankee whalemen performed their epic deeds.

GÖRAN ALGARD

**A whale is a bonanza** to Eskimos at Point Hope, Alaska (above). It means food, lamp oil, intestines for waterproof garments and bags. Here they cut out head bone for implements. Tough, horny baleen strips, comblike food strainer for the toothless plankton-eating whale, make harpoon line and seal nets.

**Twin blowholes** high astern a humpback's knobby snout (below left) confirm it is a baleen whale. Toothed whales have but one. Hunters can tell the species by the spout, for no two blow alike. Spray is condensed air, not sea water. Indians caught whales by plugging the nostrils, says 16th century legend.

Namu, famed captive killer whale, catapults from Puget Sound and lands with a five-ton splash. The 24-foot bull trapped himself in 1965 in a salmon net near the British Columbia town that gave him his name. Bought by the Seattle Public Aquarium and kept in a waterfront pen of steel netting, he performed for visitors and surprisingly allowed his keepers to cavort with him in the water. Probably driven by the desire to find a mate, Namu in the summer of 1966 battered a hole in his pen, became entangled in the broken cables, and drowned.

PAUL V. THOMAS

Flirting with death, Edward I. Griffin, Namu's owner, pries open the behemoth's mouth to reveal some 50 formidable teeth that interlock like the jaws of a steel trap. To get the first electrocardiogram ever made of an uninjured, unrestrained killer whale, a medical team used a suction cup to attach sensors directly over the whale's heart as he rolled on his back (left). Namu's heartbeat on the surface was 60 pulsations a minute but only 30 under water.

determine that whales were mammals. Though they can live only in water, whales would drown if they could not come up often to breathe. And they suckle their young on milk similar to a cow's. Dolphins and porpoises, which also breathe and nurse, are classed with the whales as cetaceans. All have smooth skins and are streamlined. All are blanketed with blubber, which prevents loss of body heat. A greasy secretion from tear glands protects eyes from salt water. Though whales have no external ears, they can detect water-borne sounds. But they sleep so soundly that ships sometimes ram them at night.

Whale flippers, used mainly to steer and balance, little resemble the forelimbs of land mammals. Vestigial hind limbs, buried deep in flesh, no longer serve; cetaceans propel themselves with powerful flukes. Unlike the tail of a fish, these are horizontal and stroke up and down.

There are two main kinds of whales: the toothed, and the whalebone or baleen. Larger toothed whales, such as the sperm and killer, have throats big enough to swallow a man. But even if the luckless human were not bitten in half, he would fall victim to the strong gastric juices. All dolphins and porpoises have teeth that enable them to capture fish and squid.

The baleen whales, on the other hand, have no teeth, and the throats of these gigantic creatures are so small that they can down nothing larger than a herring. Whalebone hangs from their upper jaws in long strips, the inner edge fringed with

Labels on illustration: RESPONSE WHISTLE, COMMUNICATION WHISTLE, BRAIN, BLOWHOLE, AIR SACS, MELON, SKULL, LOWER JAW, EYE, MIDDLE EAR, OUTER EAR

**Echolocation** gives the porpoise an acoustical picture of his underwater world. Emitting clicks, perhaps made by forcing air from two sacs near the blowhole, he sweeps his head back and forth, evaluating the echoes. To communicate with porpoise friends, he "whistles" signals. These sounds differ from the above-water squeaks so familiar to television fans of Flipper and to oceanarium visitors like those in Miami (opposite).

hairfine bristles. Mouth open, the whale swims through masses of shrimplike crustaceans that live near the surface. When the mouth is full the jaws close, then the whale's huge tongue forces water out through the baleen sieve. Water does not enter the lungs, for the nasal passages, instead of opening into the throat as in land mammals, connect directly with the windpipe.

The popular belief that the whale spouts water is untrue. Actually, air forcibly discharged from the lungs produces the geyser effect; the warm, moisture-laden breath meets the cooler atmosphere and condenses. Toothed whales have only one blowhole, baleens two. These nostrils are on top of the head, so whales can breathe without exposing much of the body.

Baleen whales migrate thousands of miles to reach the floating food banks that thrive in the high latitudes in spring and summer. In the winter they return to the tropics. Here they bring forth their young. As do all cetaceans, they normally give birth to single calves every other year. Most of the larger baleen whales display such strong family ties that whalers for centuries harpooned the young first. Refusing to abandon her dead offspring, a cow became easy prey. Dolphins and porpoises are not noted for defending their young; still the females stay close. The young dolphin can keep pace with adults from birth.

Few humans have actually seen whales mate. One who did was the famed explorer, Roy Chapman Andrews. An amorous bull humpback whale stood on his head and thrashed his great flukes to impress a female. Then "with a terrific

# Porpoise Sonar:
## HOW IT WORKS

TARGET

CLICK ECHO

STAFF ARTIST ROBERT W. NICHOLSON
GEOGRAPHIC ART DIVISION

BELOW: JOSEPH P. BLAIR III. RIGHT: WALTER A. WEBER, NATIONAL GEOGRAPHIC STAFF ARTIST

BALEEN WHALES

BLUE WHALE

RIGHT WHALE

TOOTHED WHALES

SPERM WHALE

KILLER WHALE

WHITE WHALE

PILOT WHALE

NARWHAL

COMMON DOLPHIN

**Dental equipment** divides the cetaceans into two groups. Portraits, not to scale, profile some species in North American waters.

Scientists have recently taken great interest in the dolphin, or porpoise. A friendly, intelligent aquatic jokester, he has a brain larger than man's and a sound-sensing system more accurate than man-made sonar. He uses an astonishing variety of sounds to communicate with other porpoises, and psychologists wonder: Do they really "talk"? Researchers are at work seeking to learn if we can talk to porpoises and they to us.

rush he burst from the water, throwing his entire fifty-foot body straight up in the air. . . . Falling back in a cloud of spray, he rolled over and over on his mate, clasping her with both flippers. Both whales lay at the surface, blowing slowly, exhausted with emotion."

Warm-blooded whales, like man, cannot live without air. But unlike man, they can hold their breath for long periods while submerged—an hour or more for the sperm whale and bottle-nosed species. How deep can a whale dive? No one knows for sure; when feeding it finds food at different levels. But a harpooned whale may sound to great depths. A drowned sperm whale, tangled in cable, was hoisted from more than 3,000 feet by a cable repair ship off the coast of Colombia. At that depth the whale had been subjected to 1,400 pounds pressure per square inch. When a whale dives, its heart throttles down. A diving bottle-nosed porpoise's clocked 50 beats a minute, compared to 110 on the surface. A large whale's heart may pound only eight to ten times per minute, but pump 500 gallons of blood. A huge finback's heart weighs more than 800 pounds.

Leviathan's brain is not so big; 15 to 20 pounds is about tops. But scientists were astonished to learn how closely it resembles a human's. In fact, pilot whales and porpoises may be the world's smartest creatures, after man and the chimpanzee. A captive porpoise in Florida imitated a man's voice so well that a woman burst out laughing; then the dolphin imitated her laughter. Porpoises, cavorting near a crowded beach, once intercepted a ball which veered into the water. Merrily batting it back and forth, they swam off with the new plaything.

The day may come when the commercially unimportant porpoises and dolphins will be the only survivors of the whale clan. Large-scale operations have taken a fearful toll. In one year, more than 46,000 whales were killed in the Antarctic alone. There, during the 1959-60 season, nearly 18,000 men were engaged in whaling. They manned 238 whale-catcher boats, 15 refrigeration ships, and 20 floating factories. But alarmed governments moved to give the whale a better break, and by 1971 factory expeditions were down to six, with only Russia and Japan engaged in major operations. International protection has been given to right, blue, and humpback whales, immature whales, and females accompanied by young; factory ships are barred from tropical calving grounds. Despite belated restrictions, nearly a million and a half whales have been harpooned since 1900.

Whales once roamed the oceans of the world in the millions. Today they are nearing the same fate that doomed the vast herds of bison.

*A Portfolio*    Following are biographies of the principal whales and porpoises found in North American waters, illustrated in full color by Else Bostelmann and Walter A. Weber. Lengths show the range between small and large adults.

**Bimbo, 3,000 pounds of pilot whale,** explodes from the water—for a tiny hors d'oeuvre! Master of many tricks, this nimble leviathan wolfs down 100 pounds of squid a day.

JAY JOHNSTON, NATIONAL GEOGRAPHIC STAFF

Else Bostelmann

**Whoosh! Right whale's wet breath** condenses in arctic air. Carbon-copy calf snuggles close.

# RIGHT WHALE

*Eubalaena glacialis*

FOR OLD-TIME WHALERS, the word "right" just fitted this whale. Rich in oil and whalebone, it swam slowly, fought feebly when attacked, and proved a "floater" when killed — easy for a whaleboat to tow.

Once the commonest of all whales, so "right" was it that Basque whalers eagerly pursued it in the Bay of Biscay more than a thousand years ago. Nineteenth century harpooners almost killed it off. Now rare, it's strictly protected.

A short, smooth-throated whale with a chunky body, it is often all black, though one out of five has a white or pied belly. At least 250 strips of black whalebone, some seven feet long, curtain each side of its great curved toothless maw. Near the end of the snout grows a horny, irregular "bonnet" — a mass of fibers jutting from the skin.

No one knows what it's for, except to harbor worms, whale lice, and barnacles.

As with most whales, the right cow bears a single calf. She keeps it with her for at least a year, suckling it and caring for it. Whalers have found she won't abandon it even if it has been killed.

Right whales like to float on the surface. To feed on plankton, as all baleen whales do, they usually make five or six shallow dives. Then they go deep, staying down 15 or 20 minutes. Surfacing, they blow a V-shaped spout that arches 15 feet from twin blowholes and often forms a dense cloud in the icy air.

The three groups of right whales of far northern and southern seas do not mingle. Some authorities consider them separate species.

*Length* 40–55 ft. *Range:* North Atlantic, Pacific, Antarctic (all forms). *Characteristics:* jaws curve upward; lips have scalloped borders; no dorsal fin.

The bowhead, big mouth full of whalebone, blubber rich in oil, was long the whaler's prize.

## BOWHEAD WHALE

*Balaena mysticetus*

EVEN BIGGER AND UGLIER than its cousin the right whale, the bowhead too was hunted almost to extinction. Its massive body is one-third head, with a mouth that could easily hold an ox. But no ox could pass its tiny throat designed for the minute crustaceans that swarm in northern seas.

Openmouthed, the bowhead cruises amid this brit. Then the mighty jaws close and water streams out through about 660 blades of whalebone, some 12 feet long.

The bowhead has been hunted in the Atlantic since the 1600's. In 1848 Americans began to hunt it in the Bering Sea. During the Civil War, the Confederate privateer *Shenandoah* burned the New England fleet; a few years later pack ice crushed the ships. But what rewards! Some 90 barrels of oil and 1,700 pounds of bone from one big whale, fetching up to $8,000.

Edward Nelson reported a Bering Sea bowhead that bore a harpoon with a Greenland whaler's markings. The whale had found the Northwest Passage!

*Length* 50–60 ft. *Range:* arctic waters. *Characteristics:* long head, white on jaw.

383

**Blue whale**, world's mightiest creature, spouts under the gun of a catcher boat. The **little**

*Else Bostelmann*

piked whale beside it is not worth hunting.

# FINBACK WHALE
## Balaenoptera physalus

MOST PLENTIFUL of large whales, the finback is the mainstay of today's whaling industry. Catcher boats and harpoon guns have taken more than 630,000 since 1900.

Beautifully streamlined, the finback is the fastest of all whales, rocketing through the sea at 30 miles per hour, gulping "krill" —tiny shrimplike creatures— by the barrelful. It migrates to the tropics to breed and bear its 22-foot calf, then returns to food-rich polar waters in summer.

Gray or bluish above, the finback is white-breasted and has a wedge-shaped head. Oddly, the right side of the head is always whiter than the left. In fixing quotas of whales to be killed, two finbacks—which may weigh 50 to 70 tons each—are considered equal to one blue whale.

*Length* 60–82 ft. *Range:* all oceans. *Characteristics:* long tapering body, high curved fin set far back, furrowed throat.

# BLUE WHALE
## Sibbaldus musculus

THE LARGEST MAMMAL that ever lived on earth still spouts among chunks of polar ice. The blue whale may weigh 150 tons— as much as 35 elephants. It is also called the sulphur-bottom because it sometimes has a yellowish film of diatoms, microscopic algae, on its belly.

After bearing a 26-foot baby, the mother lies on her side, raising her nipple so the calf can nurse and breathe at the same time. Each day she pumps into her youngster as much as 200 pounds of milk. It's like cow's milk, but fortified with extra minerals, proteins, and fats.

Weaned at seven months, the 52-foot youngster swims with mouth agape, taking in water and tidbits. Then the great scoop closes and the water is strained out through the baleen, leaving the "krill."

Tremendously powerful, blues cruise at 10 or 12 knots and can top 14 when frightened. One, harpooned off Alaska, towed a 90-foot whaler at six knots for more than eight hours. Much of that time the ship's engines were going full astern!

The big blubbery blue's tremendous yield—100 to 120 barrels of oil—made him profitable quarry for hunters and almost doomed him. In 1940 he numbered 100,000, in 1970 fewer than 3,000. International protection, instituted in the 1960's, may give him a new lease on life.

*Length* 70–100 ft. *Range:* summers in polar seas, both hemispheres. *Characteristics:* bluish mottled with gray; U-shaped snout, furrowed throat.

Speedy finback rolls on its side to feed; water spurts between baleen strips as jaws close.

*Else Bostelmann*

**Mother humpback** lies on her side to nurse her calf. Show-off neighbor breaches in distance.

# HUMPBACK WHALE

## *Megaptera novaeangliae*

IT'S NURSING TIME and the 15-foot baby is misbehaving. Full of playful affection, he leaps and splashes around his 40-foot mother until, exasperated, she gives him a swipe with her flipper—enough to shatter a whaleboat. The calf gets back to the business of putting on weight. He was a ton-and-a-half weakling at birth.

Spirited adult humpbacks like to hurl their entire bodies out of water and land on their sides with a bone-jarring splash. Perhaps they're trying to knock off barnacles. More likely it's courtship, carried out on the scale of a small earthquake. Humpbacks also enjoy lobtailing, standing head down in the sea and beating the surface to a froth with mighty flukes.

Whalers named the humpback for its trait of bending its back to dive. The squat, dark whale is decorated with knobs on the snout and lower jaws. One humpback, distinguishable by an odd whistle when it spouted, visited the Bay of Fundy each summer for more than 20 years.

*Length* 40–50 ft. *Range:* all oceans. *Characteristics:* knobby head, long flippers.

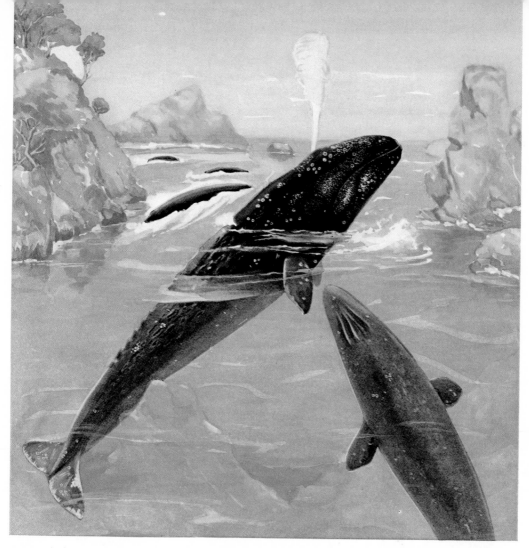

Gray whale cow and smaller male loll offshore. Bashing boats earned them the name "devilfish."

## GRAY WHALE

### *Eschrichtius glaucus*

ANYONE CAN WATCH the Pacific parade of migrating grays. Studded with barnacles, the 40-ton monsters buck the waves off San Diego's Point Loma on their 4,000-mile journey between summer haunts in the Arctic and winter breeding grounds in Lower California's lagoons. They scarcely eat during the trip or in winter quarters. Mating and calving absorb their attention.

Wallowing in shoal water, about half the cows bear their 16-foot calves. The rest mate, starting a year-long gestation. Males outnumber available cows, but breeding proceeds without fighting.

Grays stick close to shore as if recalling distant ties with land. Sometimes they venture into surf to play or escape the killer whale and man. Twice men have come within a harpoon's length of wiping them out. Now protected, gray whales pass San Diego in slowly increasing numbers.

*Length* 32–43 ft. (females are the larger). *Range:* Lower California to Bering Sea. A separate herd roves from Korea to Sea of Okhotsk. *Characteristics:* gray to black, mottled with white; no back fin.

*Else Bostelmann*

**Maddened sperm whale** eyes his foes. Harpoon lines harness him for a "Nantucket sleigh ride."

# SPERM WHALE

## *Physeter catodon*

"SHE BOLTED HER HEAD out of the water . . . then pitched the whole weight of her head on the Boat—stove ye boat & ruined her and killed the midshipman (an Indian named Sam Lamson) outwright a Sad & Awful Providence."

So wrote Nantucketer Peleg Folger of the *Phoebe* in 1754. That whale was a sperm. In 1820, a frenzied whale slammed head on into the Nantucket whaler *Essex,* backed off, and rammed her again. Stout timbers crushed, the vessel sank—1,200 miles from the Marquesas. That was a sperm too, largest of the toothed whales—prize and terror of the sea.

A newborn sperm stretches about 13 feet. Six months of nursing nearly doubles its size. Its mother guards it, even if it's dead. Many a whaler got barrels of oil by killing a calf, then the devoted parent. And many a tale was told of sperm cows carrying stricken calves in their mouths.

Protected by law, calves have a good chance to reach full growth in eight to 10 years. Bulls are bigger than cows and keep them in harems. But in summer they turn bachelor, ranging off to icy seas while the females and young stay in tropical waters.

The sperm whale lives on squid and octopus. Equipped with huge mouth and big bottom teeth, he chews up a ton of this food a day. Scars show where great tentacles have rasped him in battles with giant squid in the Stygian depths.

After sounding, the sperm wallows in the waves for perhaps 10 minutes, or makes a series of shallow dives. Then he upends, great flukes waving in the air, and down he goes again to stay as long as an hour. Finally surfacing, he blasts damp breath. "Thar she blo-o-o-ws!" would bellow the masthead lookout on old Yankee whalers.

The sperm whale made New England fortunes, braced the Nation's economy, and challenged the beaver as the most important wild animal in American history.

During the early 19th century more than 740 whaling ships sailed from American ports. New Bedford's whalers, blunt-bowed and chunky, were said to be "built by the mile and chopped off as you need 'em." Yankee whalemen charted more than 400 Pacific islands and explored polar seas in their endless search for the sperm whale. Today, not one whaler flies the Stars and Stripes—but those monstrous antagonists, the sperm whales, survive. In a recent year the world catch was 21,000.

*Length* 36–50 ft. (exceptional males to 60 ft.). *Range:* all oceans. *Characteristics:* big blunt head; slim lower jaw, heavily toothed; one blowhole at end of snout.

# CUVIER BEAKED WHALE
## *Ziphius cavirostris*

THIS SHY GLOBETROTTER, named for a 19th century French naturalist, is at home in temperate seas almost anywhere. Eluding close inspection, he seems a phantom in deep purple or gray, sometimes white-headed, sometimes spotted. But he's mortal. He's been found stranded on beaches.

Nicknamed goose-beaked whale for his tapered profile, he swims with 30 to 40 comrades. They may spout for ten minutes, then dive as if by command. They'll stay below for a half hour searching for tasty cuttlefish.

*Length* 18–28 ft. *Range:* all oceans, except polar. *Characteristics:* short beaklike face; two teeth at tip of lower jaw.

**Cuvier beaked whale** bears a rival's teeth marks. Female at his side is proof he won the fight.

# KILLER WHALE

## *Orcinus orca*

AN OMINOUS BLACK DORSAL FIN slices through water. Savage jaws gape. Sharp teeth gash white skin; then the most ferocious killer in the sea fills his belly.

His prey is the beluga or white whale (*Delphinapterus leucus*), a 15-foot denizen of northern waters that often swims up large rivers like the St. Lawrence.

But the killer whale is not choosy. He'll attack almost anything that swims, including man. Prowling the seas, he feeds on shark, smaller fish, squid, penguin, seal, young walrus, porpoise, and other whales. A 21-foot killer that was cut open had dined on 14 seals and 13 porpoises.

No wonder sea creatures panic when a bloodthirsty killer pack bores in. In the Arctic, terror-stricken sea lions have leaped upon Aleuts' large skin boats, swamping them. A floe offers little safety, for the marauders ram it from beneath, spilling their prey into the water. In the Antarctic, hungry killers once cracked eight-foot-thick ice under a fleeing photographer.

Killers plague whaling expeditions, biting chunks from dead whales before they can be towed to the factory ship. Ambushed in mid-ocean, a hulking gray whale may become paralyzed with fear and turn on its back while the pack tears out its tongue and lips. Perhaps Alaskan Eskimos are right: they believe killer whales are wolves that have changed their form.

*Length* 15−30 ft. (males are much the larger). *Range:* all oceans. *Characteristics:* black and white; high back fin, blunt snout.

**A pack of killer whales,** wolves of the sea, attacks a herd of defenseless beluga or white whales.

*Else Bostelmann*

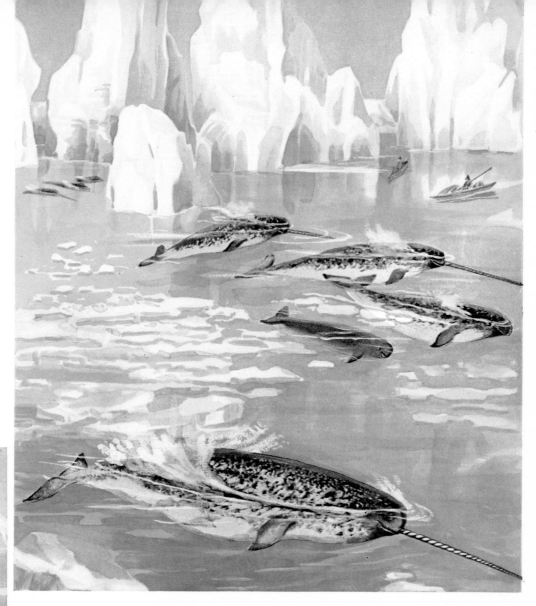

Narwhal calf in gray swims beside its tuskless mother. Eskimos stalk the school.

# NARWHAL

## *Monodon monoceros*

WHAT A MAGNIFICENT WEAPON the narwhal's tusk would be—if it were any good. Alas, this splendid hollow shaft is almost as brittle as glass.

In medieval Europe, the tusks gave "evidence" that the fabled unicorn existed. They were prized as magic cure-alls, a specific against poisons.

The male narwhal carries this long, twisted canine tooth in his left upper jaw. He munches small fish between otherwise toothless gums.

Eskimos hunt narwhals for food, oil, and ivory, catching them at openings in ice. Breaking surface close together, the beasts whistle as air rushes out. Sometimes a mother blasts a deep bass note to call her little gray calf.

*Length* 13—16 ft. *Range:* rarely south of the Arctic Circle. *Characteristics:* gray-white; male has tusk up to 9 feet long, spiraled counterclockwise.

Else Bostelmann

**Leaping common dolphins** share a seafood feast with smaller **harbor porpoise** (lower right).

# COMMON DOLPHIN

## *Delphinus delphis*

SINCE PHOENICIAN DAYS, mariners have sworn that dolphins bring good fortune, fair weather, and steady winds. Leaping gracefully, these sleek mammals, like toy whales, delight all who sail the seas. They can overtake a vessel doing 18 knots and weave in front of its bow.

Sharp teeth, curving backward, arm the dolphin's beak, allowing him to catch slippery fish and bolt them head first. He can snap a flying fish on the wing. Calves nurse as mother dolphin lies on her side.

The harbor or common porpoise *(Phocaena phocaena)* reaches six feet. It coasts the Atlantic south to Cape May, New Jersey. Relatives range the Pacific.

"Dolphin" usually applies to the beaked species; "porpoise" to other smaller kinds. But these names often are interchanged. An added confusion: dolphin is also the name of a spiny-finned ocean fish.

*Length* 6½–8½ ft. *Range:* temperate seas. *Characteristics:* black back, yellow or brown sides; "spectacles" around eyes.

# BOTTLE-NOSED PORPOISE

## *Tursiops truncatus*

CUTTING CLEANLY through the surface, the bottle-nosed porpoise leaps twice his body length, arching back into the sea. He's an impulsive show-off to passing ships, and his breed outnumbers all other dolphins that frolic off the Atlantic coast.

Herman Melville dubbed him "Huzza" porpoise: "If you yourself can withstand three cheers at beholding these vivacious fish, then heaven help ye; the spirit of godly gamesomeness is not in ye."

Porpoises enjoy people. One joined the crowd at a South African beach and let swimmers hang onto its dorsal fin while it towed them through the water.

In captivity, the bottlenose is a star performer. He can be taught to jump through hoops, even paper-covered ones. He expertly fields balls and other thrown objects, raises flags, plays bulb horns, and tows surfboards. At Florida's Theater of the Sea, Seaquarium, and Marineland, talented porpoises delight in the applause of spectators. But one visitor at a marine exhibit made the mistake of tossing a bony fish head into a tank of porpoises. He got it back in his lap.

Porpoises swallow fish whole, reserving their sharp teeth for settling disputes. For all their smiling looks and joyous ways, they are dangerous when aroused.

Gregarious, they travel in schools of up to several hundred scattered over half a mile. Sharks steer clear, for the powerful mammals can kill the menacing fish by butting with their snouts at 35 miles an hour. Naturalists saw a school of porpoises circling a shark to keep it in position for a ram. One member who had backed off came hurtling full force to stun the shark. Then all the porpoises smashed at it.

If a shark or a male bottlenose attacks a baby porpoise, the mother, sometimes aided by a female friend, shields it with her body. The calf, able to swim at birth, sticks close to its milk supply for about a year. Then it too becomes a fisherman.

*Length* 9–12 ft. *Range:* Cape Cod south to Texas and S. America. *Characteristics:* toothed beak, prominent dorsal fin.

**Mouth shape of the bottle-nosed porpoise** gives him a perpetual smile. Fish find it unamusing.
*Walter A. Weber, National Geographic staff artist*

# INDEX

Illustrated biographies are indicated in **bold face,**
other illustrations in *italics,*
text references in roman.

# INDEX

# INDEX

## For Additional Reference

Everyone interested in wildlife will find a wealth of information in the more than 930 issues of *National Geographic*. Check the Index. These stimulating National Geographic books will also make the fascinating world of nature more meaningful to you. Order from National Geographic Society, Washington, D. C. 20036. Brochure on request.

AMERICA'S WONLANDS

SONG AND GARD BIRDS OF NORTH AMERIA

WATER, PREY, A GAME BIRDS OF NORTH AM

VACATIONLAND U. S. A.

WONDROUS WORLD OF FISHES

MAN'S BEST FRIEND, *Revised Edition, National Geographic Book of Dogs*

**Enterprising black bears** breakfast in grand style on the lawn of Jasper Park Lodge, Alberta.

EDNA LEONARD—HARRY ROWED, O'NEILL & ASSOCIATES, LTD.

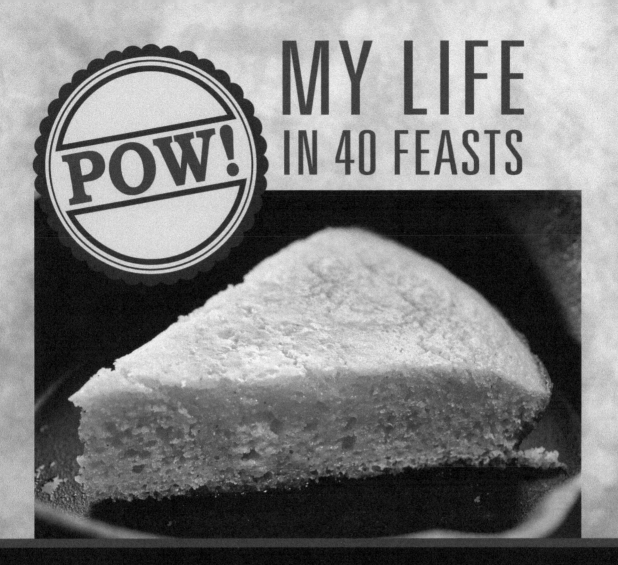

# POW!

## MY LIFE
### IN 40 FEASTS

## A COOKBOOK
## AND MEMOIR

*BY A BELOVED AMERICAN CHEF,*
*JESSE JONES AND*
*LINDA WEST ECKHARDT*

# CHEF JESSE JONES

# Table of Contents

# Chapter 10: October — 159

# November: Chapter 11 — 175

# Introduction:

The summer I was four years old, my mother, my sister, and I got on the bus in Newark, New Jersey, and went down South to my grandmother's house in Snow Hill, North Carolina.

I don't remember much about the trip, but when we got off the bus and into a taxi to my grandmother's house, I began to feel uneasy.

Her house was out in the country, a two-and-a-half-room white clapboard house set in the middle of a cornfield. I was afraid of the tall corn stalk trail that led to her house, the noises, the smells, the fact that I couldn't see around it or through it. Where was this trail leading me?

At four years old, this would be my first summer of many, staying down South with my grandmother and grandfather. It all became clear when that cab we came in would leave without me and my sister, with only my mama in the backseat. I could see her crying.

I cried so hard and I thought my life was over. But my grandmother had a way to make things better—with the greatest piece of candy. She gave me a coconut rainbow bar, my all-time favorite. Still love 'em. And it didn't take long for me to see that the love that had come to me from Mama had its roots in my grandmother's house on the farm.

My first lesson that summer came when I got burned on the hot cast-iron stove that sat in the middle of the room. Ouch. That hurt.

But my greatest memory came while helping my grandmother snap green beans. I loved helping her. She would pull up a chair to the table, and I'd stand on it and love everything I saw.

The smells that came out of that little kitchen were amazing. Grandmother was famous for her biscuits and molasses pudding. I tried everything. I loved it all. I was home there at that kitchen table. It's where I belonged.

I created my own molasses cake in honor of my grandmother.

## SPICED MOLASSES POUND CAKE

* 3 cups all-purpose flour
* 1 teaspoon baking powder
* ½ teaspoon salt
* 1 cup (2 sticks) butter, softened
* 1 cup dark brown sugar
* 1 cup granulated sugar
* ½ teaspoon cinnamon
* ½ teaspoon allspice
* ½ teaspoon nutmeg
* 5 large eggs
* 1½ cups molasses
* 1 cup milk
* 1 teaspoon vanilla extract
* ½ cup grape-seed oil

- Preheat the oven to 350°F. Combine the flour, baking powder, and salt in a bowl. Set aside.

- In a large bowl, using an electric mixer, cream the butter and sugars together until well mixed, scraping down the sides of the bowl. Beat in the eggs, one at a time. Beating well after each addition, add the flour mixture, alternating with the milk. Mix in the molasses, spices, vanilla and oil. Pour batter into a greased and floured 10-inch Bundt pan and bake for 90 minutes. Cool in the pan for 5 minutes and drizzle with a little molasses.

## CHEF JESSE'S SPICE GLAZE

* 1 cup plus 1 tablespoon powdered sugar
* 2 tablespoons evaporated milk
* ¼ cup unsalted butter, softened

* ¼ teaspoon cinnamon
* ¼ teaspoon allspice
* ½ teaspoon pure vanilla extract

—  In a medium bowl, add milk and powdered sugar, mixing well. Add softened butter, whip till smooth, and then mix in cinnamon, allspice, and vanilla. Drizzle on cool cake to make a sugar glaze.

Even though that was more than fifty-two years ago, I learned early and surely that the kitchen was where I was meant to be. I loved the sizzling sounds, the smells, the tastes, the love that came from cooking and eating food around that table.

I took a lot of teasing from the men of the family who called me a sissy for staying in there with the women. But I learned right then and there that the kitchen was a safe place and a place filled with joy. I knew it was where I belonged and I've stayed there ever since.

I always feel I have the best of both worlds, with my heart in New Jersey, but girded by the soul of the South!

My first job in a real kitchen came when I was a teenager. I stood in a basement and opened cans. But I could smell those great aromas drifting down from the stove upstairs. I knew I could get there. And I did.

This book tells you about my trip through the kitchens of America. Here are forty feasts that I love and I know you will too. Each feast gives four recipes. You can, of course, add dishes as you see fit. That's what cooking is all about. You start with a good firm foundation and then build your meal just like you'd build a house—item by item. Just know that every recipe in this book has been tested and tasted and is filled with love from the cooks who have gone before you. Welcome to my table.

With love,
Chef Jesse Jones

>>>><<<<

# Acknowledgments

First, I'd like to thank Linda West Eckhardt for helping and believing in me and for being a great co-author.

For my lovely wife, Annette Jones, love you to the moon and back.

My mother, Mildred Jones, thank you for everything. Where would I be without you?

My sister, Priscilla Durant, thank you for casting a positive light on my life.

My friend, Yvonne Durant, thanks for your input in helping us finalize the name of this wonderful book... POW!

Chef Dennis Foy, thanks for giving me an awesome experience in French cuisine.

Thanks to David Verdini, photographer extraordinaire who helped us so much.  All photos in the book were taken by David and Chef Jesse.

Thanks, News 12 New Jersey, for allowing me to showcase my talent on TV, along with PIX11 and CBS2 news.

Great towns of South Orange and Maplewood, thanks for keeping me in the spotlight and for hosting events here in my hometown.

Thanks to our inspired editor, Dana Nelson and the extraordinary editorial crew at Outskirts Press who have helped us realize our dream. We are so grateful to you. Outskirts is just the best.

And lastly, but always first in my heart, Avery Thompson, love you forever. Dream big! ... POW!

# Foreword

BY JOAN WHITLOW

Two remarkable things about this cookbook reflect what is remarkable about the author, Chef Jesse Jones.

First, you will get what you were looking for when you picked up this book: wonderful food. There is plenty of that. There are feasts to make. And a friendly warmth is infused into the instructions for executing the recipes. As I read, I hear Chef Jesse's big, encouraging, you've-got-this voice cheering you on step by step. I love the fact that he tells you about the special brand of grits he uses for his shrimp and grits—but also makes it clear there is no shame in taking the short route and using instant grits.

There are other recipe books and chefs that get all snooty about a classic French dish like cassoulet. They insist only a certain kind of little white bean will do for this oh-so-French bean and meat stew. Chef Jesse says use black-eyed peas! Cook with what you know and love—nothing wrong with keeping it simple.

But don't be afraid of those little extra steps or trying new combinations that elevate the tried and true into something truly wonderful. That's the other remarkable thing you'll get by diving into Chef's book.

I have eaten his food and loved it. I tried to be a regular patron of his Heart and Soul Restaurant. But I was a reporter who did not work the typical nine-to-five schedule. Too often, by the time I got to Heart and Soul it was closed. Chef Jesse's loyal followers had swooped down like locusts, leaving behind nothing but a menu of what I could have had.

One time I got there just as he was closing. Lamb shanks were all he had left. Most people just want their lamb shanks tender and don't seem to mind if the lamb has been cooked to tasteless mush-meat. Chef Jesse's met the prerequisite for being fork tender. But they also had texture and flavor. The succulent meat was served in a sauce that deserved its own place on the menu. POW!

A few weeks later I had pulled a long drive from my childhood home, Cleveland, Ohio. In the middle of Pennsylvania, I began obsessing about those lamb shanks and whether I could get to Heart and Soul in time. I made it.

"I've got turkey wings," Chef Jesse said. But I wanted lamb shanks. I got a friendly lecture about the concept behind his restaurant. He had certain staple offerings, of course, but the idea was to seek out the freshest, best ingredients each day—farm to table ingredients that would determine that day's menu. So I couldn't count on finding the same items day in and day out.

Chef Jesse was ahead of his time. He was working on a concept that is catching on now. But at the time I wanted lamb shanks, not concepts. I took home the turkey wings. Yes, they were fork tender and so good I didn't bother much with the fork. The turkey wings did not make me forget the lamb shanks. They just added to my obsession for Chef Jesse's cooking.

The other remarkable thing about this cookbook is the way Chef Jesse laces it with his own story. You may be tempted to just get to cookin' and skip the vignettes about his life, the people, and experiences that shaped him. But those stories provide the recipe for the making of this man. And you won't be able to miss even a little taste of Chef Jesse's life. It's a remarkable story.

He grew up in Newark, a city that is most maligned by the people who know the least about it. I won't pretend that Newark's problems are not real: too much poverty, unemployment, and miseducation; too much crime and drugs.

Chef Jesse's story speaks to young people growing up in such cities, growing up with a scream at the edge of their throats, and with anger they don't even understand firing away in their chests. Chef Jesse says he had that kind of anger; he was tempted by the streets.

He tells you how the kitchen, and his love of cooking, saved his life. He was transformed by that love and his drive to succeed as a chef. He was also transformed by the drive to help other people—particularly kids like the one he was.

I have seen that part of him in action. I was an organizer for the 2017 Newark High School Cook-Off, sponsored by the Newark Branch NAACP and Whole Foods, the first competition of its kind in Newark. We carefully chose the chefs, restaurant owners, and caterers we invited to be judges. We wanted people who would inspire Newark's African-American and Hispanic youths about the art and business of cooking. Nobody does that better than Chef Jesse Jones.

He is a big man who leans down to talk to little kids, like the students from his old elementary school, who were at the cook-off serving healthy snacks and smoothies. He was a good, fair, serious judge and leader. It was clear he also came to encourage and to teach students to respect the food, and respect themselves. Chef Jesse's sincere concern that they learn and succeed was a prize that each of the contestants took home that day.

So much of who he is comes through in this book. It is a treasure. Read the book, work the recipes. You will eat well—and feel better about the prospects of cooking up a better world.

Signed,
Joan Whitlow, completely, utterly, and happily retired *Newark Star-Ledger* columnist and editorial board member.

>>>>><<<<<

# Chapter 1: January

*The great fellowship of family and the special smells that came out of my grandmother's kitchen have sustained me my whole life. I still talk to my mother on the telephone every single day. Family is everything to me. Always has been.*

*And my relationship to fire started right then and right there. Of course, my grandmother cooked on a potbellied stove and I was fascinated by the process of feeding kindling into that stove, slamming the door shut, and smelling the pungent aroma of smoke and heat that came at me.*

*She warned me early and often not to touch that stove, not to get too close, and to respect the power that came from that stove. The food that came from it fed us, but one false move and that stove could really hurt you.*

*Lot of times, I would go out into the yard with Uncle William to cut kindling for that stove and to watch his powerful arms as he raised that hatchet over his head to break that wood into manageable pieces. I found that amazing.*

*One of my first kitchen jobs was gathering that kindling and taking it to the kitchen, where it was kept in a basket in the corner. I didn't rise from that station for many years.*

*As a teenager, I got a job back in Newark with a huge operation called Aramark and began my training right at the bottom, literally in the basement. They assigned me to a station where I opened gallon cans and washed dishes. Mountains of dishes. Every single day. I would go home and dream about those dishes and the never-ending stream of cans to be opened.*

*But one of the major blessings of my life came along about the same time. I met and married my wonderful wife, Annette, who has put up with me for more than 30 years now.*

*Between the two of us, we earned enough money so we could rent a tiny apartment. Annette has always been good with numbers and she got an office job at Prudential. Life was good.*

*Our two sons were born during that period. Wonderful Tristan, who was clearly an artist from an early age, sitting on the floor with a box of crayons. Then, a few years later, his brother, whom we call Double J. He was born with a ball in his hands and today, as we speak, is being courted for a spot in the overseas basketball professional leagues. That kid can jump! He simply flies through the air as light as a bird. And he just keeps getting better and better.*

*And both of our sons earned college degrees. We are proud of that.*

*God has been good to Annette and me. We try to give back every day. We know we owe a big debt to the universe. We try to pay it forward in every way we can. I try to help others every day. Every day.*

*But back to the stove.*

*When I finally got promoted to a station on the line, my real training began. When you work in a large operation like Aramark, you are part of the process of creating restaurant-sized portions of food. This means that some days you might be assigned to make 700 crepes during your shift. Or you might be making gallons of soup. Or you might make 200 sandwiches. It just depends on which slot you're assigned.*

*But I had an affinity for cooking, a real interest in making it the best that I could, and the patience to do the job, so eventually I rose to the rank of head cook. I have always cared about food. Always.*

*And the other part of my personality is the piece that says I want to win. I want to make that dish better than anyone has ever made it and I know I can do it.*

*I am as interested in being the best as a NASCAR driver is in winning the race. Every day. And I'm always like this. I want to win. I want to beat you. I want to make, every day, the best dish that can be made so that the food I make is as good as it can be.*

*Sometimes, when I'm in a competition it looks like I'm there to beat all the other cooks. But the truth is, I'm there to make my best time, to do my best, to come out ahead, and to know that I did it because I've dedicated my life to this craft, and I'm always in it to win.*

*This competition cooking actually started in my family, with my aunts and mother and grandmother each trying to best the next one. Fried chicken was a huge part of my growing-up years, and I'm happy to say that now that I've been trained in classical French cooking, my fried chicken is truly the best.*

*I learned from my grandmother to be my best every day. I also learned another life lesson from her that has sustained me to this day.*

*"It's not your time," she would say, rocking in her chair. "You have to be patient. Your time will come." And now as you sit here reading this book, I know. My time has come. If only my grandmother were still on this earth to see it.*

*But I carry her around with me in everything I do, and I offer her to you too. Just read these recipes. Cook them. You, too, will be blessed. That's what cooking can do. It can bring the past forward, and connect you with your own.*

⇛✦⇚

# Celebrate with a New Year's Day Buffet

✳ Chef Jesse's Black-Eyed Pea Cassoulet with Cornbread Crumb Topping
✳ Harissa Collard Greens
✳ Praline Crusted Old Fashioned Buttermilk Bundt Cake

## CHEF JESSE'S BLACK-EYED PEA CASSOULET WITH CORNBREAD CRUMB TOPPING

*My first experience with cassoulet was when I walked into Dennis Foy's Town Square Restaurant in Chatham, New Jersey. I was still just a kid and had been working at Aramark, but once I got a whiff of a real French restaurant, I was blown away. The smells were incredible. And that was before I had my first bite. Was I ever in for an education. Thank you, Chef, for three great years in your kitchen.*

*In the window that first day was a cassoulet ready to be picked up. It was in a big oval French soup tureen, with crusty garlic rosemary toast points.*

*I made this dish many times under Chef Foy's guidance, but, over the years, as I learned to make the dish, I found I wanted to make it with my spin, adding a bit of my own southern heritage. The first thing I changed were the peas. I believe black-eyed peas make a superior cassoulet, and corn bread on the top? Whooee. Is that good? POW!*

**Makes 16 servings (can be cut in half)**

There are as many cassoulet recipes as there are cooks in rural France. And now I bring my little twist on it to further the cause, as cooks have done forever.

Starting with the iconic black-eyed pea, then using traditional French ingredients and technique, including the D'Artagnan duck leg confit and finishing with a lovely corn bread crumb topping, I make it my own.

The process is long, but not hard. First you soak the black-eyed peas overnight in water. Then rinse and drain.

On the day you're going to serve, get out your biggest stew pot plus a Dutch oven, a sharp knife, and a cutting board, and prepare to be amazed. You're going to sear the meats, one at a time, in the stew pot, then add stock, soaked beans, and diced vegetables. Simmer until beans are soft, about 2 hours.

Build the dish in the Dutch oven by sautéing bacon until crispy; then sauté sausages and duck leg confit* on the whole thing once it's assembled.

Slow cook in the oven until beans are tender and dish is well married. Lift out the duck leg confit and remove the skin and bones. Replace duck meat in the mix and add more stock as needed.

Top with the corn bread crumb topping, pop it back into the oven to finish a few minutes, and then serve. Woowee, the aromas that will float through the house while it's cooking will buckle your knees.

*Confit is a traditional method for preserving meat by placing in animal fat to cover. Seals out all air borne bacteria.*

### Recipe:
- The night before, soak **1½ pounds black-eyed peas** in water to cover. Rinse and drain the next morning

- Meanwhile, sauté **1½ pounds pork shoulder** cut into ¼-inch cubes in a little olive oil in the bottom of the stew pot.

- Make a bouquet garni:
* 2 sprigs fresh parsley
* 2 bay leaves
* 2 whole cloves (or ½ teaspoon ground)
* ½ teaspoon black peppercorns

- Add these into a piece of cotton cheese cloth, tie with kitchen string, then drop the bundle into the stew pot.

- 4 quarts stock (homemade or good quality commercial)

- Soaked black-eyed peas

- Simmer until beans are tender, about 1½ hours, adding stock as needed to keep the level of stock to the top of the beans.

- Then, in a large Dutch oven, heat 1 teaspoon olive oil and sauté **1 pound thick, smoked bacon,** cut into lardons until crispy. Remove to a paper towel to drain.

- Next, brown 1 pound **country sage sausage** (remove casing, then break up in the bottom of the pan). Remove to a dish.

- Brown the vegetables in the bottom of the Dutch oven. As you cut the vegetables add them to the bottom of the pan over medium heat:
* 2 medium yellow onions, peeled and diced
* 2 medium carrots, peeled and diced
* 3 celery stalks with leaves, diced
* 5 garlic cloves, minced fine

- Next, stir **in 2 tablespoons tomato paste** plus sea salt and cracked black pepper to taste and cook about 5 minutes.

- Pour beans and meats on top of the veggies. Top with **4 duck confit**. Cover and let it cook on the stovetop until the duck can be separated from the bones, about 1 hour. Discard skin and bones.

- Chop duck and add it along with everything else back into the pot. Add any necessary stock to cover, then finish in a 275°F oven, or stovetop, covered on simmer.

- Stir from time to time. Cook until vegetables are tender.

- Once the cassoulet is cooked and meltingly tender, add corn bread crumb topping. Run it under the broiler to brown and serve.

## CHEF JESSE'S CORNBREAD CRUMB TOPPING

* 1 tablespoon fresh minced garlic
* 2 tablespoons olive oil
* 1½ cups Chef Jesse's corn bread, cubed small (make your own—see page 70—or use storebought corn bread)
* Sea salt and cracked black pepper to taste
* 2 tablespoons chopped fresh flat-leaf parsley

- In a medium skillet, cook garlic in oil over low heat about 1 minute, then toss with corn bread, seasonings, and parsley. Stir until crispy and golden brown, about 2 minutes. Sprinkle over cassoulet. Brown and serve.

## HARISSA COLLARD GREENS

*Harissa is a hot sauce that originated in Tunisia. It lifts flavors and it's so easy to use.*

**Makes 12 servings**

* 2 quarts water
* 2 lbs. smoked turkey wings
* 2 whole onions, peeled
* 2 tablespoons harissa* or to taste
* 4 bunches collard greens
* Sea salt and fresh black pepper to taste

- In a large stockpot, bring water and turkey wings to a boil. Simmer stock, then add onions and harissa. Cook 2 hours, then season to taste with salt and pepper.

- Wash greens in water to cover, remove stems, cut leaves into broad strips and then wash two more times. Drain.

- Remove turkey and onion and chop together. Heat 2 tablespoons olive oil in pot, and sweat the greens until they are limp. Then pour stock back in, adding turkey, onion, and more water to cover as needed.

- Simmer greens in stock about 2 hours, adjusting seasonings to taste.

*\*Harissa is a Tunisian version of chili paste readily available online at Amazon. Feel free to substitute Jewel hot sauce if you can't find harissa, although I predict if you start using harissa, you'll be hooked.*

# PRALINE CRUSTED OLD FASHIONED BUTTERMILK BUNDT CAKE

*I've made this cake so many times, I could do it in my sleep. It always gets rave reviews and it is easy to make, bake, and eat.*

**Makes 12-16 servings**

- Coat one 10-inch Bundt pan with butter and dust with flour. Set it aside. Preheat the oven to 350°F.

## Cake recipe

* 1 cup unsalted butter
* 2 cups granulated sugar
* 5 large eggs, room temperature
* 3 cups sifted cake flour
* 1 tablespoon baking powder
* ½ teaspoon kosher salt
* 2 teaspoons vanilla extract
* 1¼ cup buttermilk
* ¼ cup vegetable oil

- In a bowl, sift cake flour, baking powder, and salt.

- In a mixer, cream butter and granulated sugar together. Add eggs, one at a time, beating well after each addition. Stir in dry ingredients alternately with the buttermilk, beginning and ending with flour. Stir in vanilla, then oil.

- **Make the praline** and line into the pans.

* 1½ cups brown sugar
* ½ cup heavy cream
* 1 tablespoon corn syrup
* ¼ teaspoon kosher salt
* ¼ cup soft butter

* 1 teaspoon vanilla
* ½ cup chopped pecans

- Combine in a pot and cook and stir for a minute, or until it comes to a boil. Add warm mixture to the bottom of prepared 10" Bundt pan. Pour in the cake batter and spread to mix evenly. Bake 35 to 45 minutes, or until a toothpick comes out clean. Let it stand on a rack 10 minutes, then flip onto a cake plate and cool on a rack. Spread cooling praline over the cake to make a frosting.

# Make Martin Luther King Jr's January Birthday a Great Lunch

*When January rolls around, it is my honor and duty to acknowledge and remember Dr. Martin Luther King Jr. and his "I Have a Dream" speech. His fight for equal rights in America is my fight as well.*

*When I think of the civil rights movement, I'm saddened by how things were, but delighted that food played a great part in the decision making of some serious matters, because most meetings were held either around a dinner table where someone was cooking good old southern food, or in a restaurant, where they gathered to talk plans. And as a result, we have a more just and equitable society, one that I leave to my sons with pride.*

*There is one part of the "I Have a Dream" speech that I practice, live by, and hold dear to my heart.*

***"I look to a day when people will** not **be judged by the color of their skin, but by the content of their character."***

*Over the years, I have been treated in the worst way in some kitchens. But as a chef, I have always maintained my integrity and character and worked extremely hard. To make a difference, I learned to respect myself first, then expect the same respect from my peers. Like my grandmother and mother, I try to lead by example. I carry the torch now. Please enjoy my feast and look for my King dinner...POW!*

✳ Butternut Squash Soup with Hotcha Honey Shrimp

✳ Spiky Deviled Eggs

✳ Wilted Frisée and Belgian Endive with Radicchio, Bacon and a Spiked Vinaigrette

✳ Winter Pear Tarte Tatin

## BUTTERNUT SQUASH SOUP WITH HOTCHA HONEY SHRIMP

*This punched-up soup makes a great foil for the spicy shrimp.*

**Serves 8-12**

* 4 tablespoons butter
* I tablespoon grape-seed oil
* I leek, washed and chopped
* 2 garlic cloves, chopped
* I stalk celery, chopped
* I medium carrot, chopped
* 2 medium russet potatoes, peeled and cubed
* I medium butternut squash, peeled, seeded, and chopped
* I quart chicken stock
* Sea salt and freshly ground black pepper to taste
* 2 sprigs fresh thyme, minced
* 2 whole cloves, ground
* 2 whole allspice, ground

– Melt butter and oil in a large stockpot, then add leek, celery, carrot, potato, and squash as you get them prepared. Cook until lightly browned. Pour in stock, add salt, pepper, thyme, cloves and allspice and cover and bring to a boil. Reduce heat to low, cover the pot, and simmer 40 minutes, or until vegetables are tender.

– Transfer the soup to a blender and blend until smooth (or use a stick blender). Return to the pot and add stock as needed to obtain a nice thick mixture. Season with salt and pepper and serve hot.

## HOTCHA HONEY SHRIMP

* ½ cup honey
* ⅛ cup diced fresh jalapeño (stems and seeds removed) or to taste
* I pound peeled shrimp – any size

– Season shrimp with sea salt and black pepper. Sauté in a sauté pan with a bit of grape-seed oil. Sear shrimp on both sides until they turn pink. Toss with honey and pepper mixture. Add a spoonful to the top of each soup bowl and finish with minced fresh parsley

## SPIKY DEVILED EGGS

*Just a whiff of chili powder and hot paprika sprinkled on top of these traditional deviled eggs takes them to a whole new place.*

**Makes 12**

* 6 large hard-cooked eggs, peeled
* I tablespoon Hellmann's mayonnaise
* ½ teaspoon Dijon mustard
* Sea salt and black pepper to taste

– Garnish: sprinkling of chili powder and hot paprika

– Cut eggs in half lengthwise and remove yolks to a small bowl. Mix well with mayo, mustard, salt and pepper. Replace the whites, using a small spoon. Top with sprinkling of chili powder and hot paprika

## WILTED FRISÉE AND BELGIAN ENDIVE WITH RADICCHIO, BACON AND A SPIKED VINAIGRETTE

*I have loved frisée since my time in the French kitchen. It looks like a light green salad on a bad hair day. Far too wild to be tamed into a neat head, its spiny leaves just go every which way. But the hot and sweet flavor of this French chicory will win you over. The French pair it with buttery bacon cut into lardons. What a good idea. My little twist is to mix it with endive, radicchio, and shallots. Yes.*

**Makes 8 servings**

* I small head frisée, cored and cut into bite-size pieces
* I head white or red Belgian endive, cored and cut crosswise into strips ½-inch wide
* I head radicchio, cored and cut crosswise into strips ½-inch wide
* 3 shallots, minced
* 2 tablespoons chopped fresh chives
* Sea salt and freshly ground pepper, to taste
* 2 tablespoons extra-virgin olive oil
* ½ pound French lardons or other cured, unsmoked bacon, such as pancetta, cut
* into 1/4-inch dice
* 4 tablespoons sherry vinegar
* ½ teaspoon red chili flakes (optional)

– In a large bowl, combine the frisée, endive, radicchio, shallots, and chives. Season with salt and pepper and toss with 2 tablespoons olive oil. Set aside.

– Heat a heavy, nonstick skillet over medium-high heat. Add the bacon and the remaining oil, stirring constantly until the bacon is browned and has rendered much of its fat, about 2 minutes. Add vinegar and cook until syrupy, about 3 minutes. Add optional chili flakes.

– Immediately pour the hot bacon and vinegar over the greens and toss. Serve hot.


## WINTER PEAR TARTE TATIN

*One of only a few fruits that are actually at their best in the winter, choose Comice or Bosc pears and go forth!*

**Makes 8 servings**

**For the pastry dough:**
* 2 cups all-purpose flour
* ½ teaspoon kosher salt
* 9 tablespoons chilled unsalted butter
* 6 tablespoons ice water
* 3 tablespoons unsalted butter

**For tart:**
* ¼ cup granulated sugar
* 3 or 4 firm, ripe winter Bosc or Comice pears, cut in half with seeds scooped out
* (about 2 lb. total), peeled, halved, and cored
* ½ cup firmly packed brown sugar
* 2 tablespoons finely chopped crystallized ginger
* I tablespoon fresh lemon juice
* ½ teaspoon ground mace
* ¼ teaspoon EACH: ground cinnamon and cloves

– To make the pastry dough: in a bowl, stir together the flour and salt. Cut the butter into ½-inch chunks and add to the flour mixture. Using a pastry blender or 2 knives, cut in the butter until pea-size pieces form. Add the ice water, 1 tablespoon at a time, stirring lightly with a fork and then rubbing with your fingertips. Gather the dough into a ball, wrap it in plastic wrap, and refrigerate for 15 minutes.

— Preheat an oven to 375°F. Using 1 tablespoon butter, grease a 12-inch round baking dish with 2-inch sides, preferably of glass so you can watch the syrup forming. Sprinkle the granulated sugar evenly over the bottom of the dish.

— Place the pears, cut sides up, in a tightly packed layer in the prepared baking dish. Sprinkle ¼ cup of the brown sugar over the pears. Top with the crystallized ginger and the lemon juice. Cut the remaining butter into bits and dot the tops of the pears. Stir together the remaining ¼ cup brown sugar and the mace, cinnamon, and cloves. Sprinkle the mixture evenly over the pears.

— On a floured work surface, roll out the dough a little larger than the diameter of the baking dish and a scant ¼ inch thick. Drape the pastry over the rolling pin and transfer it to the baking dish. Carefully undrape the pastry over the pears. Tuck the edges of the pastry down to the bottom of the dish to form an interior rim that will encircle the pears once the tart is turned out of the dish. Prick the top all over with a fork.

— Bake until the crust is golden brown, the pears are tender, and a thickened, golden syrup has formed in the dish, about 1 hour.

— Remove from the oven and let stand for 5 minutes. To unmold, run a knife around the inside edge of the baking dish to loosen the sides of the tart. Invert a platter on top of the baking dish and, using pot holders to hold the platter and the baking dish tightly together, flip them. Lift off the baking dish. Serve warm.

# Superbowl Sunday Feast

*Here's a meal you can eat on your lap while you watch the big game. Just keep that chili hot in a Crockpot or on the back of the stove in a large stew pot. The wings can be made ahead and held in a low oven, and those cookies? POW!*

* Chef Jesse's Famous Beef Chili
* Hennessey Chicken Wings
* Red Cabbage and Radicchio Salad with Pecorino
* Garlic Tossed Toasted Pita Triangles
* Giant Chocolate Chip Cookie Pizza

## CHEF JESSE'S FAMOUS BEEF CHILI

*Who doesn't love chili? Adding a mix of beans gives the dish an added layer of texture and flavor.*

**Makes 6 to 8 servings**

* 1 teaspoon grape-seed oil
* 2 pounds lean ground beef
* 1 cup chopped onions
* ½ cup **EACH**: fresh red and yellow bell peppers
* 4 cloves garlic, chopped
* 1 tablespoon chopped canned chipotle, in adobo sauce
* 3 tablespoons ground cumin
* 3 tablespoons ground chili powder
* 1 cup tomato puree
* 2 cups beef stock
* 1 cup diced fresh plum tomatoes

* 1 cup EACH: pinto beans, kidney beans, pink beans

- Garnish: shredded cheddar, sour cream, and chopped green onions

- In a heavy sauce pot, heat oil to medium and sauté the ground beef meat until brown. Add into a strainer to discard the fat. In the same pot, add back a little oil and sauté onions, peppers, garlic, and chipotle pepper, for 3 minutes. Add cumin and chili powder and tomato puree. Let flavors meld together, and finally, add fresh diced tomatoes, cooked beans, and cook for 30 minutes, stirring from time to time so nothing sticks to the bottom of the pot. Taste and adjust seasonings. Serve in large soup bowls with shredded cheddar, sour cream, and green onions.

- Note: to prepare beans, soak dry beans in cold water overnight, Next day, in a sauce pot, bring water to boil, add 1 small onion, 1 bay leaf, and 1 thyme sprig. Add beans and cook for 2 hours or until fork tender. Reserve for later use.

## HENNESSEY CHICKEN WINGS

*If you like Buffalo wings, you're gonna love these spicy, sweet wings. POW!*

**Makes 6-8 servings**

* 3 pounds chicken wings
* ⅓ cup Hennessey whiskey
* ¼ cup pepper sauce (any brand)
* 3 tablespoons packed brown sugar

* 4 garlic cloves, minced
* 1 tablespoon grape-seed oil
* 1 teaspoon EACH: fresh squeezed lemon juice, minced tarragon
* ¼ teaspoon crushed red pepper

- Marinate the wings with a mixture of whiskey, pepper, sugar, garlic oil, lemon juice, tarragon, and crushed red pepper in a large bowl. Cover and set aside in the refrigerator overnight. (You can use a Ziploc bag too. Makes it easy to turn the wings from time to time.)

- Heat a grill or oven to 350°F. Lay out wings one layer deep and cook 30 minutes, turning wings once or twice. Serve warm.

## RED CABBAGE AND RADICCHIO SALAD WITH GOAT CHEESE AND WALNUTS

*Colors, textures, sweet, salty, and nutty. This salad has it all.*

**Makes 6 to 8 servings**

* ½ small red cabbage, finely shredded
* 1 small radicchio, finely shredded
* 2 Belgian endives, finely shredded
* 1 small fennel bulb, fronds reserved and finely shredded
* 2 tablespoons finely chopped flat-leaf parsley
* ½ cup toasted walnuts, roughly chopped
* ¼ cup crumbled goat cheese

### For the Dressing:
* 2 tablespoons apple cider vinegar
* 2 tablespoons maple syrup

* ¼ cup extra-virgin olive oil
* 2 tablespoons walnut oil
* sea salt and freshly ground pepper to taste

- Combine the thinly shredded cabbage, radicchio, endive, and fennel in a large bowl with the parsley and chopped fennel fronds.

- Whisk the vinegar, maple syrup, olive oil, and walnut oil in a small bowl. Season with sea salt and freshly ground black pepper to taste.

- Toss the salad with the vinaigrette just before serving. Top with toasted walnuts and crumbled goat cheese. Serve at once.

## GARLIC TOSSED TOASTED PITA TRIANGLES

- Quarter pitas and arrange on a baking sheet. Brush with melted butter and garlic. Heat until toasty. Serve at once.

## GIANT CHOCOLATE CHIP COOKIE PIZZA

**Makes 12 servings**

* 2 cups all-purpose flour
* 2 teaspoons cornstarch
* 1 teaspoon baking soda
* ½ teaspoon sea salt
* ¾ cup (1½ sticks) unsalted butter, softened to room temperature
* ¾ cup packed dark brown sugar
* ¼ cup granulated sugar
* 1 large egg, at room temperature
* 2 teaspoons pure vanilla extract

* 1¼ cup semi-sweet chocolate chips
* 12-inch pizza pan (one with a lip so there's no spill over the edges)

- Preheat oven to 350°F. Lightly grease a pizza pan with butter. Whisk the flour, cornstarch, baking soda, and salt together in a medium bowl. Set aside.

- Using a hand mixer or a stand mixer fitted with a paddle attachment, cream the butter and both sugars together on medium speed until smooth, about 2 minutes. Add the egg and beat on high until combined, about 1 minute. Scrape down the sides and bottom of the bowl as needed. Add the vanilla extract and mix on high until combined.

- Add the dry ingredients to the wet ingredients and mix on low until combined. With the mixer running on low speed, add the chocolate chips. Dough will be thick and soft.

- Transfer the cookie dough to the pizza pan and flatten out with your fingers or a rubber spatula until the edges reach the sides. Bake until golden, 15-25 minutes..

- Allow the cookie pizza to cool on the pan set on a wire rack before slicing with a pizza cutter. Cover leftovers and store at room temperature for 2-3 days or in the refrigerator for up to 5 days.

# Chapter 2: February

**Work is work.**

I always have kept a little spiral bound notebook and pencil in the breast pocket of my chef's coat. Wherever I am, whatever I am doing, I find it's helpful to jot down what I've learned from the experience of the moment.

Now, of course, I have boxes of these notebooks in a drawer at my house. But not a day goes by that I don't see something that needs to be written down.

I call it **TAKE NOTE**.

One way to look at it is to understand that this was the beginning of my culinary training. Just paying attention, making a note, and doing things over and over until they were burned into my brain was the plan.

Whereas the kids today go straight to culinary school, I went straight to work. I made it a practice, and still do, to get to work early, ready to work and ready to go. POW! That's how it started for me, and how it remains today.

I am the first person on the job. I am the last to leave. I come to work clean, suited up, with my notebook in my pocket, and ready to go.

Maybe Chef would tell me to make 700 crepes before the breakfast service began. Let me tell you, do that a few times and make notes and soon you are an expert. It's not rocket science, but it is work. As I tell my students today, "Work is work. Do it over and over until you are fast, accurate, and proud of what you've done." That's how you become a chef.

It's harder for your bosses to disrespect you, to call you names, or to otherwise humiliate you when you are doing your best, with no attitude except to be a part of the team that gets the job done.

And what is a chef? He's the master of the kitchen, the boss, the leader of all the cooks working under him. That word CHEF gets kicked around a lot now, but it really is quite specific.

Sometimes I think of the line in the kitchen like an orchestra, in which each person is playing their part and in great harmony. Or maybe a dance, where nobody steps on anybody else's feet.

But however you choose to see it, remember that you are a team, working together for one goal: to turn out the best food possible. It's a profession in which I take great pride.

And I've certainly had my struggles with it.

Racism is a fact of life in kitchens. Back when I started, that teamwork would be going great when we were preparing to serve offsite, but often the head of the operation would just tell me and the other black cooks to "lay back" while the others went to serve the food elsewhere.

That was hard to take. Not everybody can hold their temper and just do as they are told in a situation like that. But I had the experiences of my mother and grandmother to draw from, and I'd seen them hold their head up high, keep their dignity, do the best job possible, and draw strength from the act of the work itself, regardless of the indignities that were an inevitable part of life for black and brown people. Then. And now.

# Feast of February's Future

* Spiced Shrimp on a Bed of Cheddar Grits Cake
  with Haricots Verts

* Cold Oven Pound Cake Dusted with Coconut

*Everywhere I ever cooked this spiced-up shrimp dish, people raved. It's beautiful to look at and delicious—one of my trademark dishes. Yes. POW!*

## SPICED SHRIMP ON A BED OF CHEDDAR GRITS CAKE

**Makes 8 servings**

* Chef Jesse's spice blend (see below)
* 16 medium shrimp
* ½ cup unsalted butter (1 stick)
* ¼ cup grape-seed oil
* 1½ teaspoon fresh minced garlic
* ½ cup EACH: red and yellow bell peppers
* ½ cup shrimp stock*
* microgreens or fresh minced parsley for garnish

- Remove shrimp from their shells. Keep shells to make a shrimp stock*. Place shrimp in a small bowl, then combine Chef Jesse's seafood spice blend, and mix a couple of tablespoons with the shrimp. Marinate in the fridge for 4 hours or overnight for more flavor—I recommend overnight.

- In a medium sauté pan, melt butter and oil. On medium heat, quickly sauté shrimp on both sides. Remove from pan quickly, using tongs, and set on a plate.

- Sauté garlic and peppers in that same pan for 1 minute. Stirring all the time, add shrimp stock. Let sauce get thick, then adjust seasoning. Add seared shrimp back into the pan and stir to heat shrimp through.

Feast #4

- Serve over cheese grits cakes. Drizzle some sauce on the plate. Finish with microgreens or fresh green herbs.

*To make an instant seafood stock, boil shrimp shells in 2 cups hot water with a bit of salt, then strain to make stock. Store up to 3 days covered in the refrigerator.*

## CHEF JESSE'S SPICE BLEND

*Make up a batch of this spice mix except fresh ingredients and keep it in your pantry in a closed glass jar. Add fresh ingredients at the last minute. POW!*

* I teaspoon dried thyme
* ½ teaspoon EACH: black and white pepper, salt, granulated onion, crushed red pepper
* I teaspoon sweet paprika AND granulated garlic

- At serving time add ½ teaspoon EACH: fresh thyme, rosemary, and tarragon, finely minced

## CHEF JESSE'S CHEDDAR GRITS CAKES

### Makes 24 discs

*These POW! flavored discs make a great base for a lot of different dishes. Make up a batch and keep them in the refrigerator until serving time. Then heat them in the oven, plate them, and add toppings. POW!*

* 4 cups water
* I teaspoon kosher salt
* ½ teaspoon white pepper
* ½ cup butter (I stick)
* I cup old-fashioned or stone-ground grits*
* I cup heavy cream
* I cup cheddar cheese, shredded
* I cup pepper jack cheese, shredded

- Generously butter a 9 x 12 utility pan. Heat water to a boil in a large pot and then add salt, pepper, and butter. Whisk in the grits. Reduce heat to medium, cover, and cook 30 minutes, stirring frequently. Add cream and cook 5 minutes. Stir in cheese, then pour into the prepared pan.

- Cool grits until firm. Use a biscuit cutter to cut them. Arrange on a lightly buttered baking sheet and bake 5 minutes or until tinged lightly brown on the edges.

- To serve, place a grits cake on the dinner plate, top with shrimp, then add a sprinkle of microgreens or parsley.

*If you're in a hurry, substitute instant grits and make them following box directions. But for best flavor, use old-fashioned grits, which are sold in grocery stores under the brand Bob's Red Mill.*

## HARICOTS VERTS WITH SHALLOTS, BUTTER, AND FRESH THYME

### Nothing more French than haricots verts. POW!

### Makes 8 servings

* I pound fresh haricots verts (the French

green bean)

* 2 teaspoons grape-seed oil
* I small shallot, minced fine
* I teaspoon butter
* I teaspoon fresh thyme
* Sea salt and freshly ground black pepper to taste

— Bring a large pot of cold water to a boil. Salt generously and add haricots verts and cook 8-10 minutes, or until tender. Drain and plunge into ice water.

— Heat oil in a large sauté pan over medium heat. Add shallots, butter, and thyme, and cook until shallots are tender, 1-2 minutes. Add beans and toss to coat with the shallot mixture. Taste and adjust seasonings. Serve hot.

## COLD OVEN POUND CAKE DUSTED WITH COCONUT

**Makes 12-16 servings**

*Back in the day, when grandmothers made this cake in a wood-burning stove, they measured everything by weight. But now, we measure by volume. Nevertheless, pound cake is one of my standbys. It's easy to make, keeps well, and you can add a lot of different toppings to suit the meal. Or just serve it naked. Yum. Here, we've dusted the cake with simple coconut shreds. POW!*

* 3 cups all-purpose flour, sifted
* I tablespoon baking powder
* ½ teaspoon sea salt
* 1½ cups unsalted butter

* 2½ cups granulated sugar
* 6 large eggs
* 1½ teaspoons vanilla extract
* ¾ cup heavy cream

— Grease and flour a 10-inch tube or Bundt pan. Do not preheat the oven.

— In a medium bowl, mix flour, baking powder and salt. Set aside.

— In the large bowl of a mixer fitted with the paddle, cream butter and granulated sugar until light and fluffy. Add eggs, one at a time, mixing well each time. Add vanilla.

— Add flour mixture alternately with cream. Beat until smooth. Pour batter into tube or Bundt pan.

— Place cake on the middle rack of a cold oven, set the temperature to 350°F, and bake for 60 to 90 minutes, or until a toothpick inserted into center of cake comes out clean.

— Turn the cake out onto a wire rack to cool. Dust with confectioners' sugar and/or coconut while warm.

— Store in a covered cake plate. Keeps up to a week.

# Valentine's Day Is for Lovers

* Pecan Crusted Rack of Lamb
* Yukon Gold Mash with Truffle Oil
* Wilted Garlic Spinach
* Double Chocolate Soufflé

*My valentine for more than 30 years, Annette, loves me to cook this feast for just the two of us. It's my great pleasure.*

## PECAN CRUSTED RACK OF LAMB

**Makes 2 servings**

* 2 lamb racks, cleaned and frenched* (your choice of brand, I prefer Australian)
* 2 tablespoons extra-virgin olive oil
* 2 cloves minced garlic
* 1 tablespoon EACH: fresh minced thyme, rosemary, coarse black pepper, kosher salt
* 2 tablespoons creole mustard
* ¾ cup panko bread crumbs
* ¾ cup toasted chopped pecans

– In a medium bowl, mix oil, garlic, thyme, rosemary, and black pepper together. Rub all over lamb and marinate, covered, in the refrigerator overnight.

Next day:

– Preheat the oven to 425°F.

– Season lamb with kosher salt. In a hot skillet, sear the lamb on both sides for 4 minutes, and until golden brown. Place in a 425°F. oven for 8 minutes, remove from the oven, and let rest.

— Brush meat with creole mustard. Combine crumbs and pecans in a bowl, dredge lamb to cover, and return to oven just to toast for 5 minutes. Serve hot.

***How to French a rack of lamb***

— Ask your butcher to "French" the rack of lamb. Or, you can do it yourself. Lay the rack on the cutting board, fat side up. Cut away the fat up to the meaty portion, making a clean slice using a sharp knife.

— Flip it over, and using the sharp knife, cut the meaty part away from the bones. Now turn the fatty side UP again and begin slicing the meat away from the fat.

— Pull the fat away from the bone and trim the bones clean with your knife. Now that is a Frenched rack. Wipe the bones clean with a paper towel.

## YUKON GOLD MASH WITH TRUFFLE OIL

**Makes 6 to 8 servings**

* 6-8 medium Yukon gold potatoes, peeled and quartered
* 1 teaspoon sea salt
* ½ cup butter (½ stick)
* ½ teaspoon freshly ground white pepper
* 1 cup hot whole milk
* Sea salt to taste
* 1 tablespoon white truffle oil

— Place peeled and quartered potatoes in a pot of water. Add salt and bring to a boil. Reduce heat to medium and cook for approx. 20 minutes or until cooked through and tender. Drain and mash with potato masher or stick blender. Add butter, hot milk, pepper and salt, and combine. Add truffle oil. Beat well with a stick blender or mixer until fluffy and creamy. Serve hot.

## WILTED GARLIC SPINACH

**Makes 6 to 8 servings**

* ¼ cup grape-seed oil
* 3 cloves garlic, minced
* ½ cup shallots, finely minced
* 4 bunches fresh spinach
* ½ teaspoon EACH: kosher salt and freshly ground black pepper

— Thoroughly wash the spinach and drain in a colander.

— In a large heavy skillet, heat the oil over medium-high heat. Cook and stir garlic and shallots for 2 to 3 minutes; stir in the spinach and cook for 5 minutes. Reduce the heat, stir until wilted, and season with kosher salt, fresh black pepper.

# BLACK HAND IN THE POT

One of the big influences when I was cooking with Chef Dennis Foy, always cooking family meals for the staff where we had to use all the leftovers, like the pork backs, was when I first heard of Edna Lewis, who ran Café Nicholas in New York. She changed my life.

I was already doing farm-to-table food. We were already doing Southern, but Edna Lewis showed me how to be authentic. Chef Lewis was from Virginia. She changed the game. She said there were white people in the kitchen with her. It may seem odd to you that this fact made her stand out, but it did.

What I learned from Chef Lewis was how to be true to my roots, to my memories that came through the kitchen door, and to acknowledge and admire the truth of what I learned from my Southern family.

I give you my aunt and my grandmother. It's just a feeling you get through food. It opens up everything in your heart, and you know that though these people are a little intimidating when you start out, if you just stay true to your roots, you'll learn what you need to learn and you'll be free. I'm free now and the kitchen did that for me.

Edna Lewis was the real deal. She always told the stories. She showed people the truth that she was. This really helped me when I was starting out. My whole struggle was: "Am I worthy to work on this line?" And even when it was hard and people were really hard on me, I just smiled. I kept my dignity, my pride, and I just cooked. It has worked for me, just like it worked for Ms. Lewis.

She made this classic French dessert, the chocolate soufflé, famous in America. It was at the time when Julia Child had brought French cooking into American households and when incredible black chefs made it all look easy.

## DOUBLE CHOCOLATE SOUFFLÉ

*Chef Edna Lewis made her version of this soufflé famous in her New York restaurant, Café Nicholas. In fact, they even put the recipe on the cover of a well-known food magazine of the day.*

*The big secret is that it's so easy, it will buckle your knees with the first bite.*

### Makes 10 servings

* 2 tablespoons unsalted butter, plus more for greasing the ramekins
* ½ cup granulated sugar, plus more for dusting
* 6 ounces semi-sweet chocolate, finely chopped
* ¼ teaspoon kosher salt
* ¼ cup whole milk
* 2 tablespoons unsweetened cocoa powder
* 6 large eggs, separated

– Preheat the oven to 400°F. Grease ten 6-ounce ramekins with butter and dust with granulated sugar, tapping out the excess; set on a rimmed baking sheet.

– In a large bowl set over a saucepan of simmering water, melt the semi-sweet chocolate with the 2 tablespoons of butter and the kosher salt, stirring a few times. In another medium saucepan, bring the milk just to a simmer over moderate heat. Whisk in the cocoa powder, and then whisk in the melted chocolate.

– In a large bowl, beat the egg yolks. Gradually whisk in the chocolate mixture until smooth. In another large bowl, using an electric mixer, beat the egg whites at high speed until medium peaks form, about 2 minutes. Gradually beat in the ½ cup of granulated sugar and continue beating until the whites form stiff peaks, 2 to 3 minutes.

— Carefully fold the egg whites into the chocolate mixture until no streaks remain. Spoon the soufflé into the prepared ramekins and bake in the center of the oven until risen, about 15 minutes. Serve right away.

# Uncle William's Hunters' Lunch

\* Uncle William's Rabbit Gumbo with Jasmine Rice

\* Turnip and Mustard Green Mash

\* Hush Puppies

\* Easy Crème Brûlée

## UNCLE WILLIAM'S RABBIT GUMBO WITH JASMINE RICE

*My uncle William loved grilling rabbit and was a master rabbit catcher in the South when he was a boy. He would set the traps, then check them later. Always exciting.*

*Uncle William helped me understand where food comes from. It's not just something in the supermarket under a clear plastic wrap. He and all my North Carolina relatives had a serious respect for food and where it came from. They didn't waste a thing and they knew what they were doing. With them, work is work and has real meaning.*

**Yields 2 quarts**

*   3-4 pounds rabbit legs
*   1 cup Wondra flour + 1 cup all-purpose flour
*   ½ cup grape-seed oil
*   ¾ cup EACH: onion, green and red bell pepper, medium dice
*   ½ cup celery, medium dice
*   2 cloves garlic, minced
*   1 teaspoon jalapeño, seeded and minced
*   1 teaspoon oregano, minced
*   ½ cup tomato paste
*   ½ cup okra, sliced, lightly fried (optional)
*   2 quarts rabbit stock or chicken stock (homemade or store bought)

* 1 cup Andouille sausage (browned in a pan; reserve for later use)
* 1 dash filé* powder

— Dredge rabbit legs in Wondra flour on both sides. In a heavy Dutch oven, heat oil and brown rabbit legs on both sides. Remove and drain on paper towels. Add 1 cup of all-purpose flour to the oil in the pot, and stir slowly to make a peanut butter-colored roux, about 25 minutes.

— Add vegetables one at a time: onions, celery, peppers, garlic, jalapeño, oregano, and sauté until the vegetables are tender. Mix in tomato paste, and continue cooking about 5 minutes. Add fried okra, the stock, and browned sausage. Cook for 45 minutes or more over LOW heat. Taste and adjust seasoning. Add Filè powder, and stir to thicken.

— Serve over Jasmine Rice

*Filé (fee-lay) powder is dried sassafras leaves originating in Africa. Available at high-end grocery stores or online. It's a good thickener to keep on hand. It is often used in Cajun and other Southern stews.*

## TURNIP AND MUSTARD GREEN MASH

**Makes 8 servings**

* 1 bunch turnips with stems
* 1 bunch mustard greens
* Sea salt and butter to taste
* Water

—

— Bring to a boil a large stew pot of barely salted water. Scrub turnips and add to the pot. Chop greens and add to the pot. Cook until tender. Fish out the turnips and mash them. Pour out most of the water from the pot and add the turnips back to the greens. Season to taste with sea salt and butter. Don't forget to save that pot "likker." Not only is it delicious, but it's loaded with natural vitamins and minerals. POW!

## HUSH PUPPIES

**Makes about 24**

*What a quick and easy bread to serve.*

* 1 cup yellow corn meal
* ¼ cup all-purpose flour
* 1½ teaspoon baking powder
* ¼ teaspoon sea salt
* ¾ cup milk
* 1 large egg, lightly beaten
* 1 small onion, finely chopped
* 1½ teaspoons grape-seed oil + more to go in the pot for frying

— Combine cornmeal, flour, baking powder, and salt in a medium mixing bowl. Mix well and set aside.

— In another bowl add milk, beaten egg, onion, and oil. Make a well in the middle of the dry ingredients and add wet ingredients, mixing well.

— Heat the grape-seed oil in a deep fryer or a pot with high sides (to avoid splashing hot oil) to 365°F. Use a spoon to scoop the batter, forming oval-shaped hush puppies. Carefully drop the hush puppies into the hot oil, a few at a time. Fry on both sides until golden brown, about 3 minutes. Drain on paper towels. Serve hot.

## EASY CRÈME BRÛLÉE

*The original French dessert. I figure I made about a jillion of them working for Chef Foy. He taught me such respect for ingredients. Only the best eggs, the best cream, and pure vanilla will do. That and the classic technique will get you there.*

**Makes 6 servings**

* I large egg
* 4 large egg yolks
* ½ cup granulated sugar, plus I tablespoon for each serving
* 3 cups organic heavy cream
* I teaspoon pure vanilla extract
* I tablespoon orange liqueur

— Preheat the oven to 300°F.

— In the bowl of an electric mixer fitted with the paddle attachment, mix the egg, egg yolks, and ½ cup of the granulated sugar together on low speed until just combined. Meanwhile, scald the cream in a small saucepan until it's very hot to the touch but not boiled. With the mixer on low speed, slowly add the cream to the eggs. Add the vanilla and orange liqueur and pour into 6- to 8-ounce ramekins until almost full.

— Place the ramekins in a baking pan and carefully pour boiling water into the pan to come halfway up the sides of the ramekins. Bake for 35 to 40 minutes, until the custards are set when gently shaken. Remove the custards from the water bath, cool to room temperature, and refrigerate, covered with plastic wrap, until firm.

— To serve, spread 1 tablespoon of granulated sugar evenly on the top of each ramekin and heat with a kitchen blowtorch until the granulated sugar caramelizes evenly. Or, place on a baking sheet and run it under the broiler until it bubbles, about 3-5 minutes. Allow to sit at room temperature for a minute until the caramelized granulated sugar hardens.

— PROPANE GAS TORCH SAFETY: Propane gas torches are highly flammable and should be kept away from heat, open flame, and prolonged exposure to sunlight. When lighting a propane gas torch, place the torch on a flat, steady surface, facing away from you. Light the match or lighter and then open the gas valve. Light the gas jet, and blow out the match. Always turn off the burner valve to "finger tight" when finished using the torch.

# Chapter 3: March

**How the Kitchen Saved Me from the Streets.**

*I often wonder where would I be without the kitchen. It saved my life.*

*I grew up in Newark, on High Street. I continued running in the streets. Every day was survival of the fittest. When I walked to school, there were bullies everywhere. I had to learn to fight. But I really wasn't a fighter—just a nice kid who loved to make friends. But that was only inside my heart. On the outside, I had to play tough, act like I wasn't scared. And so I found I could draw on my anger, hit first, and never ask questions later. I could go from zero to 60 in a split second. I grew up with this street anger. It was my weapon, my sword, my salvation. Or so I thought.*

*When I went to work as a teenager, doing the lowest restaurant jobs there are, I discovered in the kitchen there are all kinds of anger—the chef screaming at the top of his lungs, lots of name calling, fights, and plain old backstabbing. I witnessed it all. For example, one day I had an issue with another cook, and bam, I went at him with a knife. I told him, "I'm from Newark. I don't play." I was serious, but something happened that day that changed my life forever.*

*Lucky for me, that kid ran away. In a split-second, my life was saved. I looked down at that knife in my hand and knew an important river had been crossed.*

*From then on, when I would feel anger welling up in me, I would just go to the walk-in, close the door, and scream my lungs out.*

*No matter how good I was, they treated me like an animal because of my anger. I knew then I couldn't get upset like that, or they would lock me up and throw away the key. I had to control this anger somehow. So I*

decided to just smile, no matter what was going on inside.

I became a "yes chef! no chef!" kind of cook, holding all my problems and issues inside. Sometimes I would, as I say, go into the freezer and scream at the top of my voice to get it all out, and then go back to work. I learned to kill them with kindness, and never let them see me sweat. The less information they knew about me, my background, and where I came from, the better for me.

But I was terribly lonely. That's the truth. So, at a young age, I started helping kids who had similar issues; like anger problems, no father, being bullied.

And guess what? When I decided to help kids like that, it helped me conquer my issues as well, giving back, making a difference in young boys' lives. I showed them that they could stay out of jail. My speech has always been, "Let's talk about it, get it off your chest. That's how I controlled my temper. And you can too"."

I had seen my mother and my grandmother always giving and smiling, and I got it. Givers get. It began to work for me. Not only did I find my place at the stove, in the kitchen, but I found a place where I could help others. And when I was focused on others, I began to feel better.

Plus, I just loved to cook—every day, every setting, every opportunity. To focus on the job at hand, to just cook it out, helped make me whole again.

Sometimes, I have to sit down and wonder what happened to that angry young kid who once pulled a knife on somebody. But I know the answer. He went to the kitchen and put that energy to work.

⟫⟪

# St. Patrick's Day: When we're all Irish for a day

＊ Honey Pineapple Glazed Ham

＊ Braised Savoy Cabbage, Carrots, and New Potatoes

＊ Waldorf Salad

＊ Blondies

## HONEY PINEAPPLE GLAZED HAM

*Life gets so much easier when you buy a fully cooked spiral sliced ham to start with. To make a ham from scratch see pp 203 for the Christmas ham. POW!*

**Makes 8 to 10 servings**

* 5-pound spiral sliced ham (fully cooked)
* 1 cup pineapple juice
* 1 cup ginger ale
* ¼ cup brown sugar
* ½ cup honey
* 2 teaspoon ground cloves
* 1 fresh orange, juiced, and zest

– Heat oven to 375°F.

– In a medium saucepan, add pineapple juice, ginger ale, brown sugar, honey, cloves and fresh orange juice with zest, and bring it to a hard boil, about 10 minutes. Then pour over the ham in a baking pan. Bake until fully hot, about 20 minutes. Glaze should be semi-thick.

– Serve alongside vegetables and potatoes. POW!

## BRAISED SAVOY CABBAGE, CARROTS, AND NEW POTATOES

**Makes 6 to 8 servings**

*To braise means to cook food low and slow so the flavors can marry. My grandmother had a pot on the back of the stove many days to braise whatever she could scare up that day.*

* I large yellow onion
* 4 medium carrots
* 6 medium red potatoes
* 3 ribs celery, with leaves on top
* I Savoy cabbage, about 6 to 8 cups
* I tablespoon extra-virgin olive oil
* 2 bay leaves
* ½ teaspoon herbes de provence
* 6 cups chicken stock or water

– Roughly chop onion. Peel carrots; then slice by cutting in half the long way (in 2 or more sections), then into half or quarter circles. Peel and slice potatoes to a similar size. Slice celery, cutting the wide end in half lengthwise. Remove dark green outer leaves from cabbage. Cut off a thick slice, avoiding the core. Lay flat, cut into 3 or 4 wedges, then thickly slice the wedges.

– Heat olive oil in a large soup pot. Add onion and sauté until it starts to get tender, about 5 minutes. Add celery and sauté 5 minutes longer. Add carrots, potatoes, cabbage, herbs, and stock. Cover and simmer until vegetables are tender (30 to 40 minutes).

## WALDORF SALAD

**Makes 8 to 10 servings**

*Here's a recipe that was invented in a fancy New York restaurant, but hitch-hiked to the South as soon as it could get there. On every Southern table for holidays.*

* I large navel orange
* 2 cups diced, unpeeled apple
* I teaspoon finely grated orange peel
* ½ cup EACH: raisins, thinly sliced celery, chopped walnuts
* ¼ cup mayonnaise
* I tablespoon granulated sugar
* ¼ cup whipping cream
* salad greens or lettuce

– Zest orange for the 1 teaspoon grated orange peel; peel and section orange over a bowl to catch any juices. Cut each orange section in half; reserve 1 tablespoon of the collected orange juice.

– In a large bowl combine diced apple, orange peel, raisins, celery, walnuts, and orange pieces.

– In a separate bowl, blend together mayonnaise, granulated sugar, and reserved orange juice. Fold in cream and gently stir into the apple salad mixture.

– Arrange salad greens on salad plates and top with salad.

# BLONDIES

**Makes 24 squares**

*Brownies' cousin, these are rich, easy to make, and easy to eat. POW!*

* ½ cup (1 stick) butter, melted
* 1 cup tightly packed dark brown sugar
* ¼ cup molasses
* 1 large egg, lightly beaten
* 1 teaspoon vanilla extract
* ½ teaspoon baking powder
* ⅛ teaspoon baking soda
* Pinch of sea salt
* 1 cup all-purpose flour
* ⅓ cup butterscotch chips
* ½ cup chopped walnuts

- Heat the oven to 375°F. Lightly grease an 8 x 11 inch baking pan with butter.

- In a large mixing bowl, add and stir together melted butter, sugar, molasses, egg, vanilla, then baking powder, soda, salt, and flour. Fold in butterscotch chips and walnuts.

- Lay out onto the baking pan and even it out. Then pop into the oven and bake until golden brown, 15 to 20 minutes. Remove to cooling rack. Cool, then cut into squares. Store in an airtight tin.

# March Madness: For Double J, Our Own Basketball Star and Hero

Can I even begin to tell you how proud Annette and I are of our son, Double J? As a recent college graduate, he is being courted by overseas professional basketball. All I can tell you is that he can fly, and when he is on the basketball court, he floats and flies and always gets that ball exactly where he wants it. We are so proud.

This is Double J's favorite celebration dinner after a big game. He is a big guy with a big appetite, and this one does it for Double J.

> ✳ Slow-Braised Veal Osso Buco over Parsnip Mash Steamed Garlic Broccoli
> ✳ Chef Jesse's Coconut Bread Pudding with Bourbon Sauce

## SLOW-BRAISED VEAL OSSO BUCO

*(allow one shank per person)*

* 4 to 6 veal shanks (12 oz.)
* Chef Jesse's Spice Blend:
* 1 teaspoon kosher salt
* ¼ teaspoon black pepper
* ½ teaspoon white pepper
* 1 teaspoon EACH: granulated garlic, onion, and sweet paprika
* ½ cup grape-seed oil + 2 tablespoons for the pan
* 4 medium carrots, peeled and cut medium dice
* 1 medium onion, cut into medium dice
* 4 celery stalks, cut into medium dice
* ½ cup tomato paste
* 2 cups dry red wine (pinot is great)
* 4 cups beef broth (homemade or store-bought)
* 6 to 8 sprigs fresh thyme

- Preheat the oven to 375°F.

- In a large oven-proof saucepot (or Dutch oven), heat 2 tablespoons oil over medium-high heat until just smoking. Add spice blended shanks and sear on all sides, turning with tongs to get an even golden color. Remove the shanks to a dish and add carrots and onions to the pot. Sauté for 2 minutes, turn once, then add celery, stirring quickly. Add tomato paste, cook for 2 minutes more. Add wine to quickly deglaze the pan.

- Now, stir in the stock, bay leaf, and thyme. Raise the heat to high and bring to a boil, stirring and scraping the bottom. Add shanks back to the saucepot, cover, and place in the oven until tender—about 3 to 3½ hours with oven turned down to 300°. Remove the shanks to a plate. Skim off fat from the pan, bring to a boil, reduce by one-third, and then add shanks back into the sauce. Simmer for 5 to 7 minutes.

## PARSNIP MASH

**Makes 8 servings**

* 8 medium parsnips, scrubbed and cut into large pieces
* Barely salted water to boil
* 1 tablespoon butter
* Sea salt and freshly ground black pepper to taste

- Add parsnips to boiling water and cook until tender, about 15 minutes. Drain, then season with butter, salt and pepper. Mash with a potato masher or stick blender. Serve hot.

## STEAMED GARLIC BROCCOLI

**Makes 8 servings**

* 4 large broccoli heads, stemmed and cut into large pieces
* Large garlic heads, smashed
* Sea salt and freshly milled black pepper

- Place broccoli in a large steamer basket over boiling water. Cover and steam until just tender, about 10 minutes. Remove from the heat, and place in a large serving bowl. In a small pan, melt butter, sauté garlic until it begins to color, then toss with the broccoli. Season to taste with salt and pepper. Serve hot.

## CHEF JESSE'S COCONUT BREAD PUDDING WITH BOURBON SAUCE

*Bake this old-fashioned dessert in a boiling water bath in the oven. It will be tender and crunchy all at once. POW!*

**Makes 8 servings**

* ½ cup sweetened flaked coconut
* ½ loaf French or white bread
* 6 eggs
* 1 cup granulated sugar
* 1 cup (½ pint heavy cream)
* 2 cups (1 pint) half-and-half cream
* ½ cup dark raisins

* ½ cup golden raisins
* 1 tablespoon almond extract
* 1 tablespoon vanilla extract
* 4 tablespoons unsalted butter

– Preheat oven to 350°F and butter a 2-quart clear baking dish. Toast coconut on a shallow pan until golden brown, about 2 to 5 minutes. Set aside. Trim crust from bread and cut bread into 1-inch cubes. In a large bowl, beat eggs until foamy. Gradually stir in granulated sugar. Stir in heavy cream, half-and-half, and extracts. Soak bread in the egg mixture until moistened. Add coconut and raisins. Mix well. Pour mixture into the baking dish. Place butter over top. Place the baking dish into a baking pan and pour hot water into the pan to a depth of about 1 inch. Bake uncovered for 45 minutes. Serve with your favorite ice cream.

## BOURBON SAUCE

**Makes 2 cups**

* ½ cup (1 stick) unsalted butter, softened
* 3 cups sifted powdered sugar
* ½ cup bourbon

– Beat butter until creamy. Mix in powdered sugar. Mix until light. Add bourbon and pour over warm bread pudding.

# Hints of Spring for an Early Easter: Fat Tuesday Begins the Feasting

Signaling the coming Easter, Fat Tuesday is a celebration of festive seasonal foods from the fried oysters to Sweet Potato Soufflé. POW!

*Hannah Lewis Jones, a monarch of a woman to me, our Queen of Southern Cooking, from Snow Hill, North Carolina. When I think of my grandmother, food always comes up first, because she was the best; her cakes, pies, and those biscuits. POW!*

*Losing my grandmother was devastating to our family. She lived to be 92 years old. A godly woman, she trusted in the Lord; her favorite saying was "You better get your soul right for Judgment Day."*

*I'm very blessed to have experienced my grandmother's teaching, through food and life, the sense of survival that what was served on the table was what you ate— no options or variety. No questions asked. Just clean your plate and say thank you.*

*So far, up to now, everything she told me has come true. Be humble, help people, and, her favorite line: "Be nice, Junior."*

*I will continue your legacy and will always bake a pie for you. That's what Hannah did; she made you either a Famous Sweet Potato Pie or Molasses Pudding.*

*On her birthday, which came on April Fool's Day, 1920, and later when we were all in North Carolina, we would take her to the all-you-can-eat raw oyster buffet that was held every Friday night. She would look that hostess in the eye and say, "Girl, you not making any money tonight, 'cause I'm gonna eat up all those oysters. And then I want a big piece of that sweet potato pie. I hope you learned to make it right, like I taught you."*

*The proudest moment in my life was when my mom let me deliver the speech at my grandmother's funeral. She died March 15, 2013. Before I approached the stage, I had been listening to folks stand up and say a few words about my grandmother. That moment decided my faith. I knew my purpose in life—my deliverance was to continue her quest to help the sick, the needy, folks who don't have a voice, and, last but not least, the young.*

*Most in the crowd at her funeral were young people whose lives my grandmother had touched. She lives on inside me, and as she always said, "Don't worry about me, God got me."*

*God took care of her for 92 years. She didn't suffer or complain—just closed her eyes forever. This is the feast I loved to cook for my grandmother. She loved oysters and here's my little twist on that sweet potato dessert. POW!*

* Fried Oysters with Basil Sauce
* Arugula Salad with a Lemon Vinaigrette
* Sweet Potato Soufflé

## FRIED OYSTERS WITH BASIL SAUCE

**Makes 8 servings**

*You've heard that you are only supposed to eat oysters in months without an "r" because of those red tides. But cultivated oysters are okay year-round. Serve one or two to each diner, just for an appetizer.*

**Basil Sauce:**
* 1 cup packed fresh basil leaves
* ½ cup extra-virgin olive oil
* Sea salt and freshly milled black pepper

**Oyster Breading:**
* ½ cup whole milk
* 1 large egg
* 1 cup panko bread crumbs
* 1 tablespoon EACH: chopped chervil, chives, and thyme
* 1 cup all-purpose flour
* 16 large oysters
* Grape-seed oil for frying

- Blanch the basil by bringing a small pan of water to a boil. Add basil and cook only 10-15 seconds. Remove basil to a bowl of ice water to stop the cooking. Lift out of ice water to a strainer and drain. Blot with paper towels.

- Purée basil with olive oil until smooth. Taste and adjust seasoning with salt and pepper. Set aside until serving time.

- Whisk in a small bowl the milk and egg. Set aside.

- Combine in another bowl the bread crumbs with the fresh herbs: chervil, chives, and thyme.

- Place flour on a sheet of parchment and season lightly with salt and pepper.

- Preheat a large frying pan with oil and heat to 375°F.

- Dip oysters first into egg mixture, then give a little shake and place in seasoned flour, coating thoroughly. Shake off excess. Finally, dredge oysters in seasoned bread crumbs and add oysters to the hot oil. Fry 2 minutes or until golden brown. Cool on a paper towel and serve with basil sauce.

## ARUGULA SALAD WITH A LEMON VINAIGRETTE

*This simple 5-ingredient salad will make your dinner say POW!*

### Lemon Vinaigrette:
* ¼ cup EACH: freshly squeezed lemon juice and white wine vinegar
* ⅔ cup extra-virgin olive oil
* ½ teaspoon sea salt
* ¼ teaspoon freshly grated black pepper

### Salad:
* 8 ounces arugula lettuce
* ¼ cup grated Parmesan
* ¼ cup shaved Parmesan

### To make the vinaigrette:
- Place the lemon juice and white wine vinegar in a small bowl and whisk in olive oil to emulsify. Season to taste with salt and pepper.

### To make the salad:
- Place the arugula in a large bowl. Pour desired amount of dressing on top and toss to coat. Add grated Parmesan and toss to mix. Add shaved Parmesan to top and serve immediately.

## SWEET POTATO SOUFFLÉ

*Oh, the competitions between my aunts over this recipe. Who made the best version? Could that one be beat? You tell me. I think mine is best. POW!*

* 2 pounds sweet potatoes, scrubbed
* ¼ cup butter, melted
* ¾ cup EACH: white granulated sugar and dark brown sugar
* ½ teaspoon sea salt
* 1 teaspoon vanilla extract
* 1 teaspoon cinnamon
* 3 large eggs
* ½ cup whole milk

- Roast potatoes in a 375°F oven until tender, about 1 hour. Let them cool before peeling.

- Place the potatoes in a large bowl and mash with butter, sugars, salt, vanilla, and cinnamon.

- In a separate bowl, beat eggs until frothy and pour over sweet potatoes along with milk. Whip until light, then transfer to a 9 x 13 baking dish.

- Bake in a 350°F. oven until golden and glistening, about 30 minutes. Serve warm.

- Because there are too many good spring menus to leave any one out, here's our favorite Spring-has-Sprung menu.

# Spring Has Sprung Menu

* Seared Spiced Salmon Filets
* Couscous Pilaf
* Polish Paczki (Sugar-Coated Rasberry-Filled Donuts)

## SEARED SPICED SALMON FILETS

***The early spring vegetables make a perfect bed for salmon***

**Makes 6 to 8 servings**

* 6 to 8 salmon fillets, 6 ounces each
* ½ teaspoon EACH: garlic powder, onion powder, cayenne, sweet paprika, black pepper, and sea salt

– Drizzle olive oil into a medium skillet over medium-high heat.

– In a small bowl, combine spices. Season all sides of salmon filets. Add to skillet when oil is glistening hot.

– Cook for 5-7 minutes on each side, or until a crispy, thin brown outside crust forms and the fish flakes easily when fork-tested. Do not overcook, or salmon will be tough. Transfer to a hot platter. Cover and hold to keep warm.

**Meanwhile, make the bed of spring vegetables to form a base for the seared salmon.**

* sea salt and freshly ground black pepper, to taste
* 4 oz. snow peas, trimmed
* ⅓ cup fresh peas
* 6 baby carrots with green tops, tops trimmed to 1" and carrots peeled and halved lengthwise
* 1 bunch pencil asparagus secured with a rubber band, trimmed

* ½ teaspoon coriander seeds
* ¼ cup plus 1 tablespoon extra-virgin olive oil
* 10 cloves garlic, peeled and smashed
* 4 bulbs baby fennel, trimmed and halved, or 2 medium fennel, quartered
* 4 bulbs spring onions, greens thinly sliced; white onions peeled, leaving stem end trimmed and attached, and halved
* 4 cups vegetable stock
* 10 sprigs thyme
* 5 whole black peppercorns
* 1 bay leaf
* 1 vanilla bean, split lengthwise
* 3 tablespoons sherry vinegar
* Cilantro sprigs, for garnish
* Crumbled sea salt, for garnish

— Bring a 6-quart saucepan of salted water to a boil. Working in batches, cook snow peas, peas, carrots, and asparagus until crisp-tender, about 1 minute each for peas, and 2–3 minutes for carrots and asparagus. Discard rubber bands from the asparagus. Transfer blanched vegetables to an ice bath until chilled; then drain and set aside.

— Wipe the pan clean and toast coriander seeds over medium-high heat until fragrant, 1–2 minutes. Add $\frac{1}{4}$ cup oil and cook garlic until golden, 3–4 minutes, and, using a slotted spoon, transfer to a bowl. Cook fennel and white onions until golden, 6–8 minutes; transfer to bowl with garlic. Add sliced onion greens, the stock, thyme, peppercorns, bay leaf, and vanilla bean. Simmer until reduced by half, about 30 minutes. Strain stock and return to pan. Whisk in remaining oil, the vinegar, salt, and pepper, and heat over medium. Stir

in all reserved vegetables. Cook, covered, until vegetables are heated through, 2–3 minutes. Divide vegetables among wide-rimmed soup bowls and ladle broth over the top. Garnish with cilantro sprigs and sea salt. Top with seared salmon filets and a side of couscous.

## COUSCOUS PILAF

*Couscous originated in Tunisia and other Northern African countries, probably by the Berbers, who learned if they formed millet into little pellets, it cooked better. Now you see couscous made from other grains, including rice and durum wheat. What we buy in the grocery stores today is pre-steamed, easy to cook, and makes a wonderful base for many dishes. But the key to a good couscous is that it should be light and fluffy, never gummy.*

* 1 teaspoon extra-virgin olive oil
* 2 garlic cloves, smashed
* 1 shallot, minced
* ½ cup whole wheat couscous
* ½ cup chicken broth
* Sea salt and freshly cracked pepper, to taste
* 1 tablespoon EACH: fresh parsley and chives, chopped

— Heat olive oil in a small saucepan over medium heat, then add the garlic and shallot and cook, stirring constantly, for 2 minutes. Add the couscous and cook, stirring often, for 2 minutes. Add the chicken broth, sea salt, and freshly cracked pepper to taste and bring to a boil. Cover, remove from heat, and let stand for 5 minutes. Add the fresh parsley and chives, then fluff with a fork. Taste and add more seasonings as needed. Serve immediately from a large bowl.

## POLISH PACZKI (SUGAR-COATED RASPBERRY-FILLED DONUTS)

*Just the thing for the spring feast. I learned to make these at Dennis Foy's restaurant. They were as important to Easter as any other holiday dessert.*

*Make these as much as 8 hours ahead and let them rest until serving time.*

* 2 cups whole milk, warmed to 110°F
* 4½ teaspoons active dry yeast (2 packages)
* ¾ cup granulated sugar, divided
* 5 to 6 cups all-purpose flour, divided
* I large egg
* 4 large egg yolks
* I teaspoon vanilla extract
* 1¼ teaspoons sea salt
* 4 tablespoons unsalted butter, melted and cooled
* Grape-seed oil, for frying
* Raspberry or other fruit preserves, for filling

– Powdered and granulated sugars, for coating

– Pour warm milk into bowl of a stand mixer. Stir in the yeast and a pinch of the granulated sugar. Let stand for 5 to 10 minutes, or until it has become bubbly.

Add 2 cups of flour to the mixture and stir with a wooden spoon until a smooth batter forms. Cover with plastic wrap and set in a warm spot for 30 minutes. The mixture rise and be very bubbly.

– In a medium bowl, whisk the egg and egg yolks until pale yellow and frothy, about 3 minutes. Add the remaining sugar, vanilla extract, and salt, and whisk until combined and smooth.

– Attach the dough hook to the mixer. Add the egg mixture to the dough and mix on medium-low speed until mostly combined. Add the melted butter and mix to combine. Gradually add 3 more cups of flour to the mixture and continue to knead until a very soft dough comes together. (It will not clean the sides of the bowl or form a ball. It may be rather slack and a bit sticky.) If necessary, add up to another 1 cup of flour, a spoonful at a time, until a soft dough forms.

– Transfer the dough to a lightly greased bowl, cover with plastic wrap, and set in a warm spot until it has doubled in size.

– Remove the dough from the bowl and turn out onto a floured work surface. With your fingers, smash down the dough into an even layer. Sprinkle flour on the dough and roll it out to ½-inch thickness. If the dough doesn't hold its shape and springs back, cover with a damp towel and let rest for a few minutes and try again.

– Use a 3-inch biscuit cutter to cut out rounds of dough. Transfer the dough rounds to parchment-lined baking sheets. Gather scraps of dough and again roll out and cut until you have used up all the dough. Cover the baking sheets loosely with plastic wrap and place in a warm, draft-free spot until almost doubled in size, about 30 minutes.

— Meanwhile, heat at least 1½ inches of oil in a heavy-bottomed pot or deep skillet over medium heat to 350°F. Place a deep-fry thermometer in the pot and carefully lower about six paczki into the hot oil (be sure not to overcrowd the pan) and fry until the bottom is golden brown. Carefully flip them over and continue to fry until the other side is golden brown. Use a slotted spoon to remove them to a paper towel-lined baking sheet to drain. Allow the oil to come back up to 350°F, then repeat until all of the paczki have been fried.

— Allow the paczki to cool on a parchment sheet until you are able to handle them easily. Using a filling tip, pipe fruit preserves into the sides of the paczki, then roll in powdered sugar. The paczki are best the same day they are made, but can be stored in an airtight container at room temperature for up to 2 days.

# The Rise and Fall of my Heart and Soul Restaurant

It was the year 2003, and I was tired of working for people and being treated unfairly, sometimes like I wasn't even a person. So I decided to open my own restaurant and be my own boss.

Well, there's a lot to running the show. You need multiple hats. Just being a great chef is only the beginning. My Heart and Soul restaurant was located on 61 Academy Street, South Orange, New Jersey.

My mission statement was to serve the freshest, free range, and farm-to-table ingredients that I could find. I think I was before my time, because folks then couldn't care less, as long as it was cheap. I was way out ahead of the millennials, who now demand to know every single thing that goes into every dish.

From where I stood in the kitchen, looking out at the dining room, I got at a glance how people perceive Southern cooking. They thought it was all about cheap and inexpensive ingredients.

I went out into the dining room and began talking to my customers. "So why are your prices so high?" These questions were not even very friendly. I could see by the looks on their faces, they thought I was trying to pull a fast one.

So first I tried to convince them. "I'm a trained chef. I have been trained by formally schooled master chefs."

I knew what I was doing, but what I hadn't counted on were the expectations of my customers. The wanted great fresh and natural food so long as it didn't cost them more than mass-produced cheap food. Period.

In the restaurant business, there is a lot of very hard work. Every day it's the same drill; work long hours, go home bone tired, then get up early the next day to go to the fresh foods purveyors to buy the best ingredients to get started and do it all over again.

And there are a million things that can go wrong every day. The sinks can back up. The vendors can get really nasty if you can't pay right on time. Just the ordinary charges for putting the key in the door every morning can be a shock. Electric bill?

You might get a run on fried chicken and run out right at the height of the dinner hour. Or you might buy too much and either have to make a quick change in the menu for the day or put that premium, high-priced fresh bird in the freezer. You can't anticipate everything that gets thrown at you, and you have to make lightning-fast decisions.

Ever wonder where the "Daily Specials" came from? Call it righting the supply and demand problem. It's an ever-present issue in a restaurant, especially one that prides itself on serving the freshest ingredients.

How could I have made more than $200,000 the first year and still be so broke? Money just seemed to fly through my hands. And the wear and tear on the body of a job that requires you be on your feet 15 hours a day—now that was a shock too.

One regret I have is dragging my family into my business. Annette, Tristan, and Jesse hated it, but they helped me and I'm grateful now for them; we are family. But it wasn't their dream, it was mine.

And a restaurant doesn't die a quick and sure death. It takes a long time, more and more sacrifices, until one day you just have to let go. After losing everything, my business, my home, my van—everything and I mean everything!—I knew it was over.

Thank God, my family stayed with me. I will forever be grateful to Annette, Tristan, and Jesse for sticking it out. That was the surest sign of love I ever had.

I had fallen, but I got back up. POW! I dream big and I never give up, but I often sit and ponder. Where did I go wrong? First, you have to maintain your hours. I opened and closed the door based on business, no restaurant walk-ins. I took a catering job and put a sign up on the door, "Be back." You can't do that or you lose the customers who have remained faithful to you. It's one of the hardest lessons to learn about retail. You gotta be open when you say you're gonna be open.

Next the old saying, "location, location, location," knew what it was talking about. Location is very important. Mine wasn't great. Still to date, I hear this from previous owners. What I didn't know then is that 90 percent of new restaurants fail within the first year. And I'm talking the big and the small—those with big bucks behind them and the bootstrap operations. The restaurant business is not for the faint of heart.

Would knowing all this have stopped me from opening Heart and Soul? Probably not. I say Heart and Soul was my graduate school. I learned more in three years there than I could ever have learned in any college.

And the last and hardest lesson I had to learn was when to be convinced you are failing. Not Chef Jesse Jones. I never fail. But maybe that's the key; the ego, the pride, wondering what my chef friends will think.

I didn't want to be a failure, but now I realize you must fail to achieve success. My restaurant lasted for 3 years, and I was out. But on a good note, because my recipes went with me and through my food, I managed to keep the Heart and Soul legacy alive. People still call me up and say, "Jesse, when you gonna open up Heart and Soul again?"

Folks are still talking about my legendary meals. Who remembers my Southern fried catfish, braised oxtails, smothered turkey wings, baby back ribs, BBQ apricot salmon and chicken, supreme roasted chicken, jumbo garlic shrimp, 5-cheese baked mac, candied yams, country potato salad, collard greens and cabbage, stewed green beans, and don't forget my honey buttermilk cornbread!

So where is Heart and Soul?

You are holding it in your hand. All of my recipes are in *40 Feasts*. Heart and Soul will never die as long as good people keep passing the recipes along, cooking and eating and enjoying the feast. Please cook it and remember Heart and Soul restaurant. It's yours now. POW!

April: Yes. March comes in like a lion and goes out like a chicken in the pot. It's April and we're not fooling.

But, I have to tell you, I think it's really true. April is the cruelest month. I always loved it because my beloved grandmother, Hannah Lewis Jones, was born on April Fool's Day. But it's bittersweet to me as well because my grandmother passed away three years ago, and we miss her every day.

But, looking on the bright side, by the time I got old enough to cook for my grandmother Hannah, I started making fried catfish with collards for her on her birthday every year. She would just beam. She loved that feast and loved that I'd make it for her.

And whenever I make she-crab soup, I think of my grandmother, who taught me how to make this gorgeous recipe and taught me about she-crabs in the process.

So, I say to you, whenever you make these April feasts, raise a glass to my beloved grandmother, Hannah Lewis Jones, and to your own grandmother as well. That's what good cooking can do. It can give you a link to your own past whenever you make your grandmother's recipes. And these are two of my favorites from my own beloved grandmother.

Maybe we should call April "Grandmother Month." A good reason to celebrate, don't you think?

# Chapter 4: April

## The French Connection

\* Chef Jesse's Chicken Gumbo

\* Carolina Gold Rice Pilaf

\* Uber Caesar Salad

\* Best Beignets

## CHEF JESSE'S CHICKEN GUMBO

**Makes 6 – 8 servings**

*Here's the French connection for sure. Pure French method in this basic Southern gumbo.*

* 4 boneless chicken breasts or thighs (6-8 ounces each)
* Chef Jesse's Spice mix:
    * 1 teaspoon EACH: kosher salt, white pepper, fresh thyme and sweet paprika
    * ½ teaspoon EACH: cayenne and black pepper
    * ¼ teaspoon EACH: garlic powder and onion powder
* ½ pound Andouille sausage (browned in a pan, then drained and saved on paper towel)
* 1 cup all-purpose flour
* 1½ cup grape-seed oil + pan drippings
* 1 cup EACH: diced onions, and green and red bell peppers
* ¾ cup chopped celery
* 1 teaspoon minced garlic
* 7 cups chicken stock or water
* 1 teaspoon gumbo filé

- Cut chicken breasts and/or thighs into large pieces. In a medium bowl combine with spice mix and place in a Ziploc bag to marinate overnight in the refrigerator.

- Next day, in a heavy skillet, heat ½ cup oil until hot, then cook chicken – a few pieces at a time – about 2 minutes per side. Remove and drain on paper towels.

- In the same pan, add remaining oil and whisk in flour gradually, cooking to make a red-brown golden roux, about 5 minutes. Remove from the heat and stir in onions, then peppers, celery, and garlic, cooking for 5 more minutes or until vegetables are limp and golden.

- Add stock slowly, bring to a boil, then simmer about a half hour. Taste and adjust seasonings. Add cooked chicken, sausage, and cook about 20 minutes. In the end, sprinkle in gumbo filé. Serve with rice pilaf.

*Gumbo filé is a powdered sassafras leaf found in specialty grocery stores or online.*

## CAROLINA GOLD RICE PILAF

**Makes 8 large servings**

* ½ teaspoon extra-virgin olive oil
* ¼ cup (½ stick) unsalted butter
* 1 small onion, finely chopped
* 2 cups Carolina Gold converted rice
* 4 cups chicken stock
* ½ teaspoon EACH: kosher salt and freshly milled white pepper

* 1 bay leaf
* 1 sprig thyme

- In a large saucepan, over medium high heat, melt oil and butter. Add onions and cook until transparent, about 3 minutes. Add rice and cook and stir to coat the rice. Once the kernels begin to turn gold, stir in chicken stock, salt and pepper, bay leaf, and thyme. Cover and bring to a boil. Reduce heat and cook about 15 minutes. Turn off heat and let it stand 5 minutes or so.

## UBER CAESAR SALAD

***You'll make this over and over. So delicious.***

**Makes 8 to 10 generous servings**

### Dressing:
* 2 cloves garlic, crushed
* 6 tablespoons grape-seed oil
* ¾ teaspoon kosher salt
* ¼ teaspoon EACH: mustard powder and black pepper
* 1½ teaspoons Worcestershire sauce
* ⅛ teaspoon cayenne pepper
* 2 tablespoons fresh lemon juice
* 1 2-ounce can anchovy filets
* 1 large egg
* 1 French baguette, cut into ½-inch pieces for croutons
* 4 tablespoons melted butter
* 1 teaspoon Italian seasoning
* ½ teaspoon Worcestershire sauce
* 1 tablespoon grated Parmigiano Reggiano cheese
* 1 large head romaine lettuce, rinsed, dried, and torn into bite-size pieces
* ½ cup grated Parmigiano Reggiano cheese

- Preheat oven to 275°F.

- Prepare the dressing in a glass jar by combining the garlic, oil, salt, mustard, pepper, Worcestershire sauce, cayenne, and lemon juice. Rinse anchovy filets under warm water, pat dry on paper towels, and roughly chop. Place anchovy in jar with other ingredients. Cover with tight-fitting lid and shake to mix.

- To coddle the egg, bring 2 inches of water to a boil in a small saucepan. Carefully lower egg in its shell into the water; remove from heat and let it stand for 1 minute. Remove the egg from the water and set aside to cool. Crack open the egg and with a spoon, scrape out all yolk (even the runny white). Use a wire whisk and whip in a small bowl until very frothy. Pour egg into the rest of the dressing and mix well.

- Prepare the croutons by combining the bread cubes, melted butter, Worcestershire sauce, and 1 tablespoon grated cheese. Toss well to coat bread, then place in a single layer on a 10 x 15 jelly roll pan and bake in preheated oven for 20 to 30 minutes.

- Prepare salad in a large bowl by combining the romaine, ½ cup grated cheese, dressing, and croutons to taste. Toss well to coat and serve.

## BEST BEIGNETS

**Makes about 36 beignets**

* 1 envelope active dry yeast (¼ ounce)
* 3 tablespoons warm water
* ¼ cup whole milk
* ¼ cup shortening
* 1 teaspoon kosher salt
* 1 large egg
* 3 cups all-purpose flour
* 4 cups grape-seed oil

- Combine yeast and warm water in a large bowl. Set aside in a draft-free place for 5 minutes to bubble and proof.

- Heat milk in a small saucepan over medium heat. Stir in sugar, shortening, and salt. Remove from the heat and cool to lukewarm, about 100°F.

- Add cooled milk mixture, beaten egg, and 2 cups flour to the yeast mixture. Stir well to combine. Gradually stir in the remaining flour to make a soft dough.

- Turn the dough out onto a lightly floured surface. Knead until the dough is smooth and elastic, about 5 to 8 minutes. Place dough in a well-greased bowl, cover with plastic wrap, and set aside to rise in a warm draft-free place for about 1 hour.

- Preheat a large, heavy pot or Dutch oven. Add oil and heat to 375°F.

- Roll dough on a lightly floured surface to a thickness just under ¼-inch. Cut into 2-½-inch squares. Fry in the hot oil, in batches, so the oil temperature will not dip below 375°F. Fry until golden brown, then cool on paper towels.

- Dust generously with powdered sugar and serve warm.

# Southern Fried Feast

* Crispy Southern Fried Catfish
* Collards with Smoked Turkey Wings
* Classic Buttermilk Corn Bread
* Grandmother's Sweet Potato Pie

## CRISPY SOUTHERN FRIED CATFISH

*An electric skillet is ideal for frying because it's so easy to control the heat.*

**Makes 6 to 8 servings**

* 6 to 8 4- to 6-ounce fresh catfish filets

**Seafood Spice Blend**
* 1 tablespoon sweet paprika
* 2 teaspoons kosher salt
* ½ teaspoon EACH: cayenne pepper, black pepper, white pepper
* 1½ teaspoons granulated garlic and onion
* 1 teaspoon EACH fresh thyme and tarragon, minced

– Combine all ingredients in a small bowl, set aside.

**Seasoned Cornmeal Mix**
* 1 cup cornmeal (Indian Head)
* ½ cup corn flour (local health food store)
* ½ cup all-purpose flour
* 2 tablespoons of Chef Jesse's spice blend

– Mix together in medium bowl and set aside

## Wet mixture

* 1½ cup light buttermilk
* 1 teaspoon or 3 dashes Frank's RedHot sauce to taste
* 1½ inches grape-seed oil for frying in the electric skillet

– In a bowl, add buttermilk, 1 tablespoon of Chef Jesse's blend, and Frank's RedHot sauce. Add catfish, mix well, marinate overnight in a Ziploc bag.

## Next-day Prep

– Remove catfish from buttermilk mixture and drain well, shaking excess. Discard buttermilk. In a shallow pan add cornmeal mixture and dredge catfish, coating well. Shake off excess. In an electric fryer or cast-iron pot, heat oil to 365°F.

– Fry catfish, a few pieces at a time, until crispy and starting to float, about 6 to 8 minutes. Drain on paper towel.


## COLLARD GREENS WITH SMOKED TURKEY WINGS

*Start two to three hours ahead of serving time. Works well to cook the day before and reheat.*

Makes 8 servings

* 2 quarts water
* 2 pounds smoked turkey wings
* 2 large onions, peeled and quartered
* ½ teaspoon red pepper flakes
* 4 bunches collard greens, stemmed and thoroughly washed
* 1 medium hot red pepper

* ¼ cup olive oil
* Sea salt and black pepper to taste

– In a large stockpot, bring water and turkey wings to a boil. Add onions and peppers. Reduce heat and simmer 2 hours. Remove turkey meat, onion, and pepper from the pot and set aside.

– In a large pot, heat oil, then sweat the greens about 10 minutes. Season with salt and pepper and red pepper flakes. Pour in the stock. Now add back the turkey, onion, and pepper. Cook an hour or so, or until greens are tender. Serve hot.

– Keeps well, covered in the refrigerator.


## CLASSIC BUTTERMILK CORN BREAD IN A BLACK SKILLET

* 1⅓ cups cake flour
* ⅔ cup yellow cornmeal
* ½ cup corn flour
* 1 tablespoons baking powder
* ⅓ cup granulated sugar
* 1¼ cups buttermilk
* ½ teaspoon sea salt
* 6 tablespoons melted butter, divided
* 1 large egg, slightly beaten
* ⅓ cup honey

– Preheat the oven to 350°F. Heat a 10-inch black skillet in the oven.

– Whisk dry ingredients into the wet, taking care not to overmix. Reserve 2 tablespoons of butter to melt in the bottom of the pan.

– Remove hot skillet from the oven. Coat with melted butter, then quickly add the batter. Bake in a hot oven until the center is no longer wet, about 25 to 35 minutes. Check with a wooden skewer or toothpick. Cool on a rack, then cut into wedges and serve.

## GRANDMOTHER'S SWEET POTATO PIE

**Makes two 9-inch pies**

* 2 pounds of sweet potatoes roasted (about 6 large potatoes)
* ½ cup of unsalted butter (softened)
* 3 large eggs, lightly beaten
* ½ cup brown sugar (or to taste)
* I teaspoon sea salt
* ½ cup evaporated milk
* ½ cup sweet condensed milk
* I teaspoon vanilla extract
* I teaspoon allspice
* I teaspoon ground cinnamon

- 2 9-inch unbaked pie shells (see pp 134 for recipe) or try those in the red box in the refrigerated section at the grocery stores)

- Place each pie shell into a baking pan. (Tip) I prefer to pre bake the pie shells first for 5 to 7 minutes, be sure to prick the pie shells with a fork so the dough want rise.

- Place sweet potatoes in a 400 degree F oven and roast until tender, about 1 hour.

- Cool then peel and mash with a potato masher, ricer or two forks.

- Set oven to 375 degrees F.

- Combine in a mixing bowl sweet potatoes, butter, beaten eggs, brown sugar, salt, evaporated milk, condensed milk, vanilla, allspice, and cinnamon.

- Beat with a hand mixer or whisk to mix well, and then divide between the two pie shells. Bake 50 to 60 minutes, or until a wooden toothpick comes out clean. Cool and cut into wedges. Great with a dollop of whipped cream on top!

# Charleston in a Bowl

* She-Crab Soup: Tart and Tangy Charleston in a Bowl
* Old Bay Biscuits
* Chocolate Soufflé (SEE PAGE 31 FOR RECIPE)

## SHE-CRAB SOUP: TART AND TANGY CHARLESTON IN A BOWL

**Makes 6 to 8 servings**

*Order anytime from mid-April to August and use only the best jumbo lump blue crab meat. One of the original Low Country specials of Poor Folks' Cooking. Yum.*

* I cup unsalted butter
* ½ cup EACH: minced yellow onions and celery
* 2 cloves garlic, smashed
* I teaspoon EACH: fresh thyme and tarragon, minced
* I½ cups all-purpose flour
* 3 cups hot whole milk
* Sea salt and freshly ground black pepper to taste
* Chef Jesse's seafood spice blend to taste (SEE PAGE 26 FOR RECIPE)
* 2 cups heavy cream
* I pound jumbo lump blue crab meat
* ¼ cup cream sherry
* Pinch cayenne pepper
* Fresh parsley, chopped for garnish

– Melt butter in a large stewpot over medium heat. Sauté onions, celery, garlic, thyme, and tarragon for about 2 minutes, stirring, until onions are clear.

– Cook and stir in flour and cook a minute or so to make a light roux. Slowly whisk in hot milk, stirring. Add salt and seasonings to taste. Whisk until smooth. Add cream and simmer about 5 minutes. Add crabmeat and cook gently about 25 minutes, barely rippling the surface with bubbles.

— Stir in sherry just before serving. Garnish with chopped parsley.

## CHEF JESSE'S OLD BAY CHEDDAR BISCUITS

**Makes 20 biscuits**

* 4 cups cake flour
* 2 tablespoons baking powder
* I teaspoon baking soda
* I teaspoon sea salt
* ½ cup grated aged cheddar cheese
* ½ teaspoon EACH: thyme, parsley and granulated garlic
* I¼ cups buttermilk
* I½ sticks unsalted butter, softened
* I cup shortening (we like Crisco) softened
* ¼ cup of unsalted butter, melted for brushing
* 2 teaspoons Old Bay Seasoning for sprinkling

— Preheat the oven to 425°F.

— In a large bowl, sift together the flour, baking powder, baking soda, and salt. Add the cheese, thyme, parsley, and garlic to the flour mix. Cut in the softened butter and shortening, using two forks, until the mixture resembles coarse meal.

— Combine with buttermilk and stir into the ingredients until moist. Turn out onto a lightly floured surface and knead lightly 3 to 4 times. Do not over-knead. Roll the dough into a rough rectangle about 1 inch

thick. Fold over and pat down again. Let the dough rest 10 minutes or so. Pat down again to a 1-inch thick rectangle.

— Cut 2-inch rounds with a biscuit cutter or floured glass, taking care NOT to twist the cutter, then place on a lightly greased or parchment-lined baking sheet. Prick with a fork and brush with melted butter. Sprinkle Old Bay on top, then bake 15 to 20 minutes on 375°F or until lightly browned on top. Cool on a rack. Serve warm.

# Crawfish Season Begins with the First Hatch

*Although you can't say exactly when crawfish season begins, you'll know it when you see it. Basically, it's when the crawfish begin to hatch, which is when the weather warms up.*

* Crawfish Creole with Fluffy White Rice
* Creole Green Beans
* Bread Pudding with Brandy Sauce

## CRAWFISH CREOLE WITH FLUFFY WHITE RICE

**Makes 8 servings**

* 7 tablespoons grape-seed oil
* 4 tablespoons butter
* ½ cup EACH: chopped onions, celery, green and red bell pepper, jalapeño (optional)
* 1 teaspoon EACH: fresh basil, thyme
* 2 cloves smashed garlic
* 1 bay leaf
* 2 teaspoons sea salt
* 2½ teaspoons white pepper
* 1 teaspoon cayenne
* ¼ teaspoon black pepper
* 1 tablespoon dried thyme leaves
* 1½ teaspoons chopped fresh basil
* 3 cups seafood stock (made from boiled shrimp shells and water, strained)
* 2 28-ounce cans peeled tomatoes and juice, chopped
* 1 15-ounce can tomato sauce
* 2 teaspoons granulated sugar
* ½ pound shelled medium shrimp, chopped

* 1½ pounds crawfish, cleaned
* 1½ teaspoons Chef Jesse spice blend (see pp 26)
* ½ teaspoon filé
* 1 cup green onions and tops, chopped

— Heat oil in a large saucepot. Add butter, onion, celery, peppers, and garlic. Cook and stir 3 minutes, or until the onion is clear. Add salt, pepper, cayenne, thyme, basil, and stock. Cook 5 minutes and add tomatoes and granulated sugar. Stir to combine. Raise to a boil. Gently stir in shrimp and crawfish. Remove from heat and let stand 5 minutes. Taste and adjust seasonings with Chef Jesse spice blend and filé. Serve over fluffy white rice made by following box directions. Garnish with green onions and tops.

## CREOLE GREEN BEANS

**Makes 8 servings**

As if green beans were not flavorful enough, punch up the flavor with garlic, shallots, peppers, and tomatoes. POW!

* ½ cup grape-seed oil
* 3 cloves garlic, minced
* 1 cup EACH: minced shallots, red and yellow bell pepper
* 1 jalapeño, seeded, minced (optional)
* 1½ pounds fresh green beans
* 2 plum tomatoes, minced
* ¼ cup tomato juice
* Sea salt and freshly milled black pepper to taste

— In a large skillet, heat oil over medium high heat; then cook garlic, shallots, red and yellow peppers, and jalapeño for about 2 minutes, or until clear.

— Add the green beans and cook and stir about 5 minutes; then add tomatoes and juice, salt and pepper. Serve hot.

## BREAD PUDDING WITH BRANDY SAUCE

* 2 cups granulated sugar
* 5 large beaten eggs
* 2 cups whole milk
* 2 teaspoons pure vanilla extract
* 3 cups cubed challah or other eggy bread, allowed to stale overnight in a bowl
* ½ cup packed light brown sugar
* ¼ cup (½ stick) unsalted butter, softened
* 1 cup chopped pecans

**For the sauce:**
* 1 cup granulated sugar
* ½ cup (1 stick) unsalted butter, melted
* 1 egg, beaten
* 2 teaspoons pure vanilla extract
* ¼ cup brandy

— Preheat the oven to 350°F. Grease a 13 x 9 x 2 inch pan with soft butter.

— Mix granulated sugar, eggs, and milk in a bowl; add vanilla. Pour over cubed bread and let sit for 10 minutes.

— In another bowl, mix and crumble together brown sugar, butter, and pecans.

— Pour bread mixture into the prepared pan. Sprinkle brown sugar mixture over the top and bake for 35 to 45 minutes, or until set. Remove from oven.

**For the sauce:**

- Mix the granulated sugar, butter, egg, and vanilla in a saucepan over medium heat. Stir together until the sugar is melted. Add the brandy, stirring well. Pour over bread pudding. Serve warm or cold.

# Chapter 5: May

*This spring, I signed on to help in a local homeless shelter. Yesterday was my first day. It's amazing how every day, you can meet awesome people! God is good. God, please continue to bless IHN, for making a difference in so many people's lives who are homeless and just need some help. I'm so happy to be on board. My mission will always be to feed the hungry.*

# Time to go Fishing

✱ Trout Mignonette

✱ Rutabaga Mash and Braised Ramps

✱ Mango Sorbet

## TROUT MIGNONETTE ON A BED OF RUTABAGA MASH WITH BRAISED RAMPS

*Springtime makes me think about fishing. But even if you don't have a ready fishing hole, you're bound to have a great fishmonger to provide you with whole trout come springtime.*

**Makes 4 servings**

* 1 cup panko bread crumbs
* 1 clove garlic, smashed
* 2 tablespoons EACH: chopped flat-leaf parsley and oregano leaves
* Pinch crushed red pepper flakes
* 3 lemons, juiced plus 1 lemon, zested and reserved
* sea salt and freshly milled black pepper to taste
* ½ cup Dijon mustard
* 4 10- to 12-ounce trout, boned, belly flap removed, rinsed and patted dry, heads and tails left on
* Extra-virgin olive oil
* Mignonette sauce (see below)

— Heat oven to 200°F.

— In a wide, flat dish, combine bread crumbs, garlic, parsley, oregano, red pepper flakes, and zest of 1 lemon, with salt and pepper to taste.

— In a small bowl, mix the mustard and the juice of 1 lemon. Brush both sides of the trout with mustard mixture. Coat the fish on both sides with the seasoned bread crumbs and press firmly to adhere the crumbs to the fish.

– Coat a large skillet with ¼ to ½ inch of olive oil and bring to a medium-high heat. Add the fish to the pan, two at a time, skin side down, and cook the fish two-thirds of the way, about 6 to 7 minutes. Carefully turn the fish over and cook the other side until the fish is brown and crispy, about 2 to 3 minutes. Remove the fish from the pan and drain on paper towels. After the first batch is done and drained on paper towels, reserve it on a rack in a warm oven.

– When all the fish has been fried, remove the oil and any brown bits from the pan. Add the butter and remaining lemon juice and swirl to combine as the butter melts. Season with salt to taste, and reduce by about half. Transfer the fish to a serving platter. Drizzle with the butter lemon sauce and serve.

### Mignonette Sauce
(serve in a small side bowl)
* I tablespoon coarsely ground black pepper
* ½ cup red wine vinegar
* 2 tablespoons finely minced shallots
* Sea salt to taste

– Mix in a small bowl, cover, and refrigerate until serving time.

# RUTABAGA MASH

**Makes 8 servings**

*A cross between a cabbage and a turnip, this large, solid root vegetable makes a great mash with more character than a potato. POW!*

* I ½ pounds rutabagas, peeled, cut into ½-inch pieces
* 2 large carrots, peeled, thinly sliced
* I large garlic clove, peeled
* I bay leaf
* 3 tablespoons butter
* 2 tablespoons chopped fresh parsley

– Boil rutabagas and carrots with garlic and bay leaf in a large pan of barely salted water until tender. Remove and discard the bay leaf. Drain, then add butter and mash with a potato masher or a stick blender. Top with parsley and serve.

# BRAISED RAMPS

*This spring vegetable is sometimes called a wild leek, but whatever you call them, when you see them in the farmer's market, or in the field, buy them. They have a delicate onion aroma and flavor. We love them.*

* I cup grape-seed oil
* 2 pounds ramps (approximately 6 bunches), cleaned and drained
* Salt and freshly ground black pepper to taste

– Place oil in a large, shallow pan with a tight-fitting lid over high heat. When oil is warm, roll a bunch of ramps in paper towels to remove excess moisture, and unwrap. Reduce heat to medium, and add ramps to pan. Toss to coat each leaf with oil. Working quickly, dry second bunch and add to the oil, tossing until ramps wilt. Continue with remaining ramps, adding more oil as needed.

— When all ramps are wilted, season to taste and reduce heat to low, then stir and cover pot. Cook 5 to 10 minutes, depending on the size of the ramps, stirring frequently to avoid burning. When ramps are very, very tender, remove pan from heat and let sit, covered, for 10 minutes. Season again if desired, and serve.

## MANGO SORBET

*Get out the ice-cream maker and get ready for warm weather desserts.*

* 4 cups ripe mangos, peeled and chopped (makes 3-½ cups)
* 1 cup simple syrup*
* Juice and grated zest of 4 limes

— Combine mangos, syrup, lime juice, and zest in an electric ice-cream maker and process until the sorbet is frozen. Store in the freezer until serving time.

— *To make simple syrup, stir together 2 cups granulated sugar and 2 cups water in a small saucepan, cook and stir until thoroughly combined. Cool and store in a jar in the refrigerator up to a week.

# Smothered Spring Vegetables with Turkey Wings

＊ Braised Turkey Wings with Smothered Red Cabbage and Escarole

＊ Roasted Spring Roots, including radishes, broccoli, peppers, and fennel

＊ Rhubarb Strawberry Cobbler

## BRAISED TURKEY WINGS WITH SMOTHERED RED CABBAGE AND ESCAROLE

**Makes 8 servings**

*Golden brown wings on top of a bed of aromatic cabbage and escarole will buckle your knees before you take the first bite. Yes.*

* 2 tablespoons grape-seed oil
* 2-3 smoked turkey wings (cut into thirds at the joint)
* sea salt and freshly ground black pepper to taste
* 2 cups finely chopped yellow onion and carrot (peeled and finely sliced into matchsticks)
* 2 teaspoons toasted cumin seeds
* 8 cups red cabbage (sliced ¼-inch thick)
* I large head escarole, chopped
* 2 cups tart apples (grated on the large holes of a box grater)
* ¼ cup red wine vinegar
* I cup freshly squeezed orange juice
* ¼ cup brown sugar
* 2 tablespoons Dijon mustard

– Preheat 325°F.

– Place a Dutch oven over medium-high heat. When the pan is hot, add the olive oil along with the smoked turkey wings. Cook until the wings are golden brown on each side, then remove from the pot and set aside. Add the onions and carrots and a pinch of salt. Push them to one side of the pan and add the cumin seeds to the pan to toast for 2 minutes. Stir together and cook until the vegetables begin to soften (5 minutes). Stir in the cabbage, escarole, and apples. Add the turkey wings back into the pot. Cover and cook until the cabbage starts to wilt (3-5 minutes).

— In the meantime, whisk together the orange juice and brown sugar. Reduce the heat to medium low. Pour into the cabbage mixture and season with a good amount of salt and pepper. Add the vinegar to the pot. Cover the pot and place in the oven to cook for 45 minutes. Stir in the mustard, then taste for seasoning, adding more salt and pepper if necessary. Serve the cabbage with the smoked turkey wings on top.

# ROASTED SPRING ROOTS, INCLUDING RADISHES, BROCCOLI, PEPPERS, AND FENNEL

**Makes 8 servings**

* 1 bunch radishes, tops removed and reserved
* 1 head broccoli and cauliflower, chopped, including stems
* 1 large fennel bulb, sliced fine
* 2 small red peppers, chopped
* 2 tablespoons honey
* 2 tablespoons unsalted butter, melted
* 1 tablespoon apple cider vinegar
* sea salt and freshly ground black pepper to taste
* ¼ cup fresh thyme, chopped

— Position a rack in the center of the oven and set a 12-inch ovenproof skillet (preferably cast iron) on the rack. Heat the oven to 450°F.

— Trim the radishes and then halve or quarter them lengthwise, depending on their size. Trim and discard the stems from the tops, wash the leaves thoroughly, and pat dry or dry in a salad spinner. Repeat with broccoli, cauliflower, fennel, and red peppers.

— In a medium bowl, combine the honey, butter, vinegar, and ½ teaspoon salt and pepper. Add thyme, and then add the radishes and other vegetables and toss until coated. Transfer to the hot skillet, spread in a single layer, and roast in the hot oven, stirring occasionally, until the vegetables are crisp-tender, 15 to 20 minutes. Remove from the oven. Add the radish tops and thyme leaves, and toss until the leaves are just wilted; serve.

# RHUBARB STRAWBERRY COBBLER

**Makes 8 servings**

*Nothing says spring like a dessert made from rhubarb and strawberries.*

* 2 pints strawberries, hulled and thickly sliced
* 8 ounces rhubarb, trimmed and cut into ½-inch pieces (2 cups)
* ½ cup granulated sugar
* 2 tablespoons quick-cooking tapioca, or 1 tablespoon cornstarch
* ⅛ teaspoon EACH: ground cinnamon, nutmeg, ginger

## Topping

* 1½ cups all-purpose flour
* ¼ cup plus 1 tablespoon granulated sugar, divided
* 1½ teaspoons baking powder
* ½ teaspoon baking soda and salt
* ¼ teaspoon EACH: ground cinnamon, ginger, and nutmeg
* 2 tablespoons cold butter, cut into pieces
* 1 cup nonfat buttermilk

- To prepare filling: Combine strawberries, rhubarb, ½ cup granulated sugar, tapioca (or cornstarch), ⅛ teaspoon cinnamon, ⅛ teaspoon ginger, and ⅛ teaspoon nutmeg in a 9-inch deep-dish pie pan and let stand for 20 minutes.

- Preheat oven to 400°F.

- To prepare topping: Stir together flour, ¼ cup granulated sugar, baking powder, baking soda, salt, ¼ teaspoon cinnamon, ¼ teaspoon ginger and nutmeg in a large bowl. Cut butter into dry ingredients with a pastry cutter, 2 forks, or your fingers until crumbly. Use a fork to stir in buttermilk just until combined.

- Using a large spoon, drop the dough in 8 dollops over the filling. Sprinkle with the remaining 1 tablespoon granulated sugar. Bake the cobbler on the middle rack of the hot oven until browned and bubbling, 40 to 50 minutes. (Cover with foil if the top is browning too quickly.) Cool slightly on a wire rack. Serve warm.

# Tristan's Birthday Faves

The artist in our family is Tristan, who could draw before he could walk, and sing before he could talk. He is our firstborn son and our treasure. We pull out all the stops to celebrate his birthday. He always asks for my fried chicken with waffles.

* Southern Fried Chicken with Sweet Potato Waffles
* Tri-Color Cole Slaw
* Tristan's Special Peach Cobbler

When I was growing up, my mama and my aunt Ella Mae both made great fried chicken; so did my aunt Minnie Mae, and don't forget Aunt Mary. They fried the best chicken and each had her own version. But after tasting a lot of chicken all around, I learned to use the methods I learned working in French kitchens. This means I brine my chicken overnight, then rinse, drain, and leave it in a buttermilk soak for the day. I'd have to say that this is a perfect example of what happens when the French chef shakes hands with his Southern cousins.

My method takes two days, but only about 20 minutes of your time, and the result is mouthwatering, with a deep, layered flavor and cooked through. The actual chicken frying is done in 10 to 15 minutes, but the preparation is mostly a matter of brining and soaking. Easy and well worth the extra steps.

The first time I fried chicken my way for Tristan's birthday, he was surprised. POW! I told him. Now that's giving it my little twist.

When it comes time to fry a chicken, I choose a smaller bird, or chicken pieces, so that the pieces will cook evenly. After brining and soaking, I just give it a quick pass through my Chef Jesse dredge and then fry that baby up. Ready to eat in 10 to 15 minutes.

Feast #17

I always use a deep fat thermometer in the oil, and an instant-read thermometer to stick in the bird to make sure it's cooked through. Tiny steps, but the result is worth it. It's important not to overload the skillet because that drops the oil temperature and results in a greasy bird. Using a 10-inch deep, heavy black skillet, preheat the oil, then fry four pieces at a time. Then drain and fry the other four.

POW! Serve that baby with some sweet potato waffles and coleslaw. Now you're talking.

## SOUTHERN FRIED CHICKEN

* 3- to 4-pound frying chicken cut into 8 pieces (or use pieces — say, legs and thighs, breasts, around 3-4 pounds)
* I quart buttermilk
* I teaspoon hot sauce (Frank's is good)

### Chef Jesse's Fried Chicken Spice Blend
*To make the blend*

* 2 teaspoons EACH: paprika, granulated garlic, and granulated onion
* I teaspoon EACH: black and white pepper + fresh thyme
* 2 cups all-purpose flour
* 2 tablespoons cornstarch

— Prepare the dredge by blending the dried herbs with the flour and cornstarch in a shallow bowl or brown paper or plastic bag.

— The day before you plan to serve, fill a large bowl with cold water and add ¼

cup kosher salt. Put chicken pieces in the brine and refrigerate, The next morning, lift the chicken out of the brine. Rinse and drain. Now place brined chicken in a bowl and cover with buttermilk. Add hot sauce. Soak in the refrigerator about 8 hours. Then drain.

— Place chicken pieces in the dredge, shake well to coat the pieces, and shake off excess flour.

— In a 5-quart heavy pot or deep skillet, add 48 ounces peanut, soy, or other vegetable oil and heat over medium-high heat to 365°F. Cook four pieces at a time, turning once, until golden brown and cooked through to an internal temperature of 140°F.

— Fry for 10 to 15 minutes, turning, then drain on paper towels or a wire rack. POW! Serve with additional hot sauce.

## CHEF JESSE'S SWEET POTATO WAFFLES

* 2 cups cake flour
* 3 teaspoons baking powder
* ½ teaspoon salt
* I teaspoon cinnamon
* ½ teaspoon allspice
* I tablespoon granulated sugar
* 2 teaspoons light brown sugar
* 3 large egg yolks, separated, save whites
* I½ cups buttermilk
* ½ cup unsalted butter, melted
* ½ cup vegetable oil
* ½ teaspoon pure vanilla extract
* I small sweet potato, baked, peeled, and mashed (about 4 ounces)

- Preheat the waffle iron.

- Sift together flour, baking powder, salt, cinnamon, and allspice and pour into a bowl.

- In a second bowl combine egg yolks, buttermilk, melted butter, oil, vanilla, and sweet potato.

- Add liquid ingredients to dry ingredients and mix gently until combined. Don't overmix. Beat the egg whites until frothy and fluffy and gently fold into waffle mix. Let rest a few minutes.

- Spray the waffle iron with oil and ladle 4 to 6 ounces of batter. Add more batter until it fills the spaces. Close and cook until golden.

- Serve waffles with fried chicken on top. POW!

## TRI-COLOR COLE SLAW

*You eat with your eyes first, and once you see this brightly colored slaw, you'll never want to go back to plain old cabbage.*

* I carrot, peeled and grated
* ½ head green cabbage (about I pound), quartered, cored, and thinly sliced
* ½ head red cabbage (about I pound), quartered, cored, and thinly sliced
* I small red onion, peeled and very thinly sliced
* ½ cup chopped parsley
* 2 teaspoons kosher salt
* ¼ cup extra-virgin olive oil

* 2 tablespoons red wine vinegar
* I tablespoon celery seed
* I tablespoon granulated sugar

- In a large colander, toss together carrot, cabbage, onion, parsley, and salt. Set colander over a large bowl and let sit 30 minutes; press firmly to remove moisture.

- In a large bowl, whisk together oil, vinegar, celery seed, and granulated sugar to combine, then add cabbage mixture and toss well to coat. Cover and chill at least 2 hours, then serve.

## TRISTAN'S PEACH COBBLER

When the peaches come in, there is nothing better than homemade peach cobbler. You can tell the peaches are ripe when you can smell them in the farmer's market from a good distance. POW!

**Makes 8 servings**

* I cup granulated sugar
* ¼ cup brown sugar
* ½ cup all-purpose flour + more to sprinkle
* ¼ teaspoon ground nutmeg
* ⅛ teaspoon ground cloves
* I teaspoon ground cinnamon
* ½ cup unsalted butter (I stick)
* I ½ cup peach juice
* 5 cups fresh peaches, peeled, pitted, and sliced
* I teaspoon pure vanilla extract
* I teaspoon fresh lemon juice + grated zest of ½ lemon

- To make filling, combine white and brown sugars, with flour, nutmeg, cloves and cinnamon in a bowl.

- Melt butter in a large Dutch oven. Add sugar mixture, peach juice and peaches. Stir to combine. Simmer over low heat until the peaches are tender, about 10 minutes. Add vanilla, lemon juice and grated lemon zest. Set it aside.

- Preheat the oven to 375° F.

### To make the biscuit dough:

* 2-1/4 cups all-purpose flour
* 2 teaspoons baking powder
* ½ teaspoon sea salt
* 1 cup cold butter (2 sticks), cut into small chunks
* ½ cup (may need a few drops more) ice water

- To make the biscuit dough, add flour, baking powder and salt to a large bowl or a food processor. Process (or rub dough between your fingers) until it resembles coarse meal. (no more than 10-12 pulses) Sprinkle with ice water and stir to barely combine. (Do not overwork the dough or it will be tough.)

- Cover with plastic wrap and let it sit for 30 minutes or so.

- Then divide the dough. Roll out half onto a barely floured board. Transfer the dough to the bottom of the 9 x 13 pan and roll out to be ¼-inch thick. Using a fork, pierce a few holes into the bottom layer and bake for 12 minutes. Remove from the oven and pour in peach filing. Roll the second dough, and add on top, piercing a few holes with a fork, bake until golden brown about 25 to 30 minutes.

*(Here's a tip... Once you have rolled out the dough, roll it onto the rolling pin to transfer to the baking pan. Then once you have the peach filling inside, roll the second sheet of dough and roll it onto the pin to easily transfer to the to of the pan.)*

- Serve warm with ice cream or whipped cream.

# Chapter 6: June

## June Is Busting Out All Over

**Juneteenth** *has been celebrated for more than 150 years as a day of freedom for African-Americans. That party started in 1865, more than two years after Abraham Lincoln issued the Emancipation Proclamation. It took nearly two years for word to get to Galveston, but those Texans always knew how to throw a party, and so declared June 19th as a day for rest and relaxation. Still in Texas, they throw parades, barbecues, and backyard parties. But the celebration of Juneteenth has spread across the South and all over the country. Let's hear it for freedom and equality for all.*

# Break Out the Grill

First time using the grill for the season? How about a Trinidadian special—jerk chicken. So what the heck is jerk chicken, you ask? That's easy. It comes from those tropical islands where preserving food was hard before refrigeration. So what to do? Often they rubbed chickens and other meats in a spicy mixture that not only flavored the food, but preserved it as well.

* Grilled Jerk Chicken

* Fresh Mango Salad

* Caribbean Rice and Beans

* Fried Plantains with a Brown Sugar Glaze

* Lemon Berry Savarin

## GRILLED JERK CHICKEN

**Makes 8 servings**

* 6 to 8 chicken breasts, thighs, or legs

– Rub the chicken with the jerk spice and marinate in the refrigerator overnight.

**To make the jerk spice blend (yields about ½ cup)**
* ½ teaspoon coriander seeds
* 5 whole cloves
* 6 cardamom pods
* 10 allspice berries
* ½ teaspoon black pepper
* 2 bay leaves, crumbled
* ½ stick cinnamon, crushed into small pieces

* 4 cloves garlic
* 8 jalapeño peppers, toasted and seeded (or to taste)
* 1 inch fresh ginger, peeled
* ½ tablespoon fresh thyme

– Toast dry spices on a small tray in the oven at 350°F, for about 10 minutes, or until aromas are released. Puree spices with garlic, jalapeños, ginger, and thyme. Add small amount of water to make a paste.

– Cook the marinated chicken on a hot grill for 10 minutes, turn the chicken over, and cook for 10 minutes more, or until completely done. Keep hot.

## FRESH MANGO SALSA

### Makes 6-8 servings

* 3 teaspoons white balsamic vinegar
* 3 teaspoons fresh lemon juice
* 2 teaspoons granulated sugar
* ½ teaspoon kosher salt
* ½ teaspoon freshly ground black pepper
* 4 tablespoons extra-virgin olive oil
* 3 (1 pound) firm-ripe mangoes, peeled and cut into ½-inch pieces
* 2 large tomatoes, cut into ½-inch pieces
* 2 small red onions, halved lengthwise and thinly sliced crosswise
* ⅔ cup fresh cilantro leaves

– Whisk together vinegar, lemon juice, granulated sugar, salt, and pepper until sugar is dissolved, then add oil, whisking until emulsified. Add remaining ingredients and toss until coated.

## CARIBBEAN RICE AND BEANS

### Makes 6 servings

*The authentic Caribbean method in the Islands is to start off with pigeon peas, but you can use whatever you like.*

* 2 cups dried beans of your choice (white, black, pinto, cannellini)
* 2 tablespoons grape-seed oil
* 1 small onion, chopped
* 3 cloves garlic, minced
* 1 cup long grain white rice
* 2 cups chicken stock
* 1 15-ounce can coconut milk
* 1 teaspoon ground cumin
* ½ teaspoon chopped cilantro, or to taste

– Soak beans overnight in water to cover. Drain beans and transfer to a medium pot. Cover with water and boil until tender, about 2 hours.

– Heat oil in a saucepan over medium heat. Cook and stir onion and garlic in hot oil until softened, 5 to 7 minutes. Add rice. Cook and stir a few minutes, or until rice begins to turn golden.

– Stir broth, coconut milk, beans, and cumin into the rice, onion, and garlic mixture. Bring to a boil. Cover and simmer until the rice is tender and the moisture is absorbed, about 20 minutes.

– Gently stir cilantro into the beans and rice.

# FRIED PLANTAINS WITH BROWN SUGAR GLAZE

**Makes 6 to 8 servings**

* 2-3 plantains, really ripe with black marks
* olive oil
* 2 tablespoons butter
* 2 tablespoons brown sugar
* I ounce rum
* Dash sea salt
* Splash lime juice

- Peel and slice the plantain in half and then long ways. Fill a saucepan with about a half inch of oil. Fry the plantains on each side for just a few seconds, until brown. Drain on paper towels.

- For the glaze, melt the butter with the brown sugar and whisk until it dissolves. Add the rum and allow to boil until most of the alcohol cooks out, about 2 minutes. Swirl the pot or whisk the mixture so that it does not burn. Season with a sprinkling of sea salt and a splash of lime juice.

- Drizzle over the plantains and enjoy.

# LEMON BERRY SAVARIN

**Makes 6 to 8 servings**

## Bread
* I tablespoon active dry yeast
* ¼ cup warm water
* I½ cups unbleached all-purpose flour
* 3 tablespoons granulated sugar
* ½ teaspoon sea salt
* 3 large eggs, room temperature
* ½ cup (8 tablespoons) unsalted butter, soft

## Syrup
* I cup boiling water
* ¾ cup granulated sugar
* 2 tablespoons lemon juice
* ¼ cup kirsch or another cherry-flavored liqueur

## Topping
* ¼ cup red currant jelly
* 4 cups (2 pints) strawberries
* whipped cream, crème fraiche, or fresh yogurt

## To make the bread:
- In a large bowl, stir the yeast into warm water to soften.

- Add the flour, granulated sugar, salt, and eggs to the yeast mixture. Beat for 2 minutes.

- Cut the butter into eight pieces. Add one piece at a time to the yeast mixture. Beat well after each addition. Cover with plastic wrap and refrigerate for 2 hours.

- Press the dough down and scrape into a well-greased 6-cup savarin mold or Bundt pan. Cover and let rise for 1½ hours.

- While the savarin is rising, preheat the oven to 375°F.

- Bake for 35 minutes, or until it is golden and firm to the touch.

- Remove the savarin from the mold and let it cool on a rack.

- While it's cooling, make the syrup. Combine the boiling water, granulated sugar, and lemon juice. Stir until the sugar dissolves.

- Bring the mixture to a rolling boil over high heat. Reduce heat to medium and cook for 5 minutes.

- Remove from heat. Add the kirsch.

- Pour ½ cup of syrup into the savarin mold. Put the savarin back in the mold. Spoon the syrup over the top until the savarin has absorbed all the syrup. Let sit for 20 minutes.

- Remove the savarin from the mold.

- Heat the jelly to a liquid state. Brush on all sides of the savarin.

- Serve with fresh strawberries and large dollops of whipped cream, crème fraîche, or yogurt.

# Burgers with a Bite

* Spicy Lamb Burger Sliders with Harissa
* Sweet Potato Fries
* Tomato Cucumber Salad with Mint Apple Cider Vinaigrette
* Lemon Squares

## SPICY LAMB BURGER SLIDERS WITH HARISSA

**Makes 4 to 6 servings**

You can make little bite-sized sliders or regular-sized burgers. Your choice.

* 2 pounds ground lamb
* 4 tablespoons grated yellow onion, with juice
* 1 clove garlic, finely chopped
* 1 tablespoon EACH: sweet smoked paprika, ground cumin, coriander, and harissa
* 1 teaspoon cinnamon
* Sea salt and freshly ground black pepper to taste
* 6 to 8 sharp cheddar slices
* 8 to 12 small hamburger rolls
* Red onion slices
* Thin sliced tomatoes
* Parsley

- In a large bowl, combine the lamb, onion, garlic, paprika, cumin, coriander, harissa, cinnamon, and salt and pepper. Divide into 6 to 8 equal portions, then form each portion into a patty. Drizzle with olive oil.

- Heat a large cast-iron skillet or grill pan over medium- high heat. Add the patties and cook, turning once, for 4 minutes for medium. Toast roll tops on the grill as well. During the last minute of cooking, divide the cheese among the patties and tent with foil to melt. Top the rolls with the patties, red onion, tomatoes, and parsley. Then add tops and serve at once.

## SWEET POTATO FRIES

**Makes 6 servings**

* 4 large sweet potatoes, scrubbed clean
* 2 tablespoons grape-seed oil
* ½ teaspoon sea salt
* 1½ teaspoon EACH: garlic powder, smoked paprika, and dried oregano
* 1 teaspoon dried (or 2 teaspoons fresh) thyme
* ¼ teaspoon EACH black pepper and cayenne pepper

— Preheat oven to 425 degrees F.

— Leave the skin on and cut sweet potatoes with a sharp knife into thin, even matchsticks.

— Transfer to two baking sheets and drizzle with grape-seed oil. Then sprinkle with seasonings, and toss. Arrange in a single layer to ensure they crisp up.

— Bake for 15 minutes and flip/stir to cook on the other side. Bake for 10 to 15 minutes more, or until brown and crispy. You'll know they're done when the edges are dark brown and crispy.

— Remove from oven.

— Serve plain or with your favorite ketchup.

## MARINATED TOMATO CUCUMBER SALAD WITH MINT APPLE CIDER VINAIGRETTE

**Makes 6 servings**

* 3 English (also known as hothouse) cucumbers, peeled and sliced
* ⅓ cup red onion, peeled and very thinly sliced (optional)
* 1 cup water
* ½ cup apple cider vinegar
* 2 tablespoons granulated sugar
* 2 teaspoons sea salt
* 1 teaspoon freshly milled black pepper
* ¼ cup grape-seed oil
* 3 medium tomatoes, chopped (or 2-3 cups of any tomato you like)
* ¼ cup chopped fresh mint

— Place the cucumbers and red onion in a bowl. Whisk together the water, vinegar, granulated sugar, salt, pepper, and oil until the sugar is dissolved. Pour over the cucumbers and onions and let sit in the refrigerator for at least 30 minutes or up to 3 hours.

— Pour off all but a few tablespoons of the liquid. Add the tomatoes and herbs and toss to combine. Serve and enjoy!

## LEMON SQUARES

**Makes 24 small squares**

### Crust
* Grape-seed oil, for greasing
* 1½ sticks unsalted butter, diced
* 2 cups all-purpose flour

* ¼ cup packed light brown sugar
* ½ cup confectioner's sugar, plus more for garnish
* ¼ teaspoon sea salt

## Filling:
* 4 large eggs, plus 2 egg yolks
* 2 cups granulated sugar
* ⅓ cup all-purpose flour, sifted
* 1 teaspoon grated lemon zest
* 1 cup fresh lemon juice (from about 8 lemons)

– Make the crust: Position a rack in the middle of the oven and preheat to 350 degrees F. Grease a 9 x 13 pan with oil and line with foil, leaving a 2-inch overhang on all sides; grease the foil with oil. Pulse the butter, flour, both sugars, and the salt in a food processor until the dough comes together, about 1 minute. Press evenly into the bottom and about ½ inch up the sides of the prepared pan, making sure there are no cracks. Bake until the crust is golden, about 25 minutes.

– Meanwhile, make the filling: Whisk the whole eggs and yolks, granulated sugar, and flour in a bowl until smooth. Whisk in the lemon zest and juice. Remove the crust from the oven and reduce the temperature to 300 degrees F. Pour the filling over the warm crust and return to the oven. Bake until the filling is just set, 30 to 35 minutes.

– Let the bars cool in the pan on a rack, then refrigerate until firm, at least 2 hours. Lift out of the pan using the foil and slice. Dust with confectioners' sugar before serving.

# Chapter 7: July

## Fourth of July Cold Lunch

* Easy Pickled Shrimp
* Iceberg Wedge Bits with Blue Cheese
* Corn Bread (SEE PAGE 70 FOR RECIPE)
* Favorite Bananas Foster

## EASY PICKLED SHRIMP

*You can make this up to a day ahead, but you'll have to keep your hungry helpers out of it. So tempting.*

**Makes 8 servings**

* 2 pounds raw shrimp, medium

**Pickling mixture:**
* 1 cup unseasoned rice vinegar
* 1 cup olive oil
* ¼ cup EACH: fresh lemon juice, paper-thin lemon slices, red onion slices, and peeled garlic cloves (about 1 large head)
* 3 fresh bay leaves, coarsely torn
* 3 teaspoons EACH: celery seeds and mustard seeds
* 1 teaspoon coarse kosher salt
* ½ teaspoon freshly ground black pepper

## Boiling mixture:

* 8 cups water
* 1 cup coarse kosher salt
* 10 bay leaves
* 6 fresh thyme sprigs
* 1 unpeeled whole head of garlic, cut crosswise in half
* ¼ cup paprika
* 2 tablespoons mustard seeds
* 1 tablespoon EACH: whole allspice, celery seeds, and cardamom pods
* 1 cinnamon stick
* 2 pounds uncooked medium OR large shrimp in shells
* Ice cubes
* Crusty bread

## For pickling mixture:

– Stir rice vinegar, olive oil, lemon juice, lemon slices, onion slices, garlic cloves, bay leaves, celery seeds, mustard seeds, coarse kosher salt, and black pepper in large bowl until salt dissolves. Chill.

– DO AHEAD: *Can be made 1 day ahead.* Cover and refrigerate overnight.

## For boiling mixture:

– Place 8 cups water in large pot. Add coarse salt, bay leaves, thyme sprigs, garlic, paprika, mustard seeds, allspice, celery seeds, cardamom pods, and cinnamon stick. Bring to boil over high heat. Boil 5 minutes. Add shrimp; stir to separate. Boil just until shells turn pink, about 2 minutes. Using large skimmer, transfer shrimp to colander to drain.

– Line rimmed baking sheet with layer of ice cubes. Scatter shrimp on ice to cool quickly, about 5 minutes. Peel and devein shrimp, leaving tails intact. Add peeled shrimp to pickling mixture. Stir to blend. Cover and refrigerate at least 3 hours and up to 6 hours.

– Using slotted spoon, lift shrimp from pickling mixture. Arrange on platter. Serve with crusty bread.

# ICEBERG WEDGE BITES WITH BLUE CHEESE AND CORN BREAD

## Makes 8 servings

* 1 large head iceberg lettuce, cut into 8 wedges

## Blue Cheese Dressing

* ⅔ cup buttermilk, well shaken
* ⅓ cup mayonnaise
* 4 ounces crumbled blue cheese (about 1 cup)
* 1 tablespoon lemon juice
* A few dashes hot sauce, such as Tabasco
* 2 tablespoons chopped chives
* Sea salt and freshly milled black pepper, to taste

– In a bowl, combine buttermilk, mayonnaise, half of the blue cheese, lemon juice, and hot sauce.

– Stir to combine and add chives, salt and pepper.

– Then drizzle over iceberg wedges and top with remaining blue cheese.

# FAVORITE BANANAS FOSTER

**Makes 8 servings**

*So easy and so satisfying.*

* ¼ cup (½ stick) butter
* 1 cup brown sugar
* ½ teaspoon cinnamon
* ¼ cup banana liqueur (good brand)
* 8 bananas cut in half lengthwise, then halved
* ½ cup dark Myers' Rum

– Serve over vanilla ice cream

– Combine the butter, brown sugar, and cinnamon in a flambé pan or skillet. Place the pan over low heat on top of the stove and cook, stirring until sugar dissolves. Stir in banana liqueur; then place the bananas in the pan. When the banana sections soften and begin to brown, carefully add the rum.

– Continue to cook the sauce until the rum is hot; then tip the pan slightly to ignite the rum. When the flames subside, lift the bananas out of the pan and place four pieces over each portion of ice cream. Generously spoon warm sauce over the top of the ice cream and serve.

# Grilling in the Garden

\* Grilled Flank Steak

\* Arugula and Beefsteak Tomato Salad

\* Grilled Peaches with Bourbon Butter Sauce and Vanilla Ice Cream

## GRILLED FLANK STEAK

**Makes 6 servings**

* 1 cup port wine
* ½ cup EACH: chopped shallots and grape-seed oil
* 2 tablespoons EACH: fresh parsley, oregano, and thyme
* 1 bay leaf
* 4 cloves garlic, minced
* 1 teaspoon EACH: white, black, and cayenne pepper
* ½ teaspoon Creole mustard
* 1 2- to 4-pound flank steak, trimmed and fat discarded

– Mix all ingredients except steak in 13 x 9 x 2 glass baking dish. Add steak and turn to coat. Cover and refrigerate 2 hours or overnight, turning occasionally.

– Prepare barbeque (medium-high heat) or preheat the broiler. Remove meat from marinade; discard marinade. Grill the steak to desired doneness, about 4 minutes per side for medium rare. (OR oven bake about 12 minutes at 375°F.)

– Transfer steak to work surface. Let it rest about 5 minutes. Cut across the grain into thin strips. Arrange on platter and serve.

## ARUGULA AND BEEFSTEAK TOMATO SALAD

* 2 pounds beefsteak tomatoes
* 3 tablespoons EACH: red wine vinegar and extra-virgin olive oil
* Coarse sea salt and freshly ground black pepper
* 1 bunch arugula (6 to 8 ounces), washed well and dried

– Core beefsteak tomatoes; cut each into 8 wedges.

– In a small bowl, whisk together vinegar and oil; season with salt and pepper. In a large bowl, toss arugula with half the dressing. Divide arugula and tomatoes evenly among four serving plates or a serving platter. Drizzle tomatoes with remaining dressing. Serve immediately.

## GRILLED PEACHES WITH BOURBON BUTTER SAUCE AND VANILLA ICE CREAM

*So easy to do, it will buckle your knees.*

**Makes 6 to 8 servings**

* 3-4 ripe peaches (optionally peeled)
* 3 tablespoons butter
* ¾ cup brown sugar
* ¾ cup bourbon
* 1 tsp cinnamon
* pinch of salt
* Optional Topping – whipped cream or vanilla ice cream

– Peel the peaches if you'd like, then cut each in half and remove the pit. Put peaches aside on a dish to await grilling.

– Combine butter, brown sugar, bourbon, and cinnamon in a medium saucepan on the stovetop over medium heat. Heat and stir until the sugar is completely dissolved and the sauce is hot and bubbly. Pour into a small pitcher to await serving.

– Grill peaches on a hot oiled grill for approximately 3-4 minutes. Remove from the grill and serve with warm bourbon butter sauce and whipped cream or ice cream.

# Roast it Right Up

* Roast Chicken with Herbes de Provence
* Red Potatoes with Parsley
* Green Beans with Hazelnuts
* Homemade Silky Strawberry Sorbet

## ROAST CHICKEN WITH HERBES DE PROVENCE

**Makes 6 to 8 servings with plenty of leftovers for chicken soup or salad**

* 1 roasting chicken, 4 to 6 pounds
* 3 garlic cloves, smashed
* 1 teaspoon EACH: sea salt and freshly cracked black pepper
* 1 teaspoon herbes de provence*
* Soft butter to rub the skin

- Heat the oven to 350°F.

- Wash and dry the chicken. Place in a large roaster on its back.

- Peel the garlic cloves by whacking with the flat of a knife. Put the garlic into the chicken's cavity, then sprinkle with salt and pepper. Add the herbes de provence. Spread soft butter over the chicken breast.

- Roast, covered, at 350°F for 60-90 minutes depending on the size of the chicken. Remove the lid and roast uncovered another 15-30 minutes until the skin is crisp and the chicken is fully cooked. Use an instant-read thermometer to check the temperature. Cook to 150°F at the thickest part of the thigh. Remove from the oven and let it rest on a cutting board up to 30 minutes before carving.

- Make au jus by dissolving a tablespoon of cornstarch in a little water. Stir

Feast #22

that into the pan juices and raise to a boil. Taste and adjust seasonings with salt and pepper. Transfer the sauce to a gravy boat for serving.

* Herbes de provence are a dry mixture of savory herbs including savory, thyme, rosemary, and bay leaves. It is often sold in good grocery stores in little cloth bags. To use, just drop this into the cavity of the bird. Want to make your own? Just make your own mixture of the dry herbs, and rub the cavity of the bird with this classic French seasoning.

## RED POTATOES WITH PARSLEY

Almost too easy to be called a recipe. Simply buy one red potato for each diner plus a couple for the pot. Scrub potatoes, then steam until tender, about 15-20 minutes.

Meanwhile mince a tablespoon or so of fresh parsley. Transfer potatoes to a serving bowl and top with parsley, melted butter, and black pepper. POW!

## GREEN BEANS WITH HAZELNUTS

Another side dish that's so easy it is barely a recipe. Pick up a couple of handfuls of fresh green beans at the farmer's market.

Steam until just tender, no more than 2-3 minutes, then blanch in an ice water bath to stop the cooking.

Transfer to a serving bowl. Top with chopped hazelnuts and salt and pepper to taste. Easy, huh?

## HOMEMADE SILKY STRAWBERRY SORBET

*No need for an ice-cream maker here. Just whiz up the berries using a stick blender, heat with cornstarch mixture, then freeze the mixture in a flat dish for a couple of hours or overnight. Then whiz it up again with a stick blender. POW! Pure silk and just as delicious as it is beautiful. Serve in ice cream bowls.*

**Makes 6 to 8 servings**

* I large basket of strawberries, hulled and quartered
* ½ cup granulated sugar or to taste
* I pinch salt
* I ½ teaspoons cornstarch
* I ½ teaspoons cold water
* 3 tablespoons lemon juice

— Place berries in a work bowl and puree until smooth using a stick blender. Combine berry puree, granulated sugar, and salt in a large saucepan. Heat until melted and just simmering. Whisk cornstarch into the cold water; stir into heated berry mixture. Remove from heat, and stir in lemon juice. Cool slightly. Freeze berry mixture until cold and slushy, about 2 hours.

— To serve, make a silky cold mixture using the stick blender. Serve immediately.

# Summer Sandwiches

* Chef Jesse's Crockpot-Style North Carolina Pulled Pork on Mini-Brioche Rolls
* Creole Green Beans (SEE PAGE 78 FOR RECIPE)
* Old-Fashioned Hummingbird Layer Cake

## CHEF JESSE'S CROCKPOT-STYLE NORTH CAROLINA PULLED PORK ON MINI-BRIOCHE ROLLS

**Makes 8 servings**

* 2 tablespoons brown sugar
* 1 teaspoon smoked paprika
* 2 teaspoons kosher salt
* 1 teaspoon EACH: granulated garlic and onion
* ½ teaspoon EACH: ground black pepper and crushed red pepper
* 1 4- to 6-pound pork butt or shoulder roast
* 2 large yellow onions, quartered
* 1 cup EACH: cider vinegar, ketchup, and chili sauce
* ½ cup creole mustard
* ⅓ cup Worcestershire sauce

— Blend brown sugar, paprika, salt, garlic, onion, black pepper, crushed pepper, and rub over the roast. Cover with plastic wrap in a shallow glass pan, and marinate overnight in the refrigerator.

**Next day:**
— Place onions in Crockpot, then add marinated roast.

— Combine vinegar, ketchup, chili sauce, creole mustard, and Worcestershire sauce. Stir to mix well. Pour about ½ of mixture over roast. Save the rest for later.

— Cover the pot. Cook the roast on low for 8-10 hours. Remove meat and onions, discard the onions, and shred the meat. Add juices from Crockpot and some remaining vinegar mixture to moisten the meat. Save some to pass at the table. Serve on mini-brioche rolls.

## OLD-FASHIONED HUMMINGBIRD LAYER CAKEE

**Makes a large three-layer cake to serve 12 to 16**

A true child of the South recipe, the banana, coconut, and pineapple flavors in this cake came up from the tropics and took over the hearts of Southern bakers about the time my grandmother learned to bake. I have always loved it.

This is one way to use up those black overripe bananas.

* Nonstick baking spray
* 2 sticks (1 cup) butter, softened
* 2 cups granulated sugar
* 1 tablespoon vanilla extract
* 4 large eggs
* 3 cups all-purpose flour
* 1 teaspoon baking soda
* 1 teaspoon ground cinnamon
* 1 teaspoon salt
* ⅓ cup buttermilk
* 1½ cups mashed overripe bananas (about 4 medium)
* 1 8-ounce can crushed pineapple and juice
* Optional garnishes: sweetened flaked coconut, pecans

### Frosting:
* 2 sticks (1 cup) butter, softened
* 2 8-ounce packages cream cheese, softened
* 2 cups confectioners' sugar
* 1 tablespoon lemon juice
* 1 teaspoon pure vanilla extract

— Preheat the oven to 350°F. Spray three 9-inch baking pans with nonstick baking spray.

— In a large mixing bowl, using metal beaters, beat the butter, granulated sugar, and vanilla at medium speed until fluffy. Add the eggs, one at a time, beating well after each addition.

— In a medium bowl, combine the flour, baking soda, cinnamon, and salt. Add to the butter mixture alternately with the buttermilk, beginning and ending with the flour mixture and beating just until combined after each addition. Add the mashed bananas and pineapple, beating until combined.

— Using a measuring cup, spoon the batter into each of the three prepared pans, one scoop at a time to ensure an even distribution. Slam the pans against the counter to get any air bubbles out of the batter.

— Bake until a wooden pick inserted in the center comes out clean, 25 to 35 minutes. Cool in the pans for 10 minutes. Remove from the pans and cool completely on wire racks.

— Spread some frosting between the layers. Spread the remaining frosting over the top and sides of the cake. Garnish with coconut and nuts if desired.

**Frosting:**

– Beat the butter and cream cheese together with a handheld electric mixer until smooth and creamy. Beat in the confectioners' sugar in increments. Lastly beat in the lemon juice and vanilla.

# Chapter 8: August

## Summer winds down
### First Quarter Moon of the Late Summer

✳ Blackened Shrimp with Cucumber Chow-Chow

✳ Sautéed Kale with Shallots and Malt Vinegar Reduction

✳ Sweet Potato Corn Bread

✳ Banana Tart

## BLACKENED SHRIMP WITH CUCUMBER CHOW-CHOW

**Makes 8 servings**

* 2 pounds medium shrimp, peeled
* Chef Jesse's Spice blend (SEE PAGE 26 FOR RECIPE)
* Grape-seed oil

*Too easy.*

– Dredge shrimp in spice blend, then heat oil in a large skillet and cook until blackened on both sides, no more than 3-4 minutes.

## CUCUMBER CHOW-CHOW

**Makes 6 to 8 servings**

* 6 cucumbers
* ¼ teaspoon EACH: sea salt and black pepper

* ½ lemon (juice and grated zest)
* 8-12 cherry tomatoes sliced in half
* ½ scotch bonnet pepper, no seeds (optional)
* 2 tablespoons cilantro, chopped
* 1 clove garlic, crushed
* ½ small red onion

- You can use any cucumber you have on hand, and the option to peel or not is totally up to you. Remember to wear gloves when handling scotch bonnet peppers and to wash your hands immediately after with soap and water.

- Cut the stems and bottoms off the cucumbers and cut into spears and place in a large bowl. I also use some cherry tomatoes, for added flavor, color, and texture. You can use any tomato you have.

- Crush or dice the garlic, chop the cilantro, and either dice the scotch bonnet or cut it into large pieces so that when you serve it, your guests can easily identify the pieces and avoid them if they wish.Top of Form

## SAUTÉED KALE WITH SHALLOTS AND MALT VINEGAR REDUCTION

*To make the reduction, boil ½ cup malt vinegar down to about 2 tablespoons.*

**Makes 8 servings**

* ¼ cup extra-virgin olive oil
* 3 cloves garlic, smashed
* 2 cups shallots, minced
* 6 to 8 cups fresh kale, rinsed and drained
* ¼ cup vegetable stock

* ½ teaspoon kosher salt
* ¼ teaspoon freshly ground black pepper
* 2 tablespoons malt vinegar reduction*

- Remove stems from kale, then wash thoroughly and spin dry. Coarsely chop kale. In a large, heavy skillet, heat oil over medium-high heat. Cook and stir garlic and shallots for 2 minutes and stir in the kale to cook for 5 minutes. Reduce heat, stir in stock, cover and steam 10 minutes. Season to taste with salt, pepper, and malt vinegar reduction.

- Toss and serve hot.

## SWEET POTATO CORN BREAD

*Cook sweet potato in oven or microwave until soft, then cool, peel, and mash.*

**Makes 1 dozen**

* 1-⅓ cups cake flour
* ⅔ cup cornmeal
* ⅔ cup granulated sugar
* ½ cup corn flour
* 1 tablespoon baking powder
* ½ teaspoon kosher salt
* 1⅓ cups buttermilk
* 5 tablespoons unsalted butter, melted
* 1 small sweet potato, cooked and mashed

- In a large bowl, combine flour, cornmeal, granulated sugar, corn flour, baking powder, and salt. Stir to mix. In a separate bowl, combine milk, butter, egg, and mashed sweet potato. Add to the dry ingredients and blend just until large lumps are dissolved.

- Pour mixture into a greased 8-inch-square baking pan or 10-inch cast-iron skillet. Bake at 350°F until done, about 25 minutes.

prick with a fork, then put cooked bananas over the pastry. Bake 30-40 minutes at 350°F or until golden. Cool and serve. Great with a scoop of vanilla ice cream.

## BANANA TART

**Makes 8 servings**

* ½ cup (1 stick) unsalted butter
* 1 teaspoon ground cinnamon
* 1 cup packed dark brown sugar
* ½ cup banana liqueur
* 8 medium bananas, peeled and sliced

**Tart dough**
**(makes 2 tarts):**
* 5¼ cups pastry flour (or all-purpose)
* 2 teaspoons granulated sugar
* 1 tablespoon kosher salt
* 4 sticks cold unsalted butter, cut into small pieces
* 1 cup ice water

- Combine flour and salt into a bowl. Add butter and mix until it resembles coarse meal. Add ice water to form a dough. Wrap in plastic and refrigerate 1 hour.

- In a large skillet, melt butter, add cinnamon and brown sugar and stir, simmering over medium heat until the sugar dissolves, about 3 minutes. Add banana liqueur and blend well. Add sliced bananas and cook about 5-6 minutes or until soft.

- Roll pastry out on a lightly floured work surface. Line a 9-inch tart tin with pastry,

# Aunt Minnie Mae Smothers It

∗ Smothered Chicken in Rosemary Gravy

∗ Homemade Papparadelle

∗ Chopped Salad

∗ Tiramisu

## SMOTHERED CHICKEN IN ROSEMARY GRAVY

*Aunt Minnie Mae was the master of smothered chicken. We all begged her to make it for family gatherings.*

**Makes 8 servings**

* 2 2½ pound frying chickens, quartered
* 1½ cups all-purpose flour
* 1 teaspoon Chef Jesse Spice Blend (see pp 26)
* ½ cup grape-seed oil
* ½ medium yellow onion, peeled and diced
* 4 cups chicken stock
* 2 tablespoons chopped fresh rosemary

– Combine flour and spice blend in a bowl. Dredge chicken in seasoned flour, shaking off excess.

– In a Dutch oven, heat the oil over medium-high heat and fry the chicken in batches, about 5-6 minutes per side. Transfer to a plate when cooked.

– Add onion to the pan and sauté 1 minute. Add ½ cup reserved flour. Stir to make a roux and cook until fragrant and a lovely nut-brown color, about 5-7 minutes. Add stock, stirring constantly to make a smooth gravy. Season with rosemary and taste and adjust seasonings with salt and pepper.

- Return the chicken to the pan and simmer, covered, until the chicken is cooked through and tender (about ½ hour).

- Serve chicken with sauce over homemade pappardelle.

## HOMEMADE PAPPARDELLE

*Get out your pasta machine. This is easy. If you need a visual, just go to YouTube and see a video of pasta-making.*

**Makes enough for 8 servings**

* 5 cups all-purpose flour, divided
* 1½ teaspoons sea salt, divided
* 6 large eggs, divided
* 6 large egg yolks, divided
* 6 tablespoons (or more) water, divided
* Pecorino cheese for dusting

- Place 2½ cups flour and ¾ teaspoon salt in processor; blend 5 seconds. Whisk 3 eggs, 3 yolks, and 3 tablespoons water in bowl.

- With machine running, pour egg mixture through feed tube. Blend until sticky dough forms, adding water by teaspoonful if dry.

- Scrape dough out onto floured work surface. Knead dough until smooth and no longer sticky, sprinkling lightly with flour as needed, about 8 minutes. Shape into ball. Cover with plastic wrap and let rest 45 minutes. Repeat with remaining flour, salt, eggs, yolks, and water.

- Divide each dough ball into 4 pieces. Cover dough with plastic wrap.

- Set pasta machine to widest setting. Flatten 1 dough piece into 3-inch-wide rectangle. Run through machine 5 times, dusting lightly with flour if sticking. Continue to run piece through machine, adjusting to next-narrower setting after every 5 passes, until dough is about 26 inches long. Cut crosswise into 3 equal pieces. Run each piece through machine, adjusting to next-narrower setting, until strip is a scant 1/16-inch thick and 14 to 16 inches long. Return machine to original setting for each piece. Arrange strips in a single layer on sheets of parchment.

- Repeat with remaining dough. Let strips stand until slightly dry to touch, 20 to 30 minutes. Fold strips in half so short ends meet, then fold in half again. Cut strips into ⅔-inch-wide pappardelle. DO AHEAD: *Can be made 1 day ahead. Arrange pappardelle in a single layer on sheets of parchment. Stack sheets in roasting pan. Cover and chill.*

- Bring a large pot of barely salted water to a boil, and cook the pasta until al dente no more than 5 minutes. Cool on a rack, then toss with butter. Dust with shredded Pecorino.

## CHOPPED SALAD

**Makes 8 servings**

### Dressing:
* ¼ cup red wine vinegar
* 1½ tablespoons finely chopped shallot
* ½ tablespoon honey
* ¼ cup hazelnut oil or extra-virgin olive oil

### Salad:
* 6 cups chopped romaine hearts
* 4 cups sliced red cabbage
* 1 large Fuji apple, halved, cored, diced
* 1 Asian pear, halved, cored, diced
* 1 mango, peeled, diced
* ¾ cup hazelnuts, toasted, husked, coarsely chopped
* ½ cup pomegranate seeds
* ½ cup crumbled blue cheese (optional)

– Whisk dressing in a small bowl.

– Toss salad ingredients in a large salad bowl, then drizzle over dressing. Toss and serve.

## TIRAMISU

**Makes 8 servings**

* 2 cups boiling water
* 3 tablespoons instant espresso powder
* ½ cup plus 1 tablespoon granulated sugar, divided
* 3 tablespoons Tia Maria (coffee liqueur)
* 4 large egg yolks
* ⅓ cup dry Marsala
* 1 pound mascarpone (2½ cups)
* 1 cup chilled heavy cream
* 36 *savoiardi* (crisp Italian ladyfingers; from 2 7-ounce packages)
* Unsweetened cocoa powder for dusting

– Stir together water, espresso powder, 1 tablespoon granulated sugar, and Tia Maria in a shallow bowl until sugar has dissolved, then cool.

– Beat egg yolks, Marsala, and remaining ½ cup granulated sugar in a metal bowl set over a saucepan of barely simmering water, using a whisk or handheld electric mixer until tripled in volume, 5 to 8 minutes. Remove bowl from heat. Beat in mascarpone until just combined.

– Beat cream in a large bowl until it holds stiff peaks.

– Fold mascarpone mixture into whipped cream gently but thoroughly.

– Dipping both sides of each ladyfinger into coffee mixture, line bottom of a 13 by 9 by 3 baking pan with 18 ladyfingers in 3 rows, trimming edges to fit if necessary. Spread half the mascarpone filling on top. Dip remaining 18 ladyfingers in coffee and arrange over filling in pan.

– Spread remaining mascarpone filling on top and dust with cocoa. Chill, covered, at least 6 hours.

– Let tiramisu stand at room temperature 30 minutes before serving. Dust with more cocoa.

# Lobster, Lobster, everywhere You Look

*Served up and down the East Coast, in diners large and small, the lobster pie is a good way to use up those little one-pounders known as chicken lobsters, and also a great way to celebrate summer when lobsters are at their peak.*

*In Maine, cooks crumble up crackers to make a crust, but Southern cooks know you will love a Southern pastry on top. Traditionally made and cooked for each person in oval ramekins, it's just a matter of cooking the lobsters in boiling water, then picking out the meat and dividing it among the ramekins. Plus, you can buy fresh cooked lobster meat in fishmonger shops too, and you don't even have to boil 'em up.*

* Downhome Lobster Pie in a Southern Pastry Shell
* Red Rice Salad
* Summer Fruit Composé with Poppy Seed Dressing
* Panna Cotta with Fresh Seasonal Berries, Honey, and Mint

## DOWNHOME LOBSTER PIE

**Makes 8 servings**

* ½ cup grape-seed oil
* ½ cup EACH: onions, carrots, celery, and leeks, chopped
* ⅓ cup garlic, minced
* ½ cup EACH: fresh thyme and tarragon
* I teaspoon EACH: white pepper and Old Bay Seasoning
* Sea salt to taste
* ½ cup all-purpose flour
* 4 cups seafood or lobster stock, heated to a boil
* 4 lobster tails, raw, medium dice
* I tablespoon brandy

- Heat the oil in a Dutch oven, then add the onions, carrots, celery, leeks, garlic and sauté until tender, about 5 minutes, stirring. Add thyme, tarragon, pepper, and Old Bay Seasoning.

- Add ½ cup oil. Stir in the flour to make a roux. Cook 3-5 minutes or until it is fragrant and a gorgeous nut-brown color.

- Add stock and brandy. Cook until thickened. Cool

- Add the raw lobster meat, mix into the blind baked shell. Add top layer of dough. Poke holes in dough.

- Bake 25 minutes.

## *BASIC SOUTHERN PIE CRUST

Makes 1 double-crust pie, 2 single crusts, or six ramekins for pot pies

*Single-Pie Crust*

* 1½ cups all-purpose flour, chilled
* ½ cup lard or vegetable shortening, chilled
* ½ teaspoon kosher salt
* 4 to 8 tablespoons ice water

*Double Pie Crust*

* 2 cups all-purpose flour, chilled
* ⅔ cups lard or vegetable shortening, chilled
* ½ teaspoon kosher salt
* 5 to 10 tablespoons ice water

*For ramekins, roll out a large rectangle, then place a ramekin on top and cut to the correct size; repeat and stack them with layers of parchment between layers while you make the filling. Place filling in each ramekin, then add the top and seal down using a little egg white for glue. Bake as directed at 350°F, about 20 minutes or so depending on the ramekin's size.*

## How to make pastry in the food processor:

Using the regular steel blade, place the flour, shortening, and salt in food processor and pulse 5 or 6 times until it looks mealy. With machine running, begin to add the water in a steady stream through the tube, just until dough begins to gather around the blade, about 10 seconds (don't over process). You may not need all the water—you don't want your dough to be wet or sticky to the touch. The dough should hold together when squeezed. If your dough is crumbly, it needs more water; add in a tablespoon at a time.

Remove dough from the machine, make a ball, and then press into a thick disc, like a giant burger—two discs if you made the double recipe. Wrap in plastic wrap and chill in the fridge for about 1 hour before rolling out. Can also be made several days in advance and stored in the fridge till needed, or frozen. Allow 2 to 3 hours for thawing before rolling out.

Roll the dough out on a lightly floured piece of waxed paper, and sprinkle a tiny bit of flour on top of the dough disc. Use a light forward motion only when rolling (don't rock the rolling pin back and forth—roll only in one direction) but periodically lift and turn the dough to prevent sticking and to keep it circular in shape. Add a bit more flour to the surface only if necessary. Roll out to about 2 inches larger than the pie plate, about ⅛ of an inch thick.

Gently roll the dough up around the rolling pin, or simply fold it over to make it easier to transport to the pie plate. Position and unroll or unfold, carefully molding from the inside of the pie plate to the edges. Trim excess dough with kitchen shears and either flute the edges by using the forefinger of one hand and pinching the dough next to it between your forefinger and thumb of the other hand and continuing around the crust, or simply take the rolling pin and roll firmly across the top to trim. Finish as directed in your recipe, as to pre-bake or not.

## Blind Baking:

If your pie requires a pre-baked crust, dock the crust before baking using the tines of a fork to poke holes all around the bottom of the crust. This will prevent the crust from bubbling. You can also line the crust with parchment paper or aluminum foil and fill the foil with pie weights. Bake at 350 degrees for about 15 minutes. Remove paper or foil and cook another 5 minutes, or until crust is dry, but not browned. Allow crust to cool before filling and proceed with recipe.

## RED RICE SALAD

**Makes 6 to 8 servings**

*Find the Piedmont Italian red rice in high-end grocery stores everywhere. Such a brilliant ruby color, and it makes a perfect base for a summer rice salad.*

* 1 cup Piedmont Italian red rice
* Sea salt and freshly grated black pepper to taste
* 2 tablespoons red wine vinegar
* 5 tablespoons extra-virgin olive oil, plus more for drizzling
* ¾ cup mixed, halved red and gold cherry tomatoes
* ½ cup corn kernels (about 1 ear)
* 4 ounces Asiago cheese, chopped (about ½ cup)
* ¼ cup EACH diced cucumber, radishes, and scallions
* ½ cup basil leaves, torn
* 4 teaspoons chopped flat-leaf parsley

– Bring a large pot of unsalted water to a boil. Add the rice and boil until the grains begin to split, 15 to 18 minutes. Salt the water heavily and cook until the grains are tender, 5 to 10 minutes longer. Drain the rice very well and spread it out on a large rimmed baking sheet. Drizzle with the vinegar and 2½ tablespoons of the olive oil. Let cool.

– Transfer the rice to a large bowl. Toss with the tomatoes, corn, cheese, cucumber, radishes, scallions, herbs, and the remaining 2½ tablespoons oil. Adjust seasonings with salt, pepper, and more vinegar to taste. Serve warm or chilled.

## SUMMER FRUIT COMPOSÉ WITH POPPY SEED DRESSING

**Makes 6 to 8 servings**

*This ad-lib salad is made with the freshest in-season fruits you see at the farmer's market and can change as the summer season progresses.*

*Arrange the bite-sized pieces of fruit on a flat platter. Serve with your own homemade poppy seed dressing on the side. (A gravy boat is ideal for this.)POW!*

### POPPY SEED DRESSING

* ½ cup grape-seed oil
* ¼ cup white balsamic vinegar
* ¼ cup granulated sugar
* I teaspoon poppy seeds
* I teaspoon Dijon mustard
* I teaspoon salt

- Stir together in a jar with a lid. Store in the refrigerator up to 2 weeks.

### PANNA COTTA W/ FRESH SEASONAL BERRIES, HONEY, AND MINT

*Such a great finish for a complicated meal. Make it ahead at your convenience.*

**Makes 6 servings**

* I cup whole milk
* I cup heavy cream
* ½ cup granulated sugar
* 2 teaspoons gelatin

* I teaspoon vanilla extract

- In medium saucepan, heat milk, cream, and granulated sugar until the sugar is dissolved.

- Soften the gelatin in 1 cup cold water and add to the hot milk mixture. Stir until dissolved, and then mix in vanilla. Pour into 3- or 4-ounce buttered ramekins, and chill until set, about 6 hours or overnight.

- (I love to go to the farmer's market to see what seasonal fruits are on display and gather some for this recipe. Also jam works well. I like strawberries, blueberries, and blackberries to serve over panna cotta.)

- In a medium bowl, toss a few seasonal fruits with a bit of honey, a squeeze of lemon, and fresh mint. Once you have turned the panna cottas out onto dessert plates, top each one with fruit. POW!

# A late-summer picnic for my mama's birthday

**We all come out for my mama's party. Everybody brings their best dish. Oh, those ladies are competitive. But I just bring what I knows my mama likes best.**

* Baby Kale Salad
* Herbed Oil Red Potato Salad
* Chef Jesse's Barbecued Pig's Feet
* Down-Home Coconut Cake

## BABY KALE SALAD

**Makes four servings**

* 1 ½ tablespoons apple cider vinegar
* 2 tablespoons grape-seed oil
* 1 tablespoon honey
* ½ teaspoon kosher salt
* 5 ounces baby kale
* ¼ cup golden raisins
* 3 tablespoons toasted pecans
* Salt and fresh-ground black pepper

- Combine the vinegar, oil, honey, and salt in a small mason jar. Seal tightly and shake to combine. Place the kale in a large salad bowl. Just before serving, add the dressing, and toss to coat the kale.

- Add golden raisins and pecans and toss again.

- Season to taste with salt and pepper, serve quickly.

## HERBED OIL RED POTATO SALAD

**Makes four servings**

* 1½ pounds red potatoes (about 15 diced medium)
* ½ cup minced fresh herbs (parsley, tarragon, chives)
* 2 scallions, sliced thin
* 1 tablespoon of whole grain mustard
* 1 tablespoon apple cider vinegar
* ½ cup diced gherkin pickles, minced fine
* ½ cup pimentos diced fine
* Kosher salt and black pepper to taste

– Fill a large pot of water and place potatoes in pot, cook for 12-14 minutes. Drain and air cool.

– In a medium bowl, mix the herbs, scallions, oil, mustard, vinegar, pickles, pepper, salt, and pepper. Adjust seasoning and toss with potatoes.

## CHEF JESSE'S BBQ PIGS FEET

**Makes 8 servings**

* 8 fresh pig feet (about 5 pounds, split in half)

– Season with Chef Jesse's Spice Blend (see pp 26), rubbing all over pig feet. Marinate overnight in a covered dish in the refrigerator.

**Next day:**
* ½ cup EACH: grape-seed oil, diced carrots, celery, and onion
* 3 garlic cloves, smashed
* 2 quarts water AND apple cider vinegar

* 2 teaspoons crushed red pepper
* 1 tablespoon EACH: kosher salt, black pepper, and pickling spice
* 4 thyme sprigs
* 1 cinnamon stick
* 2 cups of Chef Jesse's BBQ sauce (see page 162)

– Preheat oven to 425°F.

– Place marinated pig feet in a roasting pan, roast for 25 minutes or until golden brown, then remove from pan onto a plate. In same pan, add oil and sauté the carrots, celery, and onions for 5 minutes. Add garlic, stir, and cook about a minute more. Add pig feet back in, cover with water and vinegar, bring to a boil, and add crushed pepper, salt, black pepper, pickling spice, thyme and cinnamon stick. Lower oven to 300°F. Cover pan with lid or foil and braise for 2½ hours or until tender. Strain braising liquid (this can make some great broth for greens).

– Sprinkle vegetables over the pig feet, cover with Chef Jesse's BBQ sauce, and bake for about 25 minutes more. Serve hot.

## DOWN-HOME COCONUT CAKE

**Makes 12 to 16 servings**

– Preheat oven to 375°F. Grease and flour 3 9-inch round cake pans

* 3 cups cake flour
* 2½ teaspoons baking powder

* ½ teaspoon salt
* I cup (2 sticks) unsalted butter
* 2 cups granulated sugar
* 4 large eggs
* I cup milk
* I teaspoon lemon extract
* I teaspoon pure vanilla extract
* ½ teaspoon vegetable oil

## Chef Jesse's pineapple filling

* Butter cream frosting
* ½ cup coconut flakes

- Combine the flour, baking powder, and salt in a bowl. In an electric mixer, cream together the butter and granulated sugar on medium speed until light. Add the eggs one at a time, beating well after each addition.

- Add the dry ingredients to the mixture, alternating with the milk and beginning and ending with flour mixture. Stir in the lemon, vanilla extract, and oil.

- Pour the batter into three prepared 9-inch round baking pans. Bake for 20 to 25 minutes. Insert wooden pick in the center of the cake to see if it comes out clean.

- Let the layers cool. Place the bottom layer on a cake plate and spread Chef Jesse's pineapple filling between the layers. Add a little frosting in between the layers, and sprinkle coconut. Repeat process until the cake is completely covered in frosting.

# BUTTER CREAM FROSTING

**Makes 4 cups**

* I cup butter
* ½ cup shortening
* I cup granulated sugar
* 4 large egg whites
* ½ teaspoon fresh lemon juice
* ¾ teaspoon vanilla extract
* I tablespoon water (optional); for a softer butter cream, blend in the water

- In an electric mixer with paddle attachment, cream together the butter, shortening, and granulated sugar until well blended. Add the egg whites, lemon juice, and vanilla. Blend at medium speed, then mix at high speed until light and fluffy.

# FRESH PINEAPPLE FILLING

**Makes 2 cups**

1 whole pineapple (peeled, cored, and crushed)
* ¼ cup granulated sugar

- In a saucepan, add the crushed pineapple and granulated sugar, bring to a boil, and cook for 5 minutes, or until pineapple is cooked through and juice becomes syrupy. Cool for cake later.

# Chapter 9: September

## Back to School and Other Fall Feasts

* Baby Back Ribs with Honey Barbecue Sauce
* Mom's Baked Beans with Molasses
* Braised Kale with Apples
* Down-Home 7-Up Pound Cake

## BABY BACK RIBS WITH HONEY BARBECUE SAUCE

**Makes 6 servings**

*We could call these rainy day ribs, since they can be baked in the oven and you don't even have to think about an umbrella over the outdoor grill. POW!*

* ¼ cup paprika
* ½ teaspoon EACH: cayenne pepper, black and white pepper
* 2 teaspoons EACH: granulated garlic and onion
* 1 tablespoon EACH: brown sugar and smoked salt
* ½ cup EACH: water and cider vinegar
* 1 cup apple juice
* 2 pounds of baby back ribs, cleaned

– Mix all the spices above in a bowl. Add vinegar and water to form a paste. Rub the paste over the ribs, cover in plastic, and marinate overnight in the refrigerator.

**Next day:**
– Preheat the oven to 350°F.

- Roast ribs for 1 hour uncovered in a baking dish. Once the ribs have browned, add apple juice and cover them in foil to cook for 1½ more hours or until fork tender. Let rest for 10 minutes, brush on barbecue sauce, and brown for 5 minutes more. Keep hot.

## HONEY BARBECUE SAUCE

* I tablespoon grape-seed oil
* I red onion, minced
* I medium garlic, minced
* I cup EACH: ketchup and chili sauce (Heinz 57)
* 2 teaspoons hot sauce or to taste (Frank's is good)
* ½ cup EACH: cider vinegar and apple juice
* I cup EACH: honey and water
* ¼ cup Creole mustard
* I tablespoon Worcestershire sauce
* ⅓ teaspoon fresh thyme
* Sea salt and freshly ground black pepper to taste

- In a heavy saucepan, add oil over medium heat, then cook onion and garlic until soft and translucent, about 5 minutes. Stir in ketchup, chili sauce, cider vinegar, apple juice, hot sauce, honey, water, Creole mustard, Worcestershire, thyme, salt and pepper.

- Stir together and heat over medium heat about 20 minutes. Rub some on the ribs. Serve remaining sauce in a gravy boat at the table.

## MOM'S BAKED BEANS WITH MOLASSES

*As long as you've got that oven cranking, you should add a side of my mom's baked beans. POW! Remember to soak those dried beans overnight in water to cover.*

*When my mom made these beans when I was a kid, they lasted our little family for days and days. Still my favorite.*

* 2 pounds dried beans (navy, cannellini, black, or pinto beans)
* I bay leaf
* 2 smoked ham hocks
* I medium yellow onion peeled and finely chopped
* Sea salt and freshly milled black pepper to taste
* ½ teaspoon hot sauce (or to taste)
* 2 tablespoons yellow mustard
* ½ cup EACH: molasses and tomato ketchup
* ¼ cup brown sugar

- Rinse beans and place in a large bowl with water to cover. Soak overnight, then drain the beans and place in a 4-quart pot with a lid. Cover with cold water and raise to a boil. Reduce heat to low and simmer until the beans are tender, up to 2 hours, checking to make sure water remains just covering them by a couple of inches.

- Add ham hocks to simmering water in a second pot. Cook about 45 minutes, then add onion, garlic, salt, pepper, and hot sauce. Simmer about 15 to 20 minutes more so that the juices cook down to about ½ cup.

- Preheat oven to 350°F. Lightly oil a large 6-quart oven-proof bowl (or bean pot).

- Drain the cooked beans and add them to the bowl. Combine the mustard, molasses, ketchup and brown sugar. Pour over beans along with ham hocks and liquid and mix well. Place bean pot in the oven and cook, covered with a lid or foil, 3-4 hours, adding water as needed to maintain a thick soupy mix.

- Taste and adjust seasonings with additional salt and/or pepper as needed.

- About halfway through the cooking, remove the lid and turn the heat down to 300°F. Cook, checking from time to time so that it doesn't boil dry. Add water as needed.

## BRAISED KALE WITH APPLES

**When the fall gives you apples, pick from two or three varieties to create the most complex flavor in this gorgeous autumn kale dish.**

**Makes 6 to 8 servings**

* ¼ cup extra-virgin olive oil
* 1 medium yellow onion, peeled and chopped
* 3 cloves garlic, minced
* 2 cups apples, cored and chopped (Granny Smiths, Empire, Braeburns, Gravensteins) Leave the skin on the apples for texture and interest
* 2 bunches fresh kale, stemmed, thoroughly washed, and chopped

* ½ cup chicken or vegetable stock
* Sea salt and freshly milled black pepper to taste
* 2 tablespoons malt vinegar

- In a large skillet or stockpot, add oil and then heat and brown onion, then garlic. Add apples and brown them. Add kale and begin to cook it down, turning often, and cook until soft. Add stock, salt and pepper, and vinegar. Add a lid and braise until the greens are totally limp and mixed with onion, garlic, and apples. About 20 minutes.

## DOWN-HOME 7-UP POUND CAKE

*When Mom began to make this cake, we thought it was some kind of magic trick. Now I know this secret method just gives me a great tender and flavorful cake. POW! And wow. Is this a keeper? Yes.*

* 1½ cups butter
* 3 cups granulated sugar
* 5 eggs, at room temperature
* 3 cups cake flour
* 1 tablespoon lemon flavoring
* ¾ cup carbonated lemon-lime beverage (7-Up preferred)

- Preheat oven to 350°F. Grease/flour a tube or Bundt pan.

- Cream butter and granulated sugar together until light and fluffy.

- Add eggs one at a time, beating after each one.

- Add flour alternately with 7-Up. Stir in lemon flavoring.

- Bake in prepared pan until cake tests done, approximately an hour. Cool on a rack, then turn out onto a cake plate.

# The Death of Zeus

My first word to Jesse was "NO!" And then, "No dogs. Who is going to take care of him, feed him, wash him, walk him?"

Well, I finally said yes and we got this wriggly little pup that our youngest son, Jesse, named Zeus: the god of all the gods, the god of sky and fire, the god of everything. Soon Zeus was the god that ran our house.

Zeus loved it when I cooked braised oxtails. I usually started late at night, after I came home from work. Zeus would lie in the kitchen door, raising his head and patting his tail as the sizzling went on. He would take deep breaths of that good food cooking. Zeus loved him some oxtails.

I would talk to him and tell him everything that had gone on that day. We were the only two up by then; me turning the oxtails, Zeus listening to every word I said. He looked up and I knew he understood. From time to time, I'd toss him a little scrap. You would have thought I'd given that dog a filet mignon. He was so grateful.

I am writing this down with tears pouring out of my eyes. Yes, I have heard some people say, "It's just a dog, get another one." But Zeus has been in our lives for 7 years. He is family. He was the smallest in the bunch, but grew up to be the biggest. I never thought he would die.

I didn't know how hard it would be to miss him so much. Things will never be the same because I'm so used to him greeting me when I come home. Before I could even put the keys in the door, he was barking.

I miss that barking now. After a while you get to understand your dog, and he understands you. Zeus had his good days and his bad days. In my mind, I would reminisce about the good times. For example, when we gave Zeus a bath, he hated to be wet and would run all over the house trying to dry himself off. That's a classic memory I will cherish for life.

POW! I think one of the reasons I hurt so bad is that when Jesse was in college for two years, I walked Zeus, fed him, and we became friends all over again.

When Zeus first started to limp, we took him to the doctor. The doctor said it was arthritis. We were relieved. Then Zeus started to get worse. Next visit, cancer was the word. We heard that some others in his family had it before him.

We all were devastated. He just got worse. Everyone told us we were letting him suffer, and we knew that wasn't right. But we hated to let him go. But finally, we took him back to the doctor to start his journey on the Rainbow Bridge.

We all sat in that room with him a long time after he was gone. It was so hard to leave that room.

I think now we did the right thing, He wasn't living a healthy life. He couldn't run, couldn't have a good time. Soon, he was bleeding from the nose every day. And we could see the pain in his eyes. He was crying and suffering, and we were the witnesses who were watching him deteriorate day by day. As we watched Zeus take his last breath on that fateful day, I had a sense of guilt. Why couldn't I save him?

I cried so hard, and everything flashed in my mind. Zeus was human to us. He was family. We will never forget him. No other dog will take his place.

Yes, we had our ups and downs, but Zeus was always right there with us. How can we go on without him? How can we face all that life throws at us without our Zeus?

REST IN PEACE, ZEUS. Have fun running up and down that Rainbow Bridge in Heaven. No more pain. No more suffering. And a big old dinner every night. Please cook this feast in memory of our dog ZEUS! And good dogs everywhere. POW!

# Oxtails Low and Slow

* Chef Jesse's Braised Oxtails with Callaloo
* Classic Risotto
* Old Fashioned Scratch Lemon Meringue Pie

## BRAISED OXTAILS WITH CALLALOO

**Makes 6 to 8 servings**

*This is one of those all day and dinner on the grounds recipes. Cook it low and slow. Not too hard to do, just takes patience.*

## CHEF JESSE'S BRAISED OXTAILS

**Makes 4 to 6 servings**

* 5 pounds of beef oxtails (fat removed, washed)
* *Chef Jesse's Spice Blend*
    * 1 teaspoon kosher salt
    * ½ teaspoon EACH: black pepper and white pepper
    * 1 teaspoon EACH: granulated garlic, onion, and paprika
* ½ cup + 2 cups grape-seed oil, divided
* 4 medium carrots, peeled and cut medium dice
* 1 medium onion, cut into medium dice
* 4 celery stalks, cut into medium dice
* ½ cup tomato paste
* 2 cups dry red wine (pinot is great)
* 4 cups beef broth (homemade or store-bought)
* 6 to 8 sprigs fresh thyme

Feast #29

**Prepare Oxtails**

– In a bowl, add oxtails to Chef Jesse's blend with ½ cup oil. Mix well, cover, and marinate overnight.

**Next day:**

– Preheat the oven to 375°F.

– In a large oven-proof saucepan, heat 2 tablespoons oil over medium-high heat until just smoking. Sear the oxtails on all sides, then remove them, add carrots and onions to the pan, and sauté for 2 minutes. Add celery, stirring quickly.

– Add tomato paste and cook for 2 minutes more. Add wine to deglaze pan, plus stock, bay leaf, and thyme. Now raise the heat to high and bring to a boil, stirring and scraping the bottom. Add oxtails back to the saucepan, cover and place in the oven, and bake until tender, about 2 to 2½ hours at 300°F.

– Remove the oxtails to a platter. Skim off fat from the pan, bring to a boil, reduce by one-third, then add oxtails. Give it one big stir and then serve over rice. POW!

# CALLALOO

*This Trinidadian green is full-flavored and full of minerals. POW!*

**Makes 6 to 8 servings**

* 2 pounds callaloo (substitute Swiss chard or mustard greens)
* 1 tablespoon cooking oil
* 1 tablespoon butter
* 1 onion, chopped
* 3 whole scallions, chopped
* 1 sprig fresh thyme, or ½ teaspoon dried
* ½ teaspoon salt
* ½ teaspoon freshly ground black pepper
* ⅓ cup water

– Remove the small branches with leaves from the main stem and submerge the callaloo in a bowl of cold water. Let soak for a minute and remove, discarding the water. Repeat 2 more times. Finely chop the leaves and branches and set aside.

– Heat the oil and butter in a medium-size skillet over medium heat until the butter is melted. Add the onion and scallions, stirring until the onion begins to soften, about 2 minutes. Add the callaloo, thyme, salt, and black pepper. Mix all the ingredients together, add the water, and cover. Cook over medium heat until the stems are tender, about 8 minutes.

# CLASSIC RISOTTO

**Makes 6 to 8 servings**

* 5½ cups chicken stock, preferably homemade
* 2 tablespoons extra-virgin olive oil
* 1 small onion, finely chopped
* Sea salt and freshly ground black pepper
* 1½ cups Arborio rice (10 ounces)
* Pinch of saffron threads
* ½ cup dry white wine
* ½ cup freshly grated Parmigiano-Reggiano cheese

* 1 tablespoon unsalted butter
* 2 tablespoons chopped flat-leaf parsley

– In a medium saucepan, bring the chicken stock to a simmer; keep warm. In a large saucepan, heat the olive oil. Add the onion, season with salt and pepper, and cook over moderate heat, stirring until softened, about 5 minutes. Add the rice and cook for 1 minute, stirring to thoroughly coat. Crumble the saffron into the wine and add it to the rice. Cook, stirring until the wine is absorbed. Add 1 cup of the warm stock and cook over moderate heat, stirring constantly until nearly absorbed. Continue adding the stock ½ cup at a time, stirring constantly until it is nearly absorbed between additions. The risotto is done when the rice is al dente and suspended in a thick, creamy sauce, about 20 minutes total. Season the risotto with salt and pepper to taste. Stir in the cheese, butter, and parsley and serve immediately.

# OLD FASHIONED SCRATCH LEMON MERINGUE PIE

**Makes 8 servings**

*So much more flavorful than a pie that starts in a box. This is the real deal, full of great lemon flavor and a gorgeous pastry you made yourself. POW!*

## For the pastry. Makes 2 10-inch pie shells:
* 1 cup very cold butter cut into small cubes
* 2½ cups all-purpose or pastry flour
* ½ tsp sea salt

* ¼ cup to ⅓ ice water (only enough to make a dough form)

## For the filling:
* ⅓ cup corn starch
* ⅓ cup cake flour
* pinch sea salt
* 1½ cups granulated sugar
* 5 egg yolks, slightly beaten
* zest of 2 lemons, very finely chopped
* juice of 2 lemons
* 2 cups water
* 3 tablespoons unsalted butter

## For the meringue:
* 5 large egg whites
* 1¼ cups granulated sugar
* ¼ teaspoon cream of tartar
* pinch sea salt
* 1 teaspoon vanilla extract

## To make the pastry:
– Using a food processor or a pastry blender cut cold butter into flour and salt until mixture resembles a coarse meal. Small pieces of butter should still be visible.

– Pour cold water over the mixture and work in by tossing with a fork until dough begins to form. Use your hands as little as possible and work the dough as little as possible.

– Divide dough into 2 balls. Flatten into 2 rounds, wrap in plastic wrap, and place in the refrigerator to rest for a minimum of 20 minutes. You can freeze the second round for another time, but make sure you take it out of the fridge for 10 minutes to warm slightly before rolling out.

- Roll the dough into a 12-inch round and place in the bottom of a 10-inch pie plate.

- Trim and flute the edges as desired. Poke a few holes in the bottom of the pastry shell, and rest in the refrigerator for an additional 20 minutes before baking at 400 degrees F for 12 to 15 minutes or until golden brown.

- Cool completely before adding the filling.

## To make the filling:

- In a medium saucepan, combine corn starch, cake flour, granulated sugar and salt. Pour in water and stir constantly over medium-low heat until mixture comes to a slow boil.

- Remove the pan from the heat and reduce the flame to low. Pour about a cup of this mixture onto the slightly beaten egg yolks while whisking constantly.

- Pour the egg mixture back into the rest of the other mixture in the pot, whisking constantly. Return to the stove and cook for an additional 3 minutes, stirring constantly.

- Remove from heat and stir in lemon juice and lemon zest. Finally whisk in butter one tablespoon at a time.

- Pour the filling into the baked and cooled shell. Let stand for a few minutes while preparing the meringue.

## To prepare the meringue:

- Whip egg whites, vanilla, salt, and cream of tartar to soft peaks. Very gradually add the granulated sugar while continuing to beat the egg whites.

- Dollop in heaping tablespoonfuls onto pie. Gently spread over the filling, making sure that the meringue touches the crust all the way around the pie. This will help to prevent the meringue from shrinking.

- Bake in a 325°F oven for 20 to 25 minutes or until the meringue is well browned. Cool pie thoroughly in the refrigerator before serving.

- Dip a sharp knife in cold water to help with cutting the pie into slices, and clean the knife with paper towel between cuts.

# Easy Etoufee

* Shrimp Etouffee with Jasmine Rice
* Corn Flat Break with Scallions and Shredded Cheddar Crust
* Autumn Fruit Salad
* White Blondies

## SHRIMP ETOUFFEE WITH JASMINE RICE

**Makes 8 servings**

* Chef Jesse's Seasoning Mix
    * 2 teaspoons EACH: sea salt and cayenne pepper
    * 1 teaspoon EACH: white pepper, black pepper, and dried sweet basil
    * ½ teaspoon dried thyme

– Mix and store in a jar in a cool, dark place.

* 7 tablespoons grape-seed oil
* ½ cup EACH: chopped onions, celery, and green bell pepper
* 2 cloves garlic, minced
* ½ cup all-purpose flour
* 3 cups seafood or vegetable stock
* 1 cup unsalted butter (2 sticks)
* 2 pounds medium shrimp, peeled
* 1 cup green onions, finely chopped

– Stir seasonings mix into a jar. Preheat a large Dutch oven over medium heat. Add oil, onions, celery, and pepper. Cook and stir until tender, about 5 minutes. Add garlic and cook another minute, stirring.

– Stir flour into the mixture and cook and stir to make a golden roux, over medium heat. Continue cooking until it's a gorgeous nutty brown color.

- Add shrimp and seasonings mixture to the roux. Cook until the shrimp turn pink. About 5 minutes. Add stock, butter, and green onion. Simmer over low heat about 15 minutes.

- Serve over grits or rice.

## JASMINE RICE

- Cook rice with barely salted water, 1 cup rice to 4 cups water. Cover until rice is cooked through, about 20 minutes. Toss with a fork.

## CORN FLAT BREAD WITH SCALLIONS AND SHREDDED CHEDDAR CRUST

**Makes 1 10-inch black skillet full to cut into thin wedges**

* 1⅓ cups all-purpose flour
* 1 cup coarse stone-ground yellow cornmeal
* 2 teaspoons baking powder
* 1 teaspoon sea salt
* Pinch fresh-ground black pepper
* 1¼ cups whole milk
* 2 tablespoons honey
* 2 large eggs, beaten
* ⅓ cup + 1 tablespoon grape-seed oil, divided
* 1 green onion, white and tender green parts only, thinly sliced
* ½ cup shredded sharp cheddar

- Preheat the oven to 400°F.

- Place a 10-inch cast-iron skillet in the oven to heat.

- In a medium bowl, whisk the flour, cornmeal, baking powder, salt and pepper. In a small bowl, whisk the milk, honey, eggs and 1/3 cup of the oil. Add the wet ingredients to the cornmeal mixture and whisk just until combined. Stir in the scallions.

- Add the remaining 1 tablespoon of oil to the hot skillet and swirl to coat.

- Pour the batter into the skillet and bake for about 30 minutes, until the top is golden and a toothpick inserted in the center comes out clean. Top with shredded cheddar. Serve from the black skillet.

## AUTUMN FRUIT SALAD

**Makes about 6 to 8 servings**

* 1½ pounds mixed citrus fruit (such as oranges, grapefruit, pomelo, tangerines, and mandarins), peeled and cut into segments, juices reserved separately
* ¼ cup mayonnaise
* 1 tablespoon juice + zest from 1 lemon
* 1 tablespoon honey
* 2 tablespoons extra-virgin olive oil
* Sea salt and freshly ground black pepper
* 1 Belgian endive
* 1 small head radicchio (about 5 ounces)
* 1 head escarole, washed and roughly chopped (about 6 cups)
* 1 large bulb fennel (about 6 ounces), shaved on a mandoline or fine cut with a very sharp knife

- Combine ¼ cup citrus juice with

mayonnaise and lemon juice in a medium bowl (save remaining citrus juice for another use). Whisk in honey. Whisking constantly, slowly add olive oil in a thin, steady stream. Season to taste with salt and pepper.

- Toss endive, radicchio, escarole, fennel, and citrus segments in a large bowl. Drizzle in half of dressing. Season to taste with salt and pepper, toss to combine, then drizzle in more dressing to taste. Serve immediately.

sprinkle with white chocolate chips.

- Bake in the preheated oven until a toothpick inserted into the center of the pan comes out clean, 30 to 35 minutes. Allow to cool in pan for about 10 minutes before cutting into bars.

⟫⟩⟨⟪

## WHITE BLONDIES

**Makes 8 generous servings**

* 1 cup unsalted butter
* 4 (1 ounce) squares white chocolate, chopped
* 3 large eggs
* 2 cups granulated sugar
* 1 teaspoon vanilla extract
* 2 cups all-purpose flour
* 1 teaspoon sea salt
* 1 cup white chocolate chips

- Preheat oven to 350°F.

- Grease a 9 x 13 baking pan. Mix the butter and white chocolate together over low heat in a saucepan. Remove from heat, and let cool slightly. Meanwhile beat eggs with granulated sugar and vanilla extract in a mixing bowl. Mix in the butter mixture, and stir in the flour and salt until thoroughly combined. Scoop the batter into the prepared baking pan;

# Chapter 10: October

*Autumn sets in with all the football games and celebrations, including the biggest and best for this time of year: Halloween, now the second most celebrated holiday of the year. Time for a great feast. POW!*

# Friday Night Football Dinner

* Apple Cider Brined Pork Tenderloin with Honey BBQ Sauce
* Roasted Sweet Potato Mash with Candied Pecans
* Smothered Peppered Cabbage
* Applejack Bundt Cake with a Caramel Sauce

## APPLE CIDER BRINED PORK TENDERLOIN WITH HONEY BBQ SAUCE

*You want to talk about delicious? Pork tenders with my own honey BBQ sauce. POW!*

**Makes 6 to 8 servings**

* 4 to 6 pork tenderloins

**Brine:**
* I cup apple cider
* ½ cup EACH: apple cider vinegar and brown sugar
* 2 teaspoons kosher salt
* I garlic clove, crushed
* I teaspoon EACH: mustard seeds and whole black peppercorns
* 5 sprigs fresh thyme
* I teaspoon fresh ginger, chopped

— Cook brine ingredients in a large pot until dissolved. Remove from the heat and add a couple of ice cubes to speed up the cooling. Add pork tenders, cover, and refrigerate overnight.

— Next day: Preheat the oven to 350°F. Season pork tenders to taste with salt and pepper. Film the bottom of a sauté pan with grape-seed oil, then brown meat on all sides, about 2 minutes. Transfer to the oven and cook about 10 minutes more.

Serve with:

## CHEF JESSE'S HONEY BBQ SAUCE

* I tablespoon grape-seed oil
* I medium red onion, peeled and minced
* I clove garlic, minced
* I cup EACH: ketchup and chili sauce
* ½ cup EACH: apple juice and cider vinegar
* ⅓ cup (or to taste) hot sauce
* I cup EACH: honey and water
* ¼ cup Creole mustard
* I tablespoon Worcestershire sauce
* ⅓ teaspoon fresh thyme, minced
* I teaspoon coarse ground black pepper

— Sea salt and freshly milled black pepper to taste

— In a heavy saucepan, add oil over medium heat, then add onion and garlic and cook until clear and tender. About five minutes. Stir in ketchup, chili sauce, cider vinegar, hot sauce, honey, water, Creole mustard, Worcestershire sauce, thyme, salt and pepper. Bring to a boil, reduce heat, and simmer about 20 minutes. Adjust seasonings. POW! Transfer to a clear glass jar with a lid, and store in the refrigerator.

— This BBQ sauce is great with all meats.

## ROASTED SWEET POTATO MASH WITH CANDIED PECANS

— Choose one sweet potato for each diner. Roast them in a 350°F oven until tender. About 1 hour.

— Let them cool, then peel and smash them in a large bowl using a stick blender. Season to taste with salt, pepper, and butter. Stir in candied pecans:

* I cup pecan halves
* I cup granulated sugar

— Mix pecans and granulated sugar together in an oven-proof dish. Cook in the oven until golden brown and glistening. POW!

## SMOTHERED PEPPERED CABBAGE

*My cousin Velma is the Queen of Peppered Cabbage, but I tried to squeeze mine right up there against hers. POW!*

* ¼ cup bacon, chopped
* I teaspoon grape-seed oil
* 2 heads savoy cabbage, cut into thin slices
* I medium EACH: yellow onion, red and green bell peppers, seeded and chopped
* I tablespoon cider vinegar
* I teaspoon EACH: granulated sugar and Chef Jesse's spice blend (SEE PAGE 26 FOR RECIPE)
* I cup turkey or chicken stock

— In a large stewpot, cook the bacon with oil over medium heat until limp, then add cabbage, onion, and pepper. Cook and stir about 15 minutes, then add vinegar, stock, and essence to taste. Simmer about 5 more minutes, then correct seasonings and serve hot.

## APPLEJACK BUNDT CAKE WITH A CARAMEL SAUCE

**Makes 8 servings**

* 4 cups thinly peeled, cored, and sliced Granny Smith apples
* ½ cup golden raisins
* ¼ cup applejack brandy
* 2 cups all-purpose flour
* ¾ teaspoon sea salt
* 1 tablespoon cinnamon
* 1 teaspoon mace
* 1½ teaspoons baking soda
* 3 large eggs
* 1 cup vegetable oil
* 2 cups granulated sugar
* 2 teaspoons vanilla extract
* ¾ cup pecan pieces

– Preheat the oven to 350°F. Grease a Bundt pan generously with butter and dust with flour.

– Soak apples and raisins in applejack for about 10 minutes. Meanwhile, sift flour, salt, cinnamon, mace together and set aside.

– Use electric mixer with the paddle and combine eggs and oil, then mix, and now blend in granulated sugar and vanilla. Beat until creamy. Gradually add flour and beat until completely mixed. Fold in apples and raisins. Transfer to the Bundt pan, pop into hot oven, and bake until done and a toothpick comes out clean, about 45-55 minutes.

## CARAMEL SAUCE

* 1 packed cup brown sugar
* ½ cup half-and-half
* 4 tablespoons butter
* Pinch sea salt
* 1 tablespoon vanilla extract

– Mix the brown sugar, half-and-half, butter, and salt in a saucepan over medium-low heat. Cook while whisking gently for 5 to 7 minutes, until it gets thicker. Add the vanilla and cook another minute to thicken further. Turn off the heat, cool slightly, and pour the sauce into a jar. Refrigerate until cold.

– Drizzle over pieces of cake. POW!

# Southern Fried Quail

* Southern Fried Quail
* Savannah Red Rice
* Low and Slow Southern Braised Collards
* Fall Clafoutis with Pears and Apples

## SOUTHERN FRIED QUAIL

*Quail hunting season varies from state to state but usually begins mid-October and ends in February. We like to have one big blow-out dinner sometime during this late fall period. That quail is really special. POW! Marinate the birds overnight for best results.*

**Makes 6-8 servings**

* 6-12 whole picked and cleaned quail
* 1 cup buttermilk
* Pinch hot sauce

— Marinate overnight in a covered container in the refrigerator.

— Next day, make up this seasoned flour

  * 1 cup all-purpose flour
  * 1 teaspoon Lawry's seasoning
  * ½ teaspoon black pepper
  * ½ teaspoon cayenne pepper

— Lift the quail out of the buttermilk. Dredge in seasoned flour. Shake to remove excess flour.

— Heat 1-inch grape-seed oil in a heavy black cast iron skillet to 375°F. Fry quail until brown on both sides. Drain on a rack. Drain off all but 1 cup fat from the pan.

*To make gravy, simply add leftover flour mixture to the fat and stir to cook the flour, then add 2 cups chicken stock and cook and stir to make gravy, adjusting seasonings with salt and pepper. Serve in a gravy boat.

## SAVANNAH RED RICE

* 1 cup EACH: onion, red and green bell pepper chopped
* 2 tablespoons butter
* 1 cup smoked sausage, diced
* 1 (14.5 ounce) can crushed tomatoes, with juice
* 1 tablespoon hot sauce
* 1 cup tomato sauce
* 1 cup chicken broth
* Sea salt, to taste
* Freshly milled black pepper to taste
* 1 cup uncooked long grain white rice

– Preheat oven to 350°F. In a saucepan over medium heat, sauté onion and bell pepper in butter. Add sausage; heat until mixture is slightly browned. Add tomatoes, hot sauce, tomato sauce and chicken broth. Season with pepper and salt as needed. Stir in rice. Pour mixture into a greased casserole and bake for 45 minutes.

## LOW AND SLOW SOUTHERN BRAISED COLLARDS

**Makes 6-8 servings**

* 1 applewood smoked bacon slice, chopped
* ½ teaspoon crushed red pepper
* ¼ teaspoon salt
* 2 (16-ounce) package prewashed torn collard greens (or 3 bunches)
* 1 cup fat-free, less-sodium chicken broth
* ½ cup water
* ¼ cup dry white wine
* 1½ tablespoons cider vinegar

– Cook bacon in a Dutch oven over medium heat until crisp. Add pepper, salt, and greens; cook 2 minutes or until greens begin to wilt, stirring constantly. Stir in broth, water, wine and vinegar. Cover, reduce heat, and simmer 1 hour or until greens are tender.

## FALL CLAFOUTIS WITH PEARS AND APPLES

*The go-to dessert in France is basically a custard with fruits of the season. Swap out fruits for what you find in the farmer's market. Cherries are the classic. POW!*

**Makes 6 to 8 servings**

* 1 cup whole milk
* 3 large eggs
* ½ cup granulated sugar
* 1 teaspoon vanilla extract
* 2 tablespoons butter, melted
* ½ cup all-purpose flour
* 1 large pear and/or apple, seeded and cut

into pieces

* 2 tablespoons Pear Au de Vie or Calvados

– Preheat the oven to 325°F. In a large bowl, whisk together the milk, eggs, granulated sugar, vanilla, and butter until the sugar is dissolved. Add the flour and whisk until smooth. Pour the batter into a cast-iron skillet or pie pan.

– Now add fruits. Cherries are the traditional French choice. But use your favorite fruit or flavoring. Bake until the clafoutis is beautifully puffed and golden, 35–40 minutes. Serve immediately.

# Halloween Jambalaya For All

* Halloween Chicken and Sausage Jambalaya
* Jalapeño Cheddar Mini Corn Muffins
* Autumn Roasted Beet Salad with Apples
* Spiced Pumpkin Cake with Cream Cheese Pumpkin Frosting

## HALLOWEEN CHICKEN AND SAUSAGE JAMBALAYA

*Make this in the Crockpot or in a big stew pot on the back of the stove; then you'll have plenty of time to greet the trick-or-treaters as they come to the door.*

* 12 ounces applewood-smoked bacon, diced
* 1 pound EACH: smoked fully cooked sausage (such as linguiça), halved lengthwise, cut crosswise into ½-inch-thick semicircles, and andouille
* ½ pound tasso or smoked ham (such as Black Forest), cut into ½-inch cubes
* 4 large yellow onions, peeled and chopped
* 2 large celery stalks, chopped
* 1 EACH: red and green bell pepper, coarsely chopped
* 6 large skinless boneless chicken thighs, cut into 1-inch pieces
* 2 tablespoons paprika
* 1 tablespoon EACH: chopped fresh thyme and chili powder
* ¼ teaspoon (or to taste) cayenne pepper
* 3 10-ounce cans diced tomatoes and green chiles
* 2½ cups beef broth + 1 cup water
* 2 cups long-grain white rice
* 2 cups green onions, chopped
* Chopped fresh Italian parsley all at

— Position rack in bottom third of oven and preheat to 350°F.

- Cook bacon in very large pot over medium-high heat until brown but not yet crisp, stirring often, for 8 to 10 minutes. Add smoked sausage, andouille, and tasso. Sauté until meats start to brown in spots, about 10 minutes. Add onions, celery, and bell peppers. Cook until vegetables begin to soften, stirring occasionally, 10 to 12 minutes. Mix in chicken. Cook until outside of chicken turns white, stirring often, 5 to 6 minutes. Mix in paprika, thyme, chili powder, and ¼ teaspoon cayenne. Cook 1 minute. Add diced tomatoes with chiles, broth, and water. Stir to blend well. Add more cayenne, if desired. Mix in rice.

- Bring jambalaya to boil. Cover pot. Place in oven and bake until rice is tender and liquids are absorbed, about 45 minutes. Uncover the pot. Mix chopped green onions into jambalaya; sprinkle with chopped parsley and serve.

## JALAPEÑO CHEDDAR MINI CORN MUFFINS

* 6 tablespoons melted butter
* 2 cups stone ground cornmeal
* 1 cup all-purpose flour
* 1 tablespoon baking powder
* ½ teaspoon baking soda
* 1 teaspoon salt
* 3 large eggs
* 2 cups buttermilk
* 4 slices bacon, cooked and crumbled
* 2-3 tablespoons finely chopped jalapeño, seeds discarded
* ½ cup shredded cheddar

- Preheat the oven to 350°F.

- Mix all of the ingredients together with a whisk. Generously spray a mini muffin tin with nonstick spray. Fill the muffin tins almost to the top. Bake for about 15-20 minutes or until the tops spring back when touched. Turn out on a rack to cool.

## AUTUMN ROASTED BEET SALAD WITH APPLES AND PEARS

*Best time of year to enjoy root vegetables with freshly harvested fruits.*

* ¾ pound golden beets, trimmed and cut into ¾-inch wedges
* ½ pound EACH: red apples and pears, cored and cut into ¾-inch wedges
* 2 tablespoons extra-virgin olive oil
* Sea salt to taste
* 4 cups mixed sturdy winter greens (such as baby kale, tatsoi, endive, and radicchio), torn or cut into bite-size pieces
* ⅓ cup crumbled fresh goat cheese
* ¼ cup toasted chopped pecans
* 3 tablespoons dried cherries

### For the vinaigrette

* ¼ cup grape-seed oil
* ⅓ cup thinly sliced shallots
* Sea salt
* ½ teaspoon chopped fresh ginger
* 2 tablespoons balsamic vinegar
* 1 tablespoon pure maple syrup
* Juice and grated zest of one lime
* 1 teaspoon finely chopped fresh flat-leaf parsley

* I teaspoon Dijon mustard
* Freshly ground black pepper

## Roast the beets and fruit

- Position racks in the upper and lower thirds of the oven and heat the oven to 450°F.

- In a large bowl, toss the beets with 1 tablespoon of the oil and ½ teaspoon salt. Transfer to a large-rimmed heavy-duty baking sheet. Spread into a single layer.

- In another large bowl, combine the apples and pears with the remaining 1 tablespoon of oil and another ½ teaspoon salt. Transfer to a large-rimmed heavy-duty baking sheet. Spread into a single layer.

- Roast, flipping with a spatula halfway through and rotating the baking sheets until browned and tender, 20 to 25 minutes. Let cool for a few minutes on the sheets. Transfer to a large bowl.

## Make the vinaigrette

- Heat the oil in an 8-inch skillet over medium heat. Add the shallots and a pinch of salt and cook, stirring occasionally until softened and lightly browned, 2 to 4 minutes. Add the ginger and cook, stirring until fragrant and softened, about 15 seconds. Remove from the heat. Let the oil cool for 3 to 5 minutes.

- Meanwhile, in a small heatproof bowl, whisk the vinegar, maple syrup, lime juice, zest, parsley, mustard, ¼ teaspoon salt, and several grinds of fresh pepper. Whisk the warm oil into the vinegar mixture until emulsified.

- Season to taste, adding more lime juice, salt, or pepper as needed.

## Assemble the salad

- Lightly season the greens with salt and then drizzle with 2 tablespoons of the warm vinaigrette. Toss, taste, and add a little more dressing, if necessary. Arrange the greens on a platter.

- Season the roasted beets and fruit with a pinch more salt, and dress them lightly with a bit of the remaining vinaigrette. Scatter over the greens, then top with the goat cheese, pecans, and cherries. Serve right away, passing the remaining dressing at the table.

# SPICED PUMPKIN CAKE WITH CREAM CHEESE PUMPKIN FROSTING

**Makes 12 servings**

*The cake can be made up to 2 days in advance. Refrigerate until cold, and then carefully cover with plastic wrap. The cake can also be wrapped tightly and frozen for up to 1 month. Let thaw in the refrigerator, about 12 hours.*

* Butter for coating cake pans, at room temperature
* 2 cups all-purpose flour, plus extra for dusting the pan
* 2 cups granulated sugar
* 2 teaspoons EACH: baking soda and cinnamon
* I teaspoon sea salt
* ½ teaspoon freshly grated nutmeg

* ¼ teaspoon ground cloves
* 3 large eggs, beaten
* I cup vegetable oil
* 2 teaspoons pure vanilla extract
* I¼ cups canned unsweetened pumpkin purée
* I cup lightly packed sweetened flaked coconut
* ¾ cup canned crushed pineapple (do not drain)
* ⅓ cup dried currants

## CREAM CHEESE PUMPKIN FROSTING

* 2 packages (8 ounces each) cream cheese, at room temperature
* I cup (2 sticks) unsalted butter, at room temperature
* 2 tablespoons canned unsweetened pumpkin purée
* I½ cups confectioners' sugar, sifted
* I teaspoon pure vanilla extract

– Position a rack in the center of the oven and preheat to 350°F. Butter two 9-inch diameter cake pans with 1½-inch sides. Line the bottom of each pan with a circle of parchment paper. Butter the parchment paper. Sprinkle the pans with flour, tap the pans to evenly distribute the flour, and then shake off the excess flour. Set aside.

– To make the cake, in a large bowl, sift together 2 cups flour, granulated sugar, baking soda, cinnamon, salt, nutmeg, and cloves. In a medium bowl, combine the eggs, oil, and vanilla. In another medium bowl, combine the pumpkin purée, coconut, crushed pineapple, and currants.

– Add the egg mixture to the flour mixture and stir with a wooden spoon until just combined. Add the pumpkin mixture and stir just until combined. Divide the batter between the prepared pans, spreading it evenly. Bake for 35 to 40 minutes until a toothpick inserted into the center of a cake comes out clean. Transfer to wire racks and let cool in the pans for 15 minutes. Run a table knife around the edge of the pans to loosen the cakes. Invert the cakes onto the racks and peel off the parchment paper. Let cool completely before frosting the cakes.

– To make the frosting, in the bowl of an electric mixer fitted with the paddle attachment, beat the cream cheese on medium speed for about 3 minutes until smooth. Add the butter and beat for about 2 minutes until combined. Add the pumpkin purée and beat until incorporated, about 1 minute. Add the confectioners' sugar and vanilla and beat for about 3 minutes until fluffy.

– Place 1 cake layer on a cake plate or platter. Using an offset spatula, spread half of the frosting over the top of the first cake layer. Spread the frosting right to the edge of the top without frosting the sides of the cake. Carefully place the second cake on top, lining up the edges. Spread the remaining frosting over the top of the cake without frosting the sides. Swirl the frosting to decorate the top. Refrigerate the cake to set the frosting. Remove from the refrigerator 30 to 40 minutes before serving.

# November: Chapter 11

## When We Say Thanks for Every Little Thing

* Beef Bourguignon with Gratin Dauphinoise
* Glazed Baby Carrots and Brussels Sprouts
* Red Velvet Cake with Cream Cheese Frosting

## BEEF BOURGUIGNON

**Makes 8 generous servings**

* 6 slices thick bacon, coarsely chopped
* 1 tablespoon extra-virgin olive oil
* 3 pounds lean beef chuck roast, cut into 2-inch pieces
* 1 EACH: carrot and yellow onion, cut into thick slices
* Sea salt and freshly milled black pepper to taste
* 2 tablespoons all-purpose flour
* 3 cups full-bodied red wine, such as a pinot noir
* 3 cups brown beef stock
* 1 tablespoon tomato paste
* 2 cloves garlic, mashed
* 1 crumbled bay leaf
* 24 small white onions
* 1 pound quartered fresh brown mushrooms
* ½ cup all-purpose flour
* Parsley sprigs

- Preheat oven to 450°F.

- In a large heavy Dutch oven, sauté the bacon in oil over moderate heat for

2 to 3 minutes to brown lightly. Remove to a large side dish. Reheat the pot until fat is almost smoking before you sauté the beef.

– Dry the beef on paper towels. Sauté it, a few pieces at a time, in the hot oil and bacon fat until nicely browned on all sides. Add it to the bacon.

– In the same fat, brown the sliced vegetables. Pour out the sautéing fat.

– Return the beef and bacon to the Dutch oven and toss with the salt and pepper. Then sprinkle on the flour and toss again to coat the beef lightly with the flour. Set the pot uncovered in the middle position of a preheated oven for 4 minutes. Toss the meat and return to oven for 4 minutes more. (This browns the flour and covers the meat with a light crust.) Remove the Dutch oven, and turn the oven down to 325°F.

– Stir in the wine and stock so the meat is barely covered. Add the tomato paste, garlic, herbs, and bacon. Bring to simmer on top of the stove. Then cover the pot and set it in the lower third of the preheated oven. Bake slowly for 2½ to 3 hours, or until the meat is done when pierced with a fork easily.

– While the beef is cooking, prepare the onions and mushrooms. Toss each in flour, then braise in butter in a skillet. Set them aside until needed.

– When the meat is tender, distribute the cooked onions and mushrooms over the meat.

– Simmer sauce for a minute or two, skimming off additional fat as it rises. You should have about 2½ cups of sauce thick enough to coat a spoon lightly. If too thin, boil it down rapidly. If too thick, mix in a few tablespoons of stock, taste, and adjust seasoning. Pour the sauce over the meat and vegetables. Recipe may be completed in advance to this point.

– **For immediate serving:** Cover the Dutch oven and simmer for 2 to 3 minutes, basting the meat and vegetables with the sauce several times. Arrange the stew on a platter surrounded with potatoes and decorated with parsley. Transfer sauce to a gravy boat and serve on the side.

## GRATIN DAUPHINOISE

*Classic French cooking: this can be made ahead and reheated at serving time to accompany the beef. POW!*

* 3 pounds Yukon gold potatoes (about 6 large)
* 1 medium leek
* ¾ teaspoon freshly ground white pepper
* ¼ teaspoon freshly grated nutmeg
* 2 tablespoons unsalted butter
* 1 large garlic clove, minced
* 2 cups whole milk
* ½ cup heavy creamy all at

– Preheat oven to 350°F with a rack in upper third of oven.

– Peel potatoes and thinly cut into ⅛-inch-thick slices, using a mandoline.

- Discard dark green part of leek and halve white and light green part lengthwise. Rinse layers under running water to remove any dirt and grit and pat dry. Thinly slice crosswise.

- Stir together white pepper and nutmeg with 1-¾ teaspoons salt in a small bowl. Melt butter in a small heavy saucepan over medium-low heat and cook leek and garlic, stirring frequently until softened, 3 to 5 minutes.

- Spread leek and butter mixture evenly in bottom of baking dish. Arrange one-quarter of the potatoes in a slightly overlapping layer over leeks. Pour ½ cup milk over potatoes, and sprinkle lightly with ½ teaspoon salt mixture. Layer potatoes with milk and salt mixture three more times in same manner.

- Place dish on a shallow baking pan and cover with foil. Bake until potatoes are almost tender, about 1 hour.

- Remove foil and pour cream over potatoes. Continue to bake, uncovered, until cream has been absorbed by potatoes and the top is golden in spots, 30 to 40 minutes.

## GLAZED BABY CARROTS AND BRUSSELS SPROUTS

### Makes 6 to 8 servings

* 1 pound baby carrots
* 1 pound Brussels sprouts, trimmed and scored
* 1½ cups chicken broth
* 6 tablespoons butter
* ⅓ cup packed brown sugar
- Freshly milled black pepper and sea salt to taste

- Blanch carrots and Brussels sprouts in a large pot of boiling salted water until crisp-tender, about 4 minutes. Transfer to a bowl of ice water using slotted spoon.

- Bring stock, butter, and brown sugar to a boil in a heavy large skillet. Stir until sugar dissolves. Boil until reduced by half, about 7 minutes. Add carrots and Brussels sprouts. Cook until almost tender and sauce begins to coat, shaking pan occasionally, about 6 minutes. Add pepper and salt. Cook until heated through, stirring occasionally, about 4 minutes.

## RED VELVET CAKE WITH CREAM CHEESE FROSTING

### Makes 8 to 10 servings

* 2 ½ cups cake flour
* 1 ½ cup granulated sugar
* 1 teaspoon baking soda
* 1 teaspoon sea salt
* 1 teaspoon cocoa powder
* 1 ½ cups vegetable oil
* 1 cup buttermilk, at room temperature
* 2 large eggs, at room temperature
* 2 tablespoon red food coloring (1 ounce)
* 1 teaspoon, white distilled vinegar
* 1 teaspoon vanilla extract

- Preheat the oven to 350 degrees F. Lightly

oil two 9 in round cake pans.

- In a large bowl, sift together the flour, sugar, baking soda, salt and cocoa powder. In another large bowl, whisk together the oil, buttermilk, eggs, food coloring, vinegar and vanilla.

- Using a mixer, mix the dry ingredients into the wet ingredients, until smooth.

- Pour batter into 2 greased 9 inch cake pans. Bake about 30 minutes or until the top of your finger does not leave an indentation, or insert toothpick in the center of the cake and it comes out clean.

- Cool on rack at least 20 minutes before turning it out onto a cake plate. Then ready to frost.

## CREAM CHEESE FROSTING

* 1 (8 oz) cream cheese (softened)
* ½ cup butter (softened)
* 1 (1 pound) powdered sugar
* 1 ½ teaspoon vanilla extract
* 1 cup chopped pecans

- Beat cream cheese and butter until creamy; gradually add sugar and vanilla, beating well. Stir in pecans, Yield 3 cups

# A Sandwich a Day

* Croque Monseius and Madame Sandwiches
* Curly Endive Salad with a Grapefruit Vinaigrette
* French Apple Tart

## CROQUE MONSIEUR AND MADAME SANDWICHES

* 8 slices crusty bread
* Dijon mustard or mayonnaise
* 8 ounces thinly sliced ham
* 6 ounces thinly sliced cheese (such as Emmental, Comté, or Swiss)
* 4 tablespoons butter
* 4 eggs, beaten in a pie pan (optional for Madame)

- Heat a large skillet filmed with butter. Spread mustard and/or mayo onto bread slices, then lay on ham and cheese. Add second layer of bread and toast in the hot skillet.

- For a Madame sandwich: After making the sandwich, dip into beaten egg, then place in butter-filmed skillet and toast. Cut sandwich in half and serve hot.

## CURLY ENDIVE SALAD WITH A GRAPEFRUIT VINAIGRETTE

* 1 large head of curly endive, washed, dried, and torn into bite-size pieces
* ¾ cup grapefruit vinaigrette
* Kosher salt and freshly ground black pepper to taste

- Place the endive in a large salad bowl. Drizzle the vinaigrette over the greens and toss to coat.

- Season to taste with sea salt and pepper.

## Vinaigrette:

* Juice of one large grapefruit + water to make ½ cup
* ¾ cup extra-virgin olive oil
* Sea salt and freshly milled black pepper to taste

- Whisk in a small bowl, then toss with endive in a large salad bowl.


# FRENCH APPLE TART

**Serves 6**

## Dough:

* 2½ cups all-purpose flour
* 3 tablespoons granulated sugar
* ½ teaspoon sea salt
* ½ cup EACH: cold, unsalted butter and shortening
* 4 tablespoons ice water

## Apple filling:

* 4 Granny Smith apples, peeled and cored, seeds removed
* ½ cup granulated sugar
* 4 tablespoons (½ stick) cold unsalted butter

- Add the flour, granulated sugar, and salt to the bowl of a food processor. Pulse a few times to mix all ingredients, then add butter and shortening; pulse until small bits look like cornmeal. With the motor running, add ice water, and pulse just until the dough comes together into a ball (do not overmix).

- Pour the dough ball onto a floured board, knead a little, then wrap the dough ball in plastic and refrigerate for 1 hour.

- Preheat the oven to 375°F.

- Line a sheet pan with parchment paper. Use a rolling pin to roll the dough to the shape of your tart pan, about a 9-inch circle. Cut off excess dough. Transfer the dough circle to the sheet pan and refrigerate while you cut the apples.

- Slice the apples about ¼ inch thick. Remove the tart from refrigerator. Begin laying in the apple slices, overlapping apples around the pan until the dough is fully covered. Sprinkle with granulated sugar and dots of butter. Bake for 45 minutes or until glistening and golden. Cool on a rack about 15 minutes, then cut into wedges and serve warm with your favorite ice cream or jam. What a feast! POW!

# Jollof Party Time

* Jollof Party Rice
* Carolina-style Chicken Lollipops
* Roast Cauliflower with Almonds
* Lemon Pound Cake

## JOLLOF PARTY RICE

*Originally from Nigeria, this recipe travelled to the Caribbean and laid claim to Jamaica. Americans love it. Some folks chop the incendiary scotch bonnet into the mix; others just lay the little time bomb on top of the cooking rice, then discard it at serving time.*

**Makes 8 servings**

* 1 large red bell pepper, seeded and quartered
* 1 scotch bonnet pepper (depending on how hot you want it, you can mince it into the rice or just lay it on top and discard it before serving)
* 2 medium beefsteak tomatoes, quartered
* 1 tablespoon tomato paste (optional)
* 2 cloves garlic
* 1 piece fresh ginger (about the size of your thumb)
* 1 small yellow onion
* 4 tablespoons sunflower oil or palm oil
* 2 cups vegetable stock
* 2 cups dry basmati rice
* 2 teaspoons fresh thyme
* Sea salt to taste
* 4 cups water, divided
* Fresh chopped basil and cilantro for garnish (optional)

- In the food processor, blend the peppers, tomatoes, onion, ginger, and garlic with 1 cup of water to form a smooth mixture.

- Heat the oil in a large, heavy pot and add the mixture, along with seasoning. Add the remaining 3 cups of water and bring to a boil.

- Add the rice to the mixture, stirring well, and then lower the heat completely. Cook for about 30 minutes, making sure the rice doesn't stick to the bottom of the pot and stirring from time to time (you might have to add a tiny bit more water as you go along). You want all the water to be absorbed and the rice texture to be light and fluffy.

- Toss a little fresh basil and cilantro in at the end. Serve in a wide, large bowl.

## CAROLINA-STYLE CHICKEN LOLLIPOPS

**Makes 8-10 servings**

*Great for a party. Use wings or drumsticks. Either way, you get bright, fresh, delicious bites that just scream FEAST. POW!*

* 60 chicken wings (about 5 pounds) or 20 drumsticks
* I teaspoon EACH: kosher salt, smoked paprika, granulated garlic, granulated onion, and crushed red pepper
* I tablespoon brown sugar
* ½ cup apple cider vinegar

- With a paring knife, cut around the thin tip of each chicken wing to loosen the meat around the joint. While holding the base, push the meat down gently to expose the bone and form a "chicken lollipop." Remove any flesh left on the thin end with a clean towel.

- Combine dry ingredients with vinegar in a mixing bowl. Toss and cover. Store overnight in the refrigerator.

- Next day, preheat the oven to 350°F. Place chicken lollipops on a baking pan, standing up. Roast for 20 to 25 minutes. Serve immediately with your favorite barbecue sauce or Chef Jesse's honey BBQ sauce to give it a kick. POW!

## ROASTED CAULIFLOWER WITH ALMONDS

**Makes 6 servings**

*This recipe is so quick and easy, and very healthy.*

* 3 tablespoons grape-seed oil
* 2 tablespoons Chef Jesse's spice blend (see pp 26)
* I large head cauliflower, separated into florets
* I cup whole almonds (lightly toasted in a skillet)

- Preheat the oven to 450°F. Grease a 9 x 13 casserole dish with butter.

- In a medium bowl, add grape-seed oil and chef Jesse's essence. Mix with a whisk.

- Add the cauliflower and mix well to coat. Transfer cauliflower to the prepared baking dish. Bake for 25 minutes or until tender and golden. Add toasted almonds and serve. POW!

## LEMON POUND CAKE

**Makes 12-16 servings**

*Such a useful cake. This keeps well and tastes bright and clean. We love it.*

* I cup unsalted butter, softened
* 2 cups granulated sugar
* 5 large eggs
* 3 cups cake flour
* I teaspoon sea salt
* ½ teaspoon EACH: baking powder and baking soda
* ¾ cup whole milk
* Grated zest of 2 fresh lemons
* ⅓ cup fresh squeezed lemon juice

– Preheat the oven to 350°F.

– Cream together the butter and granulated sugar until light and fluffy, then add eggs, one at a time, mixing well each time.

– In a medium bowl, mix flour, salt, baking powder, and baking soda together. In a small bowl, add milk with lemon zest and juice. Then, with the mixer on low, add flour in three parts, alternately with milk mixture in two and ending with flour.

– Mix until smooth. Grease your favorite Bundt pan. Add batter and bake for 90 minutes. Let the cake cool on a rack for 15 minutes or so, then turn out onto a cake plate.

# Thanksgiving

* My Mother-in Law's Alabama Queen Roast Turkey
* Corn Bread Sage Dressing
* Down-Home Candied Sweet Potatoes
* Collard Greens with Smoked Turkey Wings (SEE PAGE 70 FOR RECIPE)
* Mashed Potatoes and Giblet Gravy
* Turkey Stock
* Jellied Cranberry Sauce
* Molasses Cake (SEE PAGE i FOR RECIPE)

## MY MOTHER-IN LAW'S ALABAMA QUEEN ROAST TURKEY

**Makes 8 to 10 servings**

*For a real family reunion, when all the cousins and kids and aunts and uncles come to your house, everybody brings something. You cook the turkey and make the sides that you can't live without.*

* 9- to 12-pound turkey, washed and giblets removed

**Brine for turkey: Day 1**
* 1 gallon of cold water
* 1 cup kosher salt
* ½ garlic clove
* 1 sprig of thyme

– In a large container (plastic only), add salt to water with garlic and thyme. Submerge turkey in container and marinate overnight, covered, in a cool place.

## Day 2

* ½ cup unsalted butter
* I tablespoon chopped rosemary needles
* I clove garlic, minced
* ⅓ cup kosher salt
* I teaspoon coarse black pepper
* 2 carrots, peeled and rough cut
* ½ cup EACH: celery and onions, rough cut

- Heat the oven to 350°F.

- Rinse the turkey well, then cream together softened butter, garlic, and rosemary. Rub under the skin, in the cavity, and all over the turkey. Place carrots, celery, and onions in the cavity. Set turkey in large pan. Roast 3 to 4 hours, or until an instant-read thermometer reads 145°F when placed in the thickest part of the thigh.

- Let the bird rest about a half hour, then transfer to a cutting board. Cut into serving pieces, including thin slices of breast. Cut the wings and legs and thighs apart and arrange on a serving platter. Garnish with parsley and/or cranberries.

*For instant help on turkey day, you can always call the turkey talk help line.*

### Butterball Turkey Talk Line
(800) BUTTERBALL (800-288-8373)

Available November 1 through December 28, weekdays 8 a.m. to 8 p.m. CST; Saturday and Sunday, 8 a.m. to 6 p.m. CST; Thanksgiving Day, 6 a.m. to 6 p.m. CST; Nov. 24 to Dec. 25, weekdays, 8 a.m. to 6 p.m. CST.

## CORN BREAD SAGE DRESSING

When I first met my mother-in-law (Annie Will Spann), I fell in love with her cooking. Everything she made was awesome, but her dressing stood out for me.

This is my rendition. RIP to Queen of Alabama cooking. Your life is remembered with your fabulous recipes. Thank you.

**Makes 6 servings**

* ¼ cup vegetable oil
* I pound sage link breakfast sausage
* I small onion, peeled and finely diced
* I rib celery, finely diced
* I EACH: red and green pepper, seeded and finely diced
* ¼ cup fresh thyme, chopped
* I teaspoon poultry seasoning
* Chef Jesse's corn bread (recipe see page 70) or make your favorite in a black cast-iron skillet
* I cup turkey stock (recipe see page 192)
* 3 large eggs, beaten well
* ⅛ teaspoon cayenne pepper (or more to taste)

- Sea salt and freshly milled black pepper to taste

- In a large skillet, over high heat, add oil and sauté sausage for 2 minutes or until beginning to brown. Remove from the pan with a slotted spoon and set aside. In the same pan with drippings, sauté onion, celery, and peppers for 3 to 4 minutes or until onion begins to look clear and peppers begin to brown. Next add thyme and poultry seasoning. Stir to mix.

- In a large bowl, combine cornbread and sautéed vegetable mix with sausage, cayenne, salt and pepper to taste. Then add beaten eggs, mix lightly, and pour in first cup of the turkey stock. Mix well. You may need more stock. The mixture should be moist. Pour into greased 9 x 13 casserole dish, and bake for 45 minutes.

## DOWN-HOME CANDIED SWEET POTATOES

**Makes 8 servings**

* 2 pounds sweet potatoes
* ½ cup (1 stick) unsalted butter
* ¼ cup granulated sugar
* Pinch of sea salt
* 1 cup maple syrup
* ½ teaspoon cinnamon
* ½ teaspoon allspice
* ½ teaspoon pure vanilla extract

- Preheat the oven to 350°F. Bake the sweet potatoes until tender, but still a little firm, about 30 to 40 minutes. Set aside to cool. When cool, peel and cut into quarters.

- In a large skillet, melt the butter over medium heat, add granulated sugar, salt, maple syrup, cinnamon, allspice, and vanilla. Mix well. Add sweet potatoes to the sugar mix and place in a 9 x 13 casserole dish; bake for 15 minutes or until golden brown. Serve hot.

## COLLARD GREENS WITH SMOKED TURKEY WINGS (SEE PAGE 70 FOR RECIPE)

## MASHED POTATOES AND GIBLET GRAVY

### Giblet Gravy
*I learned this from the Queen of Alabama. Can't make a better dressing.*

*Serve it with your favorite mashed potatoes (SEE PAGE 30 FOR RECIPE). Pow!*

**Makes about 3 cups**

* ¼ cup grape-seed oil
* 1 carrot, medium dice
* 1 medium onion, medium dice
* 2 celery stalks, medium dice
* 1 garlic clove, crushed
* 2 sprigs of thyme
* 2 quarts water
* 1 chicken neck
* 1 chicken heart
* 1 chicken gizzard
* ⅛ teaspoon black pepper
* 1 teaspoon sea salt
* ¼ cup butter
* ¼ cup vegetable oil
* ½ cup all-purpose flour

- In a large Dutch oven or stockpot, add oil and heat over medium heat. Sauté carrots, onions, celery, and garlic for about 3 minutes. Add thyme and water, then add the neck, heart, and gizzard. Bring to boil and reduce heat, simmering until it reduces to 3 cups. Remove the giblets to cool. Finely dice them and set them aside.

- Melt the butter and oil in a large skillet over medium-high heat. Add giblets and sauté them for 2 to 3 minutes. Stir in the flour to make a roux, and cook mixture until nut brown and fragrant, about 5 minutes. Stir in the stock, bring to a boil, and simmer until thick. Cook 10 minutes more, and correct seasonings with salt and pepper. Transfer to a gravy boat and pass at the table.

## TURKEY STOCK

*Carefully made stock is the basis for many a great dish. After you have lovingly made this stock, store it covered in the refrigerator. Keeps 2 weeks, or 2 years in the freezer.*

**Makes 10 cups**

* 3 pounds fresh turkey wings
* ¼ cup grape-seed oil
* 2 cups chopped onion
* 1 cup EACH: finely chopped carrots and celery
* 2 quarts cold water
* 4 sprigs EACH: fresh parsley and thyme
* 2 garlic cloves, smashed
* 2 teaspoons kosher salt (or to taste)
* ¼ teaspoon whole black peppercorns
* 1 bay leaf

- Preheat oven to 450°F.

- Chop turkey wings with a cleaver or have your butcher cut them in ½ inch pieces. place in a roasting pan then roast wings for 30 minutes, turning them to brown evenly.

- In a medium stock pot, heat oil, then cook onions, carrots and celery until soft, about 10 minutes. Add the wings to the pot, deglaze the pan with water, scraping all the solids from the bottom, then add wings and cover with water. Bring to a high boil, skimming foam off, then add parsley, fresh thyme, garlic and salt. Add peppercorns and bay leaf, then reduce to low, and simmer, uncovered, for 3 hours, adding more water as needed to keep wings covered. Strain stock through a fine sieve, skim off excess fat, taste and adjust seasonings, then transfer to clean glass jars and store in the refrigerator.

## JELLIED CRANBERRY SAUCE

*Buy this in a can if you like the clear red sauce. Or make your own. Pow!*

**Makes 1 cup**

* 1 cup granulated sugar
* 1 cup water
* 1 12-ounce package Ocean Spray fresh or frozen cranberries

**Directions**
- Combine granulated sugar and water in a medium saucepan. Bring to a boil and add cranberries. Return to a boil. Reduce heat and boil gently for 10 minutes, stirring occasionally.

- Place a wire mesh strainer over a medium mixing bowl. Pour contents of saucepan into strainer. Mash cranberries with the back of a spoon, frequently scraping the outside of the strainer until no pulp is left.

- Stir contents of bowl. Pour into serving container. Cover and cool completely at room temperature. Refrigerate until serving time.

## MOLASSES CAKE (SEE PAGE i FOR RECIPE)

# Chapter 12: December

## The Blowout Christmas Parties to Blast Off the Season

＊ Chef Jesse's Coq Au Vin

＊ Green Bean Casserole

＊ Potatoes Lyonnaise

＊ Orange Walnut Bundt Cake

### CHEF JESSE'S COQ AU VIN

**Makes 6 servings**

*Julia Child first brought this dish to American cooks in the sixties via her popular cooking show. There have been many versions. Here's mine.*

* 6 chicken legs, washed
* 4 ounces thick, smoked bacon cut into rectangles
* 2 tablespoons olive oil
* 1 teaspoon Chef Jesse's spice blend (see pp 26)
* ¼ cup cognac
* 2 cups red wine (pinot noir or burgundy)
* 2 cups homemade chicken stock (or low-sodium canned chicken stock)
* 1 tablespoon tomato paste
* 2 cloves garlic, smashed
* 1 bay leaf
* 4 sprigs fresh thyme
* 12 boiler onions or pearl onions (see recipe below for browned, braised onions)

Feast #38

* ½ pound white medium mushrooms (see recipe below)
* 3 tablespoons all-purpose flour
* 2 tablespoons butter, softened

### Browned, Braised Onion Recipe:

* 12 small boiler onions
* 1-2 tablespoons olive oil
* Sea salt to taste

– Heat oil in a medium saucepan over medium heat and add onions. Slow cook until browned. Add salt and ½ cup water. Simmer 25 minutes or until soft.

### Mushroom Recipe:

* ½ pound white mushrooms, washed and sliced or quartered
* 1 tablespoon butter + ½ tablespoon olive oil

– In a large pan heat butter and olive oil. When hot, add mushrooms and slow cook until brown, about 4-5 minutes. Set aside.

### To Make the Coq au Vin:

Dry chicken legs in a towel to assure crispy searing. Season with Chef Jesse's spice blend.

– Cook bacon in the bottom of a Dutch oven until crisp. Remove the bacon to a side dish. In the same pan, sear chicken legs on all sides until fully browned. Pour in the cognac and flambé by lighting with a match, burning off the alcohol. Pour in the red wine and chicken stock, just enough to cover the chicken legs. Stir in tomato paste, garlic, bay leaf, and thyme. Bring the liquid to a simmer, then cover the pot. Place in a 300°F oven for 45 minutes or until fork tender. When chicken legs are finished, remove them onto a platter. Bring cooking liquid to a simmer on the stovetop. In a small bowl, blend the 3 tablespoons flour and 2 tablespoons soft butter into a smooth paste. Add to liquid while stirring constantly to prevent lumps. Cook for a few more minutes. Mix in mushrooms, braised onions, bacon, and chicken. Serve hot.

## GREEN BEAN CASSEROLE

**Serves 6 to 8**

* 1 ½ pounds fresh green beans, snipped on both ends
* ½ cup unsalted butter
* 1 small yellow onion, peeled and chopped
* 2 tablespoons all-purpose flour
* 1 cup half-and-half
* 1 cup Boursin cheese
* 1 cup sharp cheddar cheese
* 1 cup panko bread crumbs

– Bring a large pot of salted water to a boil, add beans, and cook until tender, about 5 minutes. Drain, then transfer to an ice water bath. Let cool for few minutes, then drain again and reserve.

– Melt butter in a medium skillet, add onions, and sauté for 2 minutes. Add flour to make a roux. Cook for a few minutes until onions are golden, then slowly add half-and-half and cook until it thickens. Add Boursin cheese and simmer for a few minutes. Adjust seasonings to taste with salt and pepper.

– In a medium bowl, add beans, then pour cheese mixture over the beans, mix well, and transfer to a casserole dish. Sprinkle with cheddar cheese and panko bread crumbs. Bake in a 400°F oven for 20 minutes. Serve hot.

## POTATOES LYONNAISE

**Makes 6 servings**

* 2 tablespoons grape-seed oil
* 2 pounds Idaho potatoes, peeled and sliced about ¼-inch thick
* Kosher salt and freshly milled black pepper to taste
* 4 tablespoons unsalted butter
* 3 large yellow onions, peeled and cut julienne (into thin strips)
* 2 tablespoons EACH: minced garlic and parsley

– Heat oil in a Dutch oven over medium-low heat. Add 1 layer of potatoes to start the browning process. Season with salt and pepper. Add butter, onions, and garlic. Keep adding layers until they're all in the pan. Cook 10 to 15 minutes, turning and browning, slowly. When the dish is fork tender, pour onto a platter and garnish with parsley to serve.

## ORANGE WALNUT BUNDT CAKE

**(Yield -10 inch)**

* 2 cups cake flour
* 1 teaspoon baking power
* ½ teaspoon baking soda
* Pinch of sea salt
* ½ pound unsalted butter, softened
* 1 ½ cups sugar
* 3 large eggs
* 1 cup orange juice
* 1 teaspoon vanilla extract
* 1 cup chopped walnuts
* 1 tablespoon grated orange zest

– Preheat heat oven 350 degrees F. Butter and flour a ten-inch Bundt pan.

– Sift flour, baking powder, and salt together and sit aside. In a mixer cream the butter and sugar together until light. Then beat in eggs one at a time. Add the flour alternately with one cup of the orange juice and the vanilla. Fold in the orange zest and walnuts.

– Pour cake batter into greased ten-inch Bundt pan. Bake in oven 1 hour or until brown and toothpick comes out clean.

– Cool on rack for about an hour, and then turn onto a cake platter.

# Hunters' Lunch

* Chef Jesse's Venison Chili
* Cheesy Biscuits (See recipe page 74)
* Simple Marinated Cucumbers with Cider Vinaigrette
* One-Bowl Yellow Cake with a Limoncello Infusion

## CHEF JESSE'S VENISON CHILI

*If you are a hunter, you'll be glad for this great way to cook your catch. Those of you who hunt in specialty grocery stores can purchase venison in specialty stores or online.*

I came to love venison working under the great chefs at Dennis Foy's Town Square in Chatham, New Jersey. So flavorful and yet so lean. I buy it from Fossil Farms in Boonton, New Jersey.

* 1 teaspoon grape-seed oil
* 4 pounds ground venison
* 1 cup chopped yellow onions
* ½ cup fresh red peppers
* ½ cup fresh green peppers
* 4 cloves garlic, chopped
* 1 tablespoon, chopped canned chipotle, in adobo sauce
* 3 tablespoons ground cumin
* 3 tablespoons ground chili powder
* 1 cup tomato puree
* 2 cups water
* 1 cup diced fresh plum tomatoes
* 1 cup EACH: dried pinto beans and black beans*
* 4 ounces bittersweet chocolate

- In a heavy sauce pot, heat grape-seed oil to medium and sauté the ground venison until brown. Place in a strainer to discard any fat, then set aside.

- In the same pot, add a little oil, and sauté onions, peppers, garlic, and chipotle pepper, for 3 minutes. Add cumin, chili powder, and tomato puree. Let the flavors mellow together, about 10 minutes.

- Add fresh diced tomatoes and cooked beans with venison and let it cook for about 30 minutes. Add chocolate and adjust favors.

- *Start with dried beans by soaking them overnight in water to cover. You can cook them together in a pot of barely boiling water until tender, about 1 hour. OR you can start with canned beans. Simply strain and add to the pot.

## SIMPLE MARINATED CUCUMBERS WITH CIDER VINAIGRETTE

* 2 English cucumbers, peeled and sliced thin
* 1 cup cider vinegar
* ½ cup water
* 1 tablespoon EACH: granulated sugar, salt, seeded mustard
* Freshly milled black pepper to taste

- Place cucumbers in a bowl. Combine remaining ingredients in a small bowl. Whisk and pour over the cucumbers. Cover and refrigerate (keeps up to a week).

## ONE-BOWL YELLOW LAYER CAKE WITH A LIMONCELLO INFUSION

*This recipe is more than 100 years old, but once I started giving it little sips of limoncello, it began to sing. POW!*

* 2 cups all-purpose flour, spooned and leveled; sifted after measuring
* 1 + ¼ cup granulated sugar
* 1 tablespoon baking powder
* 1 teaspoon salt
* ½ cup butter, softened
* 1 cup milk
* 1 teaspoon vanilla extract
* 2 eggs

### Whipped Cream Frosting
* 1 cup heavy whipping cream
* ½ teaspoon pure vanilla extract
* 1 tablespoon granulated sugar

### Limoncello Infusion
* 2 tablespoons limoncello liqueur

- Preheat oven to 350°F. Grease and flour two 8-inch cake pans.

- In a large mixing bowl, sift together flour, granulated sugar, baking powder, and salt.

- Add butter, milk, and vanilla. Beat with a hand mixer on medium speed for 3-4 minutes, occasionally scraping sides of bowl. Add eggs and beat for 3 more minutes.

- Pour batter into prepared pans, dividing equally among both. Bake 30 to 35 minutes or until toothpick comes out clean.

- Cool in pans on wire racks 10 minutes. Turn out and cool thoroughly on wire racks. Add sips of limoncello to cake layers as they cool.

- Frost with whipped cream frosting. Refrigerate until serving time.

## Whipped Cream Frosting:

- Combine all ingredients in a large mixing bowl; cover and chill in refrigerator 30 minutes with the beaters.

- Beat on medium speed until stiff peaks form. Frost sides and top of the cake.

# Christmas Eve Family Dinner

* Pineapple-Spiked and Apple-Glazed Whole Ham

* Roasted Winter Roots, including parsnips,
carrots, sweet potatoes, andwinter squash

* Christmas Salad with Baby Kale and Dried Cranberries

* Three Cheese Baken Macaroni

* Hummingbird Cake (SEE PAGE 122 FOR RECIPE)

My Aunt Mitt (aka Aunt Bull) is the pork queen, but what makes her hams so good is that she is picky and only uses a fresh, uncured ham. Plus, she takes her time, never skipping any steps. Thanks, Aunty, for all the inspiration.

This is an example of the care taken in my family to make wonderful meals worthy of a celebration as our own family Christmas Eve dinner.

In some families, the presents are the main emphasis. In our family, it's always been all about the food.

## PINEAPPLE-SPIKED AND APPLE-GLAZED WHOLE HAM

**Makes 12 to 15 servings**

* I whole fresh ham (bone-in, uncured, 10 to 15 pounds)
* I tablespoon grape-seed oil
* I ½ cups Chef Jesse's Spice Blend (see pp 26)
* I tablespoon rendered fat from the ham
* I whole fresh pineapple (peeled, cored, and diced)
* 3 Granny Smith apples (peeled, cored, and diced)
* I cup apple juice

* ½ cup EACH: bourbon, brown sugar, maple syrup, and apple cider vinegar
* 1 teaspoon crushed red pepper
* 2 teaspoons ground cloves

- In a medium bowl, combine grape-seed oil and Chef Jesse's spice blend. Mix well, and coat the ham on all sides. Marinate overnight, covered in the refrigerator.

**Next day:**

- Preheat oven to 325°F.

- In a roasting pan with a rack, add the ham and roast for 4 hours, uncovered, or until an internal temperature of 160°F is reached. Cool on a rack at least 2 hours.

- About two hours in, make this sauce and brush half of it over the ham for glaze:

- In a medium saucepan, add 2 tablespoons rendered ham fat and sauté the pineapple and apples for 5 minutes, or until sweated down. Add the bourbon and cook for 1 minute. Add the apple juice, brown sugar, and maple syrup. Cook and stir for 10 minutes, adjust the seasoning, and remove from the heat.

- When cool, take ½ the sauce out to a bowl and puree with the stick blender, but leave the rest whole. Add the pureed sauce into the chopped mix.

- With about 1 hour left in roasting time, brush some of the glaze over the ham and then finish roasting time, reserving the rest to serve over ham.

- Let the ham rest for about 20 minutes before carving.

## ROASTED WINTER ROOTS, INCLUDING PARSNIPS, CARROTS, SWEET POTATOES, AND WINTER SQUASH

*This is a wonderful, very easy side dish that you will love to make even as a snack.*

**Makes 8 servings**

* 1 pound EACH: parsnips and carrots, peeled and cut into 1¼-inch pieces
* 1 large, sweet potato, peeled and cut into 1¼-inch pieces
* 2 pounds butternut squash, peeled and cut into 1¼-inch pieces
* ¼ cup grape-seed oil
* 3 sprigs of fresh thyme
* Sea salt and freshly ground pepper, to taste

- Preheat oven to 375°F.

- Heat the oil in large roasting pan in a hot oven and add vegetables. Toss in the oil and season to taste with sea salt, freshly ground black pepper, and thyme. Roast for 1½ hours. Every few minutes, give it a stir. Adjust seasonings and then transfer into your favorite serving vessel. Great hot or room temp. POW!

## CHRISTMAS SALAD WITH BABY KALE AND DRIED CRANBERRIES

**Makes 6-8 servings**

*This is a wonderful, quick salad to make for Christmas. It goes perfectly with the fresh ham. But the kicker is my apple-cider vinaigrette, which I use over and over. I try to make up a batch and keep it in the refrigerator. It makes any salad go POW!*

* 4 cups baby kale, washed, spun dried, and torn into bite-sized pieces
* 1 cup sweetened dried cranberries

## Apple Cider Vinaigrette:
* ½ teaspoon Dijon mustard
* 1 teaspoon EACH: fresh minced thyme, chopped shallots, hot sauce, maple syrup, and kosher salt
* 3 tablespoons EACH: apple cider vinegar and apple juice
* 1½ cups grape-seed oil
* Few cranks of fresh black pepper

– In a salad bowl, toss the baby kale and dried cranberries.

## To make the vinaigrette:
– In a blender, combine mustard, thyme, shallots, maple syrup, salt, apple cider vinegar, and apple juice. Pulse once and then with the blender running, slowly pour in grape-seed oil until mixture is thick. Adjust the taste and finish with cracked pepper.

– Transfer to a covered jar and refrigerate until serving time.

– Arrange baby kale and dried cranberries in a nice bowl, then just before service, toss with vinaigrette and serve. POW!

# THREE CHEESE BAKED MACARONI

**Makes 8 to 10 servings**

* 1 teaspoon sea salt
* 2 cups elbow macaroni, cooked following package directions
* ½ stick butter
* ½ cup all-purpose flour
* 4 cups evaporated milk
* 1 teaspoon kosher salt
* ½ teaspoon cayenne pepper
* Pinch white pepper
* 2 cups EACH: shredded white extra sharp and mild cheddar
* 1 cup Colby cheese, grated
* ( mix cheeses and blend together)
* 2 large eggs, beaten
* Sprinkling of paprika

– Preheat oven to 350 F.

– In a large heavy-duty pot, melt butter, then add flour, to make a roux, then add milk, stir until smooth with no lumps, then add salt, cayenne, white pepper, and ½ of the cheese blend. Save remainder for topping later. Melt, then turn off the heat. In a large mixing bowl, add cooked macaroni, cheese sauce, taste for salt, then add 2 beaten eggs, mix well. Pour into a buttered 2 quart casserole dish, sprinkle with saved cheese and paprika, bake uncovered, until golden brown 40 to 45 minutes.

# December New Year's Eve

**Bonus gift from me to you for a dazzling end to a splendid year.**

**Happy New Year to you and yours!**

## New Year's Eve Midnight Supper

* Roast Rack of Pork with Fig and Apple Chutney
* Potato Pancakes
* Green Broccoli Rabe with Garlic and Crushed Red Pepper
* Chef Jesse's Banana Tart with Maple Ice Cream

## ROASTED RACK OF PORK WITH FIG AND APPLE CHUTNEY

Chef's Note: Serve this dish family-style on a great big platter, laced with the fig chutney.

*Ask the butcher to cut and tie this wonderful festive dish. It will buckle your knees.*

**Makes 6 to 8 servings**

* 1 rack of pork (normally about 3 pounds)
* ½ cup grape-seed oil
* 1 teaspoon minced garlic
* 1 teaspoon minced fresh rosemary
* 1 teaspoon minced thyme
* 1 teaspoon minced sage

Feast #41

- Combine the grape-seed oil, garlic, rosemary, thyme, sage, and pork in a glass dish. Rub pork in the mixture. Cover and refrigerate overnight.

**Next Day:**
- Take out the pork. Sear on all sides and then transfer to the oven. Roast at 325°F for approximately 1½ hours or to an internal temperature of 160°F. Let it rest on the sideboard at least 20 minutes before carving. POW!

## FIG AND APPLE CHUTNEY

* 6 dried mission figs (use fresh if available)
* 2 tablespoons granulated sugar
* I cup ruby port
* ½ cup red wine vinegar
* 2 teaspoons mustard seed
* ½ teaspoon EACH: ground cinnamon and allspice
* 2 whole cloves
* ¼ teaspoon EACH: cayenne pepper and kosher salt
* I medium red onion
* 2½ pounds Granny Smith apples
* I teaspoon EACH: orange zest, lemon zest, and lemon juice

- Combine figs, sugar, port, vinegar, mustard seeds, cinnamon, allspice, cloves, cayenne pepper, and salt in a non-reactive pan. Bring to a boil on medium heat. Reduce about half 10 to 15 minutes, until the figs are tender. Stir in apples. Let simmer for 30 minutes. Transfer to a bowl.

- Serve hot or cold.

## POTATO PANCAKES

**Serves 8 to 12**

* 4 medium baking potatoes (Idaho is my go-to potato), peeled
* I small yellow onion, peeled and chopped
* ¼ cup all-purpose flour
* I egg, beaten
* I teaspoon sea salt
* I teaspoon fresh thyme
* Few cranks of fresh cracked black pepper
* ¾ cup vegetable oil, for frying

- Shred potatoes and onion in a food processor or a box grater. Squeeze potatoes and onion between paper towels to remove all moisture, then transfer to a bowl. Stir in flour, salt, thyme, and pepper, until blended. In a large skillet heated over medium high heat and filmed with hot oil, place 2 tablespoons of potato mixture individually, and fry over medium high-heat, turning once, until golden brown. Drain on paper towels.

## SEARED GREEN BROCCOLI RABE WITH GARLIC AND CRUSHED RED PEPPER

**Makes 8 servings**

* 2 bunches broccoli rabe, chopped
* ½ cup EACH: water and butter
* Sea salt and freshly milled black pepper to taste
* ½ teaspoon EACH: fresh crushed garlic and crushed red pepper

- Heat a large skillet over high heat. Add all

ingredients, stirring until the broccoli is wilted. Serve at once.

## CHEF JESSE'S BANANA TART

*One of my most requested desserts. I know you're gonna love it.*

**Makes 8 individual tarts**

* ½ cup (1 stick) butter
* 1 teaspoon ground cinnamon
* 1 cup packed dark brown sugar
* ½ cup banana liqueur
* 8 medium bananas, peeled, cut in slices

**To Make Tart Dough:**
* 5¼ cups pastry flour or all-purpose flour
* 1 tablespoon kosher salt
* 1½ cups cold unsalted butter, cut into small pieces
* 1¾ cups solid vegetable shortening, chilled
* 1 cup ice water

– Combine flour and salt into a bowl. Add the butter and shortening and mix until it resembles coarse meal. Add ice water to form dough. Wrap and place in refrigerator for 1 hour.

– In a large skillet, melt the butter. Add cinnamon and brown sugar and stir, simmering over medium heat until the sugar dissolves, 3 to 4 minutes. Add the banana liqueur and blend well. Add sliced bananas and cook for 6 minutes. Cool.

– Roll pastry out on a lightly floured work surface and line the tart tin. Prick the pastry base, and put cooked bananas over pastry. Bake for 30-40 minutes at 350°F.

## MAPLE ICE CREAM

**Yields 2 quarts**

* 1½ cups heavy whipping cream
* 1½ cups half-and-half
* 6 large egg yolks
* 1 cup maple syrup
* ¼ teaspoon sea salt
* 1 tablespoon vanilla extract

– Bring heavy cream and half-and-half to simmer in heavy, large saucepan over medium-high heat. Remove from heat.

– Combine eggs yolks, maple syrup, and sea salt in a large bowl; whisk until thick and blended. Gradually whisk hot cream mixture into yolk mixture. Return mixture to same saucepan and stir over medium-low heat until custard thickens, about 3 minutes. Remove from heat and mix in vanilla extract. Refrigerate custard, uncovered, until cold. Stirring occasionally, add to ice cream machine. Freeze, then remove the paddle from the canister. Place ice cream in the freezer until ready to serve.

# End note:

## How I Found My Spot

*And My Place in the World.*

**Faith riders, mount up. Let's get it. POW! Dream big, never give up; that's my redemption now!**

It's what I pray for every morning of my life. I say it like a chant, over and over as I walk into the park in the morning and head to the path, taking long, sure steps.

That takes me to my spot, deep in the leafy green arms of the park.

It's what I say after I've parked the car and walked over the crunchy gravel to get to the path that takes me to my spot. And I learned to say this prayer when I found my spot.

But before all of that, let me explain. I have a special park bench I call MY SPOT, located in South Orange, New Jersey, my hometown. I started going there when everything in my life seemed to turn against me. I had lost my restaurant, my home, and my self-respect. I couldn't even look myself in the mirror. I was paralyzed with fear.

I found my spot when I walked in the park because I couldn't face looking my folks in the face. When things got impossibly hard, I just started going to my spot, and now, I go there every morning to start my day. All I could do at first was slam that car door, take a few gulps of the crisp morning air, and start walking.

This is where I go to ask God questions.

"Dear Lord, what do I do now? I have lost everything."

Sometimes I just ask, "Why did you wake me up this morning? I'm a complete failure. I cannot go on."

But the miracle is this. Through planting my seat on that park bench morning after morning, in good weather and bad, in happy days and fearful ones, year after year, I have learned that my spot is special. When I go and talk to God, things happen.

Maybe I'll get a call for a job, or several jobs. And sometimes, I just get calls from people telling me how they appreciate me and how they enjoyed my food and how I have lifted them up. Sometimes people tell me how my meal made their family feel.

The one thing I know for sure is that I have to be really still, sitting on that bench, with only the birds in the trees and the wind in the leaves saying anything besides whatever it is that God is telling me on that day. I have to open up my heart and listen hard.

But this much I can tell you, my spot really changed my perspective on life. I do believe it is God talking to me, as well as my grandmother and everyone else I lost along the way, who are outstretching their hands to help me. I know I could never do this alone. Never.

Now, when I go to my spot, I just tell God, "Thank you for waking me up. I will continue to love my family, to help the sick and the homeless. I will be humble and kind." I know we often ask God for things, but we sometimes forget we need to be thankful.

I'm blessed to be alive. Every day, when I go to my spot, I say thank God. Thank you to those who have gone before me: Grandmother, everyone, and now Zeus; for everything and for everyone who is praying for me, I give thanks. POW!

# Index

CPSIA information can be obtained
at www.ICGtesting.com
Printed in the USA
BVHW020151060219
539611BV00019B/269/P